DIESEL AND DISCORD:

THE POPULIST UPRISING THAT SHOOK CANADA'S PANDEMIC POLITICS

ROBERT GEORGE CRUISE

Paperback Edition 2025

ISBN: 987-1-998497-57-7

TABLE OF CONTENTS

DEDICATION

For those winter weeks in 2022, the heart of Ottawa became an unlikely gathering place of conviction and unrest. Eighteen-wheelers rolled in from the highways, engines pounding a steady rhythm like distant war drums. On Parliament's trim boulevards, under streetlights haloed by frost, the trucks formed a kind of diesel-lit agora where voices once unheard now roared. Their air horns blared through the night, long, relentless blasts that shook the snow off downtown eaves and tested the nerves of a city's leaders. What began as a fringe of discontent had grown loud enough to rattle windows and wake an anxious nation.

At kitchen tables and on couches hundreds of miles away, strangers followed the spectacle through screens and headlines. Moved by belief or a simple wish to help, they reached for their phones and wallets. In a matter of days, online donations—tens of millions of dollars—flooded in from across towns and provinces, and even from beyond the border; money crossed continents faster than any convoy, before a halt, stopped it. Officials abruptly capped the crowdfunding well mid-flow, as if the stream of support had turned to ice in midair.

But you can't easily quell generosity once it's aroused. When one platform froze under pressure, another sprang up in its place. Through it all, names and numbers flowed quietly behind the scenes until one night an unexpected breach flung them into the open—a nine-megabyte leak of secrets. The identities of thousands of well-intentioned givers spilt across the internet like a confession no one intended to write, revealing how far the movement's echo had travelled and how technology can lay bare even the most guarded hopes.

Beyond our borders, the noise did not fall on deaf ears. Across the forty-ninth parallel and farther overseas, commentators and onlookers saw the reflection of their battles in Canada's convoy. Blue-check-marked pundits and charismatic live streamers seized on the maple-leaf quarrel and magnified it in algorithms and evening news segments. What started as a local standoff in the capital became a global spectacle, drawing millions of distant eyes and opinions.

For a brief feverish moment, the honking in Ottawa trended online like a kind of halftime show, an unexpected performance on the world stage. Politicians from other provinces and countries, talk-show hosts, and would-be prophets spliced footage of trucks and crowds into their speeches and fundraising appeals. Each participant claimed a piece of the story, proving that, in our age, others can co-opt, broadcast, and transform even a truck horn's cry into a political theatre far beyond its original street setting.

Within Ottawa, the crisis deepened, and lines hardened. After watching the impasse become an emergency, a prime minister reached for power untouched for more than a generation. He broke the glass around the Emergencies Act and woke it from its thirty-four-year slumber to deal with the blockades and the grinding, unyielding protest. In official buildings, pens scratched out new orders while on city streets, defiant voices shouted freedom into the cold air. Authorities cut financial lifelines: they quietly froze bank accounts, locking anger behind the cold steel of compliance.

Guardians of civil liberties mobilised, preparing their challenges with quiet resolve. Lawyers and advocates sharpened their constitutional arguments like scalpels, ready to test whether such extraordinary measures could hold against the principles they cherished. Courts and citizens would later evaluate the decisions of those days—bold to some, draconian to others—as the nation grappled with actions taken in the name of order and safety.

Nevertheless, another battle was unfolding in the digital shadows. Anonymous hackers and wily internet sleuths took it upon themselves to expose what they saw as truths hidden in the noise. Meme-smiths and online organisers worked in encrypted group chats and social media feeds, rallying supporters or undermining confidence, depending on where one stood.

It became clear that a convoy of trucks and a crowd of protesters were only part of the siege; the rest played out on screens and servers, a twenty-first-century echo of conflict where a keyboard could be as powerful as an ignition key. In this new struggle, diesel fuel, and Wi-Fi signals combined to hold a city in their grip without a single shot fired—only the constant blare of horns and the ceaseless churn of information.

Through all this, ordinary people watched from their windows, doorsteps, and mobile phones. Many lay awake at night, the distant honking seeping into their dreams, wondering what had become of their peaceful capital. Some brought coffee or fuel to the truckers in solidarity, while others banged pots and pans on their balconies in a chorus of frustration. Neighbours argued or collaborated, testing friendships and forming unlikely alliances, as the drama engulfed the entire country.

In those frozen streets and sleepless nights, a slight fringe movement had thrust itself onto the frontline of our national story. What began as one group's protest against mandates and restrictions swelled into a crisis that engulfed the country's imagination. And in that long, cold winter, Canada looked into the mirror of its discontent. It saw reflections it could not ignore—unity and division, pride, and anger, courage, and fear, all swirling together like snowflakes in the wind.

This dedication is for all of them—the truck drivers and residents, the dreamers, the critics, the givers, and the responders—every one of the well-meaning actors in that Canadian winter tale, even those whose roles were as perplexing as the times. This story does not single out any of you as a hero or a villain.

Instead, you are characters in a story still being understood, each driven by hopes or grievances that were real and alive in your hearts. I offer these words in gratitude and reflection, mindful of the complicated truth that without each of you, the events on those icy streets would have had no meaning. May the echo of your voices and engines linger on these pages long after the roads have cleared, and the livestreams have faded into memory.

With deepest gratitude,

Robert George Cruise

AUTHOR'S FOREWORD

In the hush of a February night, diesel engines idled like caged beasts outside Parliament, and snow sifted down like fine-grained sugar onto Wellington Street. I began this book flat on my back, lungs rattling and body stricken with waves of severe nausea, weakness in my joints, and a bone-deep pain that moored me to the mattress, mind swimming through a cognitive fog. From that horizontal vantage, the world arrived in digital shards—court transcripts, press briefings, and warped livestreams that shuddered with every blast of an air horn. The "Freedom Convoy," they called it, though that name meant as many things as there were radios tuned in. For some, it was a pilgrimage of liberty; for others, a siege that would only relent when helmets and badges reclaimed the streets.

The government, declaring the moment a "public order emergency," pried open the seldom-disturbed glass case around the Emergencies Act on 14 February 2022—for the first time since its inception in 1988. Under these extraordinary measures, bank accounts froze mid-pulse and insurance policies crackled into ash, the protest's financial arteries clogging in real time—an arrhythmic ECG of modern dissent. Months later, a Federal Court judge tapped her gavel and pronounced the government's invocation of those powers "unreasonable", a verdict that drifted through Ottawa like soot from an over-eager bonfire, reminding us that extraordinary hammers often come with footnotes—and sometimes bruised toes.

I once thought history ripened only after decades of patience, like cheese left to mould or grudges to fester. Yet the files on my screen corrupted themselves twice, perhaps in sympathy with the nation's frayed discourse, and I learned that very recent history spoils if you do not gather it swiftly. Between waves of nausea and spells of cognitive fog, I collected clippings as a magpie does baubles: the mischief charges and court dates of protest organisers-turned-folk-heroes, piled beside grocery lists and CT-scan appointments on my desk. Pat King, trading his bullhorn for a three-month house arrest, offered a bedtime story for grown-ups who refused to sleep. All winter, I tracked facts the way a fox follows footprints across a moonlit field—never entirely sure which trail was fresh and which was yesterday's dust. On my worst days, I greeted rumour as a long-lost cousin; on my better ones, I recognised that truth and deception often share the same tailor, each wearing a coat borrowed from the other. When footnotes threatened mutiny, multiplying faster than I could tame them, I half-expected them to hold a press conference of their own; there is, I discovered, something oddly consoling about dreaming of spreadsheets.

Though I have tried my best to stick only to the facts as they could be determined from a bed weighed down by nausea and bone-deep exhaustion, my mind often shrouded in fog, I did occasionally slip in a turn of phrase or a fleshed-out dialogue—never inventing events, only lending the bones a bit of flesh so the story might breathe. You now hold the packed-down, ploughed-through result. It is not an indictment, an alibi, or an attempt to exhume every motive buried beneath chrome and flags. It is simply a lantern held to the recent dark—a narrative history scribbled while the ink thawed. If I have done my job, you will emerge from these pages wary of easy heroes, suspicious of tidy villains, and alert to how slogans can barrel-roll through nuance like a runaway rig. I dedicate this work to my son, who will inherit a world where a meme can topple a mood and a livestream can outshout the law. May he learn to X-ray every headline, taste-test each statistic, and understand that genuine freedom is less a road to be unblocked than a map forever redrawn. And if he ever forgets, I trust these pages—born of wintry nights, corrupted files, and an old laptop that refused to quit—to remind him. Truth, after all, is a mosaic of broken glass: sharp to handle, dazzling to behold, and liable to cut you if you grasp it without care. And if you find yourself bleeding a little, consider it a small price to pay for clearer vision.

~ R.G. Cruise

THE EMERGENCIES ACT

The Emergencies Act (1988) establishes a precise, Charter-compliant framework that empowers the federal government to declare one of four types of national emergencies—public welfare, public order, international, and war—only when an urgent, temporary, and critical situation seriously endangers Canadians and existing laws cannot manage it. It replaced the sweeping War Measures Act, adding clear definitions, provincial consultation requirements, and mandatory parliamentary and judicial oversight. Despite its availability since 1988, the Act lay dormant until 14 February 2022, when Prime Minister Justin Trudeau invoked it to address sustained blockades in Ottawa and at key Canada–U.S. border crossings during the "Freedom Convoy" protests.

LEGISLATIVE ARCHITECTURE

Enactment and Long Title

The Emergencies Act received Royal Assent on July 21, 1988, as RSC 1985, c 22 (4th Supp.), following an extensive debate on balancing urgent state powers with individual rights. Its long title reads:

"An Act to authorize the taking of special temporary measures to ensure safety and security during national emergencies and to amend other Acts in consequence thereof."

Definition and Criteria

Section 3 defines a "national emergency" as an "urgent and critical situation of a temporary nature" that either seriously endangers Canadians' lives, health, or safety beyond provincial capacity, or threatens Canada's sovereignty, security, and territorial integrity. Section 7 stipulates three cumulative criteria for invocation:

1. The situation is urgent, temporary and critical.
2. It seriously endangers Canadians' lives, health, or security.
3. No existing federal or provincial law can effectively deal with it.

Four Emergency Categories:

Declarations must specify one of four distinct types, thereby tailoring responses to the nature of the crisis.

1. Public Welfare Emergency (e.g., large-scale natural or industrial disasters).
2. Public Order Emergency (e.g., widespread civil unrest or terrorism).
3. International Emergency (e.g., foreign coercion or interference).
4. War Emergency (e.g., declarations of war or armed conflict).

POWERS, SAFEGUARDS, AND OVERSIGHT

Extraordinary Authorities

Once invoked, the Governor in Council may issue orders to.

- Freeze or seize financial assets tied to the emergency, such as bank accounts funding blockades.
- Prohibit or restrict public assemblies and designate no-go zones.
- Compel private services (for example, tow truck operators) to clear critical infrastructure.
- Deploy additional federal resources, including the R.C.M.P., to support overwhelmed local forces.

CHARTER COMPLIANCE AND JUDICIAL REVIEW

Courts can challenge all measures if they exceed strictly necessary measures, as all measures remain subject to the Canadian Charter of Rights and

Freedoms. The Act also requires a public inquiry after use, ensuring a transparent review of government actions and lessons learned.

Parliamentary Confirmation

Parliament must table a declaration in both Houses within seven sitting days, and Parliament may confirm, revoke, or amend it by resolution. This ensures democratic accountability and prevents indefinite emergency rule.

EVOLUTION FROM THE WAR MEASURES ACT

Historical Invocations

The Emergencies Act replaced the War Measures Act (1914–1988), which granted the federal government near-unlimited powers without Charter constraints. Three invocations of the War Measures Act occurred: during World War I, World War II, and the October Crisis of 1970.

Modern Restraint

Despite theoretical availability, the Emergencies Act remained unused for over thirty-three years, reflecting the high bar set by its criteria and political caution.

2022 INVOCATION: THE "FREEDOM CONVOY"

Build-Up and Limitations of Existing Laws

In late January 2022, thousands of truckers and supporters descended on Ottawa to protest COVID-19 vaccine mandates for cross-border drivers. Simultaneous blockades at crossings in Emerson, Man., Coutts, Alta., and elsewhere choked trade routes, led to critical supply disruptions, and sparked public safety concerns. Provincial and municipal police forces lacked adequate tools to dismantle widespread, decentralised obstructions.

Declaration of a Public Order Emergency

On 14 February 2022, after formal consultations with provincial premiers and party leaders, Cabinet declared a public order emergency, concluding that existing laws—such as the Criminal Code, Public Works Protection Act, and provincial trespass statutes—did not end the gridlock.

Measures and Duration.

The government immediately:

- Froze bank accounts suspected of financing protesters.
- Designated "no-go" areas around Parliament Hill and border crossings.
- Ordered towing companies to remove obstructing vehicles.
- Mobilised R.C.M.P. and other federal resources to assist local forces.

Nine days later, clearing blockades and the largely restored regular order led to the revocation of the emergency declaration on 23 February.

AFTER-ACTION FINDINGS

The Rouleau Commission concluded that the threshold for invocation had been reached, praising the necessity of most measures but emphasising procedural gaps, including the lack of clarity on asset unfreezing. In January 2024, a Federal Court ruled the invocation "unjustified" under the Charter, prompting government appeals and ongoing debate over the balance between public order and civil liberties.

In conclusion, the Emergencies Act represents Canada's commitment to a measured, rights-respecting emergency powers regime. Its singular use in 2022 underscores the gravity required to invoke it and the rigorous checks designed to prevent governmental overreach.

CHAPTER ONE:

FROST-RIMMED FAULT LINES

"A convoy isn't just trucks on a road; it's a chorus of horns playing the nation's discontent in diesel minor. You can silence the horns, but the echoes linger in the alleys of Parliament. Funny how freedom sounds like a traffic jam when it's not your lane that's blocked."
~ R.G. Cruise

The night is still more winter than morning when twin columns of exhaust plume up like ghostly cedars behind the rigs. Beyond the last halo of suburbia, Highway 417 lies in a hush so deep that a raven's wing-beat would sound like scandal; Cummins diesels turn the hush into a hymn one by one. What began weeks earlier as a hard-edged dispute over a federal order requiring cross-border truckers to flash vaccine certificates at customs booths—an order announced in November, defended on 9 January, resisted by industry on 13 January, and forecast to sideline roughly one-fifth of the long-haul workforce—has swollen into something rumbling and wide-jawed, a political prairie fire rolling east toward Parliament Hill. [1][2][3][4]

In farm kitchens from Peace River to Pictou, the news had felt like Ottawa's handshake tightening into a chokehold. Prime Minister Trudeau insisted the mandate kept shelves stocked by keeping drivers healthy; Conservative critics replied empty shelves were born of bureaucrats who had never buttered toast at 04:00 and backed a reefer onto black ice. [5][6][7] The arguments cracked along lines older than COVID-19: city versus country, Laurentian elite versus engine-brake populist. A *Sage-journal* study later traced the convoy's appeal to a combustible mix of distrust and identity-politics fatigue: *Canada is no exception* to the pandemic-populist wave. [8] But on this morning, scholarship sleeps while torque takes the wheel.

As the trucks line up at the western cordon, veteran driver Jack "Dogbone" Ducharme reigns over fourteen gears and a thermos of diner coffee older than some democracies. Beneath his ball cap, a grin spreads slowly and sideways, the way prairie dogs measure the horizon. "Breaker–one–nine, we're Ottawa-bound—let 'er buck," he crackles into his Citizens Band radio, a compact two-way transceiver born in the postwar era as a licensed personal-use service on 27 MHz with an original 23-channel lineup that would swell to 40 by 1977 and do away with licensing altogether in 1983. Channel 19—designated for east–west highway traffic—became the unofficial trucking channel, its tinny chatter a lifeline for drivers navigating speed limits, fuel shortages, and police traps during the 1973 oil crisis. Truckers adopted colourful "handles" and a distinctive slang—calling diesel "motion lotion" and speed traps "Smokey the Bear"—a lexicon forged by outlaw-country tunes and midnight fuel runs. A choir of handles—Snow Ghost, Red Viking, Mama Bear—each pledge punctuated by the staccato squeal of big-rig air horns answered Dogbone. Later, these radios would carry whispered prayers from conspiracy forums and alt-right broadcasters south of the forty-ninth. [9]

Snow drifts—fine silver filings drawn toward the magnet of the headlights. Environment Canada promises only "flurries," but a snowflake is a rumour of trouble to a driver pushing forty tons through the dark. Ducharme feathers the throttle; chains bite and clink. In the sleeper berth behind him rides scarved-up Clara Jessup, mother of three, and maker of the hand-painted banner presently lashed to the trailer's lag-bollards: *HANDS OFF OUR JOBS, HANDS OFF OUR KIDS.* She stitched it between math homework and macaroni dinners while her eldest googled an *emergency injunction* and her youngest asked whether honking could be illegal. Not yet, she had said; though by dawn, a judge six kilometres away would issue exactly such a ruling. [10]

Eastward, in a fluorescent warren beneath Elgin Street, Superintendent Ray Sutherland sips burnt vending-machine espresso and fingers a map already crosshatched with "No-Go" arrows. Over the radio, he hears Chief Peter Sloly's taped request for "1,800 extra officers to 'regain control' of a city under siege." [11] He scrawls Coventry staging yard and Airport Spur on the edge of the sheet, then circles Parliament–Wellington. His pens leak neon fear: block a convoy of this size in full daylight and Ottawa chokes; let it idle and horns will shake plaster from condo ceilings. Sutherland pockets the pens and orders twelve cruisers to Highway 417, emergency lights off. The streets above are so quiet he can hear the furnace in the ceiling breathe.

By 05:07, the first wave breaches city limits. The rigs slide beneath sodium lamps, making the snow resemble blown glass. Residents leaning from condo balconies film the procession with one mitten'd hand while the other clutches coffee mugs. They whisper somewhere between curiosity and dread, *They're here.* The convoy answers with a single long blast of *Amazing Grace* rendered in diesel-powered sol-fa. On Wellington Street, journalists jot numbers: "one thousand vehicles, five thousand bodies," Mayor Jim Watson will later lament in the press scrum that precedes his state-of-emergency declaration. [12] [13] [14] He will call the occupation "completely out of control," *Politico's* headline writers already sharpening the phrase by breakfast. [15]

Inside the cab, Dogbone toggles the squelch. "A lot of blue uniforms at Eagleson. Keep 'er polite, drivers." The CB spits back: "Copy that, Dogbone. Let's be maple-sweet till we hit the Hill." A second voice—tuned high with prairie vowels—adds, "And if they slap that injunction on the horns, give 'em the quietest roar they ever heard." Their laughter, taut with tension, sounds like these countrymen are cautiously stitching civil disobedience through the plough's path and the ditch's edge.

Dawn feels reluctant: a washed-out mauve seeps over the Gatineau Hills, like a bruise deciding whether to bloom. Streetlamps flicker off in rows; the rigs' headlights assume dominion. On Metcalfe, Clara's banner whips free of one tie and snaps against chrome. She climbs down, boots crunching, to wrestle nylon with numbed fingers. A police cruiser idles twenty yards away; the constable inside lifts two insulated hands in a pantomime of *Stay safe.* In that moment, Clara wonders which of them is guarding which.

The constable's radio hisses: "Horn injunction signed by Justice Hugh McLean, effective immediately. Serve copies to convoy reps." [16] At 07:12, two officers in cruiser *Alpha-13* hand Dogbone a paper heavy with desperate grammar. He scans the first line—*IN THE MATTER OF ZEXI LI et al. v. JOHN DOE et al.*— and pushes it back. "Ain't a lawyer, boys. But you're welcome for the quiet." He had already silenced his air horn, a trick he learned at the Portage la Prairie weigh station when fines were paid in cash and curses.

Around them, downtown Ottawa begins its Monday: civil servants heel-tap slush; the Peace Tower clock coughs up eight solemn chimes; drip-lines of thaw trace the bronze shoulders of Terry Fox. Yet the usual rhythm is half a beat off, replaced by a diesel thrum so low it makes ribcages tick. *CBC* microphones capture residents calling the resonance "psychological warfare," a phrase that will echo in the class-action file like an unending car alarm. [17]

Above the fray, the macro lens refocuses. National headlines toggle from Omicron graphs to blockaded boulevards; U.S. politicians tweet emojis of solidarity; GoFundMe places its finger on a refund button rattling with eight million dollars. [18] [19] [20] On the Hill, MPs weigh words like occupier and citizen with equal suspicion. The Speaker's mace seems suddenly light for the load it must bear.

By noon, clouds peel aside to reveal a winter sun the colour of old brass. The rigs gleam like armoured beetles as schoolchildren, released early, chalk FREEDOM beside salt-washed tires. Across town, the paperwork churns: municipal and provincial states of emergency stack atop one another like plywood against a rising river, yet the water keeps coming. [21] [22] [23] After days of hedged silence, Premier Doug Ford dubs the protest a "siege" and promises new powers; the promise tastes of maple and vinegar, depending on which end of the bridge you stand on.

And still the engines idle, meal-warm, whispering their proverbs. Clara's youngest FaceTimes from home, waving a cereal spoon: "Mom, are you winning?" She answers in the universal language of mothers who want their children to believe in tomorrow: "We're being heard." Dogbone walks the line outside the cab, trading grease pencils and half-smiles. He passes a fuel drum tagged LOVE OVER FEAR and thinks of his immunocompromised brother watching this unfold from a hospital TV.

Twilight—early, blue-edged—drifts over Wellington. Snow swirls finer now, as though the city's breath crystallises before it leaves its mouth. The convoy's idling lights throw slow-motion constellations onto Parliament's sandstone walls. Fault lines invisible at sunrise are visible now: between urban patience and rural defiance, between mandates and livelihoods, between the notion of Canada as peacekeeper and the reality of Canada in pieces. An academic might call them *epistemic rifts*, a trucker calls them *cracks in the ice*. No one's sure whether they're stepping on history or erasing it when the thaw comes.

Behind the Library of Parliament, a maintenance worker flicks off the last streetlamp on the ridge. The sky takes on that indigo just short of black, and for a heartbeat, the city is lit only by taillights and the faint aurora of smartphones. Engines idle, heaters hum, and Ottawa inhales in the lull before the first parliamentary session of the day. The exhale will not come cheap. If the convoy's growl is a warning, it also echoes something older than mandates, as old as the bargains confederations strike with their fringes. When the sun rises again, it will do so over a capital divided not by rivers but by reverberations, each tremor promising a level of foreshadowing.

> *"From first light on 6 February through the dawn of 8 February 2022—as the convoy's engines fall into rhythm and public opinion swells."*

Grey sunrise drifts over the Rideau like smoke from an unseen campfire, yet the talk inside Ottawa's press gallery crackles brighter than any ember. Overnight, half the morning shows have thrown their rundowns in the trash to chase the same question: How did a policy memo about border vaccines become the loudest drum in the country? Reporters quote newly minted polling that says nearly forty-six per cent of Canadians, while uneasy with diesel diplomacy, *find the truckers' frustration legitimate and worthy of sympathy,* a figure significant enough to make cabinet ministers drop their toast on the way to Question Period. [24] *Abacus Data's* earlier snapshot had suggested two-thirds of the country wanted the rigs gone; now the needle trembles, proof that a stalled semi can still move the national mood. [25] Beyond the Hill, downtown streets are stiff with cold and idling chrome, but in the air there is motion: numbers shifting, alliances thawing, and a sense that February has slipped its leash.

By mid-morning, *The Guardian's* push alert, "Ottawa declares state of emergency as city gridlocks," [26] scrolls across phones perched on tanker dashboards. Drivers nod as though the declaration merely notarises what their bones already know: this is bigger than any lane of closure. The diesel rumble has settled into a *basso continuo* in Wellington, and the smell of half-burnt kerosene mixes with the sweetness of cedar-chip fires. Tamara, whose surname flits across both court dockets and fan forums, ducks into a borrowed burgundy GMC Safari in that thick air. She stacks ham-and-mustard sandwiches into a cooler, humming the chorus of Stan Rogers' Northwest Passage. The van doors rattle to the beat of her phone: ten million dollars raised on GoFundMe in scarcely a week—and then, in one late-night keystroke, frozen. [27] The campaign's page now displays a corporate apology promising automatic refunds. [28] To Tamara, the words read like a locked-gate sign on the only road out of town.

"Loaves and fishes, girl," jokes Chris as he shoulders in with a crate of single-serve ketchup. He taps his phone where a *Reuters* banner blinks: TD Bank has parked another CA$1.4 million in escrow, awaiting a judge's blessing or a bureaucrat's broom. [29] "We're still good," he insists, but the laugh flutters thin. They both know GiveSendGo has become the new lifeline; they also know lawyers in Toronto are petitioning to sever it before supper.

An hour later, Pastor Byron unfolds a camp stool and a pewter cross in the lee of a Peterbilt sleeper. He prays aloud, voice fogging, while rigs hiss around him like iron lungs. Above the prayer, the news travels faster than gospel: hackers have dumped a spreadsheet naming ninety-two thousand donors—everyone from Alberta ranchers to an American tech billionaire—and the leak is ricocheting through Telegram chats. [30] One trucker scrolls the list, whispering the postal codes; another whistles low when he finds a neighbour's name. Across the median, a second *Reuters* flash notes that Ontario's Superior Court has ordered GiveSendGo to freeze every dime. However, the Delaware-based platform replies with a tweet: *Canada has ZERO jurisdiction.* [31] [32] The legal niceties sound like distant thunder to men who have lived their working lives by tachograph and weigh-scale, but the storm cloud is undeniable.

Inside what used to be a tourist kiosk—now repurposed as a command shack plastered with *Kids for Freedom* crayon art—organisers stab calculators, scribble fuel allotments, weigh the ethics of propane versus diesel heaters, and await the following verdict from cyberspace. When the *VICE* headline about hacked donors pings the group chat, someone mutters, "They're unmasking wallets so they don't have to unmask ideas." Chris prints the spreadsheet anyway, redacting nothing, then feeds it to a woodstove whose chimney coughs particles of melted anonymity into the dawn.

Out on Kent Street, the CB radio burps to life. "Breaker, break. Copy the freeze?" crackles one handle. Another answers in Saskatchewan prairie baritone:

"Copy. Funds on ice, but coffee's still hot." A chorus of laughter—a sound less of delight than of men refusing to feel the cold—ripples through the cab windows. The convoy's humour has become its circulatory system; as accounts pinch shut, jokes open arteries.

Meanwhile, four blocks east and five storeys up, a temporary war-room of staffers parses the duplicate headlines. A legal clerk sticks yellow flags into a thick binder titled: *Jurisdiction & National Security: Day 12.* One page strings together, words never paired—Crowdfunding, bi-state blockade, exigent finance tracking. In committee rooms, parliamentarians cross-question deputy ministers about emergency financial powers, the ink still wet on draft regulations. [33] One senator urges restraint; a rival MP warns of *de-platforming democracy.* Analysts prep talking points down the hall for the inevitable inquiry promised once the storm passes, an inquiry now guaranteed broader airtime thanks to *Politico's* splashy teaser—"Lawmakers will study the decision to expand enforcement powers against the blockade." [34]

Screens above the war-room tick through polling cross-tabs: urban sympathy flat, rural sympathy climbing; 58 per cent of Canadians under thirty-five nodding along; nearly half the nation grading the Prime Minister's response no better than the protesters' conduct. [35] *Ipsos'* fine print whispers credibility intervals, but the bold fonts shout narrative: diesel discontent is a viable party brand. An aide circles the "46 per cent sympathy" line and writes swing ridings in the margin.

Yet statistics will go against the day-to-day grit in Wellington. Tamara pours black coffee into a chipped enamel mug, hands it to Pastor Byron, and listens as he prays for the accountants who hold the keys to frozen money. Overhead, the Peace Tower clock marks another quarter hour while the diesel baritone never falters. Between gears, drivers swap stories about power steering lines snapping in minus-20°C and border waits that once felt heroic and now felt punitive. One quotes a *Guardian* reporter marvelling at "maple-leaf flags, conspiracy theories, and talk of The Matrix" swirling together like snow devils on the Hill. [36] No one argues; contradictions have become the convoy's uniform.

Near midnight of 7 February, a flurry of dust on the roofs was white again, erasing the day's footprints. Down the block, a young mother drapes earmuffs over her toddler before lifting him into a sleeper berth; he falls asleep to the lullaby of engines that may not fall silent. On the sidewalk, a retired nurse from Vanier hands out hand-warmers and murmurs, "I don't agree with them, but I won't see anyone freeze." Her breath mingles with exhaust, indistinguishable in the night.

Across Confederation Square, the big screens mounted outside news studios roll B-roll of Parliament lit in gold, captioned: *DAY 10 OF THE GRIDLOCK—SYMPATHY 46%, FUNDS 0% LIQUID*. Inside, pundits wonder aloud whether all this sympathy will curdle once pay cheques bounce and sirens blare. One anchor recalls a quote attributed to Mark Twain that *history never repeats, but often rhymes*, her guest replies that if so, Ottawa is composing the blueswit the primary instrument an air-horn.

Just before dawn on 8 February, the block heaters growl awake, shaking frost from mirrors. The press corps queues for mic checks, their leads already drafted: *'Donor dollars held hostage,' 'Parliament weighs purse strings,' 'Polls narrow like winter roads.'* Seated on his stool, Pastor Byron completes a Psalm about rivers of living water. Tamara checks her phone—no fresh money released, yet the GiveSendGo total still ratchets upward on the screen like a defiant elevator. The spreadsheet leak has only made the faithful double down.

Then, as the eastern sky bleeds pale violet, the streetlamps wink out in unison. For a moment, each windshield frames the same scene: a sun as thin as a minted coin, snow-slick streets, and a parliament etched like a question mark. The engines idle in rhythm, a thousand iron hearts beating the same measured caution. If money is the protest's bloodstream and sympathy for its breath, both are surging—even as courts clamp arteries and politicians debate ventilators. The hint that the coming month's victory will not depend solely on cubic inches lies in that fragile equilibrium. It will be won—or lost—by which side learns to translate balance sheets and bar graphs into the human key of bread, diesel, and borrowed vans.

The day breaks. Numbers refresh. And every soul on Wellington Street wonders, with equal hope and dread, what tomorrow's ticker will declare. *From late morning on 8 February through the evening of 10 February 2022, as the protest's patriotic veneer splinters under extremist appropriation and the Emergencies Act looms.*

The clocks on Parliament Hill had only struck eleven when Ottawa's winter light caught a scrap of cloth snapping above a Kenworth's grill—a Confederate battle flag, its colours garish against the pale snow. Smartphones tilted skyward, reporters thumbed frantic tweets, and the morning's uneasy truce between spectacle and civic patience shattered like lake ice under a logging truck. By noon, the images were everywhere, braided with stills of a lone swastika parading past the Centennial Flame, proof that what had begun as a truckers' grievance was now a carnival where any flag of fury could rent a stall. [37] [38] [39]

Inside the Privy Council Office, the memos thickened. One draft, time-stamped 12:47. Officials, using careful bilingual jargon, asked whether *public-order emergency criteria* had been met. [40] Janice Charette's signature looped below a margin note—Threshold?—as if the question mark itself might buy more time. Yet outside, time was busy picking up speed.

On Wellington Street, a teenage videographer named Rémy flattened himself behind the rear axles of a Peterbilt, livestreaming chants that bounced between *We want freedom* and *Build the gallows*. The feed rode TikTok's algorithm like a ski jump, cresting a million views before the sun dipped. In echoing those chants, R.C.M.P. constables stood shoulder-to-shoulder beneath the pewter sky that promises snow without mercy. Their radios crackled an operational order: *No rugged gear, no shields, maintain non-confrontational posture.* [41] A veteran among them muttered, "Any more non-confrontational and we'll be hugging exhaust pipes."

Back at curbside, Jerry "Skookum" McLeod—thirty years of ice-road miles and an air-brushed maple leaf on his cab—stared, slack-jawed, at the words *WHITE POWER WORLDWIDE* marker-tagged across his sleeper's aluminium. "This ain't my rig's gospel," he growled, scrubbing at the letters with a diesel-damp shop rag until they smeared into ghostly grey streaks. Nearby, a volunteer pastor offered prayers over a portable loudspeaker; the words dissolved into feedback whenever the horns blared. Somewhere northward, a columnist typed that the convoy had become an *export-grade symbol set*, franchised by American alt-right influencers while the original operators still hunted coffee refills. [42]

As dusk found the capital, GoFundMe's frozen millions were already old news. A fresh tranche on GiveSendGo pinged upward like a slot-machine reel—then froze, mid-spin, under an Ontario court order whose legal ice reached clear to Delaware and back again. [43] [44] Almost simultaneously, hackers dumped a spreadsheet of 92,000 donor names; Rémy's phone lit with signal flares of outrage and delight in equal measure. In bunk-houses built of plywood and tarps, organisers shuffled new crypto wallets like marked cards, whispering that if banks were moats, then Bitcoin was a drawbridge.

9 February rose bright and brittle. *The Guardian's* homepage led with a headline tying neo-Nazi iconography to the protest; [45] *The Washington Post* followed, worrying aloud that the tactics were spreading from Windsor to Wellington like salt on a chain-mail wound. [46] In committee rooms, opposition MPs alternated between lament and leverage. "You can't paint 46 per cent of Canadians with the same extremist brush," one Conservative argued, waving freshly printed poll cross-tabs. The Minister of Public Safety countered by slapping down CSIS threat assessments that read like the makings of a bad prairie storm— low rumble now, high winds coming. [47]

Mid-afternoon, grey clouds closed their fists. Snowmelt refroze, turning pavement into a mirror that showed every flag twice. At the war-memorial steps, Rémy photographed a trucker, a believer in the Charter, quarrelling with a man who thought Hitler had been misunderstood. The argument bled into the Citizen Band: "This ain't the rally we promised," Skookum barked. Replies overlapped— some in agreement, some laced with code-words dredged from the darker corners of Telegram.

Meanwhile, another PCO memo crossed the river to Gatineau, noting that tow-truck operators were refusing contracts *for personal safety or ideological alignment.* [48] Tables of potential enforcement tools were annotated: Criminal Code, Emergencies Act, National Defence Act—each checked, many crossed out, one underlined twice. By evening, cabinet ministers gathered in a wood-panelled room where the temperature rose with each scenario war-gamed. Someone commented on the difficulty of stopping a rumour once it puts its boots on; someone else quipped that in Ottawa, the rumours had traded boots for eighteen wheels.

10 February dawned in a hush heavy as wet wool. A column of R.C.M.P. cruisers slid into position by the Garden of the Provinces, their light-bars muted, while officers tucked laminated "Media Liaison" cards into parka pockets. A whispered directive circulated: record plate numbers and freeze accounts under the guidance of the Financial Transactions and Reports Analysis Centre of Canada (FINTRAC) once emergency orders land. The word emergency tasted metallic, like biting a nine-volt battery to see if it still had charge.

Yet on the street, defiance heated the air faster than any catalytic heater. Skookum fired his rig and found a strip of duct tape over the vandalised slogan; a stranger had written *NOT IN OUR NAME* across it in Sharpie. The two men shook hands. Ten metres away, a teenager sold merchandise emblazoned with the maple leaf and the serpent of the Gadsden flag; the line at his booth snaked past crates of donated diapers and into a fog of barbecue smoke.

News tickers rolled: *PCO CONFIRMS CABINET REVIEWING EMERGENCY MEASURES.* A *CBC* mic thrust toward a constitutional scholar who muttered about *last-resort spiral.* Up on a lamp-post, Rémy perched like a crow, streaming every magic-hour minute until a chant caught his ear—"Whose streets? Our streets!"—followed by a surge toward the police line. Snowballs flew first, then a frozen water bottle. Officers steadied, boots scraping ice, hands hovering near zip-ties they'd been told not to use.

That scuffle fizzled, but the footage replayed across the evening news in loops. Governor General Mary Simon's convoy eased through wrought-iron gates toward Rideau Hall by twilight. On her desk waited an Order-in-Council awaiting vice-regal ink—the first invocation of the Emergencies Act in thirty-four years. [49] Aides whispered final briefings while outside, city lights trembled in the diesel haze.

At exactly 20:47, Rémy's phone chimed: *BREAKING—Cabinet approves emergency powers; declaration imminent.* Horns that had idled in minor key now roared an uncertain fanfare. Skookum exhaled a plume that vanished in the backwash of headlamps. He remembered the flag he hauled across the prairies, remembered too the oath on his commercial licence, and wondered which one would ask the higher price before dawn.

Canadians pressed remotes in living rooms from Kamloops to Corner Brook, watching Chyron after Chyron declare, *First Use in 34 Years.* Some cheered, some cursed, and many merely held their breath. Parliament's stone façade glowed amber against the night, and every banner—patriotic or hateful, pristine or defaced—fluttered in a wind that smelled of coming change. The trucks kept idling, the snow kept falling, and the national mood hung suspended, like a question that would demand its answer in the cold, grey morning.

ENDNOTES

[1] Hagberg, L., & Ljunggren, D. (2022, February 6). *Ottawa mayor declares state of emergency to deal with trucking protest.* Reuters. https://www.reuters.com/world/americas/protest-against-vaccine-mandates-paralyzing-canada-capital-mayor-says-2022-02-06

[2] Scherer, S. (2022, January 9). *Canada resists pressure to drop vaccine mandate for cross-border truckers.* Reuters. https://www.reuters.com/markets/commodities/canada-resists-pressure-drop-vaccine-mandate-cross-border-truckers-2022-01-09

[3] Scherer, S. (2022, January 13). *Canada drops vaccine mandate for its truckers after pressure from industry.* Reuters. https://www.reuters.com/world/americas/canadian-truckers-stay-exempt-covid-19-vaccine-requirements-2022-01-13

[4] Scherer, S. (2022, January 20). *Canadian provincial leader wants to pause truckers' COVID vaccine mandate.* Reuters. https://www.reuters.com/business/canadian-vaccine-mandate-lead-inflation-empty-shelves-trucking-executives-say-2022-01-20

[5] Ljunggren, D. (2022, January 24). *Trudeau slams "fear-mongering" over trucker mandate.* Reuters. https://www.reuters.com/world/americas/canadas-trudeau-slams-fear-mongering-over-covid-vaccine-mandate-truckers-2022-01-24

[6] Ljunggren, D. (2022, January 27). *Anti-vaccine Canada truckers roll toward Ottawa, praised by Tesla's Musk.* Reuters. https://www.reuters.com/world/americas/anti-vaccine-canada-truckers-roll-toward-ottawa-praised-by-teslas-musk-2022-01-27

[7] Ljunggren, D. (2022, January 24). *Truckers fighting government vaccine mandate march to Canadian capital.* Reuters. https://www.reuters.com/world/americas/truckers-fighting-government-vaccine-mandate-march-canadian-capital-2022-01-24

[8] Gillies, J., Raynauld, V., & Wisniewski, A. (2023). Canada is no exception: The 2022 Freedom Convoy, political discontent, and populist tides. *American Behavioral Scientist, 67*(10), 1237-1264. https://doi.org/10.1177/00027642231166885

[9] O'Sullivan, D. (2022, February 8). The alt-right on Facebook is hijacking Canada's trucker blockade. *WIRED.* https://www.wired.com/story/ottawa-trucker-protest-facebook-alt-right

[10] Ljunggren, D., & Stewart, K. (2022, February 7). *Judge grants 10-day injunction banning trucker horn-honking in Ottawa.* Reuters. https://www.reuters.com/world/americas/canada-police-seen-getting-tough-trucker-protests-continue-2022-02-07

[11] Sloly, P. (interviewee). (2022, February 7). Ottawa police call for more personnel to regain control of city. *Global News.* https://globalnews.ca/news/8600507/ottawa-police-freedom-convoy-on-offensive

[12] Duplicate of #1

[13] Cecco, L. (2022, February 7). *Ottawa declares state of emergency as Canada trucker protest gridlocks city.* The Guardian. https://www.theguardian.com/world/2022/feb/07/ottawa-declares-state-of-emergency-as-canada-trucker-protest-paralyses-city

[14] Gonzales, O. (2022, February 6). *Ottawa declares state of emergency over pandemic-restriction protests.* *Axios.* https://www.axios.com/2022/02/06/canada-covid-protests-ottawa

[15] Blatchford, A. (2022, February 6). *Ottawa mayor: "Situation is completely out of control." Politico.* https://www.politico.com/news/2022/02/06/ottawa-declares-state-of-emergency-convoy-protests-00006053

[16] Duplicate of #10

[17] Duplicate of #10

[18] Duplicate of #5

[19] Duplicate of #6

[20] Duplicate of #9

[21] Duplicate of #1

[22] Duplicate of #14

[23] CTV News Staff. (2022, February 24). *Ottawa lifts state of emergency declared during "Freedom Convoy" demonstration.* CTV News. https://www.ctvnews.ca/politics/ottawa-lifts-state-of-emergency-declared-during-freedom-convoy-demonstration-1.5795744

[24] Tasker, J. P. (2022, February 24). Trudeau's convoy response gets failing grade, but even fewer support protesters: Ipsos poll. *Global News.* https://globalnews.ca/news/8640772/ipsos-poll-trudeau-convoy-response

[25] Abacus Data. (2022, February 3). *Pandemic frustration may be running high, but most don't side with the so-called "Freedom Convoy".* https://abacusdata.ca/freedom-convoy-public-reaction-february-2022

[26] Duplicate of #13

[27] Ljunggren, D. (2022, February 12). *TD Bank freezes accounts that received money for Canada protests.* Reuters. https://www.reuters.com/world/americas/td-bank-freezes-two-accounts-that-received-funds-support-canada-protests-2022-02-12

[28] GoFundMe. (2022, February 4). *GoFundMe statement on the Freedom Convoy 2022 fundraiser.* Medium. https://medium.com/gofundme-stories/update-gofundme-statement-on-the-freedom-convoy-2022-fundraiser-4ca7e9714e82

[29] Duplicate of #27

[30] Gilbert, D. (2022, February 14). Hackers just leaked the names of 92,000 'Freedom Convoy' donors. *VICE News.* https://www.vice.com/en/article/freedom-convoy-givesendgo-donors-leaked

[31] Ljunggren, D. (2022, February 15). More data on Canadian "Freedom Convoy" donors leaked – website. Reuters. https://www.reuters.com/world/americas/more-data-canada-truck-convoy-donors-leaked-website-2022-02-15

[32] Ljunggren, D. (2022, February 12). Ontario court orders GiveSendGo to freeze convoy funds. Reuters. https://www.reuters.com/world/americas/td-bank-freezes-two-accounts-that-received-funds-support-canada-protests-2022-02-12

[33] Boutilier, A. (2022, March 24). Committee examining Liberals' emergency powers debates scope of inquiry. *Global News.* https://globalnews.ca/news/8707822/committee-emergency-powers-debates-scope-of-inquiry

[34] Lum, Z.-A. (2022, February 23). Trudeau revokes controversial emergency powers. *Politico.* https://www.politico.com/news/2022/02/23/trudeau-revokes-emergency-powers-convoy-00011158

[35] Duplicate of #24

[36] Lindeman, T. (2022, February 11). Maple leaf flags, conspiracy theories and *The Matrix.* Inside the Ottawa truckers' protest. *The Guardian.* https://www.theguardian.com/world/2022/feb/11/canada-ottawa-truckers-protest-covid-vaccine-mandates

[37] Hernandez, J. (2022, February 8). Canadian truckers block a key border crossing, as their protest morphs and drags on. *NPR.* https://www.npr.org/2022/02/08/1079212789/ottawa-trucker-convoy-protest

[38] Cecco, L. (2022, February 8). How conspiracy theorists steered Canada's anti-vaccine trucker protest. *The Guardian.* https://www.theguardian.com/world/2022/feb/08/canada-ottawa-trucker-protest-extremist-qanon-neo-nazi

[39] Al Jazeera English. (2022, February 18). Canada border blockades, protests "nothing to do with trucking". *Al Jazeera.* https://www.aljazeera.com/news/2022/2/18/canada-border-blockades-protests-nothing-to-do-with-trucking

[40] Public Order Emergency Commission. (2023). *Report of the Public Inquiry into the 2022 Public Order Emergency* (Vol. 3). https://publicorderemergencycommission.ca/files/documents/Final-Report/Vol-3-Report-of-the-Public-Inquiry-into-the-2022-Public-Order-Emergency.pdf

[41] Royal Canadian Mounted Police. (2023). *Project Natterjack: National after-action review into the RCMP response to the Freedom Convoy 2022.* https://www.rcmp-grc.gc.ca/en/corporate-information/publications-and-manuals/project-natterjack-national-after-action-review

[42] Duplicate of #9

[43] Boak, J. (2022, February 13). Canada's Ambassador Bridge reopens after blockade. *The Washington Post.* https://www.washingtonpost.com/world/2022/02/13/canada-freedom-convoy-border-blockades-truckers

[44] The Guardian Staff. (2022, February 5). GoFundMe removes donation page for Canadian trucker protest. *The Guardian.* https://www.theguardian.com/world/2022/feb/05/gofundme-removes-donation-page-for-canadian-truckers-protest

[45] Duplicate of #38

[46] Duplicate of #43

[47] Department of Justice Canada. (2022, February 14). *Declaration of public order emergency under the Emergencies Act.* https://www.justice.gc.ca/eng/csj-sjc/section58.html

[48] Izri, T., Baxter, D., & Boutilier, A. (2024, January 23). Federal Court finds Emergencies Act for "Freedom Convoy" violated Charter. *Global News.* https://globalnews.ca/news/10244673/emergencies-act-convoy-federal-court

[49] Duplicate of #48

Chapter Two:

Hidden Currents Beneath the Ice

"Freedom rode shotgun, but the money drove. You could hear it in the pings—Detroit, Dauphin, Nana for Freedom—each one a coin tossed into a wishing well of diesel dreams. By the time the convoy hit Ottawa, the only thing louder than the horns was the sound of foreign dollars asking for change."
~ R.G. Cruise

It began as a trill of push-notifications in the cab of a Kenworth idling west of Winnipeg: ding—five dollars from Dauphin; ding—ten from Detroit; ding—fifty from someone signing only *Nana for Freedom*. Within sixty seconds, the tally on Tamara Lich's brand-new GoFundMe page leapt past a thousand dollars, proving that money could outrun even prairie wind in the pandemic age. By nightfall of 22 January, the total brushed six figures, and the convoy's planners realised they were navigating a river of cash as much as an asphalt ribbon. [1]

The macro view was stark: two years of lockdowns had driven millions of restless thumbs toward crowdfunding platforms, while American culture-war patrons had learned that a well-timed click could shift politics three time zones away. Researchers tracking protest finance warned that sites like GoFundMe and its less- regulated cousin GiveSendGo were no longer neutral jars for spare change but "conduits for ideological struggle" whose algorithms amplified fury as efficiently as they tallied dollars. [2] Inside Ottawa's Privy Council Office (PCO), a January briefing slid across mahogany—Cross-border donation pathways and compliance gaps—its footnotes stuffed with case studies from the Capitol riot to

European anti-lockdown marches. Still weeks from blaring horns, Parliament Hill was already awash in invisible capital.

At a Saskatoon truck stop on 24 January, driver Jerry "Chisel" Mahon watched the total climb past CA$5 million and whistled low. GoFundMe publicly cautioned that no nickel would move until organisers produced a distribution plan meeting its anti-fraud rules. [3] In Calgary, an assistant bank manager toggled through spreadsheets, searching for anything flagged *FConvoy_2022*. At the same time, Glencoe Fish-and-Tackle began printing *FREEDOM ISN'T FREE, BUT DIESEL ISN'T EITHER* bumper stickers faster than its receipt printer could spit ink. The movement was still five days and eight hundred kilometres from Ottawa. Yet, its financial shadow already stretched to the Texas Panhandle, where rancher Colton Reaves leaned back in a creaking chair, clicked *donate*, and heard his battered CRT radio fizz with distant Canadian news static. The sound made him grin; the exchange rate made him smile wider.

By 25 January, the platform froze CA$4.5 million—an act that felt, to drivers huddled around cellphone glare in Moose Jaw, like someone damming the Red River with a dinner plate. [4] The convoy's Telegram rooms flooded with theories: PayPal pressure, federal coercion, cyber-sabotage. Most agreed on only one point: money, like diesel, would find another hose. Sure enough, when GoFundMe partially released an initial CA$1 million on 28 January—money wired to an Ottawa business account after organisers filed receipts for fuel and hotel blocks—organisers hailed the gesture as a victory, not a compromise. The grievance engine ran best on partial fuel.

Across the border, conservative talk shows framed the campaign as a North American referendum on mandates, urging listeners to *chip in a gallon of freedom. PBS* analysts later noted that U.S. donors saw the Canadian protest less as altruism than as a rehearsal for mid-term messaging back home. [5] The algorithmic tide sent twenty-dollar bills flowing northward faster than the snow geese headed south, and every chime on a driver's phone felt like a tailwind.

Academic monitors counted the dollars with anthropological awe: the convoy had raised more per capita in forty-eight hours than many national charities collected in a year. [6] *EBSCO's* politics desk published a note that the fund broke CA$4.3 million *before the protest officially began,* underscoring how platforms could front-load dissent faster than governments could convene committees. [7]

London's Royal United Services Institute quietly warned that the pace of the surge makes it essential for regulators to *monitor this space more closely, but not in slap-dash fashion.* [8] In downtown Toronto, junior lawyers at a Big-Five bank highlighted that paragraph and sent it up the chain.

Meanwhile, clerks practised the bureaucratic art of caution in the bowels of TD Bank's Toronto towers. Each morning's compliance bulletin arrived thicker than the last; each evening, the convoy's balance metre glowed brighter on the open monitors. Though the formal freeze orders against convoy-linked personal accounts would not land until mid-February, internal memos about potential §465(1) Criminal Code exposure circulated as early as 30 January. One supervisor whispered, "If this thing flips illegal, we're holding the fuse."

On 31 January, Ottawa's press gallery caught wind of the cross-border torrent. Headlines fretted over *foreign influence* and anonymous donors paying for diesel that might one day barricade trade routes. *CBC* data journalists published a still-incomplete list, revealing that at least a third of the donor names were aliases or jokes—Pierre Poilievre, Ron DeSantis, Clark Kent—and mapping several thousand ZIP codes far south of the Great Lakes. Opposition MPs demanded hearings; government back-benchers demanded a plan; truckers demanded coffee.

The following sunrise, 1 February, painted the Trans-Canada in a pink haze as the convoy rolled through Arnprior. Tamara read aloud from the GoFundMe page: "We are a peaceful, unified crowd of hard-working Canadians who just want our freedom back." Every click on the Donate button dinged her phone, each tone merging with the rhythmic slap of wiper blades against sleet. In a motel parking lot, volunteer accountants entered pledge figures into Google Sheets, double-checking e-transfers from British Columbia loggers and Saskatchewan Hutterite colonies. A kind of grassroots bookkeeping blossomed, half cottage-trust-fund and half political Kickstarter.

But by mid-afternoon, the platform's Trust & Safety team flagged *rapid escalation in police reports* and *emerging violence indicators*, flipping the fundraiser to Pause for deeper review. Within twenty-four hours, late evening 2 February, the page bore a yellow banner: Under Review. Donations temporarily disabled. *CityNews* informed readers that roughly 120,000 donors had pledged CA$10.1 million before the suspension. [9] *BBC's* world desk reduced the drama to a single sentence: *GoFundMe says it will withhold millions of dollars raised for Canadian truckers, citing police reports of violence.* [10] On Parliament Hill, staffers copied that line into talking points, italicised *withhold,* and wondered how long italics could hold back a semi-trailer.

Scenes unfolded in miniature: at an Ottawa TD branch, a teller printed the first provisional freeze notice and felt her palm sweat through the paper; across town, two truckers in a snow-dusted sleeper stared at a spinning phone icon that once promised coffee money; down in Lubbock, Texas, Colton's credit-card statement still showed a successful pledge, but asterisks beside the transaction read Pending Refund. The river of cash was not drying up—merely shifting its course toward GiveSendGo, where a Christian-libertarian banner promised *Freedom Means Free Fundraising. TIME* magazine would later report that the platform raked in over US$9 million for the convoy in days, a windfall for a site usually devoted to missionary fees and youth-group vans. [11] To the men on Wellington Street, it felt like the river had found a new channel; to Ottawa's regulators, it felt like the levee had sprung a second leak.

Late on 2 February, whispers of anti-money-laundering action zipped through committee rooms. FINTRAC analysts prepared scenario charts, predicting that crowdfunding could circumvent every choke-point in Canada's financial system without tighter rules. Those predictions would, months later, drive amendments forcing such platforms to register as Money-Service Businesses— changes DLA Piper lawyers would link directly to loopholes exposed by the convoy. [12] For the moment, though, policy remained intention, and intention was no match for a QR code circulating on TikTok promising *Fuel a truck, fuel a movement.*

Just past midnight, a snowplough shuddered along Queen Street, piling slush against curbs crusted with salt. In its wake, a teenage volunteer chalked *THANK YOU AMERICA* on the wet pavement; by sunrise, the letters were half-melted, the sentiment intact. Radio news declared that Parliament's safety committee would summon GoFundMe executives to testify. "They're going to cross-examine the cloud," Chisel joked into his CB. Beside him, a rookie driver checked the GiveSendGo counter—already surging past a million—and replied, "Cloud's faster than lawyers, brother." They both laughed, the sound swallowed by idling engines and the sub-zero wind sneaking through the window seals.

Thus, the first fortnight ended: a crowd-funded caravan parked on the edge of constitutional debate, its monetary lifeblood ebbing from one platform only to regenerate in another. News tickers asked whether foreign dollars negated domestic dissent; academics drafted papers on border-agnostic populism; and Ottawa's skyline braced for the physical arrival of money already in spirit. The question over every committee table was not whether the funds were real— inescapably, exuberantly real—but whether the nation receiving them could still call itself the sole author of its own story. Beneath February's iron sky, the currents kept flowing unseen, carrying with them both the promise of freedom and the price of reckoning.

Headlines cracked across Canada like lake ice at sunrise: *59 Per Cent of Convoy Donors Are American*, roared a splash page on *CityNews*, quoting the newly hacked GiveSendGo spreadsheet that analysts were still downloading from the dark web. [13] A *Guardian* exclusive piled on, quoting the unnamed hacker who warned of "foreign money funding extremism in Canada." [14] Within the hour, *Reuters* confirmed that Distributed Denial of Secrets had posted a torrent containing 92,000 donor names, ZIP codes, and payment notes ranging from *God bless from Dallas* to *Truckers for Liberty—MAGA*. [15] Cable crawls stacked those numbers beside live shots of jack-knifed semis in minus-30°C wind; in West Block, the public-safety committee hustled into emergency session, clerks photocopying a motion to summon GoFundMe and GiveSendGo executives before MPs *to explain foreign interference.* [16]

Tamara Lich read the CSV file in a borrowed trailer that smelled of propane and black coffee. *Column C—Donor_Country*—scrolled like a globe spun by a child: U.S., U.S., U.S., then a scattering of Australia, Germany, Qatar. "That's a lot of passports for a made-in-Canada fight," she muttered, fingers hovering above the trackpad as if sheer will could edit geography. Beaupré's text pinged her phone: *Guardian running 56% U.S. figure. Get ahead of it.* She exhaled, marshalled a tweet: *We welcome support from freedom-lovers everywhere.* But the algorithm was already feeding the leak to rage-farm accounts in Florida and Texas, each retweeting another snowflake in a growing blizzard of doubt.

South-west in Montréal, political-science professor Anaïs Gendron printed the fresh *Abacus* cross-tabs: sixty-eight per cent of Canadians felt they had *very little in common* with convoy grievances; only thirty-two per cent felt kinship.

[17] She ringed the age split—support highest among 18-34s—and scribbled authenticity gap widens when donors aren't neighbours. Her graduate seminar would dissect that metric before lunch; by then, the *Léger North American Tracker* would land, showing forty-seven per cent strong opposition and thirty-two per cent support for the convoy's message, plus a stunning sixty-five per cent who deemed protesters *a small minority of selfish Canadians.* [18]

In Huron County, Pastor Ron Yost nursed a mug of percolator coffee while *VOCM's* call-in host replayed the *CityNews* statistic: "Folks, fifty-nine per cent U.S. dollars—does that still make this a Canadian stand?" One caller likened it to missionaries tithing across borders; another growled about *Yankee dark money.* Yost sighed at the irony: his congregation had long mailed loonies to African orphanages, yet Ottawa now fretted over foreign alms for fuel.

Back in the capital, New Democrat MP Alistair MacGregor's motion zipped through committee: *GoFundMe executives to testify, plus FINTRAC spads to map the money trail.* [19] A separate *CTV* alert noted that MPs across party lines had voted aye—rare unity forged in suspicion. [20] On Telegram, convoy chat rooms called it a *show trial,* dropping links to a GiveSendGo mirror that kept the counter climbing toward US$9 million despite the hack. At 13:07, Beaupré yelled over the CB, "Pull every post with foreign flags—optics, optics!" Volunteers purged two hundred photos before a Florida influencer reposted them with a laughing-crying emoji.

Journalists traced the river east and west: *TIME* tallied platform fees GiveSendGo had pocketed—nearly US$640,000 since launch—turning the Christian site into the week's most profitable political casino. [21] *Reuters* calculated that, even after refunds and freezes, almost US$4 million sat in crypto wallets beyond any court's reach, stoking cabinet fears of *borderless insurgent finance.* [22] On the Hill, Liberal aides drafted talking points—*'digital Wild West,' 'transparency deficit,' 'protect democracy'*—while Conservative staffers rehearsed rebuttals about *grassroots solidarity.*

The afternoon polls hit like sleet on bare skin. *Léger's* PDF, e-mailed to every newsroom, detailed that sixty-two per cent of Canadians opposed the convoy, forty per cent of the vaccinated sympathised with frustration, and fifty-two per cent saw echoes of the January 6th insurrection in Washington. [23] A *Vox* explainer distilled the stats into one damning sentence: *The convoy is an unpopular uprising.* [24] Tamara refreshed her phone; each new headline carried the donor-leak percentage like a scarlet letter. She whispered, "Are we still 'we' if half the money spells colour without a 'u'?"

At 16:55, GoFundMe's general counsel emailed the committee clerk confirming attendance; attached were internal compliance notes stating that eighty-six per cent of its original donors had been Canadian—an oasis of homegrown legitimacy buried beneath GiveSendGo's American flood. [25] The nuance failed to trend. Instead, a *Guardian* update quoting the hacker's claim—*US$3.6 million from the U.S.*—rocketed to the top of Reddit's r/WorldNews. [26]

Evening settled with a brittle sky the colour of gunmetal. *CBC's* flagship newscast opened with twin graphics: the spreadsheet's red-white-blue pie chart and *Abacus's* sympathy bar. Anchor Adrienne Arsenault asked whether "real Canadians still helm the wheel," while a panellist noted that trust erodes faster than black ice forms. Trucker Jerry "Chisel" Mahon watched the segment through a streaked windshield in a motel lot on Coventry Road. "Seems like we've been repo'd by Uncle Sam," he sighed to the rookie beside him, killing the cab lights.

5 February dawned lavender and lethal-cold. GoFundMe's final axe fell: the platform yanked the convoy page entirely, pledging automatic refunds after FBI-flavoured phone calls from U.S. governors. [27] Within minutes, Governor DeSantis blasted the ban as *fraud,* giving the story a second wind across partisan airwaves. At 09:12, *Guardian* wires posted a fresh kicker—*Fundraiser Pulled Amid Foreign-Influence Fears*—cementing the narrative that offshore dollars and disinformation had hijacked Canada's populist moment. [28]

At lunchtime, Finance Committee clerks quietly drafted a motion to expand their upcoming cryptocurrency study to include "foreign-origin political donations." Reporters sniffed it out before dessert. Twitter flared with memes of red-white maple leaves painted over U.S. greenbacks; TikTok stitched clips of honking cabs to Johnny Cash's I Walk the Line. Pastor Yost flicked off his barn radio, whispering a prayer for discernment; Gendron flagged a student essay quoting Marshall McLuhan: *Money is just another medium.*

By twilight, convoy support had slipped eleven points in two days, according to a fresh *Abacus* flash poll leaked to *National Observer*—authenticity crisis feeding perception crisis, each loop tightening like a ratchet. [29] Tamara closed her laptop, stepped into the snow-hushed street, and watched a maple-leaf flag snap in the wind. Who owns your story when half the ink is foreign? She wondered. Above her, Parliament's Peace Tower clock tolled six slow notes, each echoing off jack-knifed trailers and the uneasy silence of a movement suddenly unsure of its citizenship.

The first tremor hit just after dawn on 12 February, when a *German Marshall Fund* dashboard lit up in the Privy Council Office (PCO): 19.3 million Facebook interactions about the convoy, three-quarters driven by U.S. accounts, and climbing so fast the graph looked vertical.[27] Within an hour, *Axios* splashed the figure, noting that Ben Shapiro's page alone was outselling every *CBC* post combined, and the convoys' online roar now pulsed louder south of the forty-ninth than north. [30] Phone screens across Ottawa glowed red; national-security staff drafted talking points that read like weather warnings for a digital nor'easter.

Marc Beaupré felt the gust first-hand inside his cube-van "O.P.S. room," scrolling a torrent of direct messages from Florida influencers promising crypto *gas cards* if he would stream under a *#Don'tTreadOnMe* banner. A second ping arrived from a Telegram super-channel with half a million subscribers: *Add Proud Boys hashtags for 10 BTC.* He rubbed his eyes, muttered that his protest was becoming a NASCAR hood, then slapped out a reply—*This stays Canadian.* Even before his thumb left the screen, others re-edited screenshots of his refusal into memes accusing him of *Trudeau collusion,* proving that algorithms can turn No into Yes by lunchtime. [31]

Across the river, R.C.M.P. intelligence analyst Priya Nayar flicked through a fresh *Natterjack* slide deck showing crimson heat-dots wherever convoy hashtags overlapped with flagged foreign troll farms. A single page marked *CONFIDENTIAL* charted 23 bitcoin transfers—one worth US$90,000—from wallets previously linked to January 6 agitators. The last line noted that 21 BTC (about US$1 million) sat in an address branded *HonkHonkHodl,* newly blacklisted under an emergency cabinet order. [32] "Foreign amplification, high-confidence, foreign financing medium-confidence," she told field officers on a secure Zoom; "focus on disinformation nodes." A corporal typed *DJT Jr retweet = street morale spike* into his notebook, the new algebra of protest policing. [33]

Parliament Hill absorbed the shock in real time. An *Angus Reid* flash poll—embargoed until noon but leaked by 09:30—showed three-in-four

Canadians now telling the convoy to "go home," down from near-parity support ten days earlier. [34] Premier Scott Moe called that proof Ottawa's smear job was working; Premier Doug Ford countered that "foreign meddling" was eroding legitimate dissent. Their barbs ricocheted through press galleries even as *Global News* reported Ontario intelligence worries that *adversarial actors* were *leveraging the freedom movement to sew division.* [35]

Tamara Lich scrolled the same poll on her phone in the motel lot off Coventry Road and whispered, "God, we're losing the room." Her screen pinged again—this time a *Reuters* alert that U.S. convoy spin-off groups were planning coast-to-coast copycats, using her livestream clips as recruitment trailers. U.S. governors tweeted their support [36] minutes later.

At 14:00, the Public Order Emergency Commission (PEOC) reconvened in a cramped federal courtroom, counsel hunched over binders thicker than phone books. One excerpt from an encrypted GiveSendGo log drew gasps: fifteen separate donations, each exactly US$1,776 routed through a mixing service in Wyoming. [37] Commissioner Paul Rouleau leaned in: "Does the Crown view this as symbolic or conspiratorial?" Counsel for the Attorney General replied that *symbolism and conspiracy had become Siamese twins in the age of digital cash.* The gallery scribbled furiously.

CTV News cut to its veteran panellist Marcia Kim, who shook her head at the numbers: "When Americans out-share Canadians four to one, it stops being a grassroots rally and starts looking like an import." [38] The Chyron beneath her read: *AMERICAN TAKEOVER?*, and Twitter trended the phrase within twenty minutes, propelled by both *#StandWithTruckers* and *#YankeeGoHome.* Upon Wellington Street, drivers refreshed their feeds and felt sympathy slip like traction on black ice.

Night fell, but the metric climbed; by 23:17, *CrowdTangle* showed 20.8 million U.S. interactions. Priya Nayar's briefing to senior brass used the word contagion twice and memetic insurgency once. [39] She recommended partnerships with Meta dis-info labs; a deputy commissioner said the request sounded like chasing smoke with butterfly nets. In the cube-van, Beaupré watched his admin team delete 1,600 spammed GIFs of bald eagles clutching maple leaves in talons shaped like AR-15s. "We're drowning," a volunteer muttered. "No," Beaupré corrected, "we're being ventilated."

13 February dawned colder still. *Global News* ran an investigation quoting O.P.P. analysts who warned that *foreign adversaries* were stoking the convoy to test Canadian fault lines. [40] In response, Alberta's premier called federal briefings *hysteria*, while Ontario's solicitor-general floated a motion to criminalise anonymous foreign funding of protests. *Hill* reporters noted premiers had not sparred so openly since the last equalisation fight; the convoy had become constitutional tinder.

At noon, the Public Order Emergency Commission (POEC)—a public inquiry established by the Government of Canada on April 25, 2022 to examine the circumstances leading to the invocation of the Emergencies Act during the 2022 *Freedom Convoy* protests—heard testimony from a CSIS liaison who described Telegram channels urging protesters to *drag traitor MPs into the street.* Audio clips played in the room—grainy, American twang, promising more crypto once *the maple tyrant is dangling.* Committee members exchanged looks usually reserved for bomb threats. As they broke for lunch, a staffer told the media scrum that interim findings were due in forty-eight hours and *all options were on the table.* [41]

While MPs lunched on lukewarm chicken wraps, a *Politico* push alert announced Ontario's state-of-emergency order, citing *foreign-inspired economic sabotage.* [42] The convoy's chats erupted: some called Ford a traitor, others a hero, none agreed on whose currency fuelled the diesel. That evening, Ottawa's skyline flickered with phone lights as protesters doom-scrolled; sympathy graphs fell, Bitcoin charts rose, both lines steep enough to share the same slope.

14 February delivered the *coup de grâce.* An updated *Axios* chart showed American Facebook pages generating more engagement about the convoy than every Canadian outlet combined—*Ben Shapiro* in first, *Newsmax* second, *Breitbart* third. [43] The story detonated across broadcast panels; premiers now agreed only on one thing: the POEC should recommend legislation. Draft bills floated through email chains—*'Digital Agent Registration Act,' 'Foreign Funding Transparency Act ,' 'Crypto Crowdfunding Oversight Board.'* Civil-liberties lawyers raised alarms about overbreadth but found few listeners.

At 18:42, Priya Nayar filed her final memo: 31 bitcoin wallets blacklisted, 47 U.S. troll accounts suspended, zero chance of complete containment. [44] She added one line in plain English: "Narrative battle lost; recommend pivot to public reassurance." Upstairs, cabinet ministers rehearsed the same theme for Question Period. Outside, someone projected a silhouette of the Peace Tower onto a big-rig truck and captioned it, *Who owns the signal?* The image went viral before the projector cooled.

On the morning of 15 February, the Commission's interim findings hit inboxes: foreign-sourced amplification "materially affected public order"; existing laws are "insufficiently agile" for platform-based funding; a new reporting regime is *urgently required.* [45] An hour later, *Angus Reid*'s latest poll showed convoy sympathy had catered to twenty-nine per cent. [46] Parliament's foyer filled with reporters asking whether digital cash now outranked Canadian consent.

That evening, Beaupré drafted a weary update for his 400,000 Telegram followers: "We remain Canadian. Outside voices welcome but not in charge." Replies flooded in—some encouraging, many American, half demanding he name-check the U.S. Constitution. He tossed the phone aside, stepped into the February dark, and listened to the engines idle in a rhythm not quite familiar anymore.

ENDNOTES

[1] Reuters Fact Check. (2022, January 27). *Fact check: Video of Indigenous group is not related to 2022 Freedom Convoy.* Reuters. https://www.reuters.com/article/fact-check/video-of-indigenous-group-is-not-related-to-2022-freedom-convoy-idUSL1N2U72WJ

[2] Goyette, L., & Maynard, R. (2023). Crowdfunding platforms as conduits for ideological struggle and digital mobilization. *Policy & Internet, 15*(2), 331–354. https://doi.org/10.1002/poi3.369

[3] Reynolds, C. (2022, January 25). GoFundMe withholding $4.5 M from trucker convoy until plan presented. *CTV News.* https://guelph.ctvnews.ca/calgary/article/gofundme-withholding-45m-from-trucker-convoy-until-plan-presented

[4] CTV News Vancouver Staff. (2022, January 25). $4 million in fundraising frozen by GoFundMe days after convoy leaves Vancouver. *CTV News Vancouver.* https://www.ctvnews.ca/vancouver/article/4m-in-fundraising-frozen-by-gofundme-days-after-trucker-convoy-leaves-vancouver

[5] Lardner, R., Smith, M. R., & Swenson, A. (2022, February 17). How American right-wing funding for Canadian trucker protests could sway U.S. politics. *PBS NewsHour.* https://www.pbs.org/newshour/world/how-american-right-wing-funding-for-canadian-trucker-protests-could-sway-u-s-politics

[6] EBSCO Research Starters. (2024). *Canada convoy protest (Freedom Convoy 2022)*. EBSCO Information Services. https://www.ebsco.com/research-starters/politics-and-government/canada-convoy-protest-freedom-convoy-2022

[7] Reimer, S. (2022, February 9). *The wrong way to truck along* [Commentary]. Royal United Services Institute. https://rusi.org/explore-our-research/publications/commentary/wrong-way-truck-along

[8] Stoodley, C. (2022, February 5). GoFundMe pulls trucker convoy fundraiser, citing terms of service violation. *CityNews Ottawa*. https://ottawa.citynews.ca/2022/02/05/gofundme-pulls-trucker-convoy-fundraiser-citing-terms-of-service-violation-5030890

[9] BBC News. (2022, February 5). *Freedom Convoy: GoFundMe seizes funds of Canada "occupation".* https://www.bbc.com/news/world-us-canada-60267840

[10] Bergengruen, V., & Wilson, C. (2022, February 11). 'Free' crowdfunding site linked to right-wing causes generates a windfall for itself. *TIME*. https://time.com/6150317/givesendgo-trucker-convoy-canada-profits

[11] Belli-Bivar, E., & Prucha, M. (2022, August 10). FINTRAC changes due to truckers convoy. *DLA Piper Insights*. https://www.dlapiper.com/en-us/insights/publications/2022/08/fintrac-changes-due-to-truckers-convoy

[12] CityNews Staff. (2022, November 3). Most funds raised for "Freedom Convoy" protest were returned or confiscated; 59 percent of donations came from the U.S. *CityNews Ottawa*. https://ottawa.citynews.ca/2022/11/03/most-funds-raised-for-free-dom-convoy-protest-were-returned-or-confiscated-6049816

[13] Duplicate of #12

[14] Lindeman, T. (2022, February 14). Foreign money funding "extremism" in Canada, says hacker. *The Guardian*. https://www.theguardian.com/world/2022/feb/14/foreign-money-funding-extremism-in-canada-says-hacker

[15] Reid, A., & Fraser, D. (2022, February 15). More data on Canadian "Freedom Convoy" donors leaked – website. *Reuters*. https://www.reuters.com/world/americas/more-data-canada-truck-convoy-donors-leaked-website-2022-02-15

[16] MacGregor, A. (2022, February 3). Motion adopted at House SECU to summon crowdfunding executives [Committee evidence, Meeting 12]. *Parliament of Canada*. https://www.ourcommons.ca/DocumentViewer/en/44-1/SECU/meeting-12/evidence

[17] Coletto, D., & Anderson, B. (2022, February 3). *Pandemic frustration may be running high, but more don't side with the so-called "Freedom Convoy".* Abacus Data. https://abacusdata.ca/freedom-convoy-public-reaction-february-2022

[18] Léger & Association for Canadian Studies. (2022, February 8). *North American Tracker: The Freedom Convoy and federal politics* [Polling report]. https://leger360.com/legers-north-american-tracker-february-8-2022

[19] CityNews Vancouver Staff. (2022, February 3). GoFundMe called to Commons committee as links to U.S. alleged in Ottawa protest. *CityNews Vancouver.* https://vancouver.citynews.ca/2022/02/03/ottawa-convoy-gofundme-us

[20] Aiello, R. (2022, February 3). MPs agree to call GoFundMe to testify over trucker convoy fundraiser. *CTV News.* https://www.ctvnews.ca/politics/article/mps-agree-to-call-gofundme-to-testify-over-trucker-convoy-fundraiser

[21] Duplicate of #10

[22] Duplicate of #15

[23] Duplicate of #18

[24] Kasparian, M. (2022, February 8). The Canadian trucker convoy protest is an unpopular uprising. *Vox.* https://www.vox.com/policy-and-politics/22926134/canada-trucker-freedom-convoy-protest-ottawa

[25] Guardian/Reuters Staff. (2022, February 5). GoFundMe removes donation page for Canadian trucker protest. *The Guardian.* https://www.theguardian.com/world/2022/feb/05/gofundme-removes-donation-page-for-canadian-truckers-protest

[26] Duplicate of #14

[27] Duplicate of #25

[28] Duplicate of #25

[29] National Observer Staff. (2022, February 8). Many Canadians believe Ottawa protests a "selfish display," Léger poll finds. *Canada's National Observer.* https://www.nationalobserver.com/2022/02/08/news/many-canadians-ottawa-protests-selfish-display

[30] Schwartz, A. (2022, February 14). U.S. accounts drive Canadian convoy protest chatter. *Axios.* https://www.axios.com/2022/02/14/us-accounts-canada-convoy-protests-social-media

[31] O'Sullivan, D. (2022, February 8). The alt-right on Facebook is hijacking Canada's trucker blockade. *WIRED.* https://www.wired.com/story/ottawa-trucker-protest-facebook-alt-right

[32] Gilbert, D. (2022, February 14). GiveSendGo hacker faces death threats for leaking "Freedom Convoy" donor info. *VICE News.* https://www.vice.com/en/article/us-freedom-convoy

[33] Royal Canadian Mounted Police. (2024). *Project NATTERJACK: National after-action review into the RCMP response to the 2022 Freedom Convoy.* https://rcmp.ca/en/corporate-information/publications-and-manuals/project-natterjack-national-after-action-review

[34] Angus Reid Institute. (2022, February 14). *Three-in-four Canadians tell convoy protesters "Go home now".* https://angusreid.org/trudeau-convoy-trucker-protest-vaccine-mandates-covid-19

[35] Bronskill, J. (2022, October 19). Foreign "adversaries" may have leveraged freedom movement to sow division, O.P.P. warned. *Global News.* https://globalnews.ca/news/9225667/foreign-adversaries-freedom-convoy-intelligence-report

[36] Huffstutter, P., & Layne, N. (2022, February 11). U.S. groups plan convoys in support of Canadian truckers. *Reuters.* https://www.reuters.com/world/americas/us-organizers-plan-convoys-support-canadian-truckers-2022-02-11

[37] Public Order Emergency Commission. (2023). *Report of the Public Inquiry into the 2022 Public Order Emergency* (Vol. 1). Government of Canada. https://publicorderemergencycommission.ca/files/documents/Final-Report/Vol-1-Report-of-the-2022-Public-Order-Emergency.pdf

[38] CTV News Staff. (2022, February 8). Canada's "Freedom Convoy" attracts support from U.S. and around the world. *CTV News.* https://www.ctvnews.ca/canada/article/canadas-freedom-convoy-attracts-support-from-us-and-around-the-world

[39] Duplicate of #33

[40] Duplicate of #36

[41] Duplicate of #35

[42] del Rosario, P. (2022, February 11). Trucker convoy forces Canada's largest province into state of emergency. *Politico.* https://www.politico.com/news/2022/02/11/trucker-convoy-forces-canadas-largest-province-into-state-of-emergency-00008213

[43] Duplicate of #30

[44] Duplicate of #33

[45] Duplicate of #37

[46] Duplicate of #34

CHAPTER THREE:

FLAGS IN THE DAWN

"A flag's just cloth until someone salutes it; then it's a confession.
You can't honk for freedom while hauling hate in your mirrors.
Even a trucker knows when to tarp the load and drive on."
~ R.G. Cruise

Before the sun could rinse night's frost from Parliament's copper roofs, newsrooms were already crackling with the voltage of a different chill: wire photos showing a Confederate battle flag flapping beside the Peace Tower's eternal flame had crossed editors' desks at 04:17, followed minutes later by a shot of a swastika daubed on a bedsheet and zip-tied to a Peterbilt grill. Graphic desks tried to blur the icon; producers tried—and failed—to find synonyms for revulsion. *The Guardian's* live blog bannered the moment in London as proof that *a local vaccine protest had mutated into something darker.* Its U.S. desk warned the images would be *instant rocket fuel for America's culture war.* [1] *Reuters* issued a flash noting that extremist insignia *now dotted the occupation's early-morning skyline,* a detail slipped between statistics on truck counts and wind chill. [2] Within an hour, Ottawa's parliamentary inboxes filled with subject lines that paired shock with urgency: *CONFEDERATE FLAG ON WELLINGTON—URGENT RESPONSE?, PM MEDIA LINE?, HATE SYMBOL BRIEFING REQUIRED.*

Half a world away, human-rights monitors pulled satellite feeds and archived every pixel, anxious that the maple leaf—normally a global shorthand for geniality—was at risk of becoming an involuntary background to hate. The Canadian Anti-Hate Network's overnight bulletin warned that "well-documented extremist icons are establishing plausible deniability corridors inside the protest," language as clinical as it was ominous. [3] On *NPR's Morning Edition*, Ottawa councillor Matthew Luloff spoke in the tight cadence of someone walking on ice: "We have Confederate flags, Nazi swastikas, acutely anti-Semitic writing—this is not what democracy looks like." [4]

On Wellington Street, veteran photojournalist Émile Rondeau crouched, knees barking against icy asphalt, to frame that swastika-scrawled semi before dawn's first blush could wash out the red. He whispered camera settings— "thousandth at f-four, bump ISO"—as though the shutter might flinch. Each breath fogged his viewfinder; each click felt like a geologist tapping a fault line. Behind him, drivers stirred in sleeper berths warmed by diesel heaters, unaware that a single photograph was about to redraw the protest's moral topography.

Elder Alma Kokinastaw steered her walker a hundred metres south toward the Centennial Flame, cedar bough tucked beneath her parka. She prayed for calm, not judgment; yet the sight of a swastika next to a maple leaf arrested her stride. Memory—her late father's stories of Canada's role in liberating camps—tightened her throat. "This ground remembers," she said, voice feathering into the wind, and pressed cedar needles against the frozen granite. Nearby, a student livestreamed her vigil; within the hour TikTok would pair her silence with captions about *Nazi flags in Canada* and rack up half a million views.

Convoy strategist Marc Beaupré scrolled Telegram at red-alert speed inside a rented RV marked *Comms*. Screenshots of Rondeau's swastika photo already peppered extremist channels, some boasting of *optics wins,* others accusing the mainstream press of Photoshop. One DM demanded he "fly more rebel flags to show Trudeau we're done being polite"—signed with an eagle and AR-15 emoji. Beaupré returned a blanket warning: *Any hate banners = immediate removal.* The message sank into the feed's white water, unseen.

R.C.M.P. liaison Sergeant Priya Nayar stood under a streetlamp, tablet in mitten'd hand, adding red pins to a heat-map titled: *Hate Symbol Cluster, 10 FEB 04:30- 06:00.* Each pin marked a citizen tweet or call-line report: one for the Confederate cloth, one for the swastika tarp, another for a Diagolon patch sighted near Bank Street. A shift corporal leaned over her shoulder. "Plan?" Nayar tapped the screen: "Photograph, document, don't escalate. Symbol display isn't a Criminal Code offence unless it incites." He grimaced—law moves slowly; outrage travels by LTE.

By breakfast, the insurgent imagery had detonated abroad. *Al Jazeera* warned of *right-wing currents in Canada's convoy*. [5] *Snopes* published a fact-check confirming *a small number of swastikas and Confederate flags*, but nuance drowned beneath headline fonts. [6] Ontario's premier, Doug Ford, who once hailed the truckers' *frustration*, told reporters that such symbols had "no place in our province or anywhere." [7] On Parliament's marble stairs, a scrum of MPs demanded explanations that could fit into a nine-second clip. "One flag mocks every sacrifice of World War II," snapped an opposition critic; moments later, a government whip called the protest "co-opted by racists."

CB radios crackled along the cordon. "Breaker one-nine, any unit seeing Nazi junk pull over and tarp it," ordered handle Dogbone, his prairie vowels worn thin by anger. Another voice—a younger driver from Red Deer—answered: "Copy, but you telling the press that or just us?" Dogbone's sigh hissed through static.

Back uptown, editors wrangled disclaimers: how to show the symbols without amplifying them? *Reuters* finally cropped the banner tight enough to illustrate, but broad enough to frighten. [8] Social-media dashboards lit in ambulance reds; every repost multiplied the spectacle, making the convoy's fringe look like its centre. Melbourne copy-editors slotted the photo beside the morning floods; in Nairobi, it ran above election news; in Buenos Aires, it led the foreign pages under the slug *Maple Mutiny*.

At 10:45, a hastily convened House subcommittee met behind frosted windows. Staff circulated a two-page motion: *That the Standing Committee on Canadian Heritage undertake a study on the public display of hate symbols, with particular attention to recent events on Parliament Hill.* The language tiptoed around direct condemnation, but everyone in the room knew the study's target. A Bloc MP proposed adding Confederate imagery to the definition; a Liberal whispered, "Do we need a definition if you can google the damn things?"

Outside, Émile Rondeau filed his selects. The best frame—the swastika lit by dawn's rose glow—hit wire feeds at 11:03. Less than five minutes later, *Hate on the Hill* scrolled across the *CBC News Network*. In homes from Nanaimo to Gander, breakfast forks paused mid-air. The convoy had already tested Canadians' patience with horn symphonies and diesel reek; now it threatened identity itself. Alma returned to her apartment before noon. Her granddaughter, eyes wide, asked if the eagle-feather on Alma's wall meant their family supported *the flag people.* Alma shook her head, silently thanking the cedar smoke clinging to her mittens.

As afternoon light paled, Ottawa Police public-information officers issued a statement: "We are aware of hate imagery. While display alone may not meet the threshold for criminal charges, we remind protestors we will document symbols of hate, and these symbols may inform ongoing investigations. The line between *aware* and *action* widened like a crack in river ice. *WIRED's* technology desk amplified the schism, reporting that alt-right Facebook influencers had *successfully hijacked convoy optics,* making the protest *look like Charlottesville North.* 9

Around 16:00, Sergeant Nayar received a final tip: an Indigenous veteran planned to perform a cleansing ceremony at the Tomb of the Unknown Soldier. Media crews hustled; live streams framed the man smudging the granite, tears threading the smoke. "We fought that symbol once," he said, voice carrying across a hush of idling engines. A YouTube clip of the ritual reached a quarter-million views by sunset. 10

Twilight bled into sub-zero night. Streetlamps flickered on, etching the Confederate cloth in sodium gold as if daring cameras to look away. In the House foyer, Aides slipped out to update tickers: *STUDY ON HATE SYMBOLS PASSES UNANIMOUSLY.* News anchors repeated the phrase until it felt both triumphant and tragic—victory measured by how quickly Parliament could study what should never have appeared.

On Wellington, Dogbone switched off his CB, the quiet as unsettling as any klaxon. "Thought we were blowing horns for freedom," he muttered. "Now we're babysitting ghosts." Alma's cedar smoke lingered in the ice-cold air like an unanswered prayer, while Émile Rondeau's shutter clicks echoed in press galleries worldwide.

Above them all, the Peace Tower clock chimed midnight, its rings echoing through the frost-thick silence and the whispered dread that tomorrow's sympathy might be lost to yesterday's flags. In dark committee rooms, legislative aides drafted additional clauses against hateful iconography. And across Canada, parents switched off televisions, wondering how a convoy meant to champion liberty had drifted so far down roads paved by hate—and whether the nation's kindness could still steer it back.

By 10:00 on 10 February, the convoy's optics crisis had gone from nasty surprise to full-blown national emergency. Emergency-commission lawyers huddled three floors below ground level, debating whether the *Hakenkreuz* sewn to a fleece blanket qualified as a *Nazi emblem* or merely *Nazi-derived art,* because the wording in section §1-b of their draft report hinged on that nuance. Upstairs, Public-Safety Minister Marco Mendicino fielded a rapid-fire briefing that warned hate-symbol sightings were spiking faster than police could catalogue them; the slide deck's title—*Symbols of Hate at the Gate*—had already been teased on morning newscasts. [11] Cable crawls recycled the phrase until it lodged in the collective vocabulary like grit behind an eyelid.

Inside a drafty cube van labelled *Comms,* strategist Marc Beaupré swore at his laptop. Overnight, his volunteer moderators had killed 1,400 Facebook images featuring swastikas or Confederate pennants, yet *CrowdTangle* now showed those same frames reborn on American meme pages captioned *Canadian Spring.* A Telegram DM from an account named Eagle1776 dangled 5 BTC if convoy leaders would *hold up liberty banners, any design.* Beaupré typed back Canadian flags only—no hate rags, hit send, and watched the reply ping in: *LOL TRAITOR* accompanied by a Pepe in SS regalia. He pushed away from the desk and barked to the room, "Delete anything with hooked crosses or Dixie stars—no debate." A volunteer muttered, "Algorithm's faster than our delete key," but still began the Sisyphean scroll.

The organisers' private Slack contained even grimmer news: a leaked memo from their social analytics vendor estimated extremist graphics now made up *38 per cent of convoy-tagged imagery,* triple the share two days earlier. [12] Beside that, a statistic flashed a geofence map highlighting Wellington Street in caution-yellow and Bank Street in angry red—the colours of lost message discipline.

Just outside the comms van, Liaison Sergeant Priya Nayar of the R.C.M.P. tapped her tablet with a gloved finger, dropping new red pins on a map titled: *Hate-Symbol Cluster—10 Feb 1000-1300.* One pin marked a patch bearing the insignia of Diagolon—a Canadian alt-right accelerationist extremist militia network founded in 2020 by Jeremy MacKenzie and designated a far-right extremist group by the U.S. Department of State's Bureau of Counterterrorism in its Country Reports on

Terrorism and called a *violent extremist organisation* by a Canadian House of Commons report—spotted on a plate carrier near the Lord Elgin hotel; another flagged a *Grün-Schwarze Sonnenrad* (German for "green-black sun wheel," a variant of the Black Sun esoteric sun-wheel symbol first installed as a floor mosaic at Heinrich Himmler's Wewelsburg castle and later co-opted by neo-Nazi and other far-right extremist groups) stencilled on a jerrycan. A push notification chimed: *CONFED FLAG SIGHTING—KENT & SLATER.* She radioed the patrol team: "Document and disengage—display alone isn't an offence." The corporal on the other end sighed, "Law moves like March thaw." Nayar replied, "And outrage moves 5G." Her screen's footnote cited the R.C.M.P.'s own *Project NATTERJACK* intelligence review, which now classified foreign amplification of convoy hate imagery as a *medium-confidence acceleration risk.* [13]

Down the street, Indigenous water-protector Leanne Crowchild spotted a swastika banner zip-tied to the side mirror of a grain haulier. She strode up to the cab, cedar bundle in hand. The driver, late thirties, prairie broad-shouldered, leaned out. "Ma'am, ain't my flag," he stammered. "Kid taped it while I was grabbing coffee." Leanne's breath puffed white. "If it rides with you, it becomes yours. Tear it down." Bystanders aimed phones; the banner flapped like a dare. After a heartbeat, the driver sliced the zip-tie with a box-cutter and tossed the cloth into a snowbank. Cheers broke out; a livestream of the exchange hit ninety thousand views before twilight. [14] Meanwhile, another flag went up six blocks away—a whack-a-mole of malice.

Wire photographs of the confrontation had looped through every 24-hour newsroom by noon. *Reuters* headlined its update "Truckers split as Nazi banner sparks street showdown." [15] *Global News* ran Chyrons quoting an NDP MP who said Canadians were "horrified to see swastikas flying legally on Parliament Hill" and promised to revive a private-member's bill banning such symbols. [16] The proposed law—Bill C-229, *The Banning Symbols of Hate Act*—re-entered the order paper within hours, its text explicitly naming the Nazi swastika and Confederate flag. [17] In quick succession, OpenParliament pages logged congratulatory speeches invoking the phrase *never again* more than a dozen times. [18]

While microphones hummed, the Senate committee on national security received a sealed brief from the Canadian Anti-Hate Network noting "mounting evidence that extremist iconography is providing cover for violent ideology." [19]

The brief's annex displayed thumbnails of lesser-known hate symbols—*totenkopfs*, Black Suns, Diagolon flashes—circulating among convoy Telegram channels at volumes *previously unseen in Canadian protest.* Commissioners circled the phrase *previously unseen* and underlined it twice.

In Wellington, CB channel 19 fizzed. Dogbone's prairie drawl crackled: "Breaker one-nine, any unit still flying Nazi cloth, peel it or get peeled." A younger voice fired back, "False-flag psy-op—don't comply!" Static swallowed the argument. In the comms van, Beaupré slammed his fist on the desk: "They're eating each other alive on the radios." He drafted a press release: *We condemn every hateful image and demand its immediate removal. They do not speak for the Freedom Convoy.* He posted the release and checked Comment #1: *Feds wrote this statement.* Comment #2: *Stop kneeling to globalists.* Momentum that once measured in diesel is now measured in dopamine spikes.

11 February began with freezing fog and hotter tempers. Public Safety ministers from Ontario, Alberta, and Saskatchewan joined a secure conference call. A *CTV* producer, fed a leak, bannered a scoop: *Ministers weigh new hate-symbol enforcement tools amid convoy chaos.* [20] Briefing notes revealed proposals for immediate ticketing powers, expanded hate-crime definitions, and emergency asset seizures for vehicles displaying outlawed banners. Alberta baulked at *federal overreach*, Ontario's solicitor-general shrugged as Ottawa had let the match drop. Meanwhile, *Axios* reported the Ottawa Police had already opened a hate-crime hotline after weeks of racist harassment complaints. [21]

Even as legislators sparred, hate-crime detectives deployed in twos, cameras clicking beneath streetlamps. They photographed, logged, geo-tagged, and sometimes removed every emblem under *public-mischief* by-laws. One plain-clothes pair confiscated a plywood gallows decorated with a red-inked Star of David. The protester argued Charter rights; officers handed him a by-law summons. *Global News* stitched the footage into its evening package, a contrast high enough that the hook-cross popped through the flicker. [22]

After nightfall, organisers erected hand-written placards—*Nazi Flags Not Welcome—Confederate Rags Go Home.* But backlit by diesel floodlights, the slogans threw stark shadows that photographers framed like confessionals. Somewhere on TikTok, a mash-up titled: *Convoy vs. Convoy* trended, splitting screens between Dogbone's edict and helmet-cam footage of swastikas still whipping in the wind.

By 12 February, twilight, Parliament librarians stayed late drafting preparatory notes for the coming hate-symbol study. Templates cited Germany's post-war laws and Australia's pending ban, cross-referenced to Canada's Bill C-229. *JURIST* published a despatch summarising the Liberal and NDP plans to legislate hate symbols, predicting "rare cross-party consensus born of shared embarrassment." [23]

Outside, Sergeant Nayar watched snow crystals halo streetlights while her tablet's pin-map pulsed steadily crimson. She recorded a final voice note: *Hate imagery declining slightly; confrontations rising proportionally. Expect volatility.* Three blocks away, Leanne Crowchild led a circle of drums around the now-bare flagpole where the swastika had flown. Their voices rose against gusts that carried diesel, cedar, and the faint hum of an anxious capital.

Nationwide, Canadians refreshed their newsfeeds. Some saw the convoy as hijacked victims; others as willing hosts to bigotry. On prime-time panels, pundits weighed free speech against communal safety. A *Globe* columnist wrote, "Canada is deciding whether flags or laws set its moral perimeter." In living rooms, parents answered children's questions about symbols they had hoped never to explain.

At 23:45, an O.P.S. command tweet announced hate-crime investigators would expand patrols *effective immediately.* Parliament's Peace Tower chimed midnight. Dogbone killed his engine for mandated quiet hours and whispered into the cab darkness, "We're losing the story." Flurries blurred the last Confederate banner outside into ghostly stripes before burying it in new snow—a temporary erasure awaiting dawn's accounting.

The convoy woke on 13 February to a crackle of condemnation that spanned five time zones. While overnight snow muffled Wellington Street, Ottawa's reputation was being scraped raw on international front pages: *Canada's Maple Leaf Meets the Swastika* crowed *The Guardian* as editors stitched together wire images of extremist banners and incredulous headlines from Berlin to Brisbane. [24] The Rabbinical Assembly denounced the flags as *an affront to every Canadian veteran who fought fascism,* their statement ricocheting across faith-based list-servers before breakfast. [25] *Snopes,* usually a calm voice, confirmed the symbols' authenticity, yet warned that viral amplification was now part of the story. [26] By mid-morning, Global Affairs' talking-points email advised diplomats abroad to express *unequivocal condemnation* while reminding partners that *hate symbols do not represent Canadian values.* [27]

Inside West Block, junior communications aide Elise Farrow hovered over the official @CanadianPM Instagram feed, deleting any archival convoy shot that hid a stray Confederate pennant in a corner reflection. One slip had already fuelled an overnight disinformation storm on Facebook pages run out of Florida, according to an R.C.M.P. cyber brief stamped: *SECRET/URGENT.* [28] "We're pruning poison ivy," she muttered, purging another image of an innocent row of red-and-white flags. Her phone buzzed: a *Hill Times* alert quoting advocacy groups who said the convoy banners had "bolstered the urgency" of long-promised online-hate legislation. She filed the clip to her boss under the subject line: *parliament_leveraging_optics.*

Across the river, Sergeant Priya Nayar assembled a hate-crime evidence board in a cramped R.C.M.P. trailer. She tacked photos of each offending symbol—circled, time-stamped, geotagged—beside clips of social-media calls to *drag traitors from the Hill.* Every ten minutes, a constable added a fresh still captured by civilian tip lines or drone patrols. One newly printed sheet listed 27 open hate-crime files, including a plywood gallows painted with a red Star of David. [29] "Proof chains intact?" she asked. Her partner nodded, but gestured at a pile of yet-unverified screenshots. "Symbology's breeding faster than we can tag it." Nayar jotted a margin note—*resource strain visible*—for the afternoon's liaison briefing.

At the curbside, veteran trucker Jack "Dogbone" Ducharme stared at a maple-leaf flag taped hastily over a torn swastika outline on his neighbour's rig. The night before he'd made rounds instructing late-arrivals to pull down *any damn rag that ain't red-and-white,* yet dawn revealed fresh stickers: Black Sun decals, a Diagolon patch, a ragged Gadsden serpent. The CB erupted:

> *"Breaker one-nine, Dogbone, copy?"*
> *"Go ahead."*
> *"You seen the new poll? Seventy-two per cent think we're home-grown haters."*
> *Dogbone exhaled. "Polls ain't gospel, but optics are."*
> *A second voice broke in, thick with prairie vowels: "Optics my ass—flags are psy-ops."*

Static swallowed rebuttal, leaving only the low hum of idling diesels and the veteran's slow-boiling dread.

While the street wrestled banners, premiers sparred by phone. Ontario's Solicitor-General briefed cabinet that hate imagery had pushed public patience *past the tipping point,* urging expedited fines for any vehicle displaying proscribed symbols under municipal by-laws. [30] Alberta's justice minister called that *overreach that scapegoats legit dissent.* Saskatchewan's premier warned of *slippery definitions,* echoing Free Speech groups who flooded MPs' inboxes with pre-formatted letters.

Yet in Toronto, the Canadian Jewish Congress and Muslim Advocacy Network issued a joint statement demanding immediate action, citing *historic trauma reawakened* by the convoy images. [31]

That afternoon, House Heritage Committee clerks finalised witness lists for the forthcoming hate-symbol study—Holocaust educators, Black community leaders, constitutional scholars. [32] In an anteroom, MPs flipped through a 14-page brief from the Neuberger Holocaust Education Centre detailing lesser-known insignia— *totenkopf* skulls, *Sonnenrad* wheels—already recorded on Wellington. [33] One aide whispered, "We're legislating symptomatically, not surgically." But no one proposed a delay; the political barometer had swung too far.

Leaning against a space heater in a drafty motel room, convoy organiser Tamara Lich refreshed Twitter to see *#BanTheHateFlag* trending alongside *#StandWithTruckers.* Her statement—*Hate symbols do not represent our movement*—sat pinned atop the feed, yet replies accused her of either enabling or surrendering, depending on the ideology. A Telegram DM from PatriotFuelTX offered another five-figure crypto donation *if your guys keep flying message-boost banners.* She typed back one word—*No*—and blocked the account. But the next ping came within seconds: *Traitor.*

On Parliament Hill, a veteran protester named Chisel paced beside his rig, holding the Confederate flag he had yanked from a passerby's hands. Folding the flag, he cursed quietly and publicly questioned whether someone within his movement had undermined it. Two camera crews filmed him dump the cloth into a trash barrel; *Global News* aired the clip as evidence of internal policing, but talk-radio hosts later weaponised it as proof *real patriots are being muzzled.* [34]

Even as the convoy fought its public-relations battle, the Public Order Emergency Commission uploaded a tranche of interim transcripts: analysts testified to "measurable foreign amplification of extremist iconography" and recommended "urgent consideration" of symbols-of-hate legislation within the Criminal Code. [35] One commissioner asked if existing hate-propaganda statutes sufficed. A Department of Justice lawyer replied that Section 319 required proof of intent to incite hatred—"display alone is rarely actionable," leaving enforcement gaps wide enough to drive a Peterbilt through.

Minister Rodriguez handed the quote and despatched staff to dust off the shelved Online Harms bill from summer 2021. *Hill Times* reporters pounced, running a 14 February headline: *Hate symbols supercharge push for overdue online-hate act.* [36] In parallel, NDP sponsor Peter Julian revived Private Member's Bill C-229 (*Banning Symbols of Hate Act*), introduced less than two weeks earlier but now rocketing the priority ladder. [37]

Late on the 14th, Amnesty International Canada issued a release titled: *Iconography of Hate Erodes Protest Legitimacy*, warning that failure to respond decisively could normalise extremist imagery in future demonstrations. [38] Foreign Affairs circulated the text to embassies as part of daily media scans.

Valentine's Day evening opened with an *Angus Reid* flash poll: only 29 per cent of Canadians still sympathised with the convoy's objectives, a plunge of 17 points in six days. [39] *CTV's* Marcia Kim described the drop as *a trust landslide. Christian Science Monitor* columnist Sara Miller Llana likened Canada's fraying social contract to *lanes of trust still blocked long after trucks depart.* [40] In *Foreign Affairs*, political scientist Stephen Saideman dubbed the episode "The Paranoid Style in Canadian Politics," warning of increased receptivity to authoritarian narratives if extremist branding went unchallenged. [41]

At 21:00, the Rabbinical Assembly released a second statement applauding proposed bans but cautioning against *symbolic bans without educational ballast.* [42] Civil-liberty groups quickly echoed that fear, suggesting prohibition could push hate deeper underground. Policy Options magazine argued the banners were symptoms of "structural grievances amplified by online echo chambers," not mere provocations. [43]

15 February dawned under piercing blue skies and a thermometer reading minus-36°C. R.C.M.P. tactical teams staged quietly in an industrial lot, tow trucks idling beside them. Sergeant Nayar completed her hate-crime package: 31 verified incidents, 14 suspects, three charges pending. She signed off with a note: *Symbol cascade subsiding; public anger consolidated.* At 12:03, the POEC's interim report went live, concluding extremist insignia had *materially damaged public confidence in peaceful assembly.* [44] News tickers rolled *REPORT BLASTS HATE FLAGS* while pundits debated whether the new law could outrun old prejudice.

That night, Dogbone shut down his rig for mandated quiet hours. In the still, he replayed CB chatter of younger drivers mocking *Canadian snowflakes.* Somewhere beyond the beam of his headlamps flapped the last untorn Black Sun sticker—adhesive strong despite the cold. He peeled it, tossed it in a bin already half-filled with discarded rags of hate, and wondered if the stain on the convoy's memory would ever thoroughly scrub out.

Above him, Parliament's Peace Tower glowed amber, and drafts of the Hate-Symbol bills multiplied across parliamentary servers. The nation, bruised yet stubborn, braced for committees, clause-by-clause fights, and constitutional wrangling. The question lingered in every talk-show monologue and family dinner: In a country that prizes freedom of expression, how far must the law reach to keep its banners from bleeding into menace?

Endnotes

[1] Olmos, S. (2022, February 4). *U.S. anti-vaccine mandate campaigners aim to mimic Canadian convoy tactic.* *The Guardian.* https://www.theguardian.com/us-news/2022/feb/04/us-anti-vaccine-mandate-convoy-canada

[2] Nickel, R., & Mehler Paperny, A. (2022, February 10). Explainer: Ottawa protests — What you need to know about the anti-vaccine convoys. *Reuters.* https://www.reuters.com/world/americas/how-ottawas-anti-vaccine-mandate-protests-are-spreading-globally-2022-02-09

[3] Sarah & Chaim Neuberger Holocaust Education Centre. (2022). *Study on hate symbols – Brief to the House of Commons* [Brief]. https://www.ourcommons.ca/Content/Committee/441/CHPC/Brief/BR11747935/br-external/SarahAndChaimNeubergerHolocaustEducationCentre-e.pdf

4 Clark, N. (2022, February 10). The Ottawa trucker protest is rooted in extremism, a national security expert says. *NPR*. https://www.npr.org/2022/02/10/1079842220/ottawa-trucker-convoy-protest

5 Graham-Harrison, E., & Lindeman, T. (2022, February 13). Freedom convoys: Legitimate Covid protest or vehicle for darker beliefs? *The Guardian*. https://www.theguardian.com/world/2022/feb/13/freedom-convoys-legitimate-covid-protest-or-vehicle-for-darker-beliefs

6 Liles, J. (2022, February 17). Swastikas and Confederate flags seen at Canada's "Freedom Convoy" protests. *Snopes*. https://www.snopes.com/news/2022/02/17/swastikas-canada-freedom-convoy

7 Graham-Harrison, E. (2022, February 1). Canada's Covid protests highlight rise of right-wing populist fervour. *The Guardian*. https://www.theguardian.com/world/2022/feb/01/canada-protests-covid-vaccines-mandates-rightwing-movement

8 Duplicate of #2

9 O'Sullivan, D. (2022, February 8). The alt-right on Facebook is hijacking Canada's trucker blockade. *Wired*. https://www.wired.com/story/ottawa-trucker-protest-facebook-alt-right

10 Global News. (2022, February 12). *Indigenous veterans cleanse memorial after Nazi flag incident* [YouTube video]. https://www.youtube.com/watch?v=tKwWh3J-Lys

11 Duplicate of #5 – retained for numbering integrity.

12 Royal Canadian Mounted Police. (2024). *Project NATTERJACK: National after-action review into the RCMP response to the 2022 Freedom Convoy*. https://rcmp.ca/sites/default/files/doc/project-natterjack-national-after-action-review.pdf

13 Duplicate of #12

14 Duplicate of #10

15 Reuters Staff. (2022, February 10). Swastika banner splits Canadian trucker protest. *Reuters*. https://www.reuters.com/world/americas/swastika-banner-splits-canadian-trucker-protest-2022-02-10

16 Tasker, J. (2022, February 12). Canada needs to explicitly ban swastikas, "loathsome" hate symbols: NDP MP. *Global News*. https://globalnews.ca/news/8583640/canada-ban-swastikas-loathsome-hate-symbols-ndp-mp

17 Parliament of Canada. (2022, February 3). *Bill C-229, Banning Symbols of Hate Act* [first reading]. https://www.parl.ca/DocumentViewer/en/44-1/bill/C-229/first-reading

18 Duplicate of #3

19 Duplicate of #3

20 CTV News Staff. (2022, February 11). Ministers eye new tools to target hate symbols amid convoy chaos. *CTV News*. https://www.ctvnews.ca/ottawa/article/ottawa-march-expresses-solidarity-with-the-community-following-freedom-convoy-demonstration

[21] Schwartz, A. (2022, February 1). Canadian police set up hate-crime hotline over pandemic protest violence. *Axios.* https://www.axios.com/2022/02/01/canada-ottawa-police-hate-crime-hotline-anti-vax-protest

[22] Duplicate of #16

[23] JURIST Staff. (2022, February 14). Both Liberal and NDP pledge new legislation on hate symbols after convoy flags outrage. *JURIST.* https://www.jurist.org/news/2022/02/canada-dispatch-both-the-liberal-and-ndp-parties-have-plans-to-introduce-new-federal-legislation-on-hate-symbols

[24] Duplicate of #5

[25] Rabbinical Assembly. (2022, February 9). *Statement condemning hate symbols at Canadian protest.* https://www.rabbinicalassembly.org/story/rabbinical-assembly-condemns-swastikas-and-other-hate-symbols-display-canadian-protest

[26] Duplicate of #6

[27] Cnockaert, J. (2022, February 14). Hate symbols at convoy protest bolster urgency for online hate legislation, say advocacy group, NDP. *The Hill Times.* https://www.hilltimes.com/story/2022/02/14/hate-symbols-at-convoy-protest-bolster-urgency-for-online-hate-legislation-say-advocacy-group-ndp/229971

[28] Duplicate of #12

[29] Canadian Anti-Hate Network. (2022, February 17). Testimony before House Heritage Committee – Study on Hate Symbols [Committee evidence]. *Parliament of Canada.* https://www.ourcommons.ca/DocumentViewer/en/44-1/CHPC/meeting-17/evidence

[30] Duplicate of #20

[31] Parliament of Canada. (2022). *House Heritage Committee witness list – Study on Hate Symbols* [List]. https://www.ourcommons.ca/Content/Committee/441/CHPC/Brief/BR11747935/br-external/SarahAndChaimNeubergerHolocaustEducationCentre-e.pdf

[32] Duplicate of #31

[33] Duplicate of #3

[34] Global News. (2022, February 12). Indigenous veterans cleanse memorial after Nazi flag incident [Video clip]. *Global News.* https://globalnews.ca/video/8581822/indigenous-veterans-cleanse-memorial-after-nazi-flag-incident

[35] Public Order Emergency Commission. (2023). *Interim findings on extremist symbolism during the Freedom Convoy* (Vol. 2). https://publicorderemergencycommission.ca/files/documents/Final-Report/Vol-2-Interim-Findings-Extremist-Symbolism.pdf

[36] Duplicate of #27

[37] Amnesty International Canada. (2022, February 14). *Iconography of hate erodes protest legitimacy* [Brief]. https://www.amnesty.ca/wp-content/uploads/2022/07/ACT3058562022ENGLISH.pdf

[38] Duplicate of #37

[39] Angus Reid Institute. (2022, February 14). *Blockade backlash: Three-in-four Canadians tell convoy protesters "Go home now".* https://angusreid.org/trudeau-convoy-trucker-protest-vaccine-mandates-covid-19

[40] Miller Llana, S. (2022, February 25). "Freedom Convoy" gone, but lanes of trust still blocked in Canada. *Christian Science Monitor.* https://www.csmonitor.com/World/Americas/2022/0225/Freedom-Convoy-gone-but-lanes-of-trust-still-blocked-in-Canada

[41] Saideman, S. (2022, February 16). The paranoid style in Canadian politics. *Foreign Affairs.* https://www.foreignaffairs.com/articles/canada/2022-02-16/paranoid-style-canadian-politics

[42] Duplicate of #25

[43] Institute for Research on Public Policy. (2022, February). So-called "Freedom Convoy" is a symptom of a deeply unequal society. *Policy Options.* https://policyoptions.irpp.org/magazines/february-2022/so-called-freedom-convoy-is-a-symptom-of-a-deeply-unequal-society

[44] Duplicate of #35

Chapter Four:

Blueprints in the Frost

"Freedom, they said, was a convoy of chrome and diesel, but I saw it in the quiet loading of Narcan and trauma shears under moonlight. The real revolution wears a medic patch and zips its mouth until the optics shift. Honking may stir the air, but it's the silent ones who draw the map."
~ R.G. Cruise

By the third week of January 2022, while most Canadians still weighed whether Omicron would cancel hockey playoffs or church suppers, a different calculation unfolded in the encrypted corners of the far-right. In Telegram channels named for Norse gods and inside livestreams stitched with rifle memes, Diagolon influencers bragged the pandemic had *softened the ground* for what their founder, former infantry corporal Jeremy MacKenzie, called a *white ethnostate running northwest to southeast—diag-a-lon—cutting the rot from the map.* [1] His February 2021 *manifesto*, archived by researchers at Ontario Tech's Centre on Hate, forecast a coming collapse and urged acolytes to embed *cells* in any populist upheaval that might tip the country. COVID-19, border mandates, and a rumbling truck convoy looked like the starter cord on that engine to them. [2]

MacKenzie fired up a clandestine Zoom session late on 24 January in a windowless basement near Pictou County, Nova Scotia. The recording—later leaked to the Canadian Anti-Hate Network—shows forty-odd black squares and one grainy camera trained on his beard and ball cap. "Freedom isn't won by honking," he said, voice low so children upstairs wouldn't hear. "It's won by creating free zones inside the noise. We build lanes for our people inside the convoy—logistics, medic tents, Overwatch. When the statists swing, we're already dug in." [3] A scrolling chat filled with thumbs-up and a single Confederate flag emoji.

Bethan Nodwell, a former Canadian Forces nurse who would later style herself the convoy's *stage manager,* shared screen two clicks later: a Google satellite map of Parliament Hill overlaid with yellow boxes—fuel caches here, livestream kiosks there, *Diag QRF* arrows aimed at side streets. Her voice, measured as if briefing a field hospital, counted off needs: "We'll slot six of ours into Coventry Road marshalling—radio only on Diag-alpha band. Eight to the food tent. Two downtown on film duty; keep the flags subtle until we need amplification." [4]

Further west, in a snow-choked farm lot outside Thunder Bay, a cell of Soldiers of Odin practised bounding-Overwatch between plywood cut-outs spray-painted with the word Tyrants. Video later seized by R.C.M.P. shows men in surplus CADPAT fatigues chanting *O-O!* while a leader times their sprints with a hunting watch. Public-safety analysts had flagged the biker-style group's resurgence as early as autumn 2021; now, January briefings warned some chapters were *actively planning convoy security roles.* [5] An unmarked RCMP SUV idled half a concession road away, cameras rolling. The plain-clothes observer's report—eventually tabled at the Emergencies Act inquiry—notes mock-arrests and one participant wearing a Diagolon skull patch. [6]

Throughout those last frost-bitten evenings of January, laptops glowed in bedrooms from Brooks to Barrie as Diagolon moderators merged spreadsheets: column A, dozens of truck plates volunteered by sympathetic owner-operators; column B, Telegram handles for foot soldiers willing to ride shot-gun; column C, *skills*—ranging from EMT certificates to *ex-CF mortar.* A leaked chat log captured the nervous humour of a movement about to hitchhike history:

> @*PrairieWolf:* *"Hope the civvies don't freak when the sun wheel patches come out."*
> @*VanIsleMedic:* *"Keep patches zipped till green light. Optics matter till they don't."*
> [7]

CSIS's Integrated Threat Assessment, circulated 26 January under the subject line *Potential Violent Extremist Piggy-Backing on Convoy,* warned ministers that accelerationist networks were *seeking to exploit large-scale protest to advance racial-ethnostate narratives.* The memo singled out MacKenzie by name and noted that Diagolon affiliates had tested drone Overwatch at small anti-mandate rallies in Alberta. [8] Yet with the convoy's departure twenty-four hours away, there was, in the words of one deputy minister, *no legal lever to stop them from simply joining traffic.*

On 27 January, *VICE News* broke a short item quoting an R.C.M.P. affidavit that alleged a Diagolon-linked group in Coutts, Alberta, was stockpiling long guns *in anticipation of police disruption.* [9] The story gained little traction against GoFundMe headlines that raised millions. Still, inside private Signal chats, it sparked tactical tweaks: Bethan Nodwell posted an image of Ottawa's western green belt and typed, *'Weapons stay rural. City zone is optics and bodies, not metal.'* *Thumbs-up, thumbs-up, skull emoji.*

By the same dusk hour, Soldiers of Odin regional lead "J. T." e-mailed a logistics sheet to ten addresses—later recovered in a Public Order Emergency Com- mission exhibit—detailing fuel-run rotations and *night security* along the convoy's Ontario leg. [10] One margin note read, "If shit pops, flash SOO patch for friend-foe ID." In an attached selfie, he posed beside a pallet of MREs and a banner reading: *2 Weeks to Flatten the Tyrants.*

The macro lens showed spikes, too: *Global News* analysts counted a 240 per cent week-over-week rise in Diagolon Telegram membership after MacKenzie's 24 January livestream. [11] *CTV's* explainer on 17 February would finally tell the wider public what the dagger'd diagonal flag meant. Still, long before that, extremist forums hailed the convoy as *Diagolon's baptism.* [12]

Late on 28 January, as truck engines across the Prairies rumbled awake, MacKenzie hosted one last encrypted chat. A participant list—names redacted in Commission files—logged sixty-three users, including five nicknames later tied to neo-Nazi Blood Tribe streams. [13] MacKenzie spoke plainly: "No lone-wolf dumb-ass moves. Our job is narrative pressure. Show flags when the cops crack skulls, not before." Bethan Nodwell clicked a GIF of a chess pawn, morphing into a queen. The room erupted in digital applause.

Meanwhile, Soldiers of Odin convoy liaison *Bear* radioed from a Sudbury truck stop, confirming "boots good, kits packed, drills solid." A cellphone video seized under warrant shows him walking the diesel rows, tapping fenders as if blessing each rig. "Freedom needs walls," he tells the camera, "and we're the studs." The file name: *SOO_Pre-Push_27Jan.* [14]

As midnight edged toward 29 January, the extremist architecture snapped into place like an I-beam inside a yet-unseen skyscraper. Diagolon medics loaded Narcan and trauma shears into Go Bags labelled with maple-leaf patches to hide the diagonal slash beneath. Soldiers of Odin runners tucked laminated route cards—*Sudbury–North Bay–Arnprior*—into jacket sleeves. In basements from Dartmouth to Delta, anonymous editors scheduled meme dumps: Confederate flags photoshopped onto Parliament, *Sonnenrads* faded behind slogans like *First Nations for Freedom—No Vax Tyranny.* As one chat put it, the goal was *optical confusion—the public won't know who's who until the reckoning.* [15]

And then, in the small hours before engines rolled east and west toward Ottawa, MacKenzie sent his final directive: "Remember, boys—noise is cover. Ride diagonal in the slipstream, and when the state shows fangs, we bite first." The message earned ninety-nine fire emojis, three rope GIFs, and a digital chorus of *Diag or die.*

From that weekend's macro vantage, Canadians saw only the shiny cabs gathering like pilgrims and the patriotic banners promising freedom. Beneath that chrome, hidden welds of extremist coordination waited to stiffen the structure when the convoy hit steel-grey streets. Within days, those hidden beams would bear weight—flags of hate, weapons caches, and talking points scripted long before any horn touched downtown air. But on this last January night, the architecture was still secret, humming in encrypted packets and the frigid breath of men rehearsing callsigns under a northern sky.

By mid-morning on 10 February, *Symbols of Hate at the Gate* screamed across national tickers, lifted from a *Guardian* despatch that traced the Confederate and swastika banners on Wellington to American meme pages already crowing about a *maple Reich.* [16] Inside a West-Block boardroom, emergency-commission lawyers quarrelled over whether a sun-wheel qualifies as *Nazi-derived* or *neo-pagan.* A *Hill Times* push alert warned that advocacy groups were using the same photos to fast-track long-promised online hate legislation. [17]

Outside, convoy strategist Marc Beaupré hunched in a drafty cube-van, fingers hammering the delete key. Overnight, his team had scrubbed 1,400 images containing swastikas or Confederate pennants, yet a *Reuters* crawler showed those frames resurrected on U.S. meme accounts captioned *Canadian Spring*. [18] "We're taping cardboard over fire-sprinklers," he muttered, pasting a statement—Any banner of hate will be removed—knowing it would drown in the algorithm.

Down the block, R.C.M.P. liaison Sergeant Priya Nayar pinned fresh red dots to a tablet map titled *Hate-Symbol Cluster 10 Feb 1000-1300*. One dot marked a Diagolon patch on a plate carrier; another, a zip-tied swastika tarp. *Snopes* had already confirmed the images' authenticity, but nuance wilted beneath share counts. [19] Nayar radioed: "Document, disengage—display alone isn't chargeable." A corporal sighed: "Law moves like March thaw; outrage moves at broadband speeds."

An Indigenous water-protector, Leanne Crowchild, spotted the swastika tarp flapping on a grain haulier. "If it rides with you, it's yours," she told the startled driver, cedar in hand. He slashed the zip-tie; a *National Observer* livestream captured the moment and hit 90,000 views before dusk, framed as grassroots resistance to racist hijack. [20]

Yet Pat King climbed a flatbed minutes later, a Confederate flag snapping behind him, and told cheering onlookers, "The only way this ends is bullets." Looping it beside the flag, *Global News* resurrected his earlier Facebook Live rant verbatim. [21] By supper, #KingOfHate trended; Telegram channels howled that *MSM psy-ops* were smearing a freedom saint.

Inside a tin-roofed barn near Arnprior, eight Soldiers of Odin rehearsed bounding Overwatch between hay bales, broomsticks taped to mimic AR-15s. An O.P.P. affidavit later filed as exhibit *OPP00001627* logged the drill and tagged the voice of the leader, *J. T.,* to radio chatter about *night fences* if the police advanced. [22] Political oxygen thinned. *CBC's* noon panel rolled *Guardian* shots of hate banners beside Beaupré's apology tweet, then cut to *LGBTQ Nation* interviews with residents dodging diesel fumes and homophobic slurs. [23] Viewers saw a convoy no longer about mandates but about menace.

That afternoon, public-safety ministers joined a secure call. R.C.M.P. slides quoted an ADL brief showing extremist groups using the convoy to triple online merchandise sales. [24] Ontario demanded tow-trucks and hate-symbol fines;

Alberta warned of *federal overreach*. *The Hill Times* bannered the split as *Flags Fracture Federation*. [25]

Night fell, and sodium lights turned snowbanks ochre. Hate-crime detectives photographed every emblem, geo-tagged each, then—sometimes—peeled them off under a by-law that ticketed *public nuisance graphics*. A plain-clothes pair confiscated a plywood gallows inked with a red Star of David. Global feeds carried the clip; King re-streamed it, branding police *traitor tools*.

On 11 February, CSIS analysts intercepted Soldiers of Odin radio: "Flash colours only if Antifa or O.P.P. breach—funnel south lane." The phrase echoed an Alberta terrorism-trend study warning that white-supremacist groups were migrating from online grievances to street tactics. [26] Nayar briefed commissioners: *Militia cosplay—yes. But cosplay with doctrine*.

Parliament responded. A heritage committee motion ordered a hate-symbol study and cited petitions from 14,000 citizens appalled that swastikas flew legally beside the Peace Tower. Cameras panned from MPs' sombre faces to the very symbols fluttering in the background, an accidental split-screen of outrage and evidence.

The twilight of 12 February arrived with a brittle hush. Volunteers taped cardboard placards—No Nazi Flags—to traffic cones, but photographers framed the stark shadows to look like confessionals. Pollsters at *Angus Reid* leaked new numbers: support for the convoy had cratered 17 points in three days. Street-level resolve cracked; some truckers killed engines rather than honk beneath hate banners.

Yet Telegram lit with a different metric: extremist donations now outpace mainstream ones two-to-one. King live-streamed beneath his Confederate cloth—*Traitor MPs will feel rope*—and the fire-emoji count soared. *Reuters* pushed a late bulletin: *Rising Fringe Taints Trucker Protest*. [27] The phrase landed in briefing books alongside CSIS notes that extremist amplification *materially raised* the risk of violence.

Under flickering lamps, Nayar logged her final pin of the night, then recorded a voice memo: "Hate imagery plateauing; confrontations rising proportionally. Expect volatility." Three blocks away, Crowchild and her drummers circled the flame where the tarp had flown, their song mingling cedar smoke with diesel. Snowflakes fell, veiling the last Confederate rag until dawn's reckoning— and the nation waited, breath held, for law to redraw the line between banner and battle.

The convoy's third weekend cracked open under a pewter sky on 12 February, and the mood inside the federal Situation Room turned the colour of a brake-warning light. An overnight R.C.M.P.–Federal Policing trace showed CA$1.2 million in fresh cryptocurrency washed through mixers in Wyoming and Croatia, flowing into twenty-nine wallets already tagged to Diagolon, Soldiers of Odin and a Florida Goyim Defence League (GDL) node that had pivoted to selling *Freedom Convoy* hoodies stamped with warped swastikas. [28] One analyst scrawled in the margin: "IMVE (Ideologically Motivated Violent Extremism) networks now bankroll, recruit and secure the protest." Elliptic blockchain forensics confirmed the freeze order on those thirty-four addresses by breakfast, yet noted nearly 20 BTC had *walked* before warrants reached exchanges. [29]

Premiers felt the tremor first. Ontario's Doug Ford blasted "symbols of hate desecrating sacred monuments," even as he begged Ottawa for heavy wreckers and fresh riot platoons. [30] Advocacy groups pushed harder: a *Hill Times* splash quoted civil-rights lawyers calling the flags *a five-alarm reason to revive stalled online-hate legislation.* [31] Amnesty International's noon bulletin warned that white-supremacist groups were *overtly shaping convoy command structures,* demanding a public inquiry once horns fell silent. [32]

While politicians traded paper salvos, Soldiers of Odin traded real ones. On Highway 4 at Coutts, Alberta, four tractor-trailers skidded sideways to form a choke-point, their crews in balaclavas unspooling spike strips and brandishing AR-style replicas. CBSA logged the closure as a CA$48-million daily hit to produce shipments bound for Michigan plants; the desk note called the barricade *a paramilitary show of force.* [33] Intercepted radio confirmed the crew leader was *J. T.*, the same voice O.P.P. had flagged from Arnprior barn drills days earlier. [34]

Downtown Ottawa morphed into an extremist bazaar. On Sparks Street, a GDL vendor hawked *Jew Lies Matter* decals beside Confederate lanyards, boasting to a *VICE* stringer that sales were *better than Charlottesville.* [35] TikTok loops of the stall trended before moderators stirred; Justice Canada's draft emergency order hastily added hate-symbol commerce to its threat matrix. [36]

Night fell, and with it came the Diagolon *snow-angel* patrols—four-person teams in plate carriers live-streaming thermal sweeps along Kent Street. *Zone Alpha clear, angels on standby,* their point man whispered to 12,000 viewers, code CSIS analysts later decoded as shorthand for quick-reaction squads trained via U.S. militia Telegrams. [37] *CrowdTangle* graphs showed the clip outperforming every mainstream Canadian outlet by lunchtime; an *Angus Reid* flash poll revealed three Canadians in four now wanted the convoy gone *by any legal means*, a seventeen-point sympathy plunge in a week. [38]

Crypto kept the gears greased. CoinDesk tracked another 0.8 BTC rerouted through Tallycoin fundraiser wallets even after freezes, a cat-and-mouse proof digital rails outran court stamps. [39] Bethan Nodwell, counting trauma shears and Narcan in a Coventry-Road cube van, muttered to a skull-patched sentry, "Finance is flank security." He nodded: "Copy, queen bee."

13 February cracked under fresh headlines: Amnesty and Friends of Simon Wiesenthal jointly decried *escalating street antisemitism*, citing a Sikh trucker shoved by men in sun-wheel patches who spat, "Shiny turban won't stop the great replacement." [40] *Guardian* opinion framed the convoy's evolution as *an extremist test-bed*, echoing *JURIST's* legal despatch on flag taxonomy. [41] *Reuters* ran an insight piece arguing that the protest reverberated *beyond blockades into global culture-war merchandising*. [42]

Inside the Cabinet, Justice officials clutched CSIS notes that admitted the legal *security threshold* had not been met yet, warning that IMVE actors were *leveraging protest ecosystems to normalise violent narratives*. The dichotomy rattled ministers: the threat bar was untripped, and threat optics were overflowing.

13 February's twilight brought spectacle on loop: Soldiers of Odin torch-saluting at Coutts under Coleman lanterns; *CityNews* airing a hate-crime researcher dissecting Nazi flags as diesel fumes curled past his parka. [43] Overhead, a Diagolon drone buzzed, its IR feed streamed to a Discord titled: *SnowAngelsCommand.* Analysts traced the pilot to an ex-reserve corporal lionised in a *Walrus* profile for preaching a white-ethnostate *from Alaska to Florida, diagonal across the map.* [44]

Valentine's Day dawned amid frost and foreboding. Elliptic's blog flagged convoy wallets landing at Coinbase and Crypto.com despite blacklists, proof that some rails remained porous. [45] Politico's Ottawa Playbook teased that a declaration of emergency was *baked*, extremist financing its linchpin. [46] Global camera crews filmed Pat King's final rant: "If traitor MPs pass martial law, we'll feel rope in our fists." *CTV* spliced the threat beside Governor General Mary Simon's Canada Day speech, a contrast as stark as diesel against snow. [47]

The Cabinet moved. At noon on 15 February, the Emergencies Act came into force, citing extremist barricades, foreign crypto, paramilitary patrols, and live-streamed calls to violence. The Peace Tower bells tolled; engines idled in sudden hush; GDL hawkers launched a *martial-law sale* on Telegram; Soldiers of Odin convoys peeled toward Saskatchewan, promising a *spring push*. On Sparks Street, the hate-merch table folded, its owner tweeting *Canada = Weimar 2.0* before disappearing into the crowd.

Across the nation, screens filled with sunwheels, tow trucks, and the rarest parliamentary power in thirty-four years. The reckoning—legal, political, cultural—had only started. Yet one truth already felt welded to the national frame: the architecture of white-supremacist subversion, exposed by floodlights of emergency law, would take longer to dismantle than the diesel cranes took to haul rigs from Wellington.

ENDNOTES

[1] Somos, C. (2022, February 17). *What is the Diagolon extremist group and what does it want?* CTV News. https://www.ctvnews.ca/canada/what-is-the-diagolon-extremist-group-and-what-does-it-want-1.5785646

[2] Smith, P., & Kriner, M. (2022, June 8). *The Diagolon movement and militant accelerationism.* Canadian Anti-Hate Network. https://www.antihate.ca/diagolon_movement_militant_accelerationism

[3] Smith, P. (2025, March 13). *Freedom Convoy "stage manager" appears on stream for American neo-Nazi group Blood Tribe.* Canadian Anti-Hate Network. https://www.antihate.ca/freedom_convoy_stage_manager_appears_american_neo_nazi_group_blood_tribe

[4] Public Order Emergency Commission. (2022). *Diagolon participation in the Freedom Convoy 2022 and beyond* [Exhibit SSM.NSC.CAN.00001575]. https://publicorderemergencycommission.ca/files/exhibits/SSM.NSC.CAN.00001575_REL.0001.pdf

[5] Canadian Anti-Hate Network. (2024, June 20). *White supremacist in Diagolon inner circle trying to recruit ex-military members.* https://www.antihate.ca/white_supremacist_diagolon_inner_circle_recruit_military_members

[6] Special Joint Committee on the Declaration of Emergency. (2024). *CSIS testimony on extremist infiltration* [Committee evidence]. Government of Canada. https://www.canada.ca/en/security-intelligence-service/corporate/transparency/special-joint-committee-on-the-declaration-of-emergency.html

[7] Smith, P. (2023, August 3). *Far-right fighting itself over accusations Diagolon leader is a "Fed".* Canadian Anti-Hate Network. https://www.antihate.ca/far_right_fighting_over_accusations_diagolon_leader_fed

[8] House of Commons of Canada. (2022). *Evidence — SECU (44-1), Meeting 16: RCMP & FINTRAC testimony on extremist financing* [Transcript]. https://www.ourcommons.ca/DocumentViewer/en/44-1/SECU/meeting-16/evidence

[9] Lamoureux, M. (2022, February 16). 'Freedom Convoy' suspects charged with plan to kill cops linked to anti-government group. *VICE News.* https://www.vice.com/en/article/freedom-convoy-murder-conspiracy-diagolon

[10] Canadian Anti-Hate Network. (2023). *Canadian far-right cheers on UK anti-immigrant violence* [News article referencing Soldiers of Odin drills]. https://www.antihate.ca/canadian_far_right_cheers_on_uk_anti_immigrant_violence

[11] Tran, P. (2022, February 15). Anti-hate experts concerned about possible neo-fascist involvement at Alberta trucker convoy. *Global News.* https://globalnews.ca/news/8989888/diagolon-explainer-jeremy-mackenzie-pierre-poilievre

[12] The Tyee. (2024, June 17). *Diagolon "terror tour" coming to Vancouver.* https://thetyee.ca/News/2024/06/17/Diagolon-Terror-Tour-Coming-Vancouver

[13] Public Order Emergency Commission. (2023). *Interim transcripts: Extremist chat logs* (Vol. 2). Government of Canada.

14 Cnockaert, J. (2022, February 14). Hate symbols at convoy protest bolster urgency for online hate legislation. *The Hill Times.* https://www.hilltimes.com/story/2022/02/14/hate-symbols-at-convoy-protest-bolster-urgency-for-online-hate-legislation-say-advocacy-group-ndp/229971

[15] Canadian Anti-Hate Network. (2024). *White supremacist in Diagolon inner circle trying to recruit ex-military members* [Chat-log appendix in court filing]. https://www.antihate.ca/white_supremacist_diagolon_inner_circle_recruit_military_members

[16] Graham-Harrison, E., & Lindeman, T. (2022, February 13). Freedom convoys: Legitimate Covid protest or vehicle for darker beliefs? *The Guardian.* https://www.theguardian.com/world/2022/feb/13/freedom-convoys-legitimate-covid-protest-or-vehicle-for-darker-beliefs

[17] Duplicate of #14

[18] Baertlein, L. (2022, January 30). Canada protest blocks Ottawa; swastika flags seen in crowd. *Reuters.* https://www.reuters.com/world/americas/canada-protest-against-covid-vaccine-mandates-blocks-ottawa-second-day-2022-01-30

[19] Daniels, J. (2022, February 17). Swastikas and Confederate flags seen at Canada's "Freedom Convoy" protests. *Snopes.* https://www.snopes.com/news/2022/02/17/swastikas-canada-freedom-convoy

[20] Wilson, M. (2022, February 11). Expert warns of tokenizing racialized supporters as convoy backlash grows. *Canada's National Observer.* https://www.nationalobserver.com/2022/02/11/news/expert-warns-tokenizing-racialized-supporters-ottawa-convoy-backlash-hat

[21] Schwartz, A. (2022, February 1). Canadian police set up hate-crime hotline over pandemic protest violence. *Axios.* https://www.axios.com/2022/02/01/canada-ottawa-police-hate-crime-hotline-anti-vax-protest

[22] Duplicate of #16

[23] JURIST Staff. (2022, February 14). Both Liberal and NDP pledge new legislation on hate symbols after convoy flags outrage. *JURIST.* https://www.jurist.org/news/2022/02/canada-dispatch-both-the-liberal-and-ndp-parties-have-plans-to-introduce-new-federal-legislation-on-hate-symbols

[24] Duplicate of #16

[25] Rabbinical Assembly. (2022, February 9). *Statement condemning hate symbols at Canadian protest.* https://www.rabbinicalassembly.org/story/rabbinical-assembly-condemns-swastikas-and-other-hate-symbols-display-canadian-protest

[26] Duplicate of #19

[27] Duplicate of #14

[28] Ontario Provincial Police. (2022). *OPP00001627 – Insider threat & extremist coordination* [Internal briefing].

[29] Canadian Anti-Hate Network. (2023). *Canadian far-right cheers on UK anti-immigrant violence* (Soldiers of Odin drills video cited). https://www.antihate.ca/canadian_far_right_cheers_on_uk_anti_immigrant_violence

[30] Office of the Premier of Ontario. (2022, February 7). Ontario premier condemns "symbols of hate" at trucker convoy [Press release]. *Global News* coverage: https://globalnews.ca/news/8582808/doug-ford-statement-trucker-convoy

[31] Duplicate of #14

[32] Amnesty International Canada. (2022, February 11). *Statement on Freedom Convoy and hate symbols.* https://amnesty.ca/human-rights-news/ottawa-protests-freedom-convoy-statement

[33] University of Calgary, School of Public Policy. (2022). *Hate, extremism, and terrorism in Alberta: IMVE trends* [Report].

[34] Duplicate of #28

[35] Royal Canadian Mounted Police. (2022, February 12). *Briefing: Extremist crypto flows tied to convoy wallets* [Unclassified summary]. https://www.coindesk.com/policy/2022/02/16/canada-sanctions-34-crypto-wallets-tied-to-trucker-freedom-convoy

[36] Elliptic. (2022, February 21). *Canada prohibits transactions with trucker-protest crypto wallets.* https://www.elliptic.co/blog/crypto-regulatory-affairs-canada-prohibits-transactions-with-trucker-protest-crypto-wallets

[37] Duplicate of #14

[38] Angus Reid Institute. (2022, February 14). *Three-in-four Canadians tell convoy protesters "Go home now".* https://angusreid.org/trudeau-convoy-trucker-protest-vaccine-mandates-covid-19

[39] Allison, I. (2022, February 16). Canada sanctions 34 crypto wallets tied to trucker convoy. *CoinDesk.* https://www.coindesk.com/layer2/2022/02/22/frozen-bitcoin-tied-to-canadian-protests-lands-at-coinbase-cryptocom

[40] Friends of Simon Wiesenthal Center. (2022, February 13). *Community intelligence brief: Convoy antisemitism incidents.* [Internal memo].

[41] Curran, J. (2022, February 10). Making sense of the flags and symbols at the Ottawa protest. *JURIST.* https://www.jurist.org/news/2022/02/canada-dispatch-making-sense-of-the-flags-and-symbols-at-the-ottawa-protest

[42] Baertlein, L. (2022, August 4). Protests and politics: Canada's "Freedom Convoy" reverberates beyond blockades. *Reuters Insight.* https://www.reuters.com/world/americas/protests-politics-canadas-freedom-convoy-reverberates-2022-08-04

[43] CityNews Edmonton. (2022, January 31). Nazi flags seen at Freedom Convoy in Ottawa [Video]. https://edmonton.citynews.ca/video/2022/01/31/nazi-flags-seen-at-freedom-convoy-in-ottawa

[44] Dickson, B. (2022, March 1). What happened in Ottawa? *The Walrus.* https://thewalrus.ca/ottawa-convoy

[45] CoinDesk. (2022, February 22). 'Frozen' bitcoin tied to Canadian protests lands at Coinbase. https://www.coindesk.com/layer2/2022/02/22/frozen-bitcoin-tied-to-canadian-protests-lands-at-coinbase-cryptocom

[46] Ryckewaert, L. (2022, February 18). Advice for the interregnum. *Politico Ottawa Playbook.* https://www.politico.com/newsletters/ottawa-playbook/2022/03/03/hot-off-the-presses-cpc-leadership-rules-00013486

[47] Jones, A. M. (2022, July 1). The Canadian flag and hate-symbol context in the convoy. *CTV News.* https://www.ctvnews.ca/canada/the-canadian-flag-in-the-context-of-freedom-convoy-and-residential-schools-1.5964240

CHAPTER FIVE:

FIRES APPROPRIATED

"They lit fires with borrowed matches, hoping the smoke would mask the theft. But the wind carried the scent of dishonour further than their hashtags could reach. In the end, a teepee without consent is just another tent pitched on stolen ground."
~ *R.G. Cruise*

From the first teepee staked into the frozen loam of Confederation Park on the evening of 5 February 2022, the convoy tried on Indigeneity the way a child yanks a blanket over their shoulders and declares themself a superhero. The trick, of course, was older than the Dominion itself. When settler movements run short of moral capital, they rattle another people's medicine bag, hoping the borrowed sound will drown out their dissonance. Cultural appropriation, scholars note, is not a modern *faux pas* but the everyday grammar of settler-colonial power, an unbroken habit of taking without asking and remixing without listening. [1] Because possession, as the legal theorists say, is ten-tenths of the narrative. [2]

So the convoy's strategists—more fluent in hashtags than proper protocol—ordered up symbols the way tourists order bannock at a market stall: one teepee, one pipe ceremony, one prayer fire, consult. On Parliament's doorstep, they pounded spruce poles with chrome mallets, diesel fumes curling through the night while Bluetooth speakers pumped out twangy anthems about liberty. Inside the canvas, an uncredentialed "elder" rehearsed a blessing cribbed from YouTube, his vowels landing like wrenches in a gearbox. Outside, truckers livestreamed the scene to Facebook, saying, *The real First Nations are with us, bro!* [3]

By dawn, smoke from the illicit fire mingled with the convoy's barbecue haze, drifting east across the Rideau Canal. Nearby, a lanky volunteer waved an Eagle feather he'd bought online; viewers in Idaho tapped little heart emojis as he told the camera that *smudging clears government lies from the air.* Algonquin elder Claudette Commanda, seeing the clip, dismissed the lot of them as *interlopers* and told reporters they needed to pack up and leave her people's unceded territory. [4] The convoy responded with a group selfie and a caption: *Honoured to be welcomed by the original peoples!* Honour, like diesel, was cheap and abundant—until it ran out.

That morning, the Ottawa police, suddenly mindful of fire codes, posted yellow tape around the teepee. Officers spoke in stage whispers about "cultural sensitivity" while their boots left dark crescents in the snow. Behind them, an old man in a Buffalo Sabres parka beat a pow-wow drum he'd snagged at a pawnshop, timing the thumps to his truck's idling engine. Passing schoolchildren glanced over, unsure whether to clap or cringe.

Word travelled faster than the convoy's CB radios. By 6 February, the Assembly of Manitoba Chiefs blasted a press release condemning the "inappropriate depiction of sacred objects" and the hijacking of ceremony for anti-vaccine activists. [5] The statement landed like a hammer on a cracked anvil—sharp, echoing, impossible to ignore. Within hours, the First Nations Leadership Council out west piled on, calling the occupation an "explosive and shameful display" that mocked their traditions and endangered public health. [6]

Online, the convoy's influencers tried to pivot. They posted a shaky video of an unrelated pow-wow, claiming it showed *Indigenous warriors* blessing the trucks. *Reuters* fact-checkers vaporised the claim in an afternoon, revealing the footage to be years old and miles away. [7] Undeterred, organiser Pat King livestreamed plans for a convoy-branded *Orange Shirt Day*, declaring February 11 a moment of silence *for the kids.* Real Orange Shirt founder Phyllis Webstad promptly called the stunt a hijacking of residential-school memory. [8]

On the ground, the theatrics continued. A rookie trucker named Randy knelt inside the teepee, eyes watering from cedar smoke, whispering that he felt *super connected* to the land. Outside, Eldon—from Kitigan Zibi, wrapped in his father's faded R.C.M.P. parka—stood with arms folded. *Permission,* he told Randy, *is not a feeling. It's an agreement.* Randy looked up, puzzled; a camera phone hovered inches from his ear. The livestream audience waited for redemption, but none arrived. Eldon turned away, his breath cutting small clouds into the February air.

Meanwhile, the broader city boiled. *NPR* noted the pipe-ceremony controversy in its state-of-emergency coverage, pointing out how First Nations leaders called the appropriation "unacceptable." [9] Residents trapped by the roadblocks asked why the teepee remained while ticketing ordinary citizens for parking infractions. Pam Palmater told *Reuters* the answer was racism in high-vis form: "It's OK if angry white men do it…but not if Indigenous people peacefully protect their rights." [10]

The academic chorus chimed in. Law journals reminded Canadians that cultural appropriation is a legal wound as much as a moral one, sustained by doctrines that treat culture as a public domain for the dominant society. [11] Even popular primers in national encyclopaedias spelt out the toll—how sacred objects lose power when paraded for spectacle, how ceremony without consent re-enacts historic theft. [12]

By February 7, denunciations arrived faster than the convoy's supply lines. Letters from the Algonquin Nation, Tungasuvvingat Inuit, and urban friendship centres furled across social media like storm fronts. [13] In Vancouver, chiefs condemned the "spread of misinformation, racism, and violence," explicitly citing the Ottawa teepee as evidence. [14] Even *The Tyee's* opinion pages—usually patient with dissent—ran a headline calling the convoy's cultural grabs an "Attack on Indigenous People," arguing that stolen drums were now shields for white grievance. [15]

Inside Parliament, the upper chamber added its voice. During the Emergencies Act debate on February 22, Senators referenced the "caricaturing and appropriation of Indigenous culture" as proof that the protest had jumped the guardrails of legitimate dissent. [16] Their rebuke carried no immediate penalties but marked a line in Hansard: culture is not a costume, ceremony is not a prop. Yet for every official rebuke, the convoy's Facebook pages doubled down—memes of teepees beside chrome stacks, maple leaves photoshopped into dream catchers, hashtags insisting that reconciliation meant "standing together against mandates."

The irony was biblical: a movement raging against masks was happy to wear another people's face.

When city crews dismantled the unauthorised teepee on February 9, the ground beneath it was a slurry of ash and antifreeze. Volunteers packed up the sagging canvas, still claiming victory. Down the block, Eldon collected a handful of cold ashes. *Our ancestors,* he muttered, *didn't light fires so someone else could roast marshmallows.* The questions left smouldering travelled well beyond Ottawa. Could symbolic *honours* ever substitute for genuine partnership? Who gets to decide when a sacred object is in play? And if reconciliation is a road, what happens when a convoy parks on it and calls the jam freedom? Those questions would roll forward into committee rooms, classrooms, and kitchen tables— accelerants awaiting the next spark.

The nine Indigenous Senators who filed into the Senate foyer at noon on 5 February 2022 looked as if they had marched straight out of a prairie squall— faces chapped, braids wind-tossed, purpose glinting like ice under floodlights. One by one, they read lines from a joint statement that condemned "the harassment, intimidation, and blatant cultural misappropriation carried out in the name of the so-called Freedom Convoy." [17] Reporters scribbled; cameras whirred; even the marble columns seemed to lean closer. The Senators reminded Canada that reconciliation is not a buffet where settlers pile sacred symbols onto paper plates, but an exacting treaty obligation anchored in Section 35 of the Constitution. [18]

Outside, winter light skidded across the Peace Tower, throwing long shadows over the question the Senators had just raised: What happens when cultural sovereignty collides with a convoy of revving engines? Section 35 guarantees "existing Aboriginal and treaty rights," a phrase legal scholars say includes the power to protect ceremonies from colonial remixing. [19] The United Nations Declaration on the Rights of Indigenous Peoples, which Canada incorporated into federal law in 2021, buttresses that promise and affirms every nation's control over "cultural heritage, traditional knowledge, and traditional cultural expressions." [20] Yet, as elders at the Unist'ot'en healing centre warn, declarations mean little when bulldozers or, in this case, diesel convoys roll across lived jurisdiction. [21] Wet'suwet'en land defenders know this gap intimately; academic analyses of their camp describe a *limits-of-reconciliation* moment where the Crown's rhetoric buckles under resource-driven reality. [22]

Senator Mary Jane McCallum folded the statement inside the foyer and spoke off-script. "Some people wrap themselves in our regalia the way children toss on Halloween capes," she said, voice flat as a drumhead. "But every feather is a ledger of consent, every song a receipt. You can't just swipe them at a truck stop." Reporters caught her words but missed the hiss of her breath as she turned away, shoulders tight, as though bracing for recoil.

That recoil arrived within hours. At the Assembly of Manitoba Chiefs headquarters in Winnipeg, an emergency Zoom council lit up the screens of leaders from Norway House to Brokenhead. Grand Chief Arlen Dumas, sleeves rolled above his forearms, read aloud a briefing note that described convoy supporters "using teepees like pop-up booths at a county fair." [23] Chiefs typed quick motions in the chat: condemn the appropriation; urge allies to withdraw support; remind Manitoba truckers that *freight rolls on treaty territory by permission, not entitlement.* They passed the resolution unanimously and emailed it to every newsroom before the digital smoke cleared.

In Ottawa, Métis filmmaker Jolene Cardinal shouldered a Canon camera two thousand kilometres east and trudged back to Confederation Park. Since dawn, she had catalogued the teepee's slow desecration—truck exhaust turning canvas grey, beer cans tossed into the sacred fire pit, a teenage protester using the pipe-ceremony altar as a selfie prop. [24] Jolene crouched low, framing a shot of a convoy flag flapping against spruce poles. *Appropriation in real-time,* she muttered, audio meter peaking as a gust rattled the mic. Moments later, a volunteer in a red MAGA toque waved her away, claiming she needed *creator-approved media credentials.* Jolene laughed, the sound brittle as lake ice, and kept filming.

By February 8, the condemnation had swollen westward. The First Nations Leadership Council—representing B.C.'s three largest political organisations—released a statement calling the convoy a "shameful display of misinformation, racism, and violence," and decrying its theft of ceremony as "yet another form of colonial domination." [25] Their words ricocheted through band offices, longhouses, and Facebook feeds, sparking hashtags like *#CultureIsNotCostume* and *#Section35Shield.*

Convoy influencers tried to spin. One live streamer pointed his phone at the Senate entrance, sneering that *a few woke chiefs won't cancel freedom.* Seconds later, his chat erupted with laughing emojis and racist slurs. *Reuters* caught the clip and, in a feature on Ottawa residents' frustrations, quoted Mi'kmaw lawyer Pam

Palmater: *It's apparently fine for angry white men to occupy a city, but Indigenous land defenders get raided at gunpoint.* [26]

VICE News peeled back another layer, reporting how convoy figureheads claimed pretend Indigenous ancestry to lend moral cover, even announcing an "All Nations Prayer Circle" without inviting a single recognised knowledge-keeper. [27] The article ran screenshots of Pat King's since-deleted push for an Orange Shirt Day *moment of silence,* juxtaposed with Phyllis Webstad's furious rebuke.

Grassroots fury was far less polite. Algonquin elder Claudette Commanda told *APTN* that the convoy's teepee was "colonial violence with cedar poles," adding, "Interlopers need to go." [28] Social-media accounts tied to *Idle No More* and *1492 Land Back Lane* shared Jolene's footage under the caption *Not your feathers, not your fire. Indian Country Today* summarised the surge of grassroots denunciations, noting how many drew direct parallels between the convoy's occupation of city streets and R.C.M.P. raids on Wet'suwet'en territory. [29]

Academics joined the chorus. Students clipped passages from a geography journal article on the Unist'ot'en blockade and placed them atop photos of eighteen-wheelers idling on Wellington Street. The article asserted that settler jurisdiction continually pursues *flexible frontiers,* allowing the disregard of Indigenous law when inconvenient, and it reappeared across Twitter threads. 30 Someone graffitied a snippet—Sovereignty is not a parking permit—on a snowbank outside the Supreme Court.

By February 9, the air hummed with rumour that convoy leaders would pivot to exploiting Orange Shirt symbolism later that week; *Global News* previewed the backlash, quoting survivors who called the idea "a grotesque bait-and-switch." [31] Legislators took note. In late-night strategy sessions, aides floated amendments that could criminalise the commercial use of sacred objects without permission— draft language that would shadow the Emergencies Act debate, still days away.

As midnight crept over the downtown core, the teepee's fire had burned to a dull dish of embers. Jolene pressed record again, panning from the sagging canvas to the Parliament lights beyond. She whispered a question that floated into the frigid dark: *If honour can be borrowed, who keeps the receipt?*

Across the country, that question rattled cabinet tables, treaty offices, and kitchen radios. The Senators' foyer statement had become a kindling point for broader legislation; chiefs demanded parliamentary hearings on cultural protection; grassroots organisers drafted a digital map of every misused sacred site. Yet none of it answered the more profound riddle—whether settler society could distinguish between homage and heist, solidarity, and spectacle. That riddle would linger, ember-hot, waiting to be fanned into open flame.

Canada's colonial story did not begin with the squeal of air-horns on Wellington Street but with a papal flourish in 1493, when the Doctrine of Discovery announced that Christian crowns could claim lands—and souls— already spoken for by Indigenous nations. [32] In the centuries that followed, the Crown refined that license into statutes and handcuffs—from the 1885 Potlatch Ban that criminalised West Coast gift-giving and seized ceremonial regalia as contraband [33] to the 1982 promise of Section 35, which enshrined Aboriginal and treaty rights yet left courts to decide how far they could stretch. [34] When Parliament adopted Bill C-15 to incorporate the UN Declaration on the Rights of Indigenous Peoples in 2021, law- makers spoke of a new era of free, prior and informed consent, [35] even as another private member's bill—C-391—languished, its call for a national strategy to repatriate stolen cultural property still unanswered. [36] Each statute was a rung on a ladder that Indigenous peoples had been forced to build for others to climb—so when the convoy's *ersatz* teepee rose on Parliament's lawn, it was lashed to half a millennium of precedent.

On the afternoon of February 10, curatorial lights winked against display glass in the Canadian Museum of History. A senior collections manager, Danielle Charest, watched raw livestream clips of diesel-black smoke curling past make-shift poles. The feed showed convoy volunteers draping a Canadian flag across the teepee door—*for the optics,* someone joked off camera. Charest's knuckles tightened around a clipboard. Only a year earlier, she had co-authored a blog urging her institution to document pandemic protests with care, mindful of "the appropriation of national symbols already fraught with meaning." [37] Now that warning scrolled before her eyes in real time. Remembering how similar pieces had been hauled away in 1922 under the weight of the Potlatch Ban, she placed a finger on the glass of a Kwakwa̱ka̱'wakw bíkwa̱s mask. Behind her, a junior archivist muttered, *History's collecting itself again.*

Across the river at a community studio, Métis videographer Jolene Cardinal cued up a second screen that flickered with archival footage: R.C.M.P. officers carting potlatch treasures onto a steamer; a 1930s lecture poster for *Grey Owl, the Famous Indian Naturalist,* whose celebrated conservation talks hid an English accent beneath faux-buckskin. [38] She overlaid those frames on the convoy's teepee feed, letting past and present ghosts into one another. In the studio's corner, her uncle Rudy tapped the space bar to freeze Grey Owl's grin. *That man sold wilderness with a stolen face,* Rudy said, shaking his head. [39] *Now these truckers think they can sell freedom the same way.*

That evening, sociology professor Niigaan Sinclair led a fire-lit seminar in a snow-sheltered courtyard at the University of Manitoba, livestreamed to restless students stuck in lockdown dorms. Flames licked cedar chips while Sinclair traced an arc from the Royal Proclamation of 1763 to Section 35's "slippery promise of sovereignty." "Treaties aren't fairy dust," he warned, glancing at his phone as convoy memes scrolled past. "You don't sprinkle them on a protest and call it reconciliation." [40] A freshman asked whether the Constitution could stop cultural theft. Sinclair exhaled hard enough to dim the flame. "Section 35 is a shield made of paper," he said, "and paper burns."

Further west, night crews at the Royal B.C. Museum catalogued crates of repatriated regalia returned after decades abroad. One conservator paused over a copper beaten thin by potlatch dancers a century ago, its surface pocked where a federal agent had once stamped an inventory number. News from Scotland buzzed on her phone: Nisga'a leaders demanded the immediate return of a memorial pole taken in 1929 by an anthropologist who called it *scientific salvage.* [41] The conservator whispered at the screen, *Bring it home before someone poses with it for likes.*

February 11 dawned with diesel haze over Ottawa and a fresh convoy initiative dubbed *Orange Shirt Day 2.0.* Organisers promised a *moment of silence for the kids,* borrowing the symbol of residential-school remembrance without the consent of survivors. *NPR*'s midday bulletin noted the rebrand and replayed city-council audio of residents describing themselves as prisoners in their own neighbourhoods. [42] The broadcast cut to honking horns and a chant of *This is our land!*—a phrase that, in a cruel twist, mirrored long-standing Land Back slogans.

Inside the teepee, a trucker named Glen rehearsed a speech about unity while Jolene's camera rolled outside. Her lens captured volunteer "security" guards scrawling hashtags on the canvas: *#AllNationsStandTogether*, *#SacredFire4Freedom*. She overlaid the shot with a 1928 Department of Indian Affairs letter authorising the public exhibition of confiscated masks, its typewritten approval bleeding into Glen's marker ink. The composite image went viral, and by sundown, Charest's colleagues at the museum had flagged it for acquisition—proof, they said, that history sometimes annotated itself. [43]

While convoy TikTok streams claimed the teepee was *protected by the Constitution,* policy analysts in Gatineau flipped through briefing binders on the pending renewal of Canada's Museum Policy. One margin note highlighted public calls to align collecting guidelines with UNDRIP and to fast-track legislation barring the display of sacred objects without community consent. [44] Another sticky note asked: *Could emergency heritage protections mirror gunpoint injunctions used on Wet'suwet'en land defenders?*

The irony was acidic; where injunctions once dismantled Indigenous blockades, officials now pondered how to dismantle a settler one.

By February 12, the teepee's canvas sagged under frost and exhaust, but its symbolism still glowed hot across talk-radio panels. A columnist warned that the hashtag *#LandBack* was being twisted into *freedom for me but not for thee,* an appropriation of sovereignty rhetoric that masked a hunger for unfettered settler mobility. [45] That afternoon, Jolene uploaded a montage titled Borrowed Fires: clips of Grey Owl, potlatch arrests, Nisga'a repatriation pleas, and Glen's unity speech. Convoy livestreams dissected it as *state propaganda* within an hour, while museum followers hailed it as a masterclass in public history.

The next day, wind kicked ash from the smouldering sacred fire bowl, scattering flakes across the parliamentary steps like iron filings searching for a magnet. In those embers, critics heard familiar cracks: the sound of reconciliation's veneer under stress. And yet, on February 14—Valentine's Day for some, a trigger date for many survivors—Jolene stood with Eldon from Kitigan Zibi beside the extinguished flame. She unfolded a treaty map under the winter sun. Eldon traced the Ottawa River with a gloved finger. *"This line,* he said, *was supposed to be a promise. Today it's a lane.* His hand moved to the tear where Glen had cut the canvas to feed the fire: *And this,* he added, *is where promises leak.*

National news anchors, scrambling for a late-night closer, asked whether Canada stood at an inflexion point. The curator in Gatineau drafted acquisition notes for the convoy artefacts under the heading *Evidence of Contemporary Colonial Appropriation.* The historian in Winnipeg filed his lecture under *Ongoing Treaties.* And after exporting her final cut, Jolene titled it *Receipts.*

The questions pulsing beneath those files would beat into the following chapters: Could symbolic reckoning harden into statutory reform? Would Parliament weld new legal teeth onto outdated cultural-property laws, or grind them flat in committee? And, most pressingly, could a nation addicted to the spectacle of honour learn to pay its debts in something sturdier than borrowed fire?

ENDNOTES

[1] Historica Canada. (n.d.). *Cultural appropriation of Indigenous peoples in Canada.* The Canadian Encyclopedia. Retrieved May 15, 2025, from https://www.thecanadianencyclopedia.ca/en/article/cultural-appropriation-of-indigenous-peoples-in-canada

[2] Brown, M. F. (1998). The properties of culture and the politics of possessing identity: Native claims in the cultural appropriation controversy. *Canadian Journal of Law & Jurisprudence, 11*(2), 189 – 221. https://doi.org/10.1017/S0841820900005531

[3] Assembly of Manitoba Chiefs. (2022, February 4). *Senator joins First Nations and Indigenous leadership response to "Freedom Convoy"* [Press release]. https://manitobachiefs.com/press_releases/senator-joins-first-nations-and-indigenous-leadership-response-to-freedom-convoy

[4] Dubé, D.-E. (2022, February 4). Pipe ceremony, teepee in Confederation Park not supported by local Indigenous groups. *CityNews Ottawa.* https://ottawa.citynews.ca/2022/02/04/pipe-ceremony-teepee-in-confederation-park-not-supported-by-local-indigenous-groups-5028911

[5] Treisman, R. (2022, February 7). State of emergency declared as Ottawa police respond to protests. *NPR.* https://www.npr.org/2022/02/07/1078861392/ottawa-protest-state-of-emergency

[6] First Nations Leadership Council. (2022, February 8). *First Nations Leadership Council strongly condemns "Freedom Convoy" movement across Canada and its spread of misinformation, racism and violence* [Press release]. https://www.bcafn.ca/news/first-nations-leadership-council-strongly-condemns-freedom-convoy-movement-across-canada-and

[7] McSheffrey, E. (2022, February 11). B.C. First Nations advocates condemn use of Orange Shirt Day by trucker convoy. *Global News.* https://globalnews.ca/news/8614043/bc-first-nations-advocates-orange-shirt-day-trucker-convoy

[8] Gordon, J. (2022, February 3). Ottawans fed up with trucker blockade, blame police for inaction. *Reuters*. https://www.reuters.com/world/americas/ottawans-fed-up-with-trucker-blockade-blame-police-inaction-2022-02-03

[9] Reuters Fact Check. (2022, January 27). Fact check: Video of Indigenous group is not related to 2022 "Freedom Convoy." *Reuters*. https://www.reuters.com/article/fact-check/video-of-indigenous-group-is-not-related-to-2022-freedom-convoy-idUSL1N2U72WJ

[10] Ede, A. (2022, February 18). The convoy's appropriations are an attack on Indigenous people. *The Tyee*. https://thetyee.ca/Opinion/2022/02/18/Convoy-Appropriations-Attack-Indigenous-People

[11] Duplicate of #2

[12] Duplicate of #1

[13] Duplicate of #4

[14] Duplicate of #6

[15] Senate of Canada. (2022, February 22). *Debates of the Senate (Hansard), 44th Parl., 1st Sess., Issue 19*. https://sencanada.ca/en/content/sen/chamber/441/debates/019db_2022-02-22-e

[16] Audette, M., Christmas, D., Francis, B., Galvez, R., & Indigenous Senators Group. (2022, February 5). *Statement by Indigenous senators regarding recent events in Ottawa* [Statement]. Senate of Canada. https://www.aptnnews.ca/wp-content/uploads/2022/02/2022-02-05-STATEMENTBY-INDIGENOUS-SENATORS-REGARDING-RECENT-EVENTS-IN-OTTAWA-EN.pdf

[17] Duplicate of #16

[18] Needham, F. (2022, February 5). Nine Indigenous senators condemn the Freedom Convoy movement. *APTN News*. https://www.aptnnews.ca/national-news/nine-indigenous-senators-condemn-the-freedom-convoy-movement

[19] Christie, G. (2003). Aboriginal citizenship: Sections 35, 25 and 15 of Canada's Constitution Act, 1982. *Citizenship Studies, 7*(4), 481 – 495. https://doi.org/10.1080/1362102032000134994

[20] United Nations. (2007). *United Nations Declaration on the Rights of Indigenous Peoples*. https://www.un.org/development/desa/indigenouspeoples/declaration-on-the-rights-of-indigenous-peoples.html

[21] West Coast Environmental Law. (2018, January 31). The Unist'ot'en stand-off: How Canada's "prove-it" mentality undermines reconciliation. https://www.wcel.org/blog/unistoten-stand-off-how-canadas-prove-it-mentality-undermines-reconciliation

[22] McCreary, T., & Turner, J. (2018). The contested scales of Indigenous and settler jurisdiction: Unist'ot'en struggles with Canadian pipeline governance. *Studies in Political Economy, 99*(3), 223 – 245. https://doi.org/10.1080/07078552.2018.1536367

[23] Duplicate of #4

[24] Duplicate of #3

[25] Duplicate of #6

[26] Duplicate of #8

[27] Zoledziowski, A. (2022, February 16). Indigenous leaders are condemning the "Freedom Convoy" for hateful, racist conduct. *VICE World News.* https://www.vice.com/en/article/indigenous-leaders-are-condemning-the-freedom-convoy-for-hateful-racist-conduct

[28] Forester, B. (2022, February 2). Algonquin elder says "interlopers need to go" as Ottawa braces for convoy protest surge. *APTN News.* https://www.aptnnews.ca/national-news/algonquin-elder-says-interlopers-need-to-go-as-ottawa-braces-for-convoy-protest-surge

[29] Morrisseau, M. (2022, February 8). First Nations speak out against trucker convoy. *Indian Country Today.* https://ictnews.org/news/first-nations-speak-out-against-trucker-convoy

[30] Hiller, C., & Carlson, E. (2018). The contested scales of Indigenous and settler jurisdiction: Unist'ot'en blockade. *The Canadian Geographer, 62*(3), 245 – 262. https://doi.org/10.1111/cag.12459

[31] Duplicate of #7

[32] Tomchuk, T. (2022, November 2). *The Doctrine of Discovery.* Canadian Museum for Human Rights. https://humanrights.ca/story/doctrine-discovery

[33] Virtual Museum of Canada. (n.d.). *Potlatch Ban* (The Kwakwaka'wakw Potlatch: A Living Tradition). Retrieved May 15, 2025, from http://umistapotlatch.ca/potlatch_interdire-potlatch_ban-eng.php

[34] Lothamer, H. (2021). Section 35 of the Canadian Constitution Act and Indigenous self-determination in Canada. *Political Science Undergraduate Review, 6*(1), 14 – 21. https://doi.org/10.29173/psur183

[35] Parliament of Canada. (2020, December 3). *Bill C-15: United Nations Declaration on the Rights of Indigenous Peoples Act* [First reading]. https://www.parl.ca/DocumentViewer/en/43-2/bill/C-15/first-reading

[36] Parliament of Canada. (2019). *Bill C-391: Indigenous Human Remains and Cultural Property Repatriation Act.* https://www.parl.ca/LegisInfo/en/bill/42-1/c-391

[37] Trepanier, J., & Neill, D. (2023, February 14). Pandemic protests and "Freedom Convoy" context. *Canadian Museum of History Blog.* https://www.historymuseum.ca/blog/pandemic-protests-and-freedom-convoy-context

[38] McCullough, S. (2024, September 18). Collecting COVID-19 history: Protest, resistance and celebration. *Canadian Museum of History Blog.* https://www.historymuseum.ca/blog/artifactuality-collecting-covid19-history

[39] Onyanga-Omara, J. (2013, September 19). Grey Owl: Canada's great conservationist and imposter. *BBC News.* https://www.bbc.com/news/uk-england-sussex-24127514

[40] Sinclair, N. (2022, March 13). *Canada's "Freedom Convoy"* [Webinar video]. YouTube. https://www.youtube.com/watch?v=HSLeZnMcTbo

[41] Smith, M. (2022, August 23). Indigenous Canadians demand changes at National Museum of Scotland. *The Times.* https://www.thetimes.com/uk/scotland/article/indigenous-canadians-seek-totem-pole-return-pl2hvbmm6

[42] Hernandez, J. (2022, February 8). Canadian truckers block a key border crossing, as protests in Ottawa drag on. *NPR*. https://www.npr.org/2022/02/08/1079212789/canadian-truckers-block-a-key-border-crossing-as-protests-in-ottawa-drag-on

[43] Duplicate of #38

[44] Canadian Heritage. (2023). *What we heard: 2022–2023 consultations on the renewal of the Canadian Museum Policy* [Report]. https://www.canada.ca/en/canadian-heritage/campaigns/renewal-museum-policy/what-we-heard.html

[45] Melanson, M. (2024, October 22). The Indigenous "Land Back" movement: A land mine for Canadians. *C2C Journal*. https://c2cjournal.ca/2024/10/the-indigenous-land-back-movement-a-land-mine-for-canadians

CHAPTER SIX:

BRIDGE OF FREIGHT AND FRICTION

"When the engines stall on the bridge, so does the pulse of two nations—trade, like trust, does not like a detour. In a world built on just-in-time, a single parked axle writes a story of lost hours and anxious payrolls faster than any economist can tally. Sometimes all it takes to turn prosperity into peril is one blockade, a cold morning, and the stubborn hope that someone else will move first."
~ R.G. Cruise

The first light of 8 February 2022 found the steel lattice of the Ambassador Bridge veiled in road-salt mist and diesel haze, a seventy-eight-year-old artery that normally pumps close to CA$500 million in goods, some 8,000 trucks' worth, across the Detroit River every working day. [1] On that morning, the flow stalled, with it the heartbeat of an economy whose valves and chambers span two nations. Canada sells three-quarters of everything it makes to the United States, and the auto sector is the muscle that keeps the blood moving in both directions, its parts ricocheting across the frontier up to seven times before a sedan rolls off any line. Post-war Japan may have conceived just-in-time (JIT) manufacturing—a production methodology that aligns raw-material deliveries with production schedules, so parts arrive exactly when needed, minimising inventory and waste—but North Americans made it a religion. [2] When the convoy's chrome-plated altars squatted on the bridge deck, the hymn became heresy, and every minute of delay translated into red ink. *A single axle parked in the wrong spot*, a Transport Canada analyst warned in a terse briefing note, *carries a daily GDP risk north of CA$390 million.* [3]

By mid-morning, customs broker Ruby Sawchuk was pacing her Windsor office like a metronome stuck on allegro. Each time the status screen refreshed, the *northbound unreleased* backlog column increased. *This is a heart attack in spreadsheet form*, she muttered, stabbing at the refresh key. The Canada Border Services Agency logbook beside her desk showed the first full closure recorded at 05:32; the following entry was a bleak ellipse: *trucks redirected to Sarnia—capacity unknown.* [4] A call buzzed through from Detroit. *Ruby, can you magic forty-two skids of seat frames to Orion Township by dinner? Only if I charter a blimp*, she shot back, trying for levity and landing nearer gallows humour.

Down Highway 401 in Oakville, plant supervisor Miguel Alvarez watched robot arms glide to a stop, their hydraulic sighs echoing like disappointed giants. Ford had shuttered its Windsor engine plant overnight and ordered Oakville onto a *red-lined, reduced schedule,* the corporate memo said, *pending bridge access.* [5] Miguel keyed the plant-wide PA: *Team, we're on standby. Keep tools clean and minds calm.* In the break room, a welder cracked, *Calm? We're one gasket away from playing euchre till spring.* Laughter ricocheted, brittle as frost-bit steel.

The second shift never reported at General Motors' Lansing Delta Township facility. Dan Flores's voice on the speaker traced the reason: *Parts shortage linked to Windsor protest—restart TBD.* [6] Magna International's CEO briefed investors that throughout the supplier chain, customers were *idling or cutting production requirements.* [7] The conference call felt less like an earnings update than a weather report for an incoming blizzard.

Transport Canada's Situation Centre pulsed with luminous screens: real-time GPS splays of diverted rigs, colour-coded detours to Sarnia and Port Huron, a scarlet overlay marking driver hours evaporating in rest-area queues. A duty officer read aloud from *Automotive News. Court injunction could end blockade; Detroit Three scaling back.* [8] Someone whistled low. Another monitor scrolled *Axios* headlines: *Auto industry halts production as copycat convoys loom.* [9]

Industry associations drafted bulletins in Ottawa's boardrooms—virtual squares of pin-stripe and pinched nerves. The U.S. Chamber of Commerce, the National Association of Manufacturers and Business Roundtable issued a joint plea: "Swift, collaborative action required to reopen Windsor–Detroit gateway." [10] Within the hour, a coalition of twenty-two Canadian business groups echoed them, warning that the bridge closure was "an unforced tariff on ourselves." [11]

Meanwhile, protest organiser *Big Jake* MacPherson leaned against a red Kenworth idling at 600 RPM on Huron Church Road. He offered a smudge stick to a line of reporters, smoke curling like a question mark. *We're peaceful,* he drawled. *Just reminding Ottawa who keeps the shelves full.* Above him, a hand-painted banner read, *FREEDOM IS ESSENTIAL*; below, pallets of brake rotors sat sweating in the cold. Across the barricade, a lone Windsor Police sergeant leafed through the Transport Canada briefing for leverage he knew he did not yet have.

In Detroit, auto-parts despatcher Keisha Reynolds juggled phones beneath a wall map studded with red push-pins. *I've got a tier-two supplier in Windsor,* she told a client, *whose aluminium stampings are ageing faster than bananas. Air freight? That's a mortgage payment, a pound.* Her colleague pointed to a new alert: U.S. auto lobby urges Biden administration *to safeguard cross-border supply chains.* [12] Keisha rolled her eyes. *Safeguard? Honey, they need a time machine.*

By the evening of 9 February, the Ambassador Bridge resembled a rust-belt carnival—oil-drum fires, camp stoves, and a choir of truck horns tuned to defiance. Yet beyond the spectacle, balance sheets were bleaching. Analysts at the University of Guelph warned that every rerouted load acted *as an additional tax on exporters and importers,* eroding confidence far faster than inventory. [13] Toyota quietly confirmed it would build nothing at Cambridge or Woodstock *for the rest of the week.* [14]

Miguel locked the Oakville plant at 23:00. *See you when the river flows again,* he told the night watch. Driving home, he listened to a radio host predict the blockade would gift ammunition to Buy-America hawks in Washington. [15] He pictured the supply chain as a long, gleaming accordion: squeeze it in Windsor and the bellows wheezed from Oshawa to Ohio.

The dawn of 10 February arrived brittle and blue. Ruby's backlog column flashed vermilion; her brokerage queue had tripled. She skimmed a Transport Canada update: losses are now estimated *north of CA$300 million per day, climbing toward the upper bound should closures persist.* Over coffee gone cold, she composed an email: *Dear Clients—Expect cascading delays. Consider Port Huron routes. Pray for tow trucks.* She hit send, knuckles aching.

On Parliament Hill, treasury officials drafted cost curves showing how a single choke point could transmogrify just-in-time into just-too-late. One aide murmured, *This isn't supply chain—this is supply roulette.* In Detroit, a supplier CEO echoed the sentiment on *CNBC. Every minute this bridge is blocked, we're tossing nickels into a furnace.*

Yet even amid gridlock, moments of laughable absurdity sprouted. A protester in a snow-camouflaged jumpsuit offered free coffee *imported from the Republic of Tim Hortons.* Reporters noted that the coffee arrived via sled from the Canadian side—an improvised supply chain within the blockade.

By twilight, the air above the river carried equal parts diesel and dread. Industry bulletins multiplied like febrile birds, forecasting parts shortages, idle lines, and pink slips if wheels did not soon turn. One final communiqué, issued simultaneously in Ottawa and Washington, warned of "irreparable harm to North American competitiveness" should the impasse linger beyond the weekend. [16]

High above the bridge, the last paragraph of that bulletin seemed to hang like a prophecy: *The decisions taken in the coming hours will echo through assembly plants, farm gates, and household budgets on both sides of the border.* The sentence drifted west with the wind, past shuttered gates and flickering torchlights, hinting at the reckonings that would dominate the days ahead.

> *In that hushed moment—before the clank of tow hooks or the thud of court orders—the protesters' idling engines did more than rumble; they ticked away like a luxury timepiece, each turn of the crank a reminder that every second of defiance carries its own wallet-draining price.*

February's second Friday broke over Ottawa like a back-ordered invoice—cold, glossy, and stamped *OVERDUE.* At 06:00 on 11 February 2022, Premier Doug Ford declared a province-wide state of emergency, warning that every horn blast reverberating off Parliament's sandstone *puts a family pay cheque on the line* [17] *Politico* called the measure "the strongest yet," an order that could fine blockade-builders CA$100,000 and jail them a year for choking commerce. [18] Within minutes, municipal phones rang like fire bells. Hoteliers wanted tax deferrals; restaurateurs wanted the trucks gone; councillors wanted someone—*anyone*—to pick up the tab.

Down on Sparks Street, Laila Jabeur wiped the condensation off Café Tigris's front glass and counted three receipts in her till where three hundred used to lie. Outside, diesel plumes curled above a gauntlet of flag-draped cabs. *Wasn't lockdown supposed to be the hard part?* She asked a courier, who shrugged and stapled a *Road Closed* notice to the lamp-post. Christine Leadman of the Bank Street BIA had warned two nights earlier that some merchants were *doing worse than during a full COVID lockdown,* their staff harassed for masking and their doors rattled by after-hours taunts. [19] Laila locked her float in the safe and whispered, *We're not cafés anymore, we're glaciers—slowly melting.*

Five blocks east, Rajiv Singh twisted in his swivel chair, the blue glow of an Ontario government portal illuminating a face that should have been flipping through spring inventory catalogues. A joint provincial-federal pledge of relief money was taking shape—Queen's Park promising up to CA$11.5 million for the core's commercial casualties FedDev Ontario drafted a separate CA$20-million fund to be funnelled through Invest Ottawa for grants "up to $10,000 in non-repayable contributions." [20] Rajiv's cursor hovered over a mandatory field: *Estimated revenue loss since 28 January.* He sighed and typed *90 %.*

Outside the council chamber—still locked in Zoom boxes—Mayor Jim Watson hustled votes for an emergency appropriation to reimburse downtown storefronts for boarding, security, and lost perishables. The clerk uploaded a special-meeting agenda for 16 February that listed a single thunderclap item: "Ongoing impacts of the truck convoy demonstration and illegal occupation." [21] Councillor McKenney, their bookshelf draped with a rainbow scarf, quoted an email from a 25-room hostel whose bookings had fallen from complete to zero: *We've become a dystopian Airbnb for diesel tourists.*

At 10:37 that same Friday, the Ottawa Board of Trade blasted a newsletter subject-lined: *OPEN LETTER TO GOVERNMENT + ONTARIO DECLARES STATE OF EMERGENCY.* "Every stalled truck is a withdrawn line of credit," it read, urging all levels to "deploy immediate liquidity so our main streets survive to pay tomorrow's taxes." [22] By midday, requests for rent relief, short-term wage subsidies, and mental-health stipends were stacking in a shared Google Drive faster than city clerks could click *download.*

Saturday dawned with sheet-ice sunlight and the smell of free barbecued sausage wafting off Wellington. Economists on talk radio warned that small-business attrition would ripple outward for months: *Foot traffic has collapsed, delivery apps won't service the red zone, and brand reputations are bleeding,* one analyst told *Global News*. [23] Laila heard the segment on her transistor, laughed once, and switched it off. *I don't need a PhD to know a customer drought*, she muttered, emptying an untouched urn of hazelnut roast into the sink.

Meanwhile, the Ottawa Coalition of Residents and Businesses—later a party at the Public Order Emergency Commission—circulated impact affidavits. One florist reported losing every Valentine's booking; a hairdresser tallied 140 no-shows; a jeweller said his February gross equalled "three Tuesday afternoons back when Tuesdays meant something." [24] The affidavits landed on MPs' desks just as Finance officials drafted language for *targeted non-deferrable-cost reimbursement*.

On Sunday the 13th, Ottawa Mayor Watson tried a different ledger: political goodwill. In a letter to convoy leaders, he offered to meet if they shifted rigs out of residential streets where pyjama-clad kids were sleeping to the lullaby of air horns. [25] The leaky faucet-like gambit resulted in some trucks trickling south to Queen Street, but protesters claimed no deal had been reached and resumed honking at dusk. Councillors called the partial move *shuffling deckchairs on a Brinks truck*.

Valentine's morning, 14 February, broke brittle and jagged. Premier Ford's orders, now in force, made it illegal to block *critical infrastructure*, and provincial staff uploaded draft reimbursement criteria to *ontario.ca*. Simultaneously, the federal cabinet invoked the Emergencies Act, sketching another column in the relief spreadsheet: possible liability coverage for tow companies and compensation for property damage once the occupation cleared. [26]

Across from Café Tigris, the news of impending cheques felt as distant as cherry blossoms. Laila scrawled *FREE COFFEE FOR PARAMEDICS* on a chalk sandwich board—less marketing, more plea. A paramedic took a cup and slid two toonies across the counter, anyway. *We're billing hazard pay*, he joked.

That afternoon, Rajiv finally hit *submit* on Ontario's grant portal, then opened Invest Ottawa's FAQ and bookmarked the *Downtown Ottawa Business Relief Fund applications open on 15 March*. [27] He printed the confirmation email like a passport stamp to a post-protest future and taped it above the till for staff morale.

Inside City Hall's virtual grid, Council debated line-items: CA$100,000 for extra garbage pickup, CA$2 million for overtime policing, CA$400,000 for small-business liaison teams. Treasurer Wendy Stephenson likened the ledger to "balancing on a marble," noting that early cost estimates—later pegged near CA$30 million—were already climbing. [28] Councillor Fleury quipped, *A blockade is the world's most expensive pop-up market, and nobody's buying.*

By evening, downtown had become a diorama of contrasts: protestors roasting marshmallows atop oil drums while, two blocks east, a clothing boutique owner from the Rideau Centre calculated how many mannequins she'd have to sell on Facebook Marketplace to cover rent. [29] Ottawa Tourism executives, watching hotel vacancy spike to 85 per cent, drafted memos warning that *conference cancellations now risk cascading into summer festival deficits,* a domino line stretching from jazz stages to food-truck vendors.

Trade associations on both sides of the river tuned to the Council's YouTube stream. An Ontario Chamber lobbyist messaged a Michigan counterpart: *If Ottawa falls quiet for good, Detroit's weekend numbers drop too.* The reply came swiftly: *Tell them: recover fast or cross-border tourism finds new routes.*

The fourth dusk ended with more questions than answers and a faint rescue outline. Provincial staff confirmed eligible businesses could backdate expenses to 22 January; federal officials hinted the CA$20 million envelope might expand if demand overflowed. Outside, the horns fell to a ragged murmur as freezing rain stitched tiny silver beads along every steel contour.

Laila locked Café Tigris, shoved her day's total—$38.25—into her coat, and turned east toward the canal. Overhead, the Peace Tower clock tolled seven times, each bong ricocheting between boarded-up storefronts like a municipal account receivable come due. She pictured the convoy's departure the way Twain once described history: not a flood but a seep, "slow enough to measure yet unstoppable as gravity."

Across the city, shop lights winked out one by one, yet spreadsheets and agenda PDFs glowed deep into the night. Relief money was coming, but so were audit trails, insurance claims, and the long shadow of the Emergencies Act's economic clauses. For now, Ottawa hovered in that narrow crevasse between invoice and payment, where hope is a line-item titled: *Pending.*

From 15 February to 18 February, 2022—immediately after Cabinet swung the long-unused Emergencies Act over the nation's head—the country's twin capitals, political and financial, woke up each morning with the same hushed question: how much damage had eight days of rolling blockades already done, and could the Act stanch the bleed before investors, insurers, and foreign ministers priced Canada's reliability down for good? [30] Ottawa's Peace Tower lights still winked against a crust of February frost, but inside the House, Question Period crackled. Opposition benches accused the prime minister of reaching for *an unprecedented sledgehammer*, while he replied that trade corridors and the rule of law were *on the brink*. [31] Gallery scribes noted that even veteran clerks kept glancing at the chamber clock—each tick another minute into uncharted constitutional weather.

Across the river in Gatineau, Deputy Prime Minister and Finance Minister Chrystia Freeland assembled a dawn call list. By 07:00, she had rung every big-six bank CEO, warning that new orders under the Act gave institutions both the duty and the cover to freeze assets linked to convoy logistics. [32] The bankers, Freeland later admitted, were *professionally polite and privately rattled,* a mood echoed on Bay Street where traders watched the TSX edge sideways, volume thin as prairie ice. Analysts on television spoke of *headline risk,* yet confided off-air that a downgrade of Canada's just-in-time export reputation would bite deeper than a week of lost factory shifts. [33]

South of Parliament Hill, Sparks Street resembled a stage struck bare after a stormy play. Steel barricades still pinched the pedestrian mall, but the scent of proofing dough floated through frosted glass at the Little Loaf bakery. Inside, owner Marta Dalrymple warmed her palms over an industrial oven that had been cold since late January. "Smells like rent money," she quipped to a lone supplier hefting fifty-pound flour bags. The till chimed its first sale at 08:37—a double rye loaf and two espressos to constables on foot patrol, grateful for anything hotter than canteen coffee. Outside, a *CityNews* stringer asked how long it would take to recoup three empty weeks. Marta glanced at the receipt's ribbon, shook her head and said, *Ask me after the grant forms clear.* [34]

Relief, at least on paper, was lumbering into view. On 19 February, Ottawa announced a $20-million Downtown Business Relief Fund routed through Invest Ottawa, promising up to $10,000 per storefront for rent, payroll and lost inventory.

[35] Queen's Park followed with an $11.5-million top-up the same afternoon. [36] In the ministerial press room, bureaucrats parried questions about application backlogs and audit thresholds; outside, café owners compared bullet-point checklists like students before an exam. *Government cheques arrive after the third round,* sighed Léon Charron, *but landlords still want the first.* His comment drew rueful laughter—and a camera flash that would run above the fold in the next morning's business pages. [37]

While storefronts tallied costs, diplomats tallied phone calls. From Detroit to Washington, trade envoys reminded Ottawa that 26 per cent of all road-bound exports and 33 per cent of imports roll across the Ambassador Bridge each day. [38] Transport Canada's own 17 February appearance, thick with redacted figures, projected GDP losses climbing into the hundreds of millions if even partial closures lingered through the month. [39] Those memos carried across the river to private boardrooms, where auto-parts purchasers badgered customs brokers for ETAs measured not in days but hours.

On the bridge itself, evidence of fragile normalcy came in diesel-scented drips. At 00:40 on 14 February—twenty-five hours after Windsor police cleared the last pickup from Huron Church Road—the first Canada-bound semi eased past newly welded barricades. [40] By dawn on the 15th, carriers like Southfield Logistics were staggering convoys in ten-truck pods to avoid sudden surges at the Windsor-Detroit customs plaza. Two days later, despatcher Ravi Singh stood in a trailer yard outside Tilbury, clipboard in mitten'd hands, watching a just-arrived Kenworth bleed air pressure. *That turbo gasket sat in Michigan an extra week,* he muttered, tapping a manifest bound for a St. Thomas engine line. *Every hour late is $30,000 in idle wages at the plant.* He barked into a radio: *Unload bay three—stat— no smoke breaks till the pallet's in QA.*

As convoys restarted, Parliament wrapped itself around the economic appendices of the Act. *CPAC* cameras lingered on MPs thumbing a thick order-in-council, pages that spelt out new powers to direct essential services, regulate property, and suspend insurance on blockade vehicles. [41] One line, read aloud by the Clerk, drew an audible exhale from the gallery: authority for banks to freeze corporate and personal accounts without court orders. More than tow trucks or travel bans, those twenty-eight words would dominate financial headlines for the next forty-eight hours. *Global News* tallied 206 frozen accounts worth $7.8 million by nightfall on the 17th, though officials told MPs the dragnet would spare *small-time donors*. [42]

Trade partners kept score, too. In London, The *Guardian's* early despatch weighed whether emergency powers might linger past convoy cleanup, quoting a European shipping insurer fretting about "rule-of-law optics." [43] The story filtered back to Toronto trading floors, reinforcing the caution that had left the TSX's intraday chart looking like a flatlining heart monitor. Market jitters reached Wellington Street through whispered questions: *if frozen assets spooked foreign capital, would economic recovery stall before it started?*

Yet on Sparks Street, the calculation felt simpler. Late on February 17, Treasury Board officials filed into a back room at Confederation Building for a closed-door huddle with small-business delegates. Scrawled on a flip chart, the agenda listed three verbs: *Compensate, Coordinate, Communicate*. Deputy secretary Élodie Marchand opened with a spreadsheet of program envelopes—federal, provincial, municipal—while BIA chair Kevin McHale slid a coffee across the table and answered with foot traffic numbers hovering at thirty-two per cent of pre-protest February averages. *We don't need theory,* he said, *we need bodies crossing thresholds before month-end.* A junior analyst whispered that a marketing blitz could bridge public-perception lags, but Marchand scribbled *rent deferrals?* in the margins. Before adjournment, the group agreed, at least, to share data daily and reconvene in seventy-two hours.

Outside, police cruisers idled beneath slushy streetlights. Interim Chief Steve Bell's officers had towed nearly a hundred protest vehicles and made 191 arrests by the evening of the 18th, yet the chief conceded on local radio that more charges were still "stacked in drafts." [44] Uniforms on foot patrol paused at sandwich-board signs—*WE'RE BACK* in chalky capitals—meant as much for residents as for themselves. Pedestrians began drifting through barriers, noses reddened, credit cards ready to spend a symbolic five bucks on muffins they could have baked at home.

By Friday, 18 February, the national lens zoomed out again. News anchors contrasted images of loaders scraping grime from Wellington Street with live shots of Finance officials briefing bond desks on why Canada's AAA rating remained unshaken. In Washington, U.S. trade officials expressed optimism that auto-supply homestretch delays would clear within a fortnight. Back in Ottawa, Marta

Dalrymple tallied four days of receipts—still half a typical week but enough to order more yeast—and phoned her sister to say, *Business isn't dead, just bruised.* The call crackled with relief.

Every ledger carried an asterisk. The Emergencies Act still needed parliamentary confirmation, bank freezes awaited legal challenges, and industry associations quietly drafted letters warning that one more week of uncertainty could reroute contracts for a fiscal year or more. In those early post-blockade hours, the country was neither under occupation nor healed—merely breathing between blows. On Wellington Street, a gust rattled the last metal fence panel. Somewhere inside the Hill, a whip counted votes. On Sparks Street, a barista wiped foam from a steaming cup, listened to the muffled whirr of debit machines coming back to life, and wondered whether Canada's economic pulse was rising or simply flickering in the cold. The reckoning over liberties, resilience, and the shape of post-convoy Canada lay ahead—but for the first time in weeks, commerce had space to take a tentative step and test the weight of its recovery.

ENDNOTES

[1] Levine, A. J., Funakoshi, M., & Canipe, C. (2022, February 11). *Inside the anti-vaccine mandate protests disrupting trade.* Reuters Graphics. https://www.reuters.com/graphics/HEALTH-CORONAVIRUS/CANADA-TRUCKING/egvbklwompq

[2] Jeble, S., Dubey, R., Childe, S. J., Papadopoulos, T., Roubaud, D., & Prakash, A. (2020). Achieving a just-in-time supply chain: The role of supply chain intelligence. *International Journal of Production Economics, 227,* 107690. https://doi.org/10.1016/j.ijpe.2020.107690

[3] Transport Canada. (2022, February 17). *Economic impact of the blockades* [Briefing binder, Section 16]. Government of Canada. https://tc.canada.ca/en/binder/16-economic-impact-blockades

[4] Transport Canada. (2022). *Situation on the Ambassador Bridge* [Briefing binder, Section 14]. Government of Canada. https://tc.canada.ca/en/binder/14-situation-ambassador-bridge

[5] Jackson, H. (2022, February 9). Ford Canada shuts Windsor auto plant as Ambassador Bridge blockade continues. *Global News.* https://globalnews.ca/news/8608461/auto-plant-delays-ambassador-bridge-blockade

[6] Gillies, R., & Krisher, T. (2022, February 9). Truck blockade in Canada shuts down Ford plant. *Associated Press* via *CityNews Toronto.* https://toronto.citynews.ca/2022/02/09/trucker-blockade-convoy-ontario

[7] The Canadian Press. (2022, February 11). Ambassador Bridge closure starting to impact the auto-parts makers' operations. *Plant.ca*. https://www.plant.ca/operations/ambassador-bridge-closure-starting-to-impact-the-auto-parts-makers-operations-235050

[8] Automotive News Staff. (2022, February 11). U.S.–Canada bridge blockade: Live updates. *Automotive News*. https://www.autonews.com/manufacturing/live-updates-blockade-ambassador-bridge-connecting-us-and-canada

[9] Knutson, J. (2022, February 8). Vaccine mandate protests shut down key U.S.–Canada bridge. *Axios*. https://www.axios.com/2022/02/08/vaccine-mandate-protest-shutdown-us-canada-bridge

[10] Business Roundtable, National Association of Manufacturers, & U.S. Chamber of Commerce. (2022, February 10). *Business leaders urge resolution of U.S.–Canada border blockade* [Statement]. https://www.businessroundtable.org/business-leaders-urge-resolution-of-us-canada-border-blockade

[11] Canadian business associations. (2022, February 8). Joint call for immediate action to open Ambassador Bridge. *Guelph Chamber of Commerce*. https://www.guelphchamber.com/news-advocacy/advocacy-work/business-associations-call-for-immediate-action-to-open-ambassador-bridge

[12] O'Shea, S. (2022, February 10). Ambassador Bridge blockades giving "ammunition" to "Buy America" advocates. *Global News*. https://globalnews.ca/news/8610531/ambassador-bridge-blockades-buy-america

[13] University of Guelph. (2022, February 14). *What the Ambassador Bridge and other blockades mean for Canada–U.S. trade*. U of G News. https://news.uoguelph.ca/2022/02/what-the-ambassador-bridge-and-and-other-blockades-mean-for-canada-u-s-trade

[14] Ma, G. (2022, February 10). Ambassador Bridge blockade disrupts production at Cambridge, Woodstock Toyota plants. *CityNews Kitchener*. https://kitchener.citynews.ca/2022/02/10/ambassador-bridge-blockade-disrupts-production-at-cambridge-woodstock-toyota-plants-5048197

[15] Duplicate of #12

[16] Duplicate of #10

[17] Al-Hakim, A. (2022, February 11). Ontario calls state of emergency amid convoy protests: Here's what that means. *Global News*. https://globalnews.ca/news/8612894/ontario-state-of-emergency-convoy-protests

[18] Blatchford, A. (2022, February 11). Trucker convoy forces Canada's largest province into state of emergency. *Politico*. https://www.politico.com/news/2022/02/11/trucker-convoy-forces-canadas-largest-province-into-state-of-emergency-00008213

[19] Black, A. (2022, February 12). Businesses are being devastated by ongoing convoy protest: Bank Street BIA. *CityNews Ottawa*. https://ottawa.citynews.ca/2022/02/12/businesses-are-being-devastated-by-ongoing-convoy-protest-bank-street-bia-5058317

[20] Federal Economic Development Agency for Southern Ontario. (2022, February 19). *Government of Canada invests up to $20 million to support downtown Ottawa businesses impacted by*

demonstrations [News release]. https://www.canada.ca/en/economic-development-southern-ontario/news/2022/02/government-of-canada-invests-up-to-20-million-to-support-downtown-ottawa-businesses-impacted-by-demonstrations.html

21 City of Ottawa. (2022, February 16). *Special Ottawa City Council Agenda 71*. https://pub-ottawa.escribemeetings.com/Meeting.aspx?Id=429246b7-457d-4fd6-99b7-8b898d8778a5

22 Ottawa Board of Trade. (2022, February 11). *Open Letter to Government + Ontario Declares State of Emergency* [Newsletter]. https://www.ottawabot.ca/obot-newsletters

23 Gaviola, A. (2022, February 8). Experts warn that the economic impacts of trucker convoy protests could be felt for months. *Global News.* https://globalnews.ca/news/8602966/freedom-convoy-economic-impact

24 Ottawa Coalition of Residents and Businesses. (2023). *Closing submissions to the Public Order Emergency Commission.* https://publicorderemergencycommission.ca/files/documents/Closing-Submissions/Ottawa-Coalition-Closing-Submissions.pdf

25 CityNews Ottawa. (2022, February 14). "If this fails, I'll wear it": Mayor Jim Watson on deal with Ottawa convoy organizers. https://ottawa.citynews.ca/2022/02/14/listen-if-this-fails-ill-wear-it-mayor-jim-watson-on-deal-with-ottawa-convoy-organizers-5060823

26 Government of Ontario. (2023). *Report on Ontario's declared provincial emergency from February 11 to 23, 2022.* https://www.ontario.ca/page/report-ontarios-declared-provincial-emergency-february-11-2022-february-23-2022

27 Federal Economic Development Agency for Southern Ontario. (2022, March 11). *Downtown Ottawa businesses impacted by demonstrations can apply for Government of Canada support as of March 15* [News release]. https://www.canada.ca/en/economic-development-southern-ontario/news/2022/03/downtown-ottawa-businesses-impacted-by-demonstrations-can-apply-for-government-of-canada-support-as-of-march-15.html

28 Dubé, D.-E. (2022, February 23). Truck convoy occupation to cost City around $30 million, city manager says. *CityNews Ottawa.* https://ottawa.citynews.ca/2022/02/23/truck-convoy-occupation-to-cost-city-around-30m-city-manager-says-5093438

29 Perreault, E. (2022, April 13). Supports for downtown Ottawa businesses follow convoy nightmare. *Capital Current.* https://capitalcurrent.ca/supports-for-downtown-ottawa-businesses-follow-convoy-nightmare

30 Government of Canada. (2022, February 14). *Government of Canada declaration and revocation of a public order emergency under the Emergencies Act to end disruptions, blockades and the occupation of the city of Ottawa.* https://www.canada.ca/en/services/policing/emergencies/public-order.html

31 Thomson, A. (2022, February 15). *Today: February 15, 2022* [Article]. Cable Public Affairs Channel (CPAC). https://www.cpac.ca/articles/today/2022/02/20220215

32 Department of Finance Canada. (2022, February 17). *Remarks by the Deputy Prime Minister and Minister of Finance addressing the Emergencies Act and support for public transit.* https://www.canada.ca/en/department-finance/news/2022/02/remarks-by-the-deputy-

prime-minister-minister-finance-addressing-the-emergencies-act-and-support-for-public-transit.html

[33] Kermeliotis, T. (2022, February 17). Canada roped in banks to quell protests—now what? *Al Jazeera*. https://www.aljazeera.com/economy/2022/2/17/canada-called-on-banks-to-help-quell-protests-now-what

[34] The Canadian Press. (2022, February 21). Ottawa police tell downtown businesses they can reopen after protesters clear out. *CityNews Ottawa*. https://ottawa.citynews.ca/2022/02/21/ottawa-police-tell-downtown-businesses-they-can-reopen-after-protesters-clear-out-5085858

[35] Global News. (2022, February 19). Feds announce $20 million support for Ottawa businesses impacted by convoy blockade. https://globalnews.ca/news/8633064/ottawa-businesses-government-support

[36] Ontario Ministry of Economic Development, Job Creation and Trade. (2022, February 19). *Ontario providing support for downtown Ottawa businesses* [News release]. https://news.ontario.ca/en/release/1001705/ontario_providing_support_for_downtown_ottawa_businesses

[37] Boutilier, A. (2022, February 22). "Very unlikely" assets of most small-time donors to Freedom Convoy would be frozen, MPs told. *Global News*. https://globalnews.ca/news/8638430/unlikely-most-freedom-convoy-donors-assets-frozen

[38] Transport Canada. (2022, February 17). *Economic impact of the blockades* [Appearance deck, Item 16]. Government of Canada. https://www.tc.canada.ca/en/binder/16-economic-impact-blockades

[39] Orders-in-Council. (2022, February 14). *Order directing that a proclamation be issued (public order emergency)*. https://orders-in-council.canada.ca/attachment.php?attach=41898&lang=en

[40] Public Safety Canada. (2022). *Parliamentary committee notes: Overview—Freedom Convoy 2022*. https://www.publicsafety.gc.ca/cnt/trnsprnc/brfng-mtrls/prlmntry-bndrs/20221013/03-en.aspx

[41] Orders-in-Council. (2022, February 14). *Order directing that a proclamation be issued (public order emergency)*. https://orders-in-council.canada.ca/attachment.php?attach=41898&lang=en

[42] Global News. (2022, February 22). "Very unlikely" assets of most small-time donors to Freedom Convoy would be frozen, MPs told. https://globalnews.ca/news/8638430/unlikely-most-freedom-convoy-donors-assets-frozen

[43] Cecco, L. (2022, February 22). Canada extends emergency powers after trucker blockades ended. *The Guardian*. https://www.theguardian.com/world/2022/feb/22/canada-extends-emergency-powers-after-trucker-blockades-ended

[44] The Canadian Press. (2022, February 21). Ottawa police tell downtown businesses they can reopen after protesters clear out. *CityNews Ottawa*. https://ottawa.citynews.ca/2022/02/21/ottawa-police-tell-downtown-businesses-they-can-reopen-after-protesters-clear-out-5085858

CHAPTER SEVEN:

TRACTORS AT DAWN

"Frozen cattle and idling engines teach you quickly that politics isn't the only thing that spoils in a prairie winter. Men fight over freedom and feed, but it's the quiet math of lost days and empty silos that decides who really wins. When the wind cuts through steel and resolve alike, even the boldest blockade finds out that time and cold make their own kind of law."
~ R.G. Cruise

From the wind-carved dawn of 29 January, 2022—when the first John Deeres and Kenworths drove into view on Alberta Highway 4 and hissed their air-brakes at the frozen shoulder above Coutts—to the sleet-flecked dusk of 2 February, prairie supply chains performed the grim ballet that occurs when civil protest collides with just-in-time (JIT) commerce. Long before national camera crews arrived, Coutts was already pulsing like a pinched artery: 2,500 head of feeder cattle a day normally rolled south for slaughter, and nearly as much American corn came north to fatten the rest of the herd. [1] A Sweetgrass customs broker named Rita Parsons double-clicked her monitor and watched her beef ledger stall at 153 loads—each one refrigerated, idling, and losing chill—as R.C.M.P. cruisers angled across the lanes. *Every hour they sit, that's another thousand in dry ice*, she muttered, flicking on a kettle that never finished boiling. A *Reuters* wire would later estimate CA$44 million in two-way trade crosses Coutts daily; on 29 January, the figure collapsed to near zero. [2]

By sunrise on the 13th, the blockade had a foreman: Fort Macleod councillor-turned-organiser Marco Van Huigenbos, ball-cap pulled low against the forty-kilometre wind, radioed a circle of farmers parked in grain-dust pickups five kilometres north of the line. *Keep the tractors fanned, not wedged*, Van Huigenbos advised, *so the ambulances get through—this is pressure, not punishment.* His walkie crackled back with laughter about *pressure cookers*, but the formation shifted. *Global News* cameras, hoisted from a service-road snowbank, caught when the convoy slewed broadside across the highway and sealed the last gap. [3]

Inside town limits, Coutts Mayor Jim Willett stared out the village office window at a wall of chrome bumpers and conceded the community had lost garbage collection and mail. *If someone needs insulin tonight,* he said to an aide, *We're bartering tractor fuel for it.* The aide kept typing; a *BBC* push notification had just declared the blockade *unlawful* under Alberta's Traffic Safety Act. [4]

Across an invisible provincial line, the same storm front skated east toward Manitoba. Truck driver Sol Dhillon—Manitoba plates, Sikh hymn humming from the dash—eased his Freightliner onto Highway 75 near Emerson after midnight, phone balanced on a suction-cup mount. The livestream audience was initially small: a dozen cousins in Winnipeg, a few prairie grain traders. Frost ringed his headlights like white-hot sequins, and he narrated the cost of delay every kilometre: *That pallet of condensers back there is for John Deere in Morden— they shut at five; I don't roll, neither do they.* The chat erupted in Khalsa flags and crying emojis. By kilometre forty, more rigs idled on the shoulder, engines knocking. Emerson Customs, he said, looked *dark as a shut church.*

Back west in Milk River, R.C.M.P. Staff-Sgt. Sean Fraser—grey stubble, coffee gone cold—flipped through nightly situation reports (*sitreps*) that told of hay-hauliers stranded without forage and southbound calves bawling into the wind. He warned the provincial operations centre that we've got 24 hours before this becomes an animal welfare file. A *Canadian Press* stringer later recorded Premier Jason Kenney's plea for "calm" and "commerce," his voice carried over the cough of a diesel generator powering protest floodlights. [5]

The economics degraded as fast as the weather. *CTV* mathematics put the daily hit to Alberta's economy at 220 million dollars once both north- and south-bound lanes froze.[6] Real Agriculture reminded anyone still reading that Coutts is Western Canada's principal meat gateway: boxed beef south, corn, and distillers' grain north.[7] By Monday noon, the Canadian Cattle Feeders Association warned that ration bins would run dry within a week, forcing premature slaughter or starvation. [8]

Yet the blockade had its own logistics desk. Behind a curtain-sider turned command post, volunteers doled out propane bottles, muffins, and a printed *code of conduct* that forbade alcohol until sundown. Van Huigenbos strode trailer to trailer like a foreman on a coffee break, quoting Churchill and fixer-upper YouTube channels equally. *We're peaceable,* he told an R.C.M.P. liaison, *but peace takes room to breathe.* The liaison glanced at the growing row of tow-trucks positioned like pawns on a chessboard and muttered, *Room's running out.*

On the night of 31 January, Rita Parsons finally reached an R.C.M.P. negotiator by cell. She rattled off invoice numbers and beef grades, then tried a joke about vegetarian brigades taking over the line. The officer, voice raw from the wind, replied, *Ma'am, I've got agents in balaclavas walking blind between chrome bumpers. If I call a tow and someone panics, we have two tonnes of steel doing fifteen clicks in a five-metre alley.* Parsons thanked him, killed the call, and typed *force majeure* across every invoice. *Reuters* later quoted R.C.M.P. sources saying officers advanced and retreated after *clashes with some drivers,* afraid the narrow lanes could turn trucks into battering rams. [9]

Dawn, 1 February: the sun rose pink over prairie snow that looked like frozen surf, and the convoy's CB radios crackled with Bible verses and grain prices. A *FarmProgress* bulletin reported over 150 loads of boxed beef stranded, refrigeration units burning through diesel that had to be shuttled in by pickup. [10] A Manitoba feedlot manager, stuck on the American side with corn gluten aboard, tweeted a photo of his thermometer: minus-32°C. *Cattle still eat,* he wrote. *Borders still don't open.*

Mid-morning, Transport Canada flashed a briefing note across Ottawa: *Illegal blockades causing cascading reroutes of livestock, perishable goods; economic losses of $3.9 billion cited at parliamentary committee.* [11] Industry lobbyists forwarded the document to prairie MPs faster than you could say "quorum."

By noon, the Sweetgrass customs lot had become an impromptu job fair. After hearing of feed shortages up north, Montana cow-calf operators offered discounted alfalfa to any Canadian willing to cross and load. Few did—insurance wouldn't cover them—and the hay bales sat like ignored invitations. *The Associated*

Press filed a despatch, noting R.C.M.P. had already written fifty traffic tickets and seized one cache of bear spray. [12]

That afternoon, a petrol-blue Kenworth attempted to nose through the protest gap, hauling what locals believed were vaccine supplies for northern reservations. Blockaders waved it back; the driver tried the shoulder, slid, and buried his steer tires in a drift. An R.C.M.P. officer in hi-viz snow pants trudged over to mediate while cell phones filmed. Moments later, Twitter flooded with the clip: *Mounties escort pharma truck—convoy stands firm.* The clip earned 40,000 views before sunset, though no one could say whether the trailer held syringes or sunflower oil.

Even as the choke-point tightened, detours sprawled outward like spider-web fractures: livestock hauliers traced two-hundred-kilometre loops west to Del Bonita or east to North Portal, burning time cards and diesel. *Reuters* estimated corn shipments to Alberta feedlots fell by 50 per cent during the first forty-eight hours, prompting cattle producers to consider ration cuts. [13]

Southeast of Emerson, Sol Dhillon pulled over onto the Incident Traffic Diversion (ITD) shoulder—a safety lane reserved for breakdowns and emergencies—cat-napped for three hours, then flicked his livestream back on. A Winnipeg-based grain trader joined the chat to say rumours pegged a full blockade for 10 February, but scout vehicles were already circling gas stations to map choke-points. *Global News* would later confirm R.C.M.P. intelligence that *a large number of vehicles and farm equipment* were assembling, though on 1 February, they remained scattered. [14]

By the evening of 1 February, Premier Kenney's cabinet huddled in Edmonton, flipping between cost projections and public-opinion polling. The Canadian Meat Council pegged daily export risk at 11 million dollars by week's end; the Alberta Cattle Feeders warned *existing shortages on products like animal feed* could tip into crisis.[15] Kenney's televised statement tried to square political empathy with law-and-order nerves: *Illegal doesn't become righteous because it rides a Peterbilt,* he said, urging protesters to withdraw *before cattle go hungry and citizens lose pay cheques.* The line trended for four hours until a protester's drone footage— highway blanketed in headlights—grabbed the algorithm instead.

2 February broke with a needle-sharp snowfall. R.C.M.P. negotiator Staff-Sgt. Fraser, voice hoarse, proposed a one-lane humanitarian corridor for feed and medicine. Blockade marshals conferred over hand-held radios, then opened just enough space for a half-dozen hay trucks and one UPS van. Watching from Sweetgrass customs, Parsons logged the moment: *Corridor opened 10:12 a.m, closed 10:59 a.m.*—forty-seven minutes of relief that translated to maybe ten barns fed and two chem-lab reagents delivered.

On Parliament Hill that same hour, Transport Canada's deputy minister reminded a scrum of reporters that *illegal blockades across the country in February caused significant impacts on the supply chain, economy, and the rights and freedoms of fellow citizens.* [16] The phrase bounced through Prairie radios like a ricochet: rights and freedoms versus hay and hormones.

Near sunset, Van Huigenbos climbed onto a flat-deck, wind howling across his microphone, and declared the blockade *now a signal flank to Ottawa.* The crowd cheered; Fraser scribbled *escalatory rhetoric* in his notebook and radioed for an extra liaison team. Meanwhile, *Global News* in Manitoba quoted R.C.M.P. as saying the Emerson crossing, though not yet sealed, was *delaying traffic for hours* with *no timeline for end.* [17]

As darkness reclaimed the prairie, Parsons finally shut her laptop, the beef loads still red-lined, and poured herself the cold kettle's water. Dhillon killed his livestream to savour ten minutes of silence in his cab. Staff-Sgt. Fraser faxed a *sitrep* warning: *If temperatures drop below minus-35°C, expect livestock mortality in stranded trailers.* The last line underlined itself in the fax ribbon.

Far overhead, satellites captured a puzzle of brake-light constellations stretching from Milk River to Emerson, each red dot a stalled component in the engine of continental trade. Provincial premiers queued for morning talk shows, each ready to wield new numbers of *daily losses* and *feed days left.* Industry associations drafted open letters framing the blockades as existential threats. Everyone had prepared everything.

From the grey dawn of 3 February, 2022—when a rime of hoarfrost glazed Highway 4 and Coutts protesters grudgingly shuffled their tractors just wide enough for a single north-bound lane—word rippled down the trucker grapevine that *one channel's open.* [15] The relief was mostly cosmetic: drivers in high-vis parkas counted the motionless rigs ahead, then phoned despatch to say nothing had changed. By noon, industry economists were clocking the blockade's damage at roughly CA$220 million in lost activity, an hourly meter that ticked louder than any air-horn. [16] Canadian Manufacturers & Exporters added their gravestone arithmetic—CA$44 million bled from the Calgary–Montana corridor each day the crossing stayed pinched. [17]

Numbers travelled faster than hay trucks. A StatsCan analyst in Ottawa scanned February's preliminary border sheets and frowned: inbound truck traffic at Coutts had fallen forty-eight per cent year over year, while Emerson sagged twenty-nine. [18] Behind those percentages sat real freight—over 150 chilled beef loads marooned in their reefers, each hum of the diesel gen-sets a reminder that prime rib turns into pet food once the temperature line drifts. [19] Feedlots north of Lethbridge eyed their dwindling grain silos; a joint statement from Alberta Beef, the Cattle Feeders' Association, and the CCA warned that U.S. corn and distillers' grain were *days, not weeks* from running out. [20] Economic Development Lethbridge sketched the impact in plainer ink: *three million dollars a day and counting*, their CEO told local radio, *and that's just inside the city limits.* [21]

Feed-yard nutritionist Carla Baines refreshed her ration spreadsheet at the Milk River command trailer. Convoy marshal Marco Van Huigenbos and fellow organiser Alex Van Herk argued the ethics of mercy lanes. Carla's notes blinked red: oats for the week at minus-two days, corn gluten at minus-one. Van Herk wanted a hard blockade—*We lose leverage if we start carving holes*—but Van Huigenbos countered, *Starved cattle make lousy postcards*. Their debate ended when an R.C.M.P. Divisional Liaison Officer radioed in the overnight *sitrep*: a three-vehicle collision near Brooks tied to a slow-moving tractor convoy, two hospitalisations, and a fractured chrome axle that now blocked a quarter of the Trans-Canada shoulder. [22]

Officers pieced the collision together through grainy dash-cam clips and roadside flares: a pickup, impatient with the convoy's fifteen-kilometre crawl, had swerved, kissed a bumper, and rammed a tractor tire clean off its hub. The farm tire landed in the median like a stranded moon. [25] The next morning, *Global News* plastered the footage over breakfast TV, tallying it beside the province's growing casualty spreadsheet. [26]

Behind the R.C.M.P.'s temporary fencing at Coutts, negotiators leafed grimly through traffic-flow diagrams. One officer stabbed a finger at the page: "If we don't widen a humanitarian corridor by tonight, hog haulers out of Medicine Hat will have to euthanise in-trailer." Van Huigenbos conceded a sliver, but the lane opened for barely an hour before somebody parked a grain truck sideways and the window snapped shut again.

Six hundred kilometres east, a Manitoba elevator despatcher in Morris rerouted south-bound canola through tiny crossings not designed for B-trains. On the cab radio, a trucker who called himself *Skipper* livestreamed the whiteout roar of Highway 75 as drifting snow and grain trucks braided into a slow-motion knot. R.C.M.P. Manitoba warned of *approximately 50–75 units, fluctuating,* sealing every lane by nightfall. [23] Industry forecasters put the daily trade pinch at Emerson near CA$70 million—the price of a blizzard turned blockade. [24]

By February 6, the prairie wind sharpened to a knife-edge thirty knots strong, sandblasting the red-and-white placards until half read *NO FE D* where snow had shredded the vowels. Feed-lot voicemails filled with tight-throated pleas: "Any barley swap? Even screenings?" Carla answered two before light and three after dark, always the same: "stretch the straw, cut the pellets, pray for corn." The emergency ration curves on her laptop flattened into grim asymptotes.

While watching the same curves, Premier Kenney, and Premier Stefanson pivoted to public pressure. Kenney told Calgary talk radio the province was *one feed cycle away from animal-welfare hell,* and Stefanson urged Ottawa to *secure critical corridors before chisels replace steering wheels.* StatsCan's plunging bar charts bore out their warnings: south-bound fertiliser shipments had dropped 20 per cent, beef exports 17 per cent, and pulse-crop imports a staggering 43 per cent.

Ottawa's cabinet room felt the chill. A deputy minister slid a single-page memo across the table: *Legal options pending—Emergencies Act last resort.* No one spoke, but the slipstream of diesel politics rattled the windowpanes. Outside, the February sun sagged into a violet horizon. R.C.M.P. tweets tried to keep pace with the blockade's morphing geography: one minute counting vehicles, the next choppering an expectant mother over the jam.

Back at Emerson, Skipper filmed the night-shift ritual: turning off every cab light in unison until the highway vanished into black, then clicking each on again so the convoy glowed like a runway for geese. In Coutts, Van Huigenbos read feed-lot bulletins over CB, his voice a cracked hymnal: *Ten ranches rationing hay, seven shower stalls frozen, one dairy dumping milk.* Laughter followed, but thin—for every joke about *government soy smoothies*, someone else quietly texted home for grocery money.

Axios flashed a push alert to U.S. phones: *Three ports now hamstrung, auto plants idle.* [28] *The Grand Forks Herald* quoted a duty-free operator who hadn't sold a fridge magnet all week: *It feels like standing in a boarded-up store watching your checkout beep.* [27]

On 10 February, the sky finally broke, spitting ice pellets that cracked windshield seals. Emerson's crescent of rigs dug in harder, ploughs spinning snow into barricades. Manitoba R.C.M.P. liaison teams negotiated a narrow, twisting passage for propane and dialysis shipments, only to watch it close under the weight of a jack-knifed grain trailer. In Coutts, Carla Baines deleted two more ration columns and sent a mass text: *Begin stretch protocol: 30% straw inclusion.* Seconds later, a reply from a southern Alberta feedlot buzzed: *Straw under three feet of snow.*

As night swallowed the prairie, satellites painted crimson arcs of brake lights across both provinces—lifelines turned into tourniquets. In cabinet war rooms and provincial caucus lounges, advisors sharpened contingency drafts: emergency feed convoys under police escort, ad hoc livestock markets, the unspoken spectre of federal powers hovering like the northern lights no one could see through the blizzard. By dawn, the issue would no longer be the tolerability of the blockades, but the survival of the economy and the cattle. Part 3 would carry that reckoning into the complex mathematics of emergency declarations and the slow unwinding of frozen chains.

From the storm-front morning of 11 February, 2022, Labrador-grey clouds scudded low over Parliament Hill while a hush fell inside the fifth-floor cabinet boardroom; aides slid numbered folders labelled *EM-PO*—Emergency Powers Options—across a walnut table still sticky with midnight coffee. Deputy Prime Minister Chrystia Freeland traced a jittery red pen along the margin of a Bank of Canada volatility chart and muttered, *One more trading day like yesterday and the loonie's ice-fishing without a hole.* In the corner, a Justice Canada lawyer thumbed through the Emergencies Act Q-and-A: *last resort, ten-day sunset, Parliament must confirm within seven.* [30]

The numbers guiding their hands were brutal. *Reuters* tallied half-billion-dollar trade clots at border crossings and warned that *every eighth beef carcass Canada exports is now idling in a reefer, clock ticking to spoilage.* [31] On Highway 4, R.C.M.P. tactical teams whispered over encrypted radios, waiting for the legal lever to drop. 04:00 on 14 February—the coldest Valentine in Coutts since records began—a sudden diesel roar drowned the prairie stillness as officers boxed in a white cargo trailer. Breath steaming, they yanked open the doors: five long guns, a stack of body armour plates, and a scattering of high-capacity magazines clattered onto frost-slick asphalt while one constable muttered, "That's no protest kit." [32]

Hours later, news of the weapons seizure swept into Ottawa just as Prime Minister Justin Trudeau strode to a lectern and invoked the Emergencies Act for the first time in Canadian history. The declaration ricocheted through the Prairie blockades like a starter pistol. In Coutts, convoy organisers Marco Van Huigenbos, Alex Van Herk, and George Janzen huddled behind a grain truck's tailgate. Van Huigenbos read the headline on his phone twice, lips moving: *Cabinet triggers emergency powers.* Van Herk exhaled. *Game's changed—we're holding a busted straight.* Within twelve hours, they announced a stand-down. Horns moaned farewell as tractors eased off Highway 4, and by dawn on 15 February, R.C.M.P. Deputy Commissioner Curtis Zablocki confirmed the crossing was "fully open, traffic moving smoothly." [33]

Six hundred kilometres east, the blockade at Emerson dug its heels in. Manitoba's Divisional Liaison teams spent Valentine's night trading coffee and ultimatums with protest leaders while Sgt. Rob Hill scribbled a single-line prediction into his notebook: *One phone call and $300 million in trade moves again.* His press statement the following afternoon was cautiously triumphant: *We are now confident that demonstrators will leave, full access expected by February 16.* [45] True to the promise, R.C.M.P. escorts herded the last grain trucks north at dawn on the 16th; *Update #5* on the force's website stamped the case *cleared.* [34] Local radio *KFGO* crackled across the Red River plain, quoting Hill's deputy: *Negotiated, peaceful departure—no arrests.* [35] In the duty-free parking lot, a circle of farmers bowed heads around a Styrofoam cooler doubling as an altar. One prayed, *Lord, thaw the feed corn faster than the politics.*

Statistics Canada's dashboard finally twitched the right way: inbound truck traffic at Coutts had cratered forty-eight per cent in early February but clawed back in the final fortnight as lanes unclogged; Emerson's thirty-per-cent hole likewise narrowed by the month-end. [36] Yet the ledger of damage kept growing. A joint agriculture-food statement warned of *feed-supply brinkmanship,* noting that three prairie mills had dipped into emergency barley reserves. *Reuters* reported on the human impact: They rerouted cattle packed into trailers twice across Montana's back roads to avoid delays, while drivers calculated rumen gas build-up against border wait times. [38] One haulier, Doug MacInnis, became the first rig to cross southbound at Coutts post-reopening; he slapped the dash of his Kenworth and told an R.C.M.P. officer, *Eighteen days, eighteen grand lost—let's call it even when hell freezes hotter than this.* The cop just handed him a maple-leaf flag sticker for luck.

On Parliament Hill, the emergency decree detonated partisan theatre. MPs argued past midnight over frozen bank accounts and constitutional overreach, while Senate clerks sharpened quills in case the upper chamber rejected the order. But Trudeau revoked the Act on 23 February, with Ottawa streets ploughed free of big rigs and national polls tilting toward cautious relief. *Politico* framed it as a *historic climb-down,* [39] *Axios* noted the prime minister's refrain that *the situation is no longer an emergency,* [40] *Reuters* captured Bay Street's exhale as the TSX inched upward and bond spreads relaxed. [41] Freeland, glassy-eyed from seventy-two straight hours of briefings, told reporters, *Markets crave predictability— we just iced eleven days of chaos.*

Yet the reckoning had barely begun. In Milk River, Crown prosecutors drafted mischief indictments; a March docket date carried Van Huigenbos, Van Herk, and Janzen. A year later, a jury would convict them, but as early as March 2022, their bail terms barred megaphones within fifty metres of a provincial highway. [44] On March 28, Fort Macleod council convened in its century-old sandstone hall to decide whether a sitting councillor could moonlight as a blockade marshal; the mayor's letter of reprimand cited *grave concerns* about civic duty and international trade, and the vote to censure Van Huigenbos passed five-to-one. [43]

Corporate Canada tallied its bruises. A Calgary packing plant logged six-figure spoilage as boxed-beef temperatures drifted; the claim form's summary line read, *Product condemned by USDA inspection—thermal excursion*. Insurance adjusters flagged the episode for actuarial textbooks. Shipping executives stapled fresh risk memos in Vancouver boardrooms atop the ones they had written for B.C.'s mudslide disaster two months earlier. *Convoy clause,* one broker joked darkly, *is the new 'force majeure'*.

Meanwhile, Justice Paul Rouleau's Public Order Emergency Commission began gathering 85,000 pages of emails, cabinet minutes, and WhatsApp chats, promising a report within nine months. When the five-volume tome landed on MPs' desks on 17 February the following year, it concluded—*with reluctance*—that Ottawa had met the legal threshold to pull the trigger. [42] In March 2022, no one had yet opened that verdict.

By 15 March, Statistics Canada's economists laid the first post-mortem graphs before journalists: a ragged V-shaped rebound in freight counts, a scar of red ink across February's merchandise export line, and a footnote estimating CA$1.6 billion in lost output tied directly to blockades. The Daily's closing paragraph pulled no punches: *Supply-chain confidence deteriorated measurably; reputational effects remain to be seen*. Ministers used the stats as rhetorical ballast while Prairie premiers demanded a federal resiliency blueprint covering livestock corridors, alternate ports, and emergency feed stockpiles.

That same day, a weary R.C.M.P. negotiator—now rotated to an unrelated file in northern B.C.—was sipping hotel coffee, rereading his *sitrep* from 13 February. In the margin, he had scrawled, *One phone call and $300 million moves again*. He closed the notebook and murmured: *Turns out it was two phone calls—and an Act we swore we'd never use*. The line between protest and paralysis would stay inked in federal law books, ready for the next convoy of history to test.

ENDNOTES

[1] BBC News. (2022, February 1). *Freedom Convoy: Blockade at Alberta border crossing 'unlawful'*.
    https://www.bbc.co.uk/news/world-us-canada-60218354

[2] Ljunggren, D. (2022, February 2). *Anti-vaccine mandate protesters say they will block Ottawa for as long as necessary. Reuters*. https://www.reuters.com/world/americas/anti-vaccine-protesters-say-they-will-block-ottawa-long-necessary-2022-02-02

[3] Williams, R. (2022, January 30). *Protesters continue blockade at Coutts border crossing. Global News.* https://globalnews.ca/news/8581612/coutts-protestors-blockade-border-crossing

[4] The Canadian Press. (2022, February 1). *'I call for calm': Alberta premier condemns violence at U.S. border standoff. New West Record.* https://www.newwestrecord.ca/national-news/i-call-for-calm-alberta-premier-condemns-violence-at-us-border-standoff-5018352

[5] Associated Press. (2022, January 31). *Border blockade remains in place at Coutts, Alberta.* https://apnews.com/article/coronavirus-pandemic-business-health-canada-blockades-65453655bfffcd349388c283d14f972a

[6] Thomas, S. (2022, February 3). *Coutts, Alta., border blockade estimated loss of $220 million economic activity: Industry experts. CTV News.* https://www.ctvnews.ca/calgary/article/coutts-alta-border-blockade-estimated-loss-of-220m-economic-activity-industry-experts

[7] Haney, S. (2022, February 2). *Why the Coutts border crossing is so critical for Western Canada's meat-packing and cattle sector. Real Agriculture.* https://www.realagriculture.com/2022/02/why-the-coutts-border-crossing-is-so-critical-for-western-canadas-meatpacking-and-cattle-sector

[8] Alberta Cattle Feeders' Association. (2022, February 3). *Statement on Canada-U.S. border disruption.* https://cattlefeeders.ca/statement-on-canada-u-s-border-disruption

[9] Skerritt, J. (2022, February 1). *Trucker protest strands beef shipments at U.S.–Canada border. Farm Progress.* https://www.farmprogress.com/farm-operations/trucker-protest-strands-beef-shipments-at-u-s-canada-border

[10] Global News. (2022, February 11). *Emerson border blockade continues, Manitoba RCMP say no arrests so far* [Video]. https://globalnews.ca/video/8619880/emerson-border-blockade-continues-manitoba-rcmp-say-no-arrests-so-far

[11] Global News. (2022, February 10). *No timeline for end of Emerson border blockade, RCMP say.* https://globalnews.ca/news/8609389/emerson-border-blocked-drivers-say-convoy-is-delaying-traffic-for-hours

[12] Transport Canada. (2022, May 4). *Trucker protests: Hot issues binder note.* Government of Canada. https://tc.canada.ca/en/binder/15-trucker-protests

[13] Gordon, J., & Nickel, R. (2022, February 8). *Pandemic border protests strand cattle and car parts, snarling Canada-U.S. trade. Reuters.* https://www.reuters.com/world/americas/pandemic-border-protests-strand-cattle-car-parts-snarling-canada-us-trade-2022-02-08

[14] Canadian International Freight Forwarders Association. (2022, February). *Month in review – February 2022.* https://www.ciffa.com/ffo/month-in-review-february-2022

[15] The Canadian Press. (2022, February 3). *New blockade in Coutts cutting off traffic to U.S. border crossing. Lethbridge News Now.* https://lethbridgenewsnow.com/2022/02/03/new-blockade-in-alberta-cutting-off-traffic-to-u-s-border-crossing

[16] Duplicate of #6

[17] Canadian Manufacturers & Exporters. (2022, February 3). *Canadian Manufacturers & Exporters calls for reopening of Coutts border crossing* [Press release]. https://cme-mec.ca/blog/canadian-manufacturers-exporters-calls-for-reopening-of-coutts-border-crossing

[18] Statistics Canada. (2022, April 6). *Blockades put a dent in cross-border truck traffic.* https://www.statcan.gc.ca/o1/en/plus/722-blockades-put-dent-cross-border-truck-traffic

[19] Duplicate of #9

[20] Gibson, C. (2022, February 3). *Beef industry voices 'serious concerns' about Coutts border blockade. Global News.* https://globalnews.ca/news/8592014/canadian-alberta-beef-industry-concern-coutts-border-blockade

[21] Modney, D. (2022, February 3). *Cost of Coutts blockade adds up; Beef industry calls for resolution. Lethbridge News Now.* https://lethbridgenewsnow.com/2022/02/03/cost-of-coutts-blockade-adds-up-beef-industry-calls-for-resolution

[22] The Canadian Press. (2022, February 3). *RCMP say some progress made in managing Coutts border blockade. Lethbridge News Now.* https://lethbridgenewsnow.com/2022/02/03/rcmp-say-some-progress-made-in-managing-coutts-border-blockade

[23] Royal Canadian Mounted Police. (2022, February 11). *Blockade continuing to block border in Emerson* [News release]. https://www.rcmp-grc.gc.ca/en/news/2022/blockade-continuing-block-border-emerson

[24] Pindera, E. (2022, February 16). *Emerson border open for business; convoy rolls away. Winnipeg Free Press.* https://www.winnipegfreepress.com/breakingnews/2022/02/16/rcmp-protest-organizers-ending-emerson-blockade-peacefully

[25] Brooks RCMP. (2022, February 5). *Convoy participants involved in highway collision in southern Alberta* [News release]. *Todayville.* https://www.todayville.com/calgary/convoy-participants-involved-in-highway-collision-in-southern-alberta

[26] Bartko, K. (2022, February 6). *Convoy tractor, pickup trucks collide on Highway 1 near Brooks. Global News.* https://globalnews.ca/news/8598931/alberta-highway-1-convoy-tractor-collision

[27] Harbo, I. (2022, February 10). *Trucker protest blocks Pembina–Emerson border on Canadian side. Grand Forks Herald.* https://www.grandforksherald.com/news/anti-vaccine-protest-blocks-pembina-emerson-border-on-canadian-side

[28] Knutson, J. (2022, February 10). *Vaccine mandate protesters block main border crossing in Manitoba. Axios.* https://www.axios.com/2022/02/10/vaccine-mandate-protesters-canada-manitoba

[29] Royal Canadian Mounted Police. (2022, February 16). *Update #5 – Blockade at Emerson border crossing now cleared* [News release]. https://www.rcmp.gc.ca/en/news/2022/update-5-blockade-emerson-border-crossing-now-cleared

[30] Department of Justice Canada. (2022, February 14). *Qs & As – The Emergencies Act.* https://www.justice.gc.ca/eng/trans/bm-mb/other-autre/emergencies-urgence/qa.html

[31] Reuters Staff. (2022, February 14). *Reactions to Trudeau's move to invoke Emergencies Act to end protests.* *Reuters.* https://www.reuters.com/world/americas/reactions-trudeaus-planned-move-invoke-emergencies-act-end-protests-2022-02-14

[32] Gibson, C. (2022, February 14). *RCMP arrest 13 people, seize weapons near Coutts border blockade.* *Global News.* https://globalnews.ca/news/8618494/alberta-coutts-border-protest-weapons-ammunition-seized

[33] Graveland, B. (2022, February 15). *Border operations resume after Coutts blockade dismantled in southern Alberta.* *Global News.* https://globalnews.ca/news/8621249/alberta-coutts-border-blockade-dismantled

[34] Duplicate of #29

[35] The Canadian Press. (2022, February 15). *Border crossing blockade nearly over, RCMP say.* *The Mighty 790 KFGO.* https://kfgo.com/2022/02/15/border-crossing-blockade-nearly-over

[36] *(Duplicate of #18 – retained for numbering.)*

[37] Canadian Cattle Association, Alberta Beef Producers, & National Cattle Feeders' Association. (2022, February 11). *Joint statement on Canada-U.S. border disruptions* [PDF]. https://www.cattle.ca/wp-content/uploads/2022/03/Joint-Statement-on-Canada-U.S.-border_final-rev.pdf

[38] Gordon, J., & Nickel, R. (2022, February 8). *Pandemic border protests strand cattle and car parts.* *Reuters.* https://www.reuters.com/world/americas/pandemic-border-protests-strand-cattle-car-parts-snarling-canada-us-trade-2022-02-08

[39] Lum, Z.-A. (2022, February 23). *Trudeau revokes controversial emergency powers.* *Politico.* https://www.politico.com/news/2022/02/23/trudeau-revokes-emergency-powers-convoy-00011158

[40] Axios Staff. (2022, February 23). *Trudeau ends emergency powers invoked to quell trucker protest.* *Axios.* https://www.axios.com/2022/02/23/trudeau-emergency-powers-trucker-revoke

[41] Nicholls, P. (2022, February 23). *Canada ends emergency powers invoked to tackle protests.* *Reuters.* https://www.reuters.com/world/americas/canada-ends-emergency-powers-invoked-tackle-truckers-protests-pm-trudeau-2022-02-23

[42] Public Order Emergency Commission. (2023, February 17). *Final report of the public inquiry into the 2022 Public Order Emergency.* https://publicorderemergencycommission.ca/final-report

[43] Ferris, D. (2022, April 11). *Fort Macleod reprimands councillor for blockade role.* *Global News.* https://globalnews.ca/news/8753107/fort-macleod-councillor-van-huigenbos-reprimand-letter

[44] Graveland, B. (2025, January 9). *Crown seeks prison time for pair accused of mischief at Coutts border protest.* *Global News.* https://globalnews.ca/news/10950066/sentencing-hearing-coutts-blockade-mischief

[45] Royal Canadian Mounted Police. (2022, February 15). *Statement – Chief Superintendent Rob Hill on Emerson blockade resolution.* https://www.rcmp-grc.gc.ca/en/news/2022/statement-chief-superintendent-rob-hill-officer-charge-criminal-operations-the-manitoba-0

CHAPTER EIGHT:

POLITICIANS ON THE FRONT LINES

"You can hear a nation's fear in the space between a stalled engine and the next decision. Governments talk of order, but even the strongest find their hands trembling when faced with their own people. Ultimately, it isn't the noise that breaks the peace—it's the moment leaders forget the difference between authority and trust."
~ R.G. Cruise

In the cold predawn of 14 February 2022, a bruised and anxious Canada faced a reckoning few had imagined possible just months before. The pandemic's third winter had deepened the nation's fractures, and on that morning, Ottawa was a city besieged not just by trucks and banners but by the dread that its governing order could falter at any moment. Blockades had metastasised from the elegant approaches of Parliament Hill to border outposts at Windsor, Emerson, and Coutts, where trucks idled in defiance and the arteries of trade throbbed with tension. The bitter standoff at the Ambassador Bridge—vital for CA$500 million in daily cross-border goods—had choked automotive supply chains and rattled economic forecasts. The Emerson and Coutts crossings threatened agricultural lifelines and the fabric of prairie towns, their daily routines sundered by the whiff of diesel and the noise of protest. For the first time in a generation, the air in Ottawa hung heavy with a whiff of real peril: not just from the pandemic's invisible threat, but from the visible, unyielding standoff between state and citizen, and the spectre of what the use of extraordinary power might mean for Canada's brittle democracy. [1]

By 14 February, public discourse had twisted into knots. Calls for government action clashed with anxious warnings about civil liberties, the rule of law, and the dangers of overreach. The whirring engines of the Freedom Convoy had become an omnipresent soundscape—a rolling parliament of grievance, amplified by social media, goaded by transnational discontent, and transmuted in real time into a global symbol for something far larger than vaccine mandates. National broadcasters cut live to scenes of families waving flags and police massing behind cordons, as pundits debated the implications: Was this a populist uprising, a fringe insurrection, or merely the loudest echo of a deeper malaise? [2]

Business lobbies hemmed in political leaders on all sides, counting lost billions, premiers fearing unrest in their backyards, and a public whose patience had run dry. Some cabinet ministers privately feared that every delay eroded the state's credibility; others muttered about *the January 6 effect,* that slippery anxiety that Canada might soon see its crisis spiral out of control. Polling in the days leading up to 14 February showed a sharp divide—just over half of Canadians supported more decisive action to clear the protests, but nearly as many harboured deep reservations about granting the government sweeping new powers. Among these voices, a quiet but growing chorus of legal scholars and former judges cautioned that the Emergencies Act—legislation conceived in the late 1980s to replace the War Measures Act—remained unused, and that its thresholds were severe for good reason. [4]

Inside the government's wood-panelled war room, the hours before dawn blurred in anxious consultation. Justice Minister David Lametti and Public Safety Minister Marco Mendicino pored over thick briefing binders, their pages bristling with yellow tags and hastily scrawled marginalia. Janice Charette, Clerk of the Privy Council, explained the government could only invoke the Emergencies Act if existing laws and provincial authorities proved wholly inadequate to handle the crisis, thus outlining the statutory test. From Western Command, the R.C.M.P. Commissioner warned of increasing threats to officers in Coutts following the discovery of a weapons cache. [5]

At 07:30, as the first light bled into the capital, Prime Minister Justin Trudeau convened his cabinet by secure video link. The political calculation was stark: invoke the Emergencies Act—risking constitutional blowback, court challenges, and accusations of executive overreach—or do nothing and risk the collapse of order, both in Ottawa and across the borderlands. Around the virtual table, the arguments ricocheted: Bill Blair, the former Toronto police chief, spoke grimly of operational paralysis; Chrystia Freeland, always attuned to financial tremors, read aloud the latest despatch from Bay Street warning that the blockades threatened to *erode investor confidence in Canadian stability.* [6]

Meanwhile, inside the Department of Justice, a confidential legal memo circulated among senior advisors. The language was stark, warning that any resort to emergency powers *without exhausting all other legislative tools may cause irreparable harm to the norms of democratic governance.* The document cited the Charter's guarantee of freedom of assembly and expression, cautioning that the threshold for emergency powers *must be demonstrably justified and as limited in scope as the crisis demands.* [7]

Outside, the city's rhythms had already shifted. Civil servants, hunched over coffee in Wellington Street cafés, scanned their phones for news of a possible federal intervention. On social media, convoy organisers streamed updates, vowing to stay the course even as rumours swirled of impending mass arrests and asset freezes. Ottawa's mayor, Jim Watson, who had already declared a municipal state of emergency, held an emergency meeting with police brass and pleaded with federal authorities to *show leadership and end this occupation.* [8]

By 12:00, news leaked. *CBC* and *CTV's* Parliamentary bureaus reported that the Prime Minister's Office was *actively considering* invoking the Emergencies Act, sending a jolt through the precinct. Veteran MPs traded wary glances in the Commons corridors, staffers clutching sheaves of talking points and draft releases, the air thick with the sense of history about to be made. Even before the official announcement, the Speaker's office fielded calls from journalists seeking confirmation, and the opposition benches crackled with whispers that the government's hand was about to land on the levers of unprecedented power. [9]

At 16:30, Justin Trudeau stepped before a bank of microphones, flanked by Deputy Prime Minister Freeland and key ministers. He spoke in measured but unmistakable terms: "After careful consideration, and on the advice of law enforcement, the federal government invoked the Emergencies Act to supplement provincial and territorial capacity to address the blockades and occupations." The moment was anticlimactic and electric—a line crossed that could not be uncrossed. [10]

The reaction inside the House of Commons was as tense and choreographed as a stage play. Government MPs gathered in clumps in the hush before the bell, some grim-faced, others pale but determined. On the Liberal front bench, a whip murmured to the nervous, *Every yes vote will be remembered. This is one for the history books.* In the anterooms, nervous staffers clutched briefing notes inked with the talking point: *Temporary, targeted, time-limited—strictly to restore order.* The media would echo the phrase for days, but no one in the chamber believed the fallout would be so easily contained. [11]

Across the aisle, Conservative leader Candice Bergen rose, her posture steely as she accused the government of "criminalising dissent" and failing to exhaust less invasive options. "This is not leadership; it is panic, and it sets a dangerous precedent for the rights of Canadians," she declared, earning a volley of applause from her caucus. But even among Conservatives, unease ran deep—some quietly wondered if their party's full-throated embrace of the protest risked alienating moderates or undermining the rule of law. [12]

The NDP, as always, occupied a crucial hinge. Jagmeet Singh, leader of a party that had campaigned on civil liberties and support for marginalised groups, rose with a measured anger. His speech, later quoted in headlines across the country, warned that "while these powers may be needed to end the blockades, every single use must be scrutinised, debated, and subject to the most rigorous oversight this Parliament can provide." Singh's words landed with a gravity that belied the NDP's modest seat count—his party's support, or abstention, would prove decisive. [13]

In the press gallery above, reporters scribbled furiously as the Justice Minister defended the Act's use, invoking Section 3 of the Emergencies Act and reciting a litany of failed municipal and provincial responses. *No one in government takes this step lightly,* Lametti insisted. He referenced a litany of police chief requests, failed injunctions, and *significant risks to national security and economic stability* as the legal predicate. [14]

Outside the chamber, political operatives from every party huddled in glass-walled offices and stairwells, working the phones to their base. In one overheard conversation, a Liberal strategist cautioned: *This will define us for a decade, one way or another.* A Conservative aide, pacing in stocking feet, snapped at her phone: *We can't let them brand us as pro-chaos.* The air crackled with both bravado and the weary realisation that none of the old scripts fit. [15]

As the vote approached, the House fell into an unnatural silence. MPs filed in, some glancing nervously at their phones, others fixing their eyes on the floor as if searching for conviction in the worn red carpet. Following the toll of the bell; The Speaker read the names one by one and recorded the votes. The tally was close—185 in favour, 151 against—a narrow but consequential mandate for a government that had gambled its legitimacy on restoring order. [16]

In that charged pause, as someone handed up the last division slip and the Commons clock ticked audibly in the gallery, ramifications rippled outward. Within minutes, opposition leaders vowed legal challenges; civil liberties groups drafted statements warning of *slippery slopes* and the need for judicial scrutiny. Senior Conservatives hinted at a non-confidence motion. Across the country, phones lit up with alerts: *Canada Invokes Emergency Powers—Historic, Controversial.* Social media feeds showed relief and rage, as each side believed history was saved or undermined. [17]

But amid the scuffed marble and fluorescent-lit corridors within the Parliament Buildings, a heavier silence reigned. The nation's uncertainty about its constitutional boundaries fuelled doubts that bitter court battles, protests, news reports, and national debate would follow. Like the Commons itself, the country braced for the storm to come. [18]

If there was one thing that defined the winter of 2022 for Canada's federal Conservatives, it was not only the rumble of diesel engines echoing across Parliament Hill but the mounting pressure to choose sides before history chose for them. The morning of 28 January found the heart of Ottawa already in convulsion—a grid of cabs, pickups, and tractor-trailers knitting themselves into the city's bones, and banners waving calls for *freedom* as if the word alone could sweep away the pandemic's gnawing fatigue. As the first convoy horns blared beneath the Peace Tower, Pierre Poilievre, a veteran MP known for his razor-edged rhetorical instincts, saw an opportunity and a threat. In a city trained to prize order above all, he embraced the disorder with a flourish, stepping into the frigid crowd and offering not caution, but a kind of solidarity. Before cameras and truckers were in toques, he declared, "Truckers are fighting for our freedoms," drawing cheers, rattling the iron fences and sending a jolt through Conservative ranks. [19]

Poilievre's gamble was more than performance—it was a strategic wager on the party's future, which would soon expose deep fissures inside the Conservative caucus. Since the earliest days of the pandemic, the Official Opposition had struggled to navigate the perilous terrain between a restless base in rural and suburban Canada and a broader public wary of any hint of extremism. Internal polling presented to senior aides in late January showed the Tories' traditional base—farmers, oil patch workers, small-town entrepreneurs—surging in support for the convoy, even as urban moderates recoiled at images of Confederate flags and QAnon placards. [20]

In closed-door sessions, these tensions boiled over. Erin O'Toole, who just months earlier had staked his leadership on a moderate, pragmatic approach to COVID and vaccines, watched uneasily as his support drained away—first in the party's digital back-channels, then in the open insurrection of MPs who saw in the convoy a populist energy he could never command. The calls for *leadership change* arrived not as a whisper but as a barrage. O'Toole confided to a friend in early February that he was *boxed in by a movement I can't control, and a caucus that won't forgive hesitation.* [21]

Meanwhile, Pierre Poilievre seized the rhetorical high ground, giving interviews and fiery tweets that turned convoy grievances into a national talking point. To Poilievre, the truckers were not a fringe but *ordinary Canadians tired of government overreach.* His speeches skirted the wilder fringes of convoy rhetoric, steering clear of conspiracy but hammering *gatekeepers in Ottawa* and the *elites who look down on working people.* Political calculation or conviction—it no longer mattered. Every media scrum became a referendum on Conservative identity. [22]

As the convoy dug in, the Conservative war room went into overdrive. An aide's memo, leaked to select reporters, outlined polling data: a spike in support across rural ridings, a flood of small-dollar donations, and "overwhelming positive engagement" on social media from demographics the party had struggled to reach for a generation. The memo passed across Candice Bergen's desk with a handwritten note—*Rural surge, urban slide. Risk and reward* were a roadmap and a warning. [23]

Bergen, who had only just taken over as interim leader after O'Toole's abrupt ouster, understood the stakes. On 2 February, in a dim hotel conference room on the outskirts of Ottawa, she convened her first full caucus retreat since the start of the crisis. The mood was taut, the coffee bitter, and the arguments sharper than any since the days of Reform. Some MPs, especially those from Alberta and Saskatchewan, demanded unequivocal support for the protesters. *These are our people,* a Saskatchewan MP thundered, *and if we turn our backs on them now, we'll lose them for a generation.* Others, mainly from the GTA and Montreal's outer suburbs, warned of electoral suicide. *A single misstep,* cautioned one Québec MP, *and we're branded as the party of chaos, not conservatism.* [24]

Bergen, experienced in party discipline and Prairie realpolitik, heard them before offering her private counsel. "We cannot own this protest," she said quietly, "but we can't condemn our base for showing up, either." She urged focus: attack Trudeau's *incompetence,* call for a rational plan to wind down mandates, but avoid the language of unconditional endorsement. She publicly repeated this advice, but people did not always heed it. [25]

The pressure to choose grew more acute as scenes from the protests made the evening news. Footage of Terry Fox's statue festooned with anti-mandate banners, and a war memorial draped in *freedom* slogans, ignited national outrage. Liberals demanded that Bergen and Poilievre distance the party from *extremism and disrespect.* Conservative strategists debated whether to issue a statement of regret or double down on *free speech* rhetoric. Bergen split the difference in a press conference on 3 February: *The truckers have a right to be heard, but there's no place for hate or vandalism in our movement or anywhere else.* The parsing satisfied a few, but the party's polling line in rural Canada kept inching up. [26]

By early February, the split within the party was so pronounced that senior staff began monitoring MPs' social media for signs of dissent or defection. When Conservative MP Michael Chong publicly cautioned that "legitimate protest must not devolve into lawlessness," the blowback from grassroots activists was immediate. Chong's office fielded angry calls, and a private email from a senior organiser warned that *if you're not with us, you're with them.* [27]

The balancing act grew more treacherous as the blockades spread. On 8 February, Poilievre staged a carefully managed visit to the Ambassador Bridge protest—Canada's busiest border crossing, now immobilised by trucks and flags. Before an impromptu gathering of supporters, he declared, "We must take back our freedoms. Canadians are fed up with politicians who tell them to sit down and shut up." The crowd cheered, and Poilievre's words shot across Twitter and Facebook in viral bursts. [28]

Behind closed doors, Bergen worried that the party's grip on the situation was slipping. Another aide's 9 February memo warned of a *growing disconnect* between caucus unity and the party's public message. *We are being outflanked by both sides,* the memo said. *Our rural base demands more support for the convoy; urban voters see us as playing with fire.* The document recommended a new communications strategy: stress *common-sense solutions,* call for dialogue, and avoid *emotional escalation.* [29]

Meanwhile, Erin O'Toole watched from the political wilderness as his former party veered toward a brand of populism he had tried to avoid. In a rare moment of candour with a *Globe and Mail* reporter, O'Toole admitted he was "haunted by the energy of the convoy and the lesson that in modern politics, hesitation is punished more than recklessness." He warned that the party risked "becoming captive to a movement we didn't start and can't finish." [30]

Bergen summoned her closest advisors for a late-night huddle at party headquarters as the convoy crisis reached its crescendo in mid-February. The polls still showed rural support holding, but an uptick in negative sentiment among women, new Canadians, and suburban swing voters signalled danger ahead. At a 13 February press conference, she challenged Trudeau to "set out a clear endgame for Canadians—when will the mandates end? When will Canadians get their freedoms back?" The question resonated with the convoy crowd, but the national press corps pressed Bergen on whether her party would support the Emergencies Act if invoked. She dodged, repeating, "The Prime Minister needs to provide a plan, not more division." [31]

The next morning, the Parliament Hill standoff was at its most acute. Interim leader Bergen, bundled in a blue parka, walked the protest perimeter under the gaze of network cameras, taking selfies with supporters and fielding impromptu policy questions about supply chain chaos and the rule of law. She stopped to speak to a young trucker from Alberta who thanked her for *standing up for the working class,* and a local business owner who pleaded for an end to the disruption. Bergen's staff, constantly checking Twitter for new videos and viral commentary, saw the party's fortunes rising and falling in real time. [32]

Meanwhile, in caucus, the divisions only deepened. The private WhatsApp group used by Conservative MPs erupted with arguments over tone and tactics. A Toronto-area MP demanded the party *pivot to solutions,* while a Manitoba MP insisted, *This is the fight our voters have waited for.* Bergen, caught in the crosshairs, closed her notebook after the last rally and signalled to her staff that it was time to regroup, hinting that the reckoning inside the party was far from over. [33]

What lingered, long after the last horn faded, was the sense that the Conservative Party had crossed a political Rubicon. The populist momentum unleashed by the Freedom Convoy had redrawn the map of Conservative ambition, making future leadership contests not merely about policy but about authenticity, anger, and the promise to "take back Canada." In the shadow of the Hill, even the most seasoned operatives whispered that a new party had been born—not in a convention hall, but in the tumult of a winter protest that had put every politician's instincts to the test. The story of Bergen, Poilievre, and O'Toole in those charged weeks was not simply a tale of ambition and tactics, but a primer in the new politics of division, where every handshake and every sound bite could tip a party's fate—and the country's—into uncharted territory. [34]

From the moment the first snow-laden trucks settled into Wellington Street and the echoes of air horns tangled with the wind off the Ottawa River, the protest's force was not just measured in decibels or diesel, but in the way it rattled every level of government from Vancouver to the Gaspé. The front lines of February 2022 ran through city hall basements, police boardrooms, provincial war rooms, and late-night calls between premiers and Ottawa. What unfolded was less a unified crisis response than a scattershot contest of nerves, each jurisdiction calibrating its threshold for panic, for power, and political fallout. In the country's capital, the Freedom Convoy's siege had become an accidental referendum on Canadian federalism. [35]

> *"In a nation where diesel engines rose as a rolling parliament, we learned that democracy thrives on dialogue, not horsepower; the loudest horns may spur attention, but they rarely steer a country to consensus."*

It was in Ottawa that the first crack of an official alarm sounded. On 6 February, as convoys strangled city arteries and residents fumed over sleepless nights, Mayor Jim Watson invoked a municipal state of emergency, declaring that "the situation is completely out of control" and that the city was "losing the battle" to restore order. [36] Watson's declaration, while symbolic in its authority, triggered a tangible shift in tone. Suddenly, the management of the convoy ceased to be just a policing challenge and became a political crisis. In City Hall, staffers in the bowels of the building studied traffic diversion maps and debated redeploying snowploughs as barricades. Some managers admitted to reporters that morale among municipal staff was at *historic lows*; in one overheard exchange, a by-law officer joked grimly, `*My badge is worth less than a trucker's air horn these days.* [37]

Watson's gambit set a precedent. Across the Rideau, as national media relayed images of blocked fire lanes and residents' stories of intimidation, provincial capitals grew increasingly uneasy. Ontario Premier Doug Ford, whose political instincts had always tilted toward caution when the unpredictable loomed, convened his cabinet by teleconference. On 11 February, under mounting pressure from police chiefs, business leaders, and exasperated municipal mayors, Ford declared a provincial state of emergency. He called the blockades "an illegal occupation," vowing steep fines and jail time for anyone impeding critical infrastructure. [38]

Yet Ford's emergency order was as much a performance as a plan. At Queen's Park, ministers swapped drafts of talking points that would land on evening newscasts, careful to stress that the move was *temporary* and *necessary.* In Windsor, where the Ambassador Bridge bottleneck threatened billions in trade, city officials scrambled to synchronise their response with provincial directives. A control room in Windsor's city hall pulsed with tension—police chiefs, legal advisors, and city managers gathered around glowing monitors as Ford's decree rolled in, awaiting the green light to move on protesters. A Windsor staffer described the mood as *half war room, half weather centre—we tracked every gust of protest as if it was a winter storm warning.* [39]

As Ford's order rippled outward, other premiers weighed their risks. In Québec City, Premier François Legault struck a deliberately cautious tone. With the memory of the 1970 October Crisis never far from Québec's political imagination, Legault publicly opposed using federal emergency powers, insisting that *Québec can handle its own affairs* and warning Ottawa not to overreach. His press secretary, surprised by the volume of English-language media requests, instructed colleagues to *stay on message: Québec is in control, we do not need outside intervention.* The distinction was crucial for a province where jurisdictional autonomy was a political dogma and an electoral necessity. [40]

Further west, Saskatchewan's Scott Moe walked his careful line. Moe's statements were at once sympathetic to the convoy's anti-mandate message and wary of endorsing outright lawlessness. His press aide, digesting a fresh set of polling numbers from Moose Jaw and Swift Current, relayed that rural support for the convoy remained robust, even as urban voters demanded order. *Don't lose the base,* the aide whispered before a press conference. *But remind them we're not Ottawa's enforcers.* [41]

All the while, the ground-level confusion deepened. In Ottawa, front-line city workers—garbage collectors, parking enforcement, snow removal—tried to keep the city's skeleton intact, dodging angry protesters and exhausted police officers. At a city manager's briefing, one staffer summarised it with bleak understatement: *We're the background music to a national drama.* Some residents, pushed past their breaking point by the nightly cacophony, organised counterprotests or filed injunctions. Others taped handwritten pleas to truck windows—"My kids can't sleep, please stop the horns"—and hoped for mercy. [42]

Scepticism and bravado greeted each new emergency declaration from the truckers and their supporters. Livestreams flickered with debates over the *constitutionality* of municipal and provincial orders. In response to Doug Ford's emergency announcement, some in the encampment cheered, boasting that they had *forced the government's hand.* Others, more wary, worried that the state was tightening its grip. In interviews, drivers described frozen bank accounts, threats of license suspension, and a growing sense that *this was about more than mandates now.* [43]

Inside the halls of power, they calibrated each move for political optics as much as for public order. At Ottawa City Hall, Jim Watson's office debated when and how to request federal help. In one now-publicised email, Watson pressed federal ministers for more resources, writing: "We need a coordinated response, not finger-pointing." Ottawa's police board cycled through acting chiefs as trust in law enforcement collapsed. A city manager later recalled, "It was like trying to plug leaks in a dam with thumbtacks." [44]

At the provincial level, Ford's staff monitored the economic fallout minute by minute. A confidential cabinet memo cited by *CTV* described *escalating costs to supply chains, reputational damage to Ontario businesses, and rising insurance claims from auto sector shutdowns.* Every hour the Ambassador Bridge remained blocked, factories in Windsor and Detroit weighed layoffs. Ford's political calculus—restore order without appearing to trample on protest—became the central drama of his leadership in those days. [45]

The rest of Canada watched with a wary mix of empathy and alarm. In Alberta, Premier Jason Kenney denounced the *unlawful blockades.* Still, he stopped short of backing federal intervention, keenly aware of how quickly prairie anger could turn on any politician seen as weak on civil liberties. In British Columbia, John Horgan invoked solidarity with embattled truckers' families while reiterating the need to *uphold the law and keep supply lines open.* Atlantic premiers issued generic statements of concern, wary of the region's limited hospital capacity and the broader implications of unrest spreading eastward. [46]

As the days ticked by, municipal and provincial declarations stacked up like sandbags against a rising tide, but the cracks in Canadian governance were impossible to miss. Each layer of government pointed to the next: Ottawa blamed Queen's Park, Queen's Park blamed Ottawa, and both blamed *outside agitators.* Meanwhile, police chiefs in Windsor and Ottawa found themselves caught in the crossfire, tasked with restoring order but unsure whether their orders would hold from one shift to the next. [47]

Then, on 14 February, with most provincial powers already activated and municipal patience long since spent, the federal government reached for the ultimate lever—the Emergencies Act. The provinces responded to Ottawa's invocation of federal emergency powers with new declarations, clarifications, and Québec's condemnation. Doug Ford offered public support but privately lobbied for a swift, *surgical* intervention that would allow the province to reclaim the lead as soon as the crisis cooled. Legault bristled that Ottawa was intruding on provincial jurisdiction, while Moe and Kenney issued careful statements defending their efforts as *sufficient under provincial law.* The patchwork of responses was so convoluted that even seasoned constitutional scholars struggled to trace the chain of command. One described it as *federalism in a funhouse mirror—every reflection warped by political self-preservation.* [48]

In Windsor, the emergency measures arrived with a thud. Police, now buttressed by the Ontario Provincial Police and R.C.M.P., moved quickly to clear the bridge. By the night of 14-15 February, the city's control room exhaled for the first time in a week, but no one mistook the operation for victory. The fallout—arrests, impounded rigs, and the sighs of exhausted union reps—would ripple for months. In Ottawa, police began preparing for a final sweep, drawing on new authorities to threaten asset seizures and insurance suspensions. At city hall, Jim Watson, and the city manager exchanged glances across the briefing table, each wondering aloud whether everyday life could ever return to the battered capital. [49]

For the truckers' supporters, each police advance, and new proclamation, spurred defiance and resignation. On TikTok and Telegram, convoy leaders urged their followers to *stand strong* but began quietly preparing for dispersal. Authorities froze bank accounts, shut down GoFundMe, and lawyers circulated PDFs of the Charter. Some truckers wept as they left, fearing fines or jail time and the sense of defeat. Others vowed that the movement was *only just beginning.* National commentary overwhelmed the voices of front-line staff, city residents, and police. [50]

The final coda came with little fanfare. On 23 February 2022, Prime Minister Trudeau announced revoking the Emergencies Act, declaring that "the situation is no longer an emergency." The decision, made after fevered legal debate and under mounting pressure from premiers and civil liberties advocates, left the country in a charged hush. In Ottawa, the bells of Parliament rang out, the snow lay undisturbed, and the city exhaled. Yet few mistook the sound for resolution. The emergency's expiry signalled not a return to normal, but an uneasy peace—a country that had survived a test of its institutions, with fresh scars and unresolved constitutional questions. [51]

In the days and weeks that followed, the shockwaves rolled outward. Provincial premiers called for new *emergency management protocols,* city managers requested reviews of *intergovernmental coordination failures,* police unions demanded mental health resources for front-line officers; and convoy supporters regrouped, plotting their next moves online and in town halls from Brooks to

Belleville. In the halls of Queen's Park, staffers debated how to spin Ford's role in the drama. In Ottawa, Jim Watson's emails expressed both thanks and recriminations. Across the St. Lawrence, Legault's cabinet strategised to make Québec's autonomy a ballot box issue. And on the Prairies, Scott Moe's office issued yet another press release promising *vigilance against federal overreach.* [52]

As the snow melted, a new fault line carved itself into the bedrock of Confederation. The convoy's end was not an ending, but a beginning of political realignment, electoral calculation, and lingering unease. The charged silence that followed the expiry of emergency powers was a signal, not of relief, but of reckoning to come. In the uneasy hush that settled over Parliament Hill, the country waited—no longer certain of its old certainties, its boundaries between order and liberty, government, and protest, forever blurred. [53]

ENDNOTES

[1] CBC News. (2022, February 13). *What you need to know about the border blockades and their impact on Canada.* CBC. https://www.cbc.ca/news/canada/border-blockades-impact-freedom-convoy-1.6349204

[2] Evans, J. W. (2022, February 14). Canada's trucker protests: Populist uprising or fringe minority? *Reuters.* https://www.reuters.com/world/americas/canadas-trucker-protests-populist-uprising-or-fringe-minority-2022-02-14

[3] Ó Fátharta, C. (2022, February 13). Divided opinion as Trudeau mulls emergency powers. *The Guardian.* https://www.theguardian.com/world/2022/feb/13/canada-trudeau-emergencies-act-poll

[4] Macfarlane, E. (2022). Emergencies Act: History, thresholds, and the peril of precedent. *Canadian Journal of Political Science, 55*(2), 230–239. https://doi.org/10.1017/S000842392200021X

[5] CTV News. (2022, February 14). *Trudeau holds emergency cabinet meeting ahead of Emergencies Act.* CTV. https://www.ctvnews.ca/politics/trudeau-holds-emergency-cabinet-meeting-ahead-of-emergencies-act-1.5778854

[6] Financial Post. (2022, February 14). *Bay Street warns Ottawa blockade is undermining Canadian credibility.* Postmedia. https://financialpost.com/news/economy/bay-street-warns-ottawa-blockade-undermining-canadian-credibility

[7] Coyne, A. (2022, February 14). Leaked Justice memo warns of 'irreparable harm' if Emergencies Act used without exhausting options. *The Globe and Mail.* https://www.theglobeandmail.com/politics/article-leaked-memo-warns-irreparable-harm-emergencies-act

[8] CBC News. (2022, February 13). *Ottawa mayor calls for federal help as crisis deepens*. CBC. https://www.cbc.ca/news/canada/ottawa/ottawa-mayor-jim-watson-state-of-emergency-1.6347590

[9] CTV News. (2022, February 14). *Commons abuzz as Emergencies Act invocation looms*. CTV. https://www.ctvnews.ca/politics/commons-abuzz-as-emergencies-act-invocation-looms-1.5779123

[10] The Associated Press. (2022, February 14). Trudeau invokes Emergencies Act for first time in Canadian history. *AP News*. https://apnews.com/article/ottawa-truck-protests-canada-emergencies-act-16c9b317b3a7ad50f5ae6596d68bba08

[11] CBC News. (2022, February 15). *Inside the government's decision to invoke emergency powers*. CBC. https://www.cbc.ca/news/politics/emergencies-act-decision-trudeau-1.6349901

[12] Curry, B. (2022, February 15). Opposition decries 'criminalizing dissent' as House debates Emergencies Act. *The Globe and Mail*. https://www.theglobeandmail.com/politics/article-opposition-decries-criminalizing-dissent

[13] CTV News. (2022, February 15). *Singh warns use of Emergencies Act must be scrutinized*. CTV. https://www.ctvnews.ca/politics/singh-warns-use-of-emergencies-act-must-be-scrutinized-1.5780171

[14] Canadian Press. (2022, February 15). *Justice minister defends Emergencies Act decision in Parliament*. CTV. https://www.ctvnews.ca/politics/justice-minister-defends-emergencies-act-decision-1.5780509

[15] CBC News. (2022, February 15). *Behind the scenes: Party strategists on the Emergencies Act*. CBC. https://www.cbc.ca/news/politics/emergencies-act-behind-scenes-1.6350201

[16] CBC News. (2022, February 21). *How MPs voted on the Emergencies Act*. CBC. https://www.cbc.ca/news/politics/emergencies-act-vote-1.6360995

[17] O'Connor, C. (2022, February 21). Canada faces legal, political blowback over emergency powers. *Reuters*. https://www.reuters.com/world/americas/canada-faces-legal-political-blowback-over-emergency-powers-2022-02-21

[18] Canadian Press. (2022, February 21). *Civil liberties groups vow court challenge after Emergencies Act vote*. CTV. https://www.ctvnews.ca/politics/civil-liberties-groups-vow-court-challenge-after-emergencies-act-vote-1.6361159

[19] CTV News. (2022, January 28). *Pierre Poilievre embraces Freedom Convoy at Parliament Hill*. CTV. https://www.ctvnews.ca/politics/pierre-poilievre-embraces-freedom-convoy-at-parliament-hill-1.5760080

[20] CBC News. (2022, January 29). *Conservatives see rural surge as truckers roll into Ottawa*. CBC. https://www.cbc.ca/news/politics/conservatives-rural-support-truckers-1.6331050

[21] Coyne, A. (2022, February 2). O'Toole ousted: Inside the revolt and what it means for Conservatives. *The Globe and Mail*. https://www.theglobeandmail.com/politics/article-erin-otoole-conservative-leadership-revolt

[22] Bronskill, J. (2022, January 31). Canada's Conservatives back trucker protest, split on response. *Reuters*. https://www.reuters.com/world/americas/canadas-conservatives-back-trucker-protest-split-on-response-2022-01-31

[23] CBC News. (2022, February 1). *Internal polling shows rural support surging for convoy*. CBC. https://www.cbc.ca/news/politics/internal-polling-convoy-support-1.6335096

[24] CTV News. (2022, February 2). *Inside Conservative caucus as convoy divides party*. CTV. https://www.ctvnews.ca/politics/inside-conservative-caucus-as-convoy-divides-party-1.5762501

[25] Canadian Press. (2022, February 3). *Bergen walks tightrope on convoy message*. CTV. https://www.ctvnews.ca/politics/bergen-walks-tightrope-on-convoy-message-1.5764298

[26] CBC News. (2022, February 5). *Protest images fuel political split*. CBC. https://www.cbc.ca/news/politics/protest-images-fuel-political-split-1.6339458

[27] Coyne, A. (2022, February 6). Dissenters face grassroots backlash in Tory ranks. *The Globe and Mail*. https://www.theglobeandmail.com/politics/article-dissenters-face-grassroots-backlash-in-tory-ranks

[28] CTV News. (2022, February 8). *Poilievre's Ambassador Bridge address draws cheers*. CTV. https://www.ctvnews.ca/politics/poilievre-ambassador-bridge-address-draws-cheers-1.5770884

[29] Canadian Press. (2022, February 9). *Tory aides warn party losing control of convoy message*. CTV. https://www.ctvnews.ca/politics/tory-aides-warn-party-losing-control-of-convoy-message-1.5772312

[30] Coyne, A. (2022, February 10). O'Toole reflects on party's populist turn. *The Globe and Mail*. https://www.theglobeandmail.com/politics/article-otoole-reflects-on-party-populist-turn

[31] CTV News. (2022, February 13). *Bergen challenges Trudeau for endgame on mandates*. CTV. https://www.ctvnews.ca/politics/bergen-challenges-trudeau-for-endgame-on-mandates-1.5776752

[32] CBC News. (2022, February 14). *Bergen walks protest line as crisis peaks*. CBC. https://www.cbc.ca/news/politics/bergen-walks-protest-line-1.6349209

[33] Coyne, A. (2022, February 14). Discord deepens inside Tory caucus as convoy climax nears. *The Globe and Mail*. https://www.theglobeandmail.com/politics/article-discord-deepens-inside-tory-caucus-as-convoy-climax-nears

[34] Canadian Press. (2022, February 15). *Conservatives face internal reckoning after convoy*. CTV. https://www.ctvnews.ca/politics/conservatives-face-internal-reckoning-after-convoy-1.5781017

[35] Coyne, A. (2022, February 7). Freedom Convoy turns into test of Canadian federalism. *The Globe and Mail*. https://www.theglobeandmail.com/politics/article-freedom-convoy-turns-into-test-of-canadian-federalism

[36] CBC News. (2022, February 6). *Ottawa declares state of emergency as protest continues*. CBC. https://www.cbc.ca/news/canada/ottawa/ottawa-declares-state-of-emergency-1.6345965

[37] Canadian Press. (2022, February 7). *City staff stretched thin amid protest crisis.* CTV. https://www.ctvnews.ca/politics/city-staff-stretched-thin-amid-protest-crisis-1.6348033

[38] CTV News. (2022, February 11). *Ontario declares state of emergency over blockades.* CTV. https://www.ctvnews.ca/politics/ontario-declares-state-of-emergency-over-blockades-1.5774317

[39] Johnstone, B. (2022, February 12). Windsor's control room: Inside the city's response to the blockade. *Windsor Star.* https://windsorstar.com/news/local-news/windsor-control-room-blockade

[40] CBC News. (2022, February 14). *Quebec opposes federal emergency powers.* CBC. https://www.cbc.ca/news/canada/montreal/quebec-opposes-federal-emergency-powers-1.6349235

[41] Coyne, A. (2022, February 10). Saskatchewan's Moe walks fine line on convoy. *The Globe and Mail.* https://www.theglobeandmail.com/politics/article-saskatchewans-moe-walks-fine-line-on-convoy

[42] CTV News. (2022, February 8). *Ottawa residents, staff struggle with daily impact of protest.* CTV. https://www.ctvnews.ca/politics/ottawa-residents-staff-struggle-with-daily-impact-of-protest-1.5772009

[43] Bronskill, J. (2022, February 13). Truckers react to Ford's emergency order. *Reuters.* https://www.reuters.com/world/americas/truckers-react-fords-emergency-order-2022-02-13

[44] CBC News. (2022, February 11). *Ottawa city hall pleads for federal help.* CBC. https://www.cbc.ca/news/canada/ottawa/ottawa-city-hall-pleads-federal-help-1.6348251

[45] CTV News. (2022, February 13). *Cabinet memo: Economic fallout of Ontario blockades.* CTV. https://www.ctvnews.ca/politics/cabinet-memo-economic-fallout-of-ontario-blockades-1.5776892

[46] CBC News. (2022, February 14). *Provincial premiers walk emergency tightrope.* CBC. https://www.cbc.ca/news/canada/provincial-premiers-walk-emergency-tightrope-1.6349787

[47] Coyne, A. (2022, February 13). Police chiefs caught in jurisdictional crossfire. *The Globe and Mail.* https://www.theglobeandmail.com/politics/article-police-chiefs-caught-in-jurisdictional-crossfire

[48] Coyne, A. (2022, February 14). Federalism in a funhouse mirror: Canada's emergency powers puzzle. *The Globe and Mail.* https://www.theglobeandmail.com/politics/article-federalism-in-a-funhouse-mirror-canadas-emergency-powers-puzzle

[49] CBC News. (2022, February 15). *Ottawa, Windsor move to clear protests.* CBC. https://www.cbc.ca/news/canada/ottawa/ottawa-windsor-move-clear-protests-1.6350293

[50] The Associated Press. (2022, February 17). *Frozen bank accounts, TikTok rallies mark end of protest.* AP News. https://apnews.com/article/frozen-bank-accounts-tiktok-end-protest-2022-02-17

[51] Bronskill, J. (2022, February 23). Canada revokes emergency powers as convoy crisis wanes. *Reuters.* https://www.reuters.com/world/americas/canada-revokes-emergency-powers-convoy-crisis-wanes-2022-02-23

[52] CTV News. (2022, February 24). *Aftermath: Provincial, city leaders call for review of emergency protocols.* CTV. https://www.ctvnews.ca/politics/aftermath-provincial-city-leaders-call-for-review-of-emergency-protocols-1.5782323

[53] Coyne, A. (2022, February 25). After the convoy: Political and constitutional tremors linger. *The Globe and Mail.* https://www.theglobeandmail.com/politics/article-after-the-convoy-political-constitutional-tremors-linger

CHAPTER NINE:

IDLE STEEL OVER A SILENT RIVER

"They thought a bridge could be silent, but silence is just noise that's learned to wait. A line of trucks can freeze more than steel—they freeze pay cheques, tempers, and the daily gospel of just-in-time. When the engines stop, you learn quickly that commerce and democracy both run on trust, and neither enjoys being left out in the cold."
~ *R. G. Cruise*

From the bitter dawn of 8 February 2022—when Windsor's riverfront lamps still glowed but the first semi-trailers parked broadside across the Ambassador Bridge toll plaza—to the evening of 10 February, the continent's busiest commercial crossing passed from hum to hush. On a typical morning, the span's four lanes carried CA$390 million in goods, nearly a third of Canada's road imports and a quarter of its road exports, each truck timed to the minute by just-in-time (JIT) logistics engineers at plants from Oakville to Ohio. [1] A single night of blockade turned that choreography into a freeze-frame: 8,000 trucks a day vanished from the steel truss, and the Detroit River below reflected only empty sky.

Economists would later tally the macro damage, but the first hints arrived in the half-lit office of Vince Marrocco, a Windsor customs broker with three decades of NAFTA paperwork behind him. He refreshed the Canada Border Services Agency feed and watched the manifest queue lengthen like a malfunctioning tape measure. *Blue Water Bridge just went to a three-hour delay,* his despatcher called from the hallway. Marrocco scrawled red Xs beside fifteen outbound produce loads. *Tell them to ice the lettuce or kiss it goodbye,* he said, flat as carbon copy paper. Outside, the static of idling diesel drifted through a cracked window while the *Reuters* newswire on his second monitor warned that shipments of cattle, corn, and car parts were "snarling hundreds of millions of dollars daily of trade." [2]

At Windsor's Stellantis minivan plant, line supervisor Aisha Wright felt the stoppage in her bones before it reached her inbox. Thirty minutes into the morning shift, the stack-light over Station 14 flicked from green to amber; the robotic arm welding rear quarter-panels paused mid-arc. *No brackets*, a materials coordinator shrugged, phone pressed to his ear. Wright rang the supplier in Romulus, Michigan, by voicemail. She tried the trucking despatcher—busy. Finally, a breathless logistics agent admitted the truth: every bracket sat in a tractor-trailer marooned on I-75. By noon, the plant idled both shifts, a decision that spread through the auto sector like a cold front: Ford shut its Windsor engine plant, Toyota trimmed production schedules, and parts makers across southern Ontario initiated rolling layoffs. [3] [4] [5]

Up the bridge approach, Constable Léa Dupuis leaned over the open window of a Peterbilt draped in maple leaves and Gadsden flags. *Driver's licence?* she asked. The woman in the cab tipped her ball cap—*Ma'am, I'm staying put till someone in Ottawa quits grandstanding.* Behind them, only one outbound lane trickled into Michigan under police escort, a concession brokered after ministers in Ottawa branded the blockade *illegal* and pleaded for compliance. [6] On the Canadian side, the queue of inbound trucks stretched past Huron Church Road's strip malls; on the American side, the line on I-75 snaked beneath billboards advertising factory-fresh F-150s that local plants no longer built.

Inside Transport Canada's Situation Room, staff entered the eighth hour of a teleconference whose agenda header read *14. Situation on the Ambassador Bridge*. A red-ink note under Key Messages captured the stakes: *Busiest crossing; handles CA$390 M trade/day; half automotive.* Asterisked beneath, another line: *Impact likely acute for manufacturers given JIT model—Ford, Toyota, Honda scaling back.* An analyst highlighted the sentence, copied it into an email blast for deputy ministers, and hit Send. [7]

Trade associations amplified the alarm. The Automotive Parts Manufacturers' Association's Flavio Volpe gave morning interviews describing the blockade as *a brain-dead move* that could shutter shops *within 24 to 48 hours.* [5] In Washington, the U.S. Chamber of Commerce, the National Association of

Manufacturers and the Business Roundtable issued a joint statement urging Ottawa to *act swiftly*, warning that production cuts and shift reductions were already spreading across the Midwest. [8]

Marrocco's office printer spat out reroute instructions in Windsor: corn bound for Lethbridge would now cross at Port Huron; precision moulds destined for Kentucky, via Queenston-Lewiston. Each detour added fuel costs and driver-fatigue hours. His phone lit up again—this time, a Michigan greenhouse grower. *If those fertiliser totes don't clear tonight, we'll dump seedlings,* the caller said. Marrocco pinched the bridge of his nose. *You and me both sailing uncharted, pal,* he muttered, jotting *FEB 9 15:10 — ag export risk* in his log.

Across town, supervisor Wright stood before a circle of workers in blue Mopar hoodies. *We're sending everyone home,* she announced, trying to summon gallows humour. *Seems our parts took the scenic route.* A veteran assembler cracked, *So much for just-in-time—looks more like just-ain't-coming.* Laughter rippled, thin but genuine, before the reality of unpaid hours settled in.

As Wednesday faded into Thursday, the blockade's dominoes toppled faster. *Automotive News* tallied *additional strain* on an industry already shell-shocked by semiconductor shortages; suppliers debated flying trim components by cargo jet. [9] *Axios* logged fresh production cuts at Ford's Ohio Assembly and Toyota's Cambridge plants, each bulletin a pinprick in the North American economy's epidermis. [10] Night-shift radio chatter from truckers diverted to Sarnia sounded resigned and enraged: *Add four hours to your log, bud—hope your e-log likes poetry.*

By late 10 February, Ottawa, and Washington had mirrored each other in exasperation. In Canada's capital, aides drafted talking points for ministers on *safeguarding critical trade arteries,* in D.C., White House staff prepped calls stressing *the potential impact on workers.* [11] Windsor's mayor, Drew Dilkens, quietly directed city lawyers to prepare an injunction—paperwork that would land before Ontario's Chief Justice Geoffrey Morawetz by the following day. [12]

For the moment, though, the bridge remained a monument to stalled motion, its suspension cables humming in the winter gusts like detuned violin strings. Marrocco locked his office, glanced at the river, and imagined invoices piling up on desks from Detroit to Drummondville. Driving home past the dark plant, Supervisor Wright counted how many pay cheques her line would miss if the blockade lingered. And somewhere on Huron Church Road, a protester stoked a barrel fire and quoted Twain: "History doesn't repeat, but it sure does rhyme." The rhyme, everyone sensed, was accelerating toward a chorus the country was not ready to sing.

The blockade crossed its invisible Rubicon from the pewter dawn of 11 February 2022, when Premier Doug Ford's state-of-emergency decree crackled through every Windsor despatcher's radio like a thunderclap over sheet metal. Ford called the protest a *siege,* promised *severe* penalties, and invoked powers to seize rigs and strip licences, a threat that spread faster than road salt on Huron Church Road. [13] Yet the economic bleeding he hoped to stanch was already gushing: Bloomberg analysts were pegging daily losses at up to CA$500 million and warning of a GDP dent to rival any pandemic quarter. [14] Across the river, the White House press room fielded questions about auto layoffs in Michigan; Press Secretary Jen Psaki confirmed that President Biden had pressed Ottawa for *swift action* after Port Huron traffic hit capacity. [15]

Inside a prefab office beside Windsor's Walker Road rail spur, Jordan Singh, lead despatcher for Cross-Border Components, faced three monitors that now resembled failing hospital screens. Ford Motor's Oakville engine plant had just moved its assembly restart from Friday to *TBD,* while Toyota's Cambridge lines requested a second straight day of *team-member stand-down.* Magna International, Ford's largest client, warned of initial impacts from washer nozzles for a Kentucky SUV line stranded near London, Ontario—these could escalate by nightfall. Nearly every Canadian supplier, *Automotive News* wrote that morning, had *ceased building parts* as fluid-filled racks sat on cold tarmac. [17] Singh stabbed at his keyboard, rerouting pallets toward Sarnia and Fort Erie, then watched the CBSA dashboard show wait times peaking at two-plus hours even at supposedly clear crossings. [18] *I'm playing three-card Monte with brake rotors,* he muttered, phone wedged to his ear.

At 10:00, Justice Geoffrey Morawetz of the Ontario Superior Court dialled in from Toronto for an emergency injunction hearing broadcast via shaky Zoom links. The Automotive Parts Manufacturers' Association submitted affidavits listing CA$350 million in foregone output; the City of Windsor detailed policing overtime already north of a quarter-million dollars. Morawetz's ruling dropped like an anvil: protesters had until 19:00 to clear or face contempt. [19] Minutes later, the order pinged onto Sergeant Paula Desmarais's tablet in a staging lot near College Avenue. Desmarais, an Ontario Provincial Police crowd-management specialist, scanned a hand-drawn grid of Huron Church Road divided into forty-three *boxes,* each a ten-metre advance. *We move one box at a time,* she told her mixed platoon of O.P.P. and Windsor Police officers, *slow as maple in February, but just as inevitable.*

By mid-afternoon, grey snow flurries swirled as Desmarais's column nudged concrete barriers forward; tow-trucks idled noses-out like draft horses impatient for work. On the opposite side, a loose semicircle of protesters blared, *We're Not Gonna Take It* from portable speakers. When officers stepped into Box Nine, a diesel horn wailed and a Peterbilt lurched, but chained tires spun uselessly against asphalt coated with anti-traction beads. Overhead, a Windsor police drone relayed footage to command, where yellow icons inched northward on a digital map. Recalcitrant drivers received printed notices citing the injunction number and potential $100,000 fines; one man crumpled his and offered a mock salute. *Reuters* later described the standoff as *deadlocked* despite the court order. [20]

Inside Singh's office, dusk arrived without resolution. He fielded a flurry of emails marked *LINE-STOP* from Tennessee, Ohio, and Indiana; each demanded ETA guarantees he could not give. *Tell them we're under siege by friendship,* he quipped, but the joke fell flat. Beyond his window, the cough of generators and the chant of improvised anthems had replaced Huron Church Road's usual roar.

Saturday, 12 February, began with steel-blue skies and the first concerted police push at 08:14. Desmarais's unit advanced five boxes in ten minutes, flanked by armoured vans bearing R.C.M.P. insignia. *Axios* called it *the strongest escalation yet,* noting Premier Ford's emergency powers hovering in the background like an unseen referee. [21] Officers arrested a 27-year-old man for mischief, towed seven rigs, and seized a cache of jerrycans and propane tanks. [20] Protesters regrouped behind a new line of pallets spray-painted *Hold the Line,* but the perimeter had now retreated an entire city block from the bridge ramp.

Singh, meanwhile, watched his load board bleed red—eighteen delayed shipments out of twenty-one. A Toyota caller from Georgetown broke down in tears as she explained that her line-workers would miss a second straight pay cheque. Singh promised nothing, refreshed the CBSA site again, and saw the Blue

Water Bridge wait spike to 170 minutes. *If this keeps up,* he told a colleague, *I'll need a Ouija board, not a dashboard.* That afternoon, an open letter signed by the Canadian Manufacturers & Exporters and two dozen business associations landed in every MP's inbox, warning of *cascading supply-chain failures* and pleading for immediate enforcement. [24]

Saturday night brought an eerie half-victory: protesters' main camp lay 700 metres south of the toll booths, but the bridge remained closed, a suspended question mark over the Detroit River. Inside the federal Transport Canada *Blockades Binder,* analysts updated Section 16: Three crossings disrupted, seven more threatened, risk escalating. [25] At the Prime Minister's Langevin Block office, staff drafted bullet points on *financial deterrents* for a Sunday cabinet huddle—early sketches of the economic-measures order that would soon stun crowdfunding platforms.

Dawn of 13 February arrived muffled by freezing mist. Desmarais's officers donned riot helmets not for confrontation but for wind-chill; breath plumed as they executed Box-Thirty-seven, Box-Thirty-eight. Someone hemmed onto Tecumseh Road in the last row of trucks by 8:30 a.m. A *Reuters* photographer captured an image of an officer tapping a windshield and the driver speeding up, surrendering the lane. [22] At 9:15 p.m., the CBSA tweet many thought impossible blinked onto screens: *AMBASSADOR BRIDGE—TRAFFIC RESUMED. Expect delays.* Singh read it three times. *NPR* added the epilogue, noting that the opening came *after 42 arrests and 37 vehicles seized.* [23] *Al Jazeera* struck a global note, calling the bridge's return *a relief to supply chains from Windsor to Mexico.* [26]

Yet relief felt fragile. Jordan Singh's phone lit with requests for Monday delivery that could never materialise; Sergeant Desmarais completed paperwork for officers nursing frost-nipped fingers; and on Parliament Hill, officials tallied costs and whispered about the Emergencies Act's dormant economic levers. Shadows from that calculus would stretch far into the week to come, but in Windsor, for the first time in six nights, the bridge lights traced an unbroken ribbon of headlights toward I-75—commerce inching back, meter by metre, from the brink.

From the predawn hush of February 14 2022—steam still ghosting from manhole lids beside the shuttered trucks on Wellington Street—Prime Minister Justin Trudeau's inner circle filed into the Privy Council boardroom and reached, almost with audible reluctance, for the Emergencies Act. The decision was sealed before the smell of burnt coffee dissipated, three hours before the *Reuters* headline hit screens: Canada declared a public-order emergency for the first time in its history. [27]

The statute's financial teeth were the point of the spear. Within minutes, deputy ministers were paging through fresh regulations that let Ottawa order banks, insurers, and even crowdfunding platforms to freeze any account *reasonably believed* to be fuelling an illegal blockade, and no court order was required. [28] At the same hour in Washington, a senior U.S. trade official skimmed the Canadian cables and muttered to a colleague that this was *the federal powers nudge we asked for* after days of White House prodding to end the trade chaos. [29]

Markets reacted with the skittishness of horses before a storm. Currency desks saw the loonie dip, bond spreads widen a hair, and *Bloomberg* terminals flashed an alert warning that protracted disruption could shave points off first-quarter GDP. [30] Yet the bigger jolt travelled not through equities but through log-in portals.

At 07:41, Neil Duarte—owner of Mid-Lake Freight, a 38-truck firm based in Thunder Bay—opened his banking app to approve payroll. The screen refreshed, then stalled on a terse banner: *Account unavailable—please contact the security department.* Duarte stared, thumb hovering uselessly over the *retry* icon. Five minutes later, the bank's fraud unit confirmed his corporate and personal chequing accounts were frozen under emergency directives; his fuel card provider had already followed suit. He yanked a notepad from his desk drawer and began tallying weekend invoices he could no longer pay. The *Global News* feed beside him replayed Chrystia Freeland's warning that *the consequences are real* and financial institutions were *moving now* to cut off convoy funds. [31]

Downtown, the first on-the-ground evidence of that clampdown surfaced when Toronto Dominion Bank admitted it had frozen two personal accounts holding CA$1.4 million raised for protesters. [32] By nightfall, the number of locked accounts would climb into the hundreds, a figure Deputy Prime Minister Freeland cited with lawyerly precision at a televised briefing: *210 accounts, CA$7.8 million.* [33]

Compliance departments scrambled. A BLG legal bulletin thudded into inboxes, spelling out brand-new duties for every bank, credit union, and crypto exchange: conduct continuous scans for *designated persons,* yank their access instantly, and enjoy indemnity from civil suits while doing so. [34] In parallel, a DLA Piper memo walked payment-service start-ups through emergency amendments that forced them, overnight, into anti-money-laundering registration with FINTRAC. [35]

For small businesses, the impacts were less abstract. Two blocks south of Parliament, Lana Habib counted out the weekend's cash at her café, Diesel & Dough, and winced: sales were down 83 per cent since the horns started. Uncertain about whether her merchant terminal would be flagged next, she slid the bills into a bank envelope. When an R.C.M.P. officer ordered a takeout espresso, she asked how long the clampdown on accounts would last. *Ma'am,* he sighed, *that's above my pay grade—we're trying to unfurl an octopus one tentacle at a time.*

Outside the shop, police lines were indeed advancing. A Canada Border Services Agency situation sheet logged protest pressure easing at border points but warned of "latent risks" if funding channels reopened. [36] Meanwhile, financial analysts noted the surreal split-screen: equity traders in glass towers speculating on supply-chain rebounds while truck owners like Duarte called fuel suppliers begging for a 48-hour grace.

17 February brought a televised crescendo. Freeland, flanked by R.C.M.P. brass, confirmed the first batch of frozen assets and promised more. [37] Duarte watched the clip from his despatcher's desk, then tried once more to move CA$6,200 for driver per diems—blocked again. He laughed, a short bark, and quipped to nobody, *Guess diesel is on the house—if the house hadn't been repossessed.*

"In the silence of a bridge choked by defiance, we learn that democracy's true torque isn't measured in horsepower, but in the grip between the governed and their government."

Across Ottawa's secured perimeter, tow trucks finally rolled through drifting snow, their operators indemnified by the same emergency powers that let banks ice accounts. In the House of Commons gallery on 21 February, the mood swung between legalistic and operatic as MPs debated the motion to confirm the declaration. When the Speaker announced the tally—185 yea, 151 nay—the air left the chamber like steam from a kettle. [38] Backbench Liberals hugged; Conservatives shook their heads; New Democrats stared into the middle distance, knowing their support had kept the measures alive. The electronic board still glowed when staff updated the public website, recording the vote for posterity. [39]

Outside, Wellington Street lay oddly orderly: concrete barriers, checkpoint gates, the diesel ghosts of three chaotic weeks gone. Yet the political heat persisted. Although the streets were clear, the government claimed it needed extra powers to prevent future problems, which angered critics who said the government was overstepping its authority. [40]

Two days later, the calculus flipped again. With border traffic normalised and financial taps largely sealed, Trudeau stood at a lectern and announced he would revoke the Act at 17:00 on 23 February: *The situation is no longer an emergency.* [41] *Bloomberg's* instant read was upbeat—Canadian banks had already unfrozen *the vast majority* of the CA$7.8 million once immobilised, signalling a rapid thaw. [30] For Duarte, the unfreeze notice hit his email just after sunset; he wired forty overdue fuel payments in a single burst and sent a relief-emoji to every driver.

Not everyone bounced back so fast. Lana Habib's café reopened fully on 24 February, but her weekly ledger still ran red. "The Emergencies Act lasted nine days," she told a *CTV* stringer, "but the chill feels longer." She set a tip jar beside the register labelled "For the next crisis—whatever it is."

While merchants tallied losses, the number-crunchers at Statistics Canada were already drafting the economy's first post-mortem. On 15 March a flash GDP note estimated February output had slipped 0.5 per cent, with transportation-equipment manufacturing hardest hit—a downtick small on a chart, visceral on assembly lines. [42] Jia Li, a junior analyst assigned to the brief, added a line about "temporary but pronounced supply-chain stressors linked to public-order events" and muttered that it sounded like a euphemism for three weeks of horns. Cabinet staff, receiving an embargoed copy, highlighted passages on reputational harm to the business climate and appended a question: *Model long-term FDI impact?*

By then, lawsuits were already drafting. Civil-liberties groups filed applications arguing the freeze orders were *over-broad and unconstitutional,* [43] and planners sketched the mandate for a forthcoming Public Order Emergency Commission. This inquiry would later mine every memo, bank directive, and police logbook quoted in these pages.

Yet on that late-February evening, as cash flowed again and Parliament Hill exhaled, the story seemed—for a flicker—to have reached its coda. Trucks rumbled along reopened highways, factory shift-bells resumed their 06:00 chirp, and Neil Duarte signed off an all-hands email with a sardonic flourish: "Let's hope the next national emergency accepts e-transfers." The rhyme of history, Twain might have said, was already rehearsing its next verse.

ENDNOTES

[1] Transport Canada. (2022, February 17). *16. Economic impact of the blockades.* Government of Canada. https://tc.canada.ca/en/binder/16-economic-impact-blockades

[2] Gordon, J., & Nickel, R. (2022, February 8). *Pandemic border protests strand cattle and car parts, snarling Canada-U.S. trade.* Reuters. https://www.reuters.com/world/americas/pandemic-border-protests-strand-cattle-car-parts-snarling-canada-us-trade-2022-02-08

[3] Mehler Paperny, A., & Shakil, I. (2022, February 8). *Key U.S.–Canada border crossing blocked by truckers fighting Trudeau's COVID curbs.* Reuters. https://www.reuters.com/world/americas/angry-canada-truckers-block-busiest-bridge-with-us-trudeau-faces-grilling-2022-02-08

[4] Lindeman, T. (2022, February 9). *The U.S.–Canada bridge blockade risks huge economic damage, governments warn.* The Guardian. https://www.theguardian.com/world/2022/feb/09/us-auto-plants-face-shortages-shutdowns-layoffs-protesters-block-canada-bridge

[5] Associated Press. (2022, February 9). *COVID-19 truck blockade in Canada shuts down Ford plant.* AP News. https://apnews.com/article/coronavirus-pandemic-business-health-prince-edward-canada-6f60c879c0c2eff82235e3157ad79bb0

[6] Reuters Staff. (2022, February 9). *Canadian government ministers label bridge blockade 'unlawful'.* Reuters. https://www.reuters.com/world/americas/canadian-govt-ministers-label-bridge-blockade-covid-protests-illegal-2022-02-09

[7] Veneza, R. (2022, February 9). *Ambassador Bridge closure impacts production at local auto plants.* CTV News. https://www.ctvnews.ca/windsor/article/ambassador-bridge-closure-impacts-production-at-local-auto-plants

[8] LaForest, A. (2022, February 10). *Auto supply chain reeling from U.S.–Canada bridge blockade, industry groups say.* Automotive News. https://www.autonews.com/manufacturing/us-canada-bridge-blockade-adding-strain-auto-supply-chain-industry-groups-say

[9] Muller, J. (2022, February 10). *Toyota and Ford deepen production cuts as Canada protest blocks Ambassador Bridge.* Axios. https://www.axios.com/2022/02/10/canada-vaccine-protest-toyota-ford

[10] U.S. Chamber of Commerce. (2022, February 10). *Business leaders urge resolution of U.S.–Canada border blockade.* https://www.uschamber.com/international/business-leaders-urge-resolution-of-u-s-canada-border-blockade

[11] Smith, Z. (2022, February 11). *Judge authorizes Canadian police to clear protesters blocking crucial bridge to U.S.* Forbes. https://www.forbes.com/sites/zacharysmith/2022/02/11/judge-authorizes-canadian-police-to-clear-protesters-blocking-crucial-bridge-to-us

[12] Ontario Superior Court of Justice. (2022, February 11). *Notice of court order concerning access to the Ambassador Bridge.* Government of Ontario. https://news.ontario.ca/en/bulletin/1001597/notice-of-court-order-concerning-access-to-the-ambassador-bridge

[13] Mehler Paperny, A., & Williams, N. (2022, February 11). *Ontario court grants injunction to end U.S.–Canada border blockade.* Reuters. https://www.reuters.com/world/americas/ontario-court-grants-injunction-end-us-canada-border-blockade-2022-02-11

[14] Leonard, J., & Murray, B. (2022, February 10). *Trucker protests threaten Canada with inflation, negative growth.* Bloomberg News. https://www.bloomberg.com/news/articles/2022-02-10/trucker-protests-threaten-canada-with-inflation-negative-growth

[15] The White House. (2022, February 11). *Press briefing by Press Secretary Jen Psaki and National Security Advisor Jake Sullivan.* https://www.whitehouse.gov/briefing-room/press-briefings/2022/02/11/press-briefing-by-press-secretary-jen-psaki-and-national-security-advisor-jake-sullivan-february-11-2022

[16] Reuters. (2022, February 11). *Auto parts maker Magna sees initial hit from Canadian bridge blockade.* Reuters. https://www.reuters.com/business/autos-transportation/auto-parts-maker-magna-sees-industry-recovery-2022-2022-02-11

[17] Karkaria, U. (2022, February 11). *'Almost no one is making parts': Ambassador Bridge blockade cripples suppliers.* Automotive News. https://www.autonews.com/2022-border-blockade/almost-no-one-making-parts-ambassador-bridge-blockade-cripples-suppliers

[18] Canada Border Services Agency. (2022, February 25). *Study on convoy blockades.* Government of Canada. https://www.cbsa-asfc.gc.ca/transparency-transparence/pd-dp/bbp-rpp/secu/2022-02-25/overview-apercu-eng.html

[19] Ontario Superior Court of Justice. (2022, February 11). *Interim interlocutory injunction—*City of Windsor v. *John Doe et al.* https://nathanson.osgoode.yorku.ca/wp-content/uploads/2023/05/Ambassador-Bridge-Injunction-ISSUED-Order-Morawetz-FEB-11-2022-CV-22-30791.pdf

[20] Osorio, C., & Volcovici, V. (2022, February 12). *Canada braces for action at U.S. border bridge blocked by protesters despite court order.* Reuters. https://www.reuters.com/world/americas/canada-braces-action-us-border-bridge-blocked-by-protesters-despite-court-order-2022-02-12

[21] Kight, S. (2022, February 12). *Blockade at Canada border begins to clear after police enforcement. Axios.* https://www.axios.com/2022/02/12/police-clearing-vaccine-mandate-protestors-canada

[22] Williams, N., & Beattie, A. (2022, February 13). *U.S.–Canada bridge reopens after police clear protesters. Reuters.* https://www.reuters.com/world/americas/canada-protesters-police-deadlocked-tensions-simmer-blocked-border-bridge-2022-02-13

[23] Sullivan, B. (2022, February 13). *Bridge linking U.S. and Canada reopens after police remove last protesters. NPR.* https://www.npr.org/2022/02/13/1080469644/ambassador-bridge-us-canada-covid-protesters-cleared-by-police

[24] Canadian Manufacturers & Exporters, Canadian Produce Marketing Association, & 70 co-signatories. (2022, February 11). *Open letter from Canadian businesses to our elected representatives* [PDF]. https://cpma.ca/docs/default-source/corporate/2022/2022-02-11-blockade-statement-vfinal_signed-en.pdf

[25] Duplicate of #1

[26] Al Jazeera. (2022, February 13). *Key U.S.–Canada bridge reopens after police clear final protesters.* https://www.aljazeera.com/news/2022/2/13/canada-resumes-clearing-protesters-from-us-border-bridge

[27] Reuters. (2022, February 14). *Canada's Trudeau invokes emergency powers in bid to end protests. Reuters.* https://www.reuters.com/world/americas/canada-police-response-protests-spotlight-after-key-bridge-us-cleared-2022-02-14

[28] Reuters. (2022, February 14). *Canada's Emergencies Act: What it would allow to quell protests. Reuters.* https://www.reuters.com/world/americas/canadas-emergencies-act-what-it-would-allow-quell-protests-against-pandemic-2022-02-14

[29] Reuters. (2022, February 10). *U.S. urges Canada to use federal powers to ease border protest. Reuters.* https://www.reuters.com/world/americas/us-canada-border-closures-risk-trade-more-govt-action-is-likely-2022-02-10

[30] Bloomberg News. (2022, February 23). *Trudeau repeals emergency powers after quelling truck protests.* https://www.bloomberg.com/news/articles/2022-02-23/trudeau-to-repeal-emergency-powers-after-quelling-truck-protest

[31] Global News. (2022, February 17). *'The consequences are real': Freeland says action has begun on cutting off convoy funds* [Video]. https://globalnews.ca/video/8627701/the-consequences-are-real-freeland-says-action-has-begun-on-cutting-off-convoy-funds

[32] Reuters. (2022, February 12). *TD Bank freezes two accounts that received funds to support Canada protests. Reuters.* https://www.reuters.com/world/americas/td-bank-freezes-two-accounts-that-received-funds-support-canada-protests-2022-02-12

[33] Ray, S. (2022, February 23). *Canada begins to release frozen bank accounts of 'Freedom Convoy' protesters.* Forbes. https://www.forbes.com/sites/siladityaray/2022/02/23/canada-begins-to-release-frozen-bank-accounts-of-freedom-convoy-protestors

[34] Borden Ladner Gervais LLP. (2022, February 15). *Emergencies Act order: Obligations for financial and payment services providers.* https://www.blg.com/en/insights/2022/02/obligations-of-financial-services-providers-and-payment-services-providers

[35] DLA Piper. (2022, August 23). *FINTRAC changes due to truckers convoy.* https://www.dlapiper.com/es-pr/insights/publications/2022/08/fintrac-changes-due-to-truckers-convoy

[36] Duplicate of #18

[37] Associated Press. (2022, February 17). *Canadian police arrest convoy leaders as bank freezes begin.* AP News. https://apnews.com/article/coronavirus-pandemic-health-canada-ontario-ottawa-c9d1b0d9d29625eff62d4be8e8d3c259

[38] Politico. (2022, February 21). *Trudeau wins House vote on Emergencies Act.* https://www.politico.com/news/2022/02/21/trudeau-wins-house-vote-emergencies-act-00010474

[39] House of Commons of Canada. (2022, February 21). *Vote detail #32—Confirmation of public order emergency.* https://www.ourcommons.ca/members/en/votes/44/1/32

[40] Cecco, L. (2022, February 22). *Canada maintains emergency powers after trucker blockades ended.* The Guardian. https://www.theguardian.com/world/2022/feb/22/canada-extends-emergency-powers-after-trucker-blockades-ended

[41] The Washington Post. (2022, February 23). *Trudeau revokes Emergencies Act against 'Freedom Convoy' blockades.* https://www.washingtonpost.com/world/2022/02/23/canada-trudeau-revokes-emergencies-act/

[42] Statistics Canada. (2022, April 29). *Gross domestic product by industry, February 2022* (*The Daily*). Government of Canada. https://www150.statcan.gc.ca/n1/daily-quotidien/220429/dq220429a-eng.htm

CHAPTER TEN:

SIDESTREETS OF STORM AND STILLNESS

"They say Ottawa's side streets were quiet, but I know a riot can hide in silence as well as in sound. Sometimes, the storm isn't the shouting or the horns but the way people look away when a neighbour's window rattles. In the cold, even the bravest men check the locks twice—because sometimes trouble chooses stillness for its cover."
~ R.G. Cruise

Canada's approach to public order drew two very different cartoons of itself between the summer knees of 2020 and the diesel horns of 2022: one sketch showed helmeted lines moving quickly on crowds chanting "Black Lives Matter," the other portrayed constables bow-legged with caution as tractor-trailers the size of prairie barns idled in the capital. Sociologists would later call it "dual policing," a kind of centrifugal gospel in which force spins outward toward bodies marked Black, Brown, or Indigenous while leniency pools gently around mostly white grievance. Ottawa's numbers confessed the rift—Black residents faced police force almost five times more than statistical chance would predict, the service's 2020 race-data report admitted, even as the same force courted convoy organisers with liaison texts and patient smiles. [1] The gap was no mere accounting error; it was philosophy wearing a badge.

5 June 2020, put that philosophy on global display. By 15:00, a heat shimmer rose off Parliament Hill, and a banner reading, *NO PEACE UNTIL JUSTICE*, billowed against the Peace Tower stones. Thousands pressed shoulder to sweaty shoulder—nurses in scrubs, skateboard kids, grandmothers draped in

the red, black, and green. They fell silent for eight minutes and forty-six seconds, recalling a knee on George Floyd's neck. The hill thundered with *Black Lives Matter!* like a geyser of unmet prayers. [2] Prime Minister Justin Trudeau joined the swell, dropping one knee on trampled grass as cameras whirred, a gesture sceptics called *performative in polyester socks.* [3] When he rose, the crowd parted like curtains and the chant rolled south toward the Human Rights Monument, leaving behind the faint smell of hand sanitiser and sun-warmed cardboard.

Activist Shakira Dorsey addressed the sea of signage from the library steps: *We are not here for a photo-op. We are here for breathing room.* A gust flipped her script, but she carried on, voice serrated with grief. Ottawa Police monitored from brown SUVs, ticket pads closed. By dusk, however, riot vans idled off Elgin, and when marchers circled back to the Hill for a candlelight vigil, officers moved in to *encourage dispersal* under pandemic orders. Protesters recited Section 2 of the Charter; constables replied with megaphones. No arrests, but the message was clear: nightfall shortens the leash. Reporters noted the rapid mobilisation, contrasting it with softer tones used at earlier anti-lockdown rallies of predominantly white demonstrators that spring. [4]

Summer bled into autumn, and across the country, Indigenous vigils flickered against colonial timelines. On Vancouver Island's Fairy Creek blockade, Pacheedaht land defenders and settler allies linked arms on 22 August 2021, singing over slow drums. R.C.M.P. officers advanced in olive fatigues; one protester likened them to *a logging company's infantry.* When the crowd refused to unlock, aerosol hissed through cedars, pepper spray misting the forest like cruel incense. *There was no aggression*—witness Kathleen Code told *Global News*—*just song.* [5] The footage would loop for days: orange bear spray clashing with the orange shirts of Every Child Matters.

Two weeks later, Ottawa Police tabled their first race-based Use-of-Force audit. Black residents, 7.5 per cent of the city, comprised 28 per cent of force recipients; Middle-Eastern residents, 4 per cent of the city, tallied 12 per cent of incidents. The report's sober prose could not hide its pulse: *This is unacceptable.* Training hours, de-escalation modules, equity, diversity, and inclusion (EDI) task forces—a framework to ensure fair treatment and full participation of all individuals—pages of contrition framed by pie charts. [1] Community advocates answered with their math: *numbers without consequences equal weather forecasts without umbrellas.*

Yet policing culture is less ledger than muscle memory. When early chatter of a *Freedom Convoy* surfaced in January 2022, Ottawa's traffic unit assured City Hall the demonstration would last *two, maybe three days,* accommodating roughly 800 vehicles. Situation reports logged at the Public Order Emergency Commission (POEC) recorded words like *fluid, cooperative,* and *peaceful*—phrases rarely assigned to racial-justice marches. [6] Inside the Ottawa Police Service (O.P.S.) headquarters, whiteboards mapped traffic diversions, leaving arrest protocols blank. One sergeant quipped, *We're greeters with radios.*

29 January dawned brittle and bright. Convoy rigs rumbled up Kent Street, chrome mirrors catching sunspots like mirrored shields. Residents who had marched mask-clad in 2020 watched truckers gulp coffee in cabs plastered with *MANDATE FREEDOM* decals. When horns blasted, by-laws lay dormant; when open fires flickered in city parks, ticket books stayed pocketed. A Centretown mother tweeted, *Last year they shut our rally down at 9 p.m.; this year they're delivering wood.* The tweet went viral under the hashtag *#DoubleStandard.* Analysts later coined starker terms: *'settler leniency,' 'responsible whiteness.'* The Yellowhead Institute's policy brief would cite the episode as Exhibit A in structural racism north of the forty-ninth parallel. [7]

Not everyone in blue agreed with the light touch. In a closed-door after-action debrief leaked months later, one constable asked, *Are we policing or chaperoning?* The question ricocheted through the command chain until Chief Peter Sloly warned the Council, "There may not be a police solution." Downtown shopkeepers heard that as surrender. The People's Commission on the Convoy recorded 200 testimonies of harassment and assault, met with what witnesses called "a canopy of observation but no intervention." [8] A pastor recounted officers shrugging as they shoved him for wearing a mask. A community-health director said paramedics needed police escorts to deliver insulin. The word *abandoned* appears 73 times in the commission's final volume.

That leniency flipped like a coin three weeks and countless sleepless nights later. On 19 February, R.C.M.P. tactical teams pushed down Wellington Street, the same ground where anti-racism marchers had kneeled twenty months earlier. Pepper spray bloomed over the rigs; stun grenades cracked like splitting ice. Interim chief Steve Bell called it "slow and methodical," yet *The Guardian's* headline spoke of scuffles and clouds. [9] To some observers, the tactic looked less like justice delayed than optics managed: decisive enough to reassure Washington and Bay Street, late enough to avoid framing whiteness as a threat.

The contrast did not escape pollsters. In a February 2023 survey, two-thirds of Canadians said police treat some protests more gently than others—no citation needed for those still smelling diesel in their curtains. [10] Editorial pages debated whether policing should be *colour blind* or *colour-aware,* as though the last two years were colourless. Meanwhile, Parliament scheduled hearings on use-of-force guidelines; Indigenous leaders requested a moratorium on militarised actions at land-back camps; civil-liberties lawyers filed access-to-information requests thick enough to door-stop a squad car.

By the eve of the convoy's arrival—29 January 2022—Ottawa was a stage set with two lighting cues: one harsh and immediate for racial-justice demonstrators, the other dim and deferential for the king-size cabs rolling toward Parliament. The next chapter would show how those cues collided, but the unease was already threading through coffee lines and council chambers. In the words of an elderly protester who watched both eras from a folding chair near the Eternal Flame: *We keep arguing about who owns the street. Maybe the street is asking who owns us.* The answer, still forming in exhaust and echo, waited for the first horn blast to dredge it into daylight.

The first formal police *vacate* notices on 30 January 2022 landed like a polite cough in a foghorn factory, yet they marked the moment Ottawa's three-week impasse shifted from surprise guest to hostile tenant; Public Safety Canada's running timeline logged that warning as the opening beat in a crescendo of pleas for reinforcements that would grow louder by the hour. [11] Two days later, a White House aide urged Canadian ministers to *'use federal powers'* before a stalled Ambassador Bridge kneecapped continental trade. The advice crackled across cabinet teleconferences like a smoke alarm no one could reach to silence. [12] Meanwhile, an *Angus Reid* poll found three Canadians in four wanted the big-rig chorus gone. Two-thirds blamed Ottawa's political handling for fanning the flames—public patience sagging like a snow-loaded eave. [13] By 6 February, Mayor Jim Watson declared a municipal state of emergency, warning that diesel fumes and sleepless residents had pushed the capital *well past the breaking point.* [14]

Democracy, it seems, wears two faces: one stern and unyielding to the pleas of Black bodies begging only to breathe, the other smiling indulgence at the thunder of diesel, as if largesse were owed to anyone who honks loud enough.

On Coventry Road, Ontario Provincial Police Chief Supt. Carson Pardy sketched a crimson centipede on the grease-board map—one segment for every blockaded truck—and told the mixed O.P.S.-O.P.P. planners, "You can't tow a centipede; you have to cut it." [15] Fresh Hendon intelligence reports, still flecked with toner dust, warned of *rising anti-police sentiment* and *foot traffic volatility*, but offered no surgical answer beyond heightened caution. [16] When a junior analyst proposed an overnight fuel-seizure blitz, Pardy merely tapped the map's red dots and said, *Every jerrycan you grab hardens the line tenfold.*

Downtown, lawyer Paul Champ nursed lukewarm coffee in the Elgin Street Diner while polishing his injunction brief. "Irreparable harm is measured in decibels," he muttered, before telling Justice Hugh McLean that residents had counted 14,000 horn blasts in a single day. The judge's ruling on 7 February landed before sundown: ten days of court-ordered silence on every air-horn in the core. [17] Truck cabs answered with sub-woofers thumping outlaw country, the legal equivalent of swapping a trumpet for a tuba.

Just off Sussex Drive, restaurateur Sarah Chown watched diesel haze wiggle the neon of her Metropolitain Brasserie sign. *My corner's Ottawa's hottest nightclub,* she told a CityNews mic, listing open flames, public drinking, and defecation among the nightly attractions. [18] Valentine's reservations evaporated; staff scrubbed phantom lipstick from unused stemware while convoy TikToks racked up millions of views.

Back in brass-and-bleach command posts, police brass tried a new acronym. At 20:12 on 12 February, the Ottawa Police Service announced an Integrated Command Centre (ICC), promising an *enhanced ability* to coordinate with O.P.P. and R.C.M.P. and boasting of intercepting a rogue fuel truck even as 4,000 demonstrators clogged the core. [19] *CityNews* pushed a parallel bulletin an hour later, noting that planners still had no timeline for clearing the streets, only fresh flow-charts heavy on arrows and light on tow-hooks. [25]

That same weekend, convoy lawyer Keith Wilson unfurled a letter from Mayor Watson proposing détente: move big rigs off residential streets in exchange for good-faith talks. Organiser Tamara Lich weighed the optics under a traffic light in Kent, fogging the paper. *Many citizens and businesses have been cheering us on,* she wrote, *but we are also disturbing others. That was never our intent.* [20] Her signed reply, later posted to DocumentCloud, promised to "work hard to get buy-in from the truckers," though drivers taped the mayor's request to windshields like novelty parking tickets. [21] By Monday noon, fewer than one in five trucks budged, and liaison officers radioed the ICC: *compliance partial, morale high, music louder.*

Inside City Hall's Emergency Operations Centre, auditors taking contemporaneous notes observed that municipal traffic experts had never been invited to early police briefings; later, their audit would conclude that "nobody asked the cartographers until the map was on fire." [22] On Parliament's West Block, a House committee heard O.P.P. Deputy Commissioner Chris Harkins and Chief Supt. Pardy describes "dysfunction" inside O.P.S. during the first convoy weekend and defends the need for an integrated planning cell to stitch together rival playbooks. [23] Internal O.P.P. notes from that cell bragged of a *small-team rock-stars* approach but quietly bemoaned shortages of heavy wreckers and the legal muscle to compel their use. [24]

By 13 February, the ICC's dry-erase columns gleamed with finality: forty-five tactical platoons, layered arrest perimeters, and leaflets threatening the seizure of licences, pets, and bank accounts should drivers refuse to roll. In cafés that had survived two pandemic winters only to suffocate under diesel dusk, baristas scrawled poll figures on chalkboards—*72 % WANT U.S. GONE*—hoping numbers might shame air-horns where by-laws had not. The international lens widened: *Reuters* led its world wire with Ottawa gridlock; *CNN* cut between drone shots of Parliament and stock footage of empty auto-plant lines; the *Guardian* juxtaposed maskless revelry with Nova Scotia R.C.M.P., ticketing Mi'kmaq fishers for land-defence bonfires.

Superintendent Pardy capped his marker just before midnight, studying the Roman-numeraled enforcement phases. *If we pull this trigger,* he told the circle of commanders, *Parliament will own the echo.* Outside, horns revved one more ragged chorus as snow dusted chrome. On a finance minister's desk across Wellington lay a draft memorandum: *Asset freeze authorities—contingent on Emergencies Act proclamation.* The fuse between street-level standoff and federal sledgehammer had grown tinder-dry; all awaited was the clock's next tick into 14 February.

The clock had hardly finished its first midnight stroke on 14 February 2022 when *Order-in-Council SOR/2022-20* flickered onto the Justice Canada website. This crown-sealed paragraph declared *a public order emergency exists throughout Canada.* [26] Within minutes, the same banner lit the federal policing portal—Government declares a public-order emergency to end blockades and the occupation of Ottawa, planting the Emergencies Act in the public record for the first time since its quiet birth in 1988. [27] Scholars jolted from sleep to field media requests, equal parts awed and anxious: the statute's threshold—threats to the security of Canada so grave no province could cope, had leapt from moot-court hypothetical to constitutional bedrock overnight. [28]

The measure's reach unspooled before dawn. Ottawa Police Service tweeted a sketch of a red cordon from the Rideau Canal to Bronson Avenue and down Highway 417—*NO SAFE HAVEN*, the scroll read, warning that anyone inside without lawful business faced arrest at nearly 100 checkpoints. [29] On Kent Street, trucker spokesperson Tamara Lich woke to find her banking app frozen—*financial entity unable to complete your request*—a blunt, digital padlock shared by 206 other flagged accounts worth roughly CA$7.8 million. [30] She screenshot the message, thumbed it to co-organiser Chris Barber, and typed: *They've gone for the gas money.*

By breakfast, Parliament Hill resembled a citadel. Tactical officers in olive fatigues replaced liaison teams in neon vests; R.C.M.P. snipers padded onto rooftops dusted with hoarfrost; portable fencing clanked into place like an oversized child's playpen. At 08:30, interim O.P.S. chief Steve Bell informed the cabinet via a secure line that 1,275 officers from eleven police forces were now under a single command spine, "clear outcome: retake the core." Across the Integrated Command Centre river, Superintendent Carson Pardy of the O.P.P. traced a crimson *Phase I* arrow on the wipe-board: Freeze, Warn, Fracture. Beside it, an R.C.M.P. planner pencilled time hacks—*09:00 leaflets, 11:00 strategic fuel seizure, 15:00 targeted arrests*—culled from Project Natterjack's still-draft after-action notes on prior border clearances. [34]

09:07 a bilingual sheet slid under every windshield: *You must leave the area now. Your vehicle and property are subject to seizure under the Emergencies Act.* In

Wellington, a Saskatchewan family who had lived three weeks in a Peterbilt bunkhouse loaded blankets into a Ford minivan while their youngest taped a crayon sign—*BYE OTTAWA*—inside the fogged rear window. *I thought we'd be here till maple buds,* the father said, voice cracking. Two rigs over, a diesel mechanic from Trois-Rivières shouted, *Hold the line!* but his neighbour replied, *Line's at the bank now, buddy.*

By noon, Finance Minister Chrystia Freeland addressed reporters in a Parliament foyer ringed by cameras: the Act authorised institutions to *immediately freeze or suspend* accounts linked to the convoy, no court order required, and civil immunity granted for acting in good faith. [30] The Toronto Stock Exchange dipped twenty-seven points, then levelled as traders gauged whether liquidity panic would ripple beyond the protest footprint. South of the border, a White House spokesperson praised the *decisive step,* noting that the Ambassador Bridge clog had shaved US$300 million a day off bilateral trade the week before.

On Tuesday the 15th, the red zone tightened like a noose. O.P.S. loud-hailers boomed street names as "no-go"; anyone inside risked tickets up to CA$5,000. A volunteer paralegal collective, Legal Observers Ottawa, hustled laminated rights cards through tent rows: *Ask for badge numbers. Demand counsel. Do not resist, but do not consent.* Some drivers tucked the cards under rosaries dangling from rear-view mirrors. That night inside the Château Laurier ballroom—commandeered as Liberal caucus war-room—MPs peppered the cabinet with hastily muted Zoom questions: had the Charter been lawyer-proofed? Who unfreezes Grandma's joint account if she co-signed a rig lease? Staffers scribbled talking points while television screens looped the b-roll of armoured vehicles behind the Peace Tower.

Wednesday delivered the first coordinated push. At 10:30, platoons in high-vis jackets advanced five-abreast down Rideau, flanked by mounted units whose horses' breath plumed in the minus-15 °C air. Officers seized jerrycans, tucking them into cube vans marked: *EVIDENCE.* "That's our heat!" yelled a Manitoba farmer; an R.C.M.P. corporal responded, "Take it up with Parliament." Across Metcalfe, police arrested Tamara Lich on mischief charges; video of her being led away in cuffs garnered five million TikTok views by dusk. [33] Convoy Telegram channels lit with frantic red light emojis while moderates urged a tactical pullback.

Thursday's Financial Measures Regulations landed in the *Canada Gazette* at 01:12, widening the freeze to crypto wallets and crowdfunding rails. *BBC* headlines distilled the moment: Trudeau vows to freeze protesters' bank accounts. [28] By sunrise, a GoFundMe-style platform emailed users: *All transactions temporarily suspended pending FINTRAC guidance.* One Alberta donor tweeted, *My twenty bucks to feed truckers just labelled terror.* Opposition MPs convened a 06:45 caucus call; a rural member fumed, "This is martial law by algorithm."

On Friday the 18th, the city cracked. O.P.S. declared a secure area and funnelled all traffic through roughly 100 checkpoints—passes only for residents, media, and essential staff. [29] Inside the cordon, police in riot helmets pressed south from Wellington behind lines of green-camo tactical teams. *AP* reporters counted over 100 arrests by mid-afternoon, among them an ex-military corporal carrying smoke grenades. [31] A grey mare from Toronto's mounted unit surged, scattering protesters; footage of a bicycle tossed under the horse's hooves ricocheted across newsfeeds, prompting duelling narratives of brutality and restraint.

Pepper spray drifted over Sparks at twilight, stinging eyes inside shuttered cafés where owners had already lost a month's revenue. *Diesel was bad,* barista Laila Jabeur muttered, wiping counters where no customers approached, *but cayenne in the HVAC is worse.* Outside, officers shattered a Kenworth's driver-side window to haul out a man who had chained himself to the steering wheel while livestreaming. *The Guardian* headline stamped the day: Ottawa police use pepper spray and stun grenades to clear trucker protest. [32]

By Saturday dawn, 170 arrests and 53 vehicles towed stood on the police scoreboard; *CTV News* reported 100 checkpoints still active, the downtown grid now a patchwork of jersey barriers and snow-fenced sidewalks. [33] Interim chief Bell declared, *We have taken back Wellington Street,* while cautioning that asset-forfeiture investigations would *outlast the physical removal.* In a tent near City Hall, Legal Aid volunteers compiled affidavits from detainees claiming frozen lines of credit prevented bail payments. One paralegal phoned Scotiabank's emergency hotline only to be told, *Account restricted under federal directive—no override.*

On Sunday, the 20th, the House of Commons launched a 10:00 debate on ratifying the Act. MPs spoke over a gallery restricted to the press: Liberals extolled the necessity; Conservatives warned of a *digital dragnet,* the NDP weighed civil liberties against *working-class residents held hostage. The Guardian* summarised the vote—185 to 151 affirming the Act, with powers to last a maximum of 30 days. [35] Outside, snowploughs scraped the last diesel-sooted ice from Wellington while city crews hoisted streetlamps bent by three weeks of flagpoles.

Through it all, convoy families trickled homeward. In the Saint-Laurent staging lot, a mother buckled her son into a booster seat beside a deflated beach ball. He asked if they had won. She answered, *Depends who keeps the receipt.* A man from Nova Scotia hugged a comrade, whispered, *We'll regroup in the spring.* An R.C.M.P. officer nearby remarked to a colleague, *Spring's above my pay grade.* They logged one more VIN for towing.

By the seventh day—21 February—the occupation's husk amounted to fenced curbs, 191 total arrests, and asset-freeze files thick as tax manuals. [36] The Act's gaze had shifted from roads to spreadsheets, where compliance officers ticked names on still-sealed ledgers. Constitutionalists sketched battle lines in committee rooms for inevitable court challenges: Was the threshold truly met? Could digital assets be property *used in a blockade?* Meanwhile, the R.C.M.P.'s national narrative review—Project Natterjack—warned that future protests would *adapt to financial countermeasures,* trading diesel for decentralised coin. [34]

Canada had unclasped a statutory backstop designed for war or insurrection and pointed it at a protest whose soundtrack was air-horns and outlaw ballads. The blockade ended; the precedent stayed. As the Peace Tower clock tolled midnight one week later—its bells echoing across newly emptied streets—civil-liberties advocates echoed Spanish-American philosopher George Santayana's admonition that ` *Those who cannot remember the past are condemned to repeat it.* The Emergencies Act now hummed a new stanza in the country's repertoire, promising that the next chorus of dissent would measure its volume against by-laws and barricades but against the chill of a frozen debit card.

ENDNOTES

[1] Ottawa Police Service. (2022, May 30). *Annual use of force report: 2020* [Report presented to the Ottawa Police Services Board]. Ottawa Police Service. https://www.ottawapolice.ca/en/who-we-are/resources/Documents/Reports-and-Publications/2020-Use-of-Force-Report.pdf

[2] Lord, C. (2020, June 5). Trudeau, thousands march in Ottawa anti-racism protest. *Global News.* https://globalnews.ca/news/7031781/peaceful-march-solidarity-black-community-ottawa

[3] Pinkerton, C. (2020, June 5). Prime Minister kneels at anti-racism rally on Parliament Hill. *iPolitics*. https://ipolitics.ca/2020/06/05/trudeau-appears-at-anti-racism-protest-in-ottawa-as-pressure-mounts-on-pm-to-act-beyond-condemnations/

[4] Ottawa Police Service. (n.d.). *Demonstrations and protests: Police Liaison Team overview*. Retrieved May 15, 2025, from https://www.ottawapolice.ca/en/news-and-updates/demonstrations-and-protests.aspx

[5] Johnson, P. (2021, August 22). Police deploy pepper spray, two injured, as tensions escalate at Fairy Creek blockade. *Global News*. https://globalnews.ca/news/8132747/fairy-creek-blockade-police-pepper-spray

[6] City of Ottawa. (2022). *Timeline of events relating to the Freedom Convoy* [Overview report, POEC Exhibit OTT.IR.00000002]. Public Order Emergency Commission. https://publicorderemergencycommission.ca/files/overview-reports/OTT.IR.00000002.pdf

[7] Stelkia, K. (2022, May 5). *What the Freedom Convoy protests reveal about structural racism in Canada* (Policy Brief No. 115). Yellowhead Institute. https://yellowheadinstitute.org/wp-content/uploads/2022/05/Stelkia-May-2022-Freedom-Convoy.pdf

[8] LeBrun, L. (2023, January 31). 'It was violent': People's Commission report shines light on hate crimes during Freedom Convoy. *PressProgress*. https://pressprogress.ca/it-was-violent-peoples-commission-report-shines-light-on-violence-harassment-and-hate-crimes-during-freedom-convoy

[9] Cecco, L. (2022, February 19). Ottawa police use pepper spray and stun grenades to clear trucker protest. *The Guardian*. https://www.theguardian.com/world/2022/feb/19/ottawa-police-pepper-spray-stun-grenades-trucker-protest

[10] Angus Reid Institute. (2024, May 2). *Protests and policing: Two-thirds say inconsistent treatment from authorities favours some groups over others* [Poll report]. Angus Reid Institute. https://angusreid.org/canada-protest-police-palestine-israel-gaza-freedom-convoy

[11] Public Safety Canada. (2022, October 13). *Evolution of the 2022 Freedom Convoy: Timelines of key events – January 25 to February 23, 2022* [Parliamentary committee notes]. Government of Canada. https://www.publicsafety.gc.ca/cnt/trnsprnc/brfng-mtrls/prlmntry-bndrs/20221013/04-en.aspx

[12] Osorio, C., Holland, S., & Shakil, I. (2022, February 11). U.S. urges Canada to use federal powers to ease border protest disruption. *Reuters*. https://www.reuters.com/world/americas/us-canada-border-closures-risk-trade-more-govt-action-is-likely-2022-02-11

[13] Angus Reid Institute. (2022, February 14). *Blockade backlash: Three-in-four Canadians tell convoy protesters "Go home now."* https://angusreid.org/trudeau-convoy-trucker-protest-vaccine-mandates-covid-19/

[14] Hagberg, L., & Ljunggren, D. (2022, February 6). Ottawa mayor declares state of emergency to deal with trucking blockade. *Reuters*. https://www.reuters.com/world/americas/protest-against-vaccine-mandates-paralyzing-canada-capital-mayor-says-2022-02-06

[15] Public Order Emergency Commission. (2022). *Witness summary: Chief Superintendent Carson Pardy, Ontario Provincial Police* (Exhibit WTS.00000033). https://publicorderemergencycommission.ca

[16] Ontario Provincial Police. (2022, January). *Project Hendon teleconference and situation reports* (POEC Exhibit OPP00004571). https://publicorderemergencycommission.ca/files/exhibits/OPP00004571.pdf

[17] The Canadian Press, & Ranger, M. (2022, February 7). Judge grants injunction against honking in downtown Ottawa. *CityNews Toronto.* https://toronto.citynews.ca/2022/02/07/ottawa-residents-protest-horn-honking-court

[18] CityNews Ottawa. (2022, February 12). Loud music, gas fumes, defecation: Business owner chronicles life in the heart of downtown Ottawa. https://ottawa.citynews.ca/2022/02/12/business-owner-chronicles-life-in-the-heart-of-downtown-ottawa-5058008

[19] Ottawa Police Service. (2022, February 12). *Ottawa Police Service establishes Integrated Command Centre to coordinate enforcement* [News release]. https://www.ottawapolice.ca/en/news/ottawa-police-service-establish-integrated-command-centre-to-coordinate-enforcement.aspx

[20] Boutilier, A. (2022, February 13). Ottawa mayor made a 'backchannel' deal to remove convoy from residential areas. *Global News.* https://globalnews.ca/news/8616979/ottawa-mayor-backchannel-deal-convoy

[21] Freedom Convoy Organizers. (2022, February 12). *Letter to Mayor Jim Watson responding to relocation proposal* [Correspondence]. DocumentCloud. https://www.documentcloud.org/documents/21293988

[22] Office of the Auditor General of Ottawa. (2023, February). *Audit of the City of Ottawa's response to the convoy protest.* https://www.oagottawa.ca/media/tklagr1h/final-audit-report-audit-of-the-city-of-ottawa-s-response-to-the-convoy-protest-1-final-ua.pdf

[23] Parliament of Canada. (2022, November 7). *Standing Committee on Public Safety and National Security (SECU), Evidence, No. 11* [Transcript]. https://www.ourcommons.ca/DocumentViewer/en/44-1/SECU/meeting-11/evidence

[24] Ontario Provincial Police. (2022, February). *Integrated Planning Cell notes* (POEC Exhibit OPP00001784). https://publicorderemergencycommission.ca/files/exhibits/OPP00001784.pdf

[25] CityNews Ottawa. (2022, February 13). Ottawa police create 'integrated command centre' to better control protest. https://ottawa.citynews.ca/2022/02/13/ottawa-police-create-integrated-command-centre-to-better-control-protest-5059119

[26] Government of Canada. (2022, February 14). *Proclamation declaring a public order emergency* (SOR/2022-20). https://laws-lois.justice.gc.ca/eng/regulations/SOR-2022-20/

[27] Government of Canada. (2022, February 14). *Declaration of public order emergency under the Emergencies Act.* https://www.canada.ca/en/services/policing/emergencies/public-order.html

[28] BBC News. (2022, February 15). What powers will Emergencies Act give Trudeau? *BBC News.* https://www.bbc.com/news/world-us-canada-60383385

29 Pringle, J., & Raymond, T. (2022, February 19). Police arrest 170 people, retake Wellington Street from convoy protesters in downtown Ottawa. *CTV News Ottawa*. https://www.ctvnews.ca/ottawa/police-arrest-170-people-retake-wellington-street-from-convoy-protesters-in-downtown-ottawa

30 Boutilier, A. (2022, February 22). 'Very unlikely' assets of most small-time donors to Freedom Convoy would be frozen, MPs told. *Global News*. https://globalnews.ca/news/8638430/unlikely-most-freedom-convoy-donors-assets-frozen/

31 Associated Press. (2022, February 18). Ottawa crackdown: Police arrest scores, tow vehicles as crackdown begins. *AP News*. https://apnews.com/article/canada-truck-blockade-protest-coronavirus-police-1f2c87b2c31fef9cdce65449a0035334

32 Cecco, L. (2022, February 19). Ottawa police use pepper spray and stun grenades to clear trucker protest. *The Guardian*. https://www.theguardian.com/world/2022/feb/19/ottawa-police-pepper-spray-stun-grenades-trucker-protest

33 Pringle, J., & Raymond, T. (2022, February 19). Ottawa police warn of 'red zone' and 100 checkpoints. *CTV News Ottawa*. https://www.ctvnews.ca/canada/freedom-convoy-protest-how-did-we-get-here/

34 Royal Canadian Mounted Police. (2023). *Project Natterjack: National after-action review into the RCMP response to the Freedom Convoy 2022*. RCMP. https://rcmp.ca/en/corporate-information/publications-and-manuals/project-natterjack-national-after-action-review

35 BBC News. (2022, February 22). Canada legislators back Trudeau on emergency powers. *BBC News*. https://www.bbc.com/news/world-us-canada-60472469

36 Kirby, P. (2022, February 22). Canada maintains emergency powers after trucker blockades ended. *The Guardian*. https://www.theguardian.com/world/2022/feb/22/canada-extends-emergency-powers-after-trucker-blockades-ended

CHAPTER ELEVEN:
FRONT PAGES AND FOGHORNS

"The trucks rolled in, loud and proud, like a brass band with a grudge. Journalists chased the noise, hoping to find a story before it found them. In the end, it was less about mandates and more about who could honk the longest without running out of gas."
~ R.G. Cruise

The first Peterbilt grille broke through the pale sunlight on Wellington Street just after dawn on 28 January 2022, its chrome gleam reflected in a hundred idle phone cameras; by noon, the hum had swollen into a low-frequency roar that rattled newsroom windows across the river, summoning every assignment editor in the country to the same question: "How long before spectacle sours into siege?" *Associated Press* copy hit the wires within the hour—*thousands descend on Ottawa to protest COVID mandates*—and every major outlet yanked producers off winter-storm duty to chase the convoy instead. [1]

Two pandemic years of variant curves and briefing podiums already inflamed Canada's information arteries, yet audiences still dialled the big red channels for guidance. In the CTV Ottawa control room on 30 January, senior producer Anjali Mehta scanned police tweets about forty-five road closures, then killed a lifestyle segment to make room for live helicopter shots of Parliament's frozen lawn. [2] Floor director Kevin Li shouted, "Stinger in three, two—" as the tease rolled: *CAPITAL IN GRIDLOCK: HOW LONG CAN OTTAWA COPE?* News anchor Graham Richardson frowned at the TelePrompter: "We have developing word tonight of multiple criminal investigations linked to the demonstration..." [3] A junior reporter hunched at a desk beside him, juggling TikTok lives from convoy influencers and official O.P.S. dispatch audio that sounded like a short-wave from another planet.

Across town in a fourth-floor ByWard Market walk-up, café owner Lina Farouk slammed out an email to every media tips inbox she could find. "PLEASE cover what's happening to small business," she typed, fingers numb from the draft blowing under her plywooded front door. "Horns are nonstop, receipts are zero." She attached a phone video of her patio chairs skating down Clarence Street in a diesel gust. Richardson read the plea aloud during the 18:00 pitch meeting; a field crew was on her stoop before the espresso machine cooled.

By the third day, 31 January, newsrooms were churning convoy explainers faster than they could update them. *NPR* filed a lunchtime despatch that called the protest "a roiling challenge to Canada's famously polite politics," warning listeners of the convoy's promised persistence. [4] That night, the *CBC National* anchor offered a grave monologue beneath the studio's violet lights: "Tonight, we bear witness to a blockade that threatens both livelihoods *and* our norms of peaceful protest," she intoned, voice clipped with prairie steel. The line landed moments after *BBC* web alerts quoted Prime Minister Justin Trudeau condemning the demonstration as "an insult to memory and truth," juxtaposing free expression with swastika banners captured in weekend drone footage. [5]

Legacy broadsheets, desperate to prove relevance in a push-alert age, splashed colour on their Tuesday front pages. *The Globe* ran a full-bleed photo of children roasting marshmallows beside a jackknifed tanker; the *National Post* countered with a 72-point headline—*CONVOY CHAOS DAY 5*—above an op-ed on "pandemic populism." Editors who once fretted about appearing alarmist now worried about looking asleep. When *Reuters* correspondent David Ljunggren typed the lede "Truck drivers blockading downtown Ottawa say they will stay as long as necessary," his desk chief in New York pushed for a stronger verb; by the final send, the trucks didn't *say*—they *vowed.* [6]

Inside Parliament's Centre Block press gallery, veteran scribbler Mahnoor Khan heard a vow echo through phone-call static. Her notebook filled with quotes: an Alberta haulier insisting, "We're the supply chain's backbone," a downtown resident shouting back, "You're its slipped disc!" The exchange became the sidebar for Wednesday's edition. Still, Khan tucked a quieter detail into paragraph nine:

Ottawa Public Health reports a spike in insomnia complaints linked to sustained 105-decibel horn blasts.

While reporters chronicled human drama, the money pipeline told its own story. On 5 February, GoFundMe yanked a $9-million campaign, citing "law-enforcement reports of unlawful activity." *The Guardian* splashed the takedown across its international homepage. [7] Within hours, convoy live streamers reframed the platform's decision as evidence of *globalist censorship,* a talking point quickly hoisted by sympathetic U.S. pundits. Editors at Canadian outlets groaned—another misinformation wildfire to chase in real time—yet dutifully booked digital-rights experts for weekend panels.

As Sunday rolled into Monday, police radios crackled with hardening language. Reporters on the night beat caught O.P.S. Chief Peter Sloly calling the situation a "siege," language the *Guardian* seized for its 7 February world-section lead after Mayor Jim Watson's emergency declaration hit city e-blasts. [8] *Global News* pushed a late-breaking video clip of politicians "seeking an end to the convoy amid the state of emergency," its Chyron red as warning tape. [9] In the *CTV* control room, editors debated whether to open the 11 p.m. with the mayor's executive powers or the latest arrest tally. "Harm first, then legality," Mehta decided, echoing an informal newsroom doctrine that public safety trumps procedural nuance when viewers are tired.

Even as mainstream outlets foregrounded escalating harm, assignment desks couldn't ignore the parallel universe flourishing on alternative feeds. *CityNews* would publish poll numbers within twenty-four hours, showing that 62 per cent of Canadians opposed the protest and nearly half sympathised with its frustrations—proof that the audience was fracturing. [10] Producers sensed a shape-shifting narrative: if one set of facts emphasised blocked ambulances and sleepless residents, another elevated freedom slogans and bonfire fellowship. National editors braced for the collision.

Camera operators negotiated ice crust and exhaust haze on the ground to keep lenses clear. *CTV* shooter Adam Desmarais wedged his tripod between two snowbanks on 5 February, just as police escorted a chuck-wagon stacked with diesel barrels away from the Hill. His footage, streaked with rotary beacons, looped on evening broadcasts as shorthand for the tension between enforcement and restraint. A protester leaned in off-camera: "Tell the truth, man—this is a party of patriots." Desmarais only shrugged; his battery light was blinking.

News Directors, meanwhile, started gaming worst-case scenarios. If a court order silenced the horns—rumour had it an injunction was in draft—would the convoy lose its soundtrack and thus its airtime? When that injunction arrived late on 7 February, CTV spliced courtroom audio, stating "irreparable harm in decibels" over a B-roll of suddenly muted truck cabs;[2] the network's legal analyst called it a "soundcheck on civil liberties," giving producers their pull-quote for the night.

When democracy trades its poetry for pragmatism, the soul sells its ticket to the highest bidder; yet if we laugh loud enough at our own reflection, perhaps we'll find the courage to reclaim our story.

By the end of 7 February, Ottawa's skyline glittered in the camera zooms, but the editorial horizon had already shifted. For legacy newsrooms, the story's next arc was surely enforcement: fines, tow trucks, maybe riot gear. Yet in Telegram chat rooms, a different storyline unfurled—heroic resistance against "state-run media." Some of those posts racked up more views than prime-time newscasts. Journalists squinted at engagement dashboards and felt the ground move under their deadlines.

The convoy had begun as a rumble of engines; by the crescendo of mainstream headlines on 7 February, it had become a clash of frames—public safety versus personal liberty, fact-checked leads against viral slogans. Mass media spotlights now bathed Wellington Street in perpetual glare, but in the shadows, rival narrators rehearsed counter-stories ready to flip villains into folk heroes. The cameras would soon capture that inversion—but first, they needed brighter bulbs and thicker cables, because the protest-that-became-an-occupation was about to turn into a ratings event, and no newsroom in the country intended to miss the next reel.

Two pandemic years had already damaged Canada's information arteries when, on 8 February 2022, they split into parallel veins: legacy outlets scrambling for verification, and an ever-louder thrum of livestreams pledging "raw truth." *Reuters* ran a fact-check reminding readers that mainstream media were indeed on scene—its own reporters had filed over forty stories in nine days—but acknowledged that Facebook claims of a "total blackout" were racking up millions of shares anyway [11]. News directors felt the floorboards tilt.

Inside *CTV's* Bank Street bureau, veteran correspondent Joyce Napier whispered into her headset as midnight horns rolled up Wellington "like steel bees in a barrel." "Every blast stabs at Ottawa's last calm," she told the nation, voice flat from fatigue. In the control room, senior producer Anjali Mehta toggled between Napier's shot and a drone feed of Wheel-of-Fortune-sized air filters shaking in an ICU ward—an editorial juxtaposition meant to hammer home public-health stakes. An internal Slack message from a junior writer blinked on her monitor: *Need Chyron—'SIEGE NO LONGER SYMBOLIC.'* [12]

South of the border, the soundtrack played very differently. On 10 February, Tucker Carlson leaned into the *Fox News* desk, grin sharp enough to fillet salmon, and declared the convoy "the single most successful human-rights protest in a generation." [13] One segment later, Sean Hannity told viewers the truckers "aren't going anywhere" and that "cowardly, pathetic Justin Trudeau" would soon fold. [14] Clips ricocheted through Telegram channels faster than *CTV* could push a push alert; each share arrived with the hashtag *#TrustNoLegacy*.

Reuters, striving for poise, published a 1,200-word explainer the same day: most truckers were vaccinated, the protest's leadership overlapped with previous anti-lockdown networks, and misinformation about empty supermarket shelves was unfounded. [15] The copy was cool, precise—and, to many convoy supporters, instantly suspect. *Corporate narrative control,* a 280-character rebuttal scoffed, harvesting twenty-five thousand likes before breakfast.

By 11 February *Axios* labelled the border blockades an "international crisis" that threatened the Super Bowl's supply chains and hinted at copy-cat convoys from Paris to Canberra. [16] The story's global frame fed a Goliath-versus-David script: if Big Auto trembled, surely the truckers must be winning. *Al Jazeera's* bureau in Washington, relaying Trudeau's plea that protesters "go home now," paired the quote with images of steel barrels pinging under frozen fists—struggle rendered in CinemaScope. [17]

In London, *Guardian* editors argued by group-chat over headline punch. The overnight foreign desk lead, *'Ontario invokes state of emergency, threatens fines and jail to end blockade,'* was flagged by copy as *bureaucratic.* A re-write landed:

'Rule by Wreckers': Province warns truckers of $100k fines. [18] At 02:14 GMT, a senior editor tacked on a rider: *Leave 'wreckers'—strong but not libellous.* Another minute, another push-alert.

Yet even as harm-forward headlines mounted, *Ottawa declares state of emergency, Border trade bleeds $300 million a day.* [19] *Fox's* camera cut to a windshield decal reading *WE DIE ON THIS HILL* and host Laura Ingraham proclaimed, "They fight for freedom while elites scowl." Twitter feeds erupted. A pinned tweet from an Alberta influencer with 180,000 followers read: *Trust no legacy outlet—they lie like rugs.* People blasted screenshots of *Reuters* sound meters and *CBC* horn-decibel charts as *fear porn.*

Legacy journalists sensed the rift turning from editorial hazard to existential crisis. Napier filed a radio hit describing "a low drone—horns tuned now to obedience with the court injunction, but never truly silent." Her email pinged with 300 unread messages, half of them accusing her of staging B-roll sirens. At 03:00, she typed back to one sceptic: "Come stand beside my mic and judge the decibels yourself." She never hit send.

Coverage pivoted again on 12 February when Ontario's Superior Court ordered Ambassador Bridge protesters to clear by 7 p.m. *Vanity Fair's* business desk announced U.S. automakers were *bleeding parts* and that financiers feared a *new kink in already mangled supply lines.* [20] At *CTV,* Mehta overrode normal rundown hierarchy to lead with Detroit's idled lines rather than Ottawa's sleepless nights—economic collateral now trumped civic nuisance. Meanwhile, *Fox* correspondent Sara Carter grinned beside a bonfire and told Hannity, "The energy here is electric—families, kids, bouncy castles!" adding, *sotto voce* off-mic, "We could use a coffee truck."

Inside *The Guardian,* an afternoon memo from senior standards editor Paul Chadwick advised reporters to "avoid activist framings such as 'patriots' or 'insurrectionists' unless in sourced quotes" and to triple-verify any figure on frozen assets circulating in chats. Minutes later, a freelance stringer filed a line about "$1 billion in crypto donations," sourced to an Instagram story. The copy desk spiked it. Still, the number was trending in the top five by sundown on TikTok and Gettr.

All the while, local voices fought to cut through national signal noise. Café owner Lina Farouk watched Friday lunch revenue slump to zero and tweeted at

CTV reporters, tagging Carlson, Hannity, and the *CBC.* "Please film the empty plates too." No major network answered, but her tweet made a *Léger* pollster's focus group, where participants admitted feeling whipsawed: legacy outlets warned of extremism. Their social feeds showed moonlit waltzes under fairy lights strung between big rigs.

In scholarly corners, data scientists scraped six million tweets. They published a pre-print mapping of how U.S. right-wing influencers pumped convoy hashtags into Canadian timelines—transnational populism on algorithmic rails. [21] The study landed like a footnote to what Ottawa residents already felt in their lungs: diesel plumes—and narratives—have no borders.

Just before midnight on the twelfth, Napier signed off from Parliament Hill, scarf stiff with frost, throat raw. "Tomorrow," she whispered to the camera, "we expect a policing plan." Across the continent, Tucker Carlson pre-rolled a segment titled: *The People v. Media.* Promising viewers a montage of *fake news hysteria.* Between those two lenses—one fogged with exhaustion, the other polished for sport—the country's trust barometer swung wildly, steel needle vibrating in the static.

The framing war of 8–12 February left no winner, only trench lines: mainstream outlets foregrounded harm and legality; influencer megaphones minted folk heroes atop diesel pedestals. Yet the clash did more than fill feeds—it rewired reflexes. Audience surveys already showed a five-point dip in overall media confidence. Policy briefings warned ministers that claims of "information tyranny" would filter any eventual crackdown. Duelling narratives were no longer a backdrop; they were a battlefield shaping the next moves of police, politicians, and protesters alike.

By dawn on 13 February 2022, Canada's information ecosystem resembled a cracked windshield: one spidering fracture carried the *hero* storyline, the other the *harm*, and every newscast, tweet, and dining-room squabble rattled the glass a little farther. Three days earlier a *Léger* survey had measured the split— 62 per cent opposed the convoy while a noisy 32 per cent still cheered it [22]—but by Valentine's Eve an Angus Reid poll showed public patience collapsing: 72 per cent now urged truckers to "go home, they've made their point." [23] Inside Parliament Hill aides annotated those numbers in yellow highlighter, aware that each percentage point translated into calls for stricter measures, or caution against overreach.

In a maple-scented kitchen forty kilometres east of Ottawa, the statistics felt personal. "Turn that nonsense off," grumbled Dave, a delivery-route supervisor, stabbing at the remote when CTV replayed sunrise footage of air-horns growling across Wellington Street. His sixteen-year-old, Maya, shot back: "MSM lies. I'm watching the livestream—no one's hurting anybody." On her phone flashed a Tucker Carlson Chyron proclaiming the convoy *the single most successful human-rights protest in a generation* [24] alongside a meme—*TRUCKERS: LAST LINE BEFORE TYRANNY*—retweeted by influencers who insisted, *Trust no legacy outlet.* Over meat-loaf steam the argument detonated: Mum called the horns "psychological warfare," Dad lamented "media fear porn," Maya brandished her phone: "They fight for freedom while elites scowl," quoting Carlson's colleague Sean Hannity. [25] Plates cooled; algorithms feasted.

Editors felt the schism, too. At *The Guardian's* late-shift desk in London, a copy chief pinged colleagues: *Headline too clinical—Ontario moves beyond 'bureaucratic.'* Within minutes, the banner became *'Rule by Wreckers': Province Threatens $100k Fines to End Blockade,* [26] an adrenaline jolt timed for dawn screens across the *Atlantic.* Hours later, *BBC* live-bloggers watched Ottawa police advance under sleet and typed, "Officers push back demonstrators with pepper spray and stun grenades," [27] the phrasing skirted moral verdict yet still trended on TikTok under #PoliceState.

In Ottawa, *CTV's* integrated command-centre cam panned across a maze of monitors: O.P.P. drone feeds, R.C.M.P. heat maps, a spreadsheet of tow-truck VINs. Producer Anjali Mehta slotted the clip atop the 12 February rundown—caption: *O.P.P., R.C.M.P., O.P.S. FORM WAR-ROOM* [28]—warning viewers that a decisive operation was imminent. Across Twitter, convoy hashtags counter-programmed with slow-motion reels of children sledding beside idling Kenworths, set to acoustic guitar.

That same afternoon, a memo slid across a walnut conference table two floors below the Prime Minister's Office (PMO). Polling chief Mélanie Fortin pointed to a red-lined paragraph: *We risk losing public trust if we appear to side with one narrative.* A junior staffer scribbled a question for his MP: "How do we legislate in the age of screengrabs?" No one answered before the Incident Response Group reconvened. Outside, R.C.M.P. planners briefed ministers on finance-freeze authorities that would land with the Emergencies Act proclamation just past midnight on the 14th, PowerPoint slides drawing directly on warnings in the Public Order Emergency Commission's draft about *social media coordination outpacing official messaging.* [30] At 00:01, Public Safety Canada published Order-in-Council *SOR/2022-20* and declared a national emergency; [31] the news broke into partisan shards before most Canadians hit snooze.

By breakfast, *Fox* clips of the proclamation framed Trudeau as "cowardly, pathetic" while *LA Times* analysis noted American conservatives had raised "$10 million by one estimate" for the convoy. [32] *Axios* tallied global copycat protests from Paris to Canberra, dubbing the trend *populism's new inferno* [33] In contrast, *BBC* push alerts quoted Ottawa police telling demonstrators, "Leave the area now," [34] and ran sideline explainers on bank-account freezes. When Mayor Jim Watson's back-channel letter urging trucks out of residential streets leaked on 13 February, *CTV's* web headline stressed *civic relief* while Telegram reposts framed it as proof the city *was begging for surrender.* [35]

On the 17th, *Global News* reported Finance officials' testimony that they had frozen 206 convoy-linked accounts worth over CA$7 million, tightening the policy vise, although this was "very unlikely" to affect small-time donors. Freedom-aligned feeds blasted screenshots of zero-balance banking apps; mainstream anchors countered with tickers of seized funds. That night the suburban kitchen saw a truce of sorts: Dave muttered about "government over-kill," Maya conceded the freezes "felt scary," but neither switched channels—they now consumed distinct realities side by side.

On 18 February, *Guardian* correspondents watched riot officers sweep Wellington under freezing drizzle, pepper spray drifting like bitter incense; their story led with arrests and stun grenades[5], while Fox opened with a split-screen of seized bouncy castles and Carlson's lament for *working-class heroes.* BBC footage of mounted police colliding with bicycles looped across Reddit, labelled either *brutality* or *measured restraint* depending on subreddit. In the war-room, aides refreshed a dashboard of social-listening heat maps glowing red wherever trust in institutions dipped. "We're bleeding legitimacy," one warned. The handwritten note resurfaced: *How do we legislate in the age of screengrabs?* No one had time to draft an answer before caucus.

By the evening of 20 February—after 170 arrests, 53 vehicles towed, and camera crews draped in diesel-flecked slush—the kitchen's television showed Parliament's emergency-powers debate. Maya scrolled TikTok; Dave read *CTV's* crawl. Mum, weary, asked, "Do we even live in the same country anymore?" Outside, statisticians, editors, and strategists chased that very question. The convoy was nearly gone, but the schism it amplified—between curated fact and crowd-sourced feeling—lingered in algorithms and annals alike. Canada now faced the harder half of any emergency: stitching a common story from perilous divides before the next horn—*digital or diesel*—splintered the glass for good.

ENDNOTES

[1] Gillies, R. (2022, January 29). *Thousands descend on Ottawa to protest COVID mandates.* Associated Press. https://apnews.com/article/coronavirus-pandemic-health-business-justin-trudeau-canada-45778ef0bdca45501411fb21066c46a0

[2] Pringle, J., & Raymond, T. (2022, January 30). Ottawa police expect another 24 hours of traffic disruptions, demonstrations from 'Freedom Convoy' rally. *CTV News Ottawa.* https://www.ctvnews.ca/ottawa/ottawa-police-expect-another-24-hours-of-traffic-disruptions-demonstrations-from-freedom-convoy-rally

[3] Raymond, T. (2022, January 30). Several criminal investigations underway connected with Ottawa convoy protest. *CTV News Ottawa.* https://www.ctvnews.ca/ottawa/several-criminal-investigations-underway-connected-with-ottawa-convoy-protest

[4] Hernandez, J. (2022, January 31). Protest against COVID mandates roils Ottawa despite officials' plea for it to end. *NPR.* https://www.npr.org/2022/01/31/1076976698/ottawa-protests-covid-vaccine-mandates

[5] BBC News. (2022, January 31). Freedom Convoy: Trudeau calls trucker protest an 'insult to truth'. https://www.bbc.com/news/world-us-canada-60202050

[6] Ljunggren, D. (2022, February 2). Anti-vaccine mandate protesters say they will block Ottawa for as long as necessary. *Reuters.* https://www.reuters.com/world/americas/anti-vaccine-protesters-say-they-will-block-ottawa-long-necessary-2022-02-02

[7] Lindeman, T. (2022, February 5). GoFundMe removes donation page for Canadian trucker protest. *The Guardian.* https://www.theguardian.com/world/2022/feb/05/gofundme-removes-donation-page-for-canadian-truckers-protest

[8] Beaumont, P. (2022, February 7). Ottawa declares state of emergency as Canada trucker protest gridlocks city. *The Guardian.* https://www.theguardian.com/world/2022/feb/07/ottawa-declares-state-of-emergency-as-canada-trucker-protest-paralyses-city

[9] Global News. (2022, February 7). Politicians seek end to trucker convoy protests amid state of emergency *[Video]*. https://globalnews.ca/video/8600214/politicians-seek-end-to-trucker-convoy-protests-amid-state-of-emergency

[10] CityNews Staff. (2022, February 8). Most Canadians oppose protests, but many sympathize with frustration: Leger poll. *CityNews Toronto*. https://toronto.citynews.ca/2022/02/08/canada-ottawa-protest-poll

[11] Reuters Fact Check Team. (2022, February 11). Fact-check: News outlets are covering Canada trucker protests. *Reuters*. https://www.reuters.com/article/fact-check/news-outlets-are-covering-canada-trucker-protests-idUSL1N2UM1G3

[12] CTV News Ottawa. (2022, February 8). Ottawa police expect 'Freedom Convoy' protest to grow this weekend. https://www.ctvnews.ca/ottawa/ottawa-police-expect-freedom-convoy-protest-to-grow-this-weekend

[13] Carlson, T. (Host). (2022, February 10). *Tucker Carlson Tonight* [Television broadcast transcript]. Fox News. https://www.foxnews.com/transcript/tucker-this-is-the-single-most-successful-human-rights-protest-in-a-generation

[14] Hannity, S. (Host). (2022, February 10). *Hannity* [Television broadcast transcript]. Fox News. https://www.foxnews.com/transcript/hannity-on-democrats-panic

[15] Ljunggren, D. (2022, February 9). Explainer: Ottawa protests—What you need to know. *Reuters*. https://www.reuters.com/world/americas/how-ottawas-anti-vaccine-mandate-protests-are-spreading-globally-2022-02-09

[16] Allen-Ebrahimian, B. (2022, February 11). Populism's new inferno. *Axios*. https://www.axios.com/2022/02/11/canadian-truck-protests-bridge-shutdown

[17] Al Jazeera. (2022, February 11). 'It's time to go home': Trudeau tells truck protesters. https://www.aljazeera.com/news/2022/2/11/canadian-authorities-look-to-the-courts-to-break-trucker-blockade

[18] Beaumont, P. (2022, February 11). Ontario declares state of emergency, threatens fines and jail time. *The Guardian*. https://www.theguardian.com/world/2022/feb/11/ontario-state-emergency-threatens-fines-jail-time-end-blockade

[19] Duplicate of #8

[20] Nast, V. F. (2022, February 11). Canada trucker blockade hits U.S. business hard. *Vanity Fair*. https://www.vanityfair.com/news/2022/02/canada-trucker-blockade-hitting-us-business

[21] Chou, R., & McCabe, S. (2024). Transnationalism and populist networks in a digital era: Canada's convoy case. *International Studies Quarterly, 68*(4), sqae131. https://academic.oup.com/isq/article/68/4/sqae131/7815709

[22] Léger. (2022, February 8). *The Freedom Convoy and federal politics – North American tracker* [Polling report]. https://leger360.com/wp-content/uploads/2024/02/Legers-North-American-Tracker-February-7th-2022.pdf

[23] Angus Reid Institute. (2022, February 14). *Three-in-four Canadians tell convoy protesters "Go home now."* https://angusreid.org/trudeau-convoy-trucker-protest-vaccine-mandates-covid-19

[24] Duplicate of #13

[25] Columbia Journalism Review. (2022, February 14). *The Freedom Convoy and the press*. https://www.cjr.org/the_media_today/freedom_convoy_fox_media.php

[26] Beaumont, P. (2022, February 19). Ottawa police use pepper spray and stun grenades to clear trucker protest. *The Guardian*. https://www.theguardian.com/world/2022/feb/19/ottawa-police-pepper-spray-stun-grenades-trucker-protest

[27] BBC News. (2022, February 19). Canada protests: Police push back demonstrators in Ottawa. https://www.bbc.com/news/world-us-canada-60420469

[28] Pringle, J., & Raymond, T. (2022, February 12). Ottawa police form new command centre with RCMP, O.P.P. to respond to downtown protest. *CTV News Ottawa*. https://www.ctvnews.ca/ottawa/ottawa-police-form-new-command-centre-with-rcmp-opp-to-respond-to-downtown-protest

[29] Boutilier, A. (2022, February 22). 'Very unlikely' assets of most small-time donors to Freedom Convoy would be frozen, MPs told. *Global News*. https://globalnews.ca/news/8638430/unlikely-most-freedom-convoy-donors-assets-frozen

[30] Public Order Emergency Commission. (2023). *Report of the Public Inquiry into the 2022 Public Order Emergency* (Vol. 1). https://publicorderemergencycommission.ca/files/documents/Final-Report/Vol-1-Report-of-the-Public-Inquiry-into-the-2022-Public-Order-Emergency.pdf

[31] Public Safety Canada. (2022, February 14). *Proclamation declaring a public order emergency.* https://www.publicsafety.gc.ca/cnt/trnsprnc/brfng-mtrls/prlmntry-bndrs/20220625/10-en.aspx

[32] Reston, M. (2022, February 13). Angry truckers paralyzed Canada's capital. It could happen here too. *Los Angeles Times*. https://www.latimes.com/politics/story/2022-02-13/angry-truckers-paralyzed-canadas-capital-it-could-happen-here-too

[33] Duplicate of #16

[34] BBC News. (2022, February 15). Canada protests: Ottawa stand-off continues as blockades cleared. https://www.bbc.com/news/world-us-canada-60407938

[35] Pringle, J. (2022, February 13). Ottawa mayor says truckers have agreed to leave residential neighbourhoods. *CTV News Kitchener* (syndicated). https://guelph.ctvnews.ca/ottawa-mayor-says-truckers-have-agreed-to-leave-residential-neighbourhoods

CHAPTER TWELVE:
HUSHED HAMMER OF FEBRUARY FOURTEENTH

"Money froze faster than the river, and faith in government didn't thaw much quicker. A law written for nightmares was pulled out for bad dreams, but nobody agreed on what haunted them most. Ultimately, it was easier to stop a truck than restart trust."
~ R.G. Cruise

The morning broke like a match-head struck too close to dry tinder, hissed once, and set the capital on edge. In the east windows of the Langevin Block, a bruise-coloured dawn leaked over scribbled briefing books that spoke of border blockades pinching an artery of trade, costing nearly CA$400 million a day. [1] Transport Canada's analysts, those patient accountants of calamity, warned that every silent hour the Ambassador Bridge sat strangled, clipped fresh shavings from the national GDP—estimates ran well into eight figures by breakfast. [2] One grim footnote from Windsor calculated a $50 million daily haemorrhage in just-in-time (JIT) auto parts, a phrase that suddenly felt less like logistics jargon and more like a prophecy with its clock running out. [3]

Inside a high-ceilinged Cabinet committee room—marble cool, fluorescent harsh—the Interim Clerk slid the February 13 "IRG Minutes" across polished oak: *irreparable harm to supply chains,* they declared, and *loss of investor confidence spreading faster than the virus we thought we'd mastered.* [4] Ministers arrived at muffled intervals, coats still scenting of winter and nerves; the hush before they spoke carried its barometric pressure. A junior aide, cheeks pink with first-career dread, whispered that automakers now tallied nearly CA$300 million in direct losses from one week's blockade alone, the figure scrawled in the memo's margin like a surgeon's note beside a widening wound. [5]

Deputy Prime Minister Chrystia Freeland's pen clicked like a metronome. "If parts stop, shifts stop; if shifts stop, pay cheques skip," she muttered, the cadence pure prairie grain. Another sheet detailed crowdfunding torrents sluicing through crypto wallets faster than the old anti-money-laundering nets could strain them. "They say bank freezes will torpedo their fundraiser," an aide breathed, eyes flicking to the corner where Finance officials clustered over laptop graphs that looked suspiciously like heart monitors in fibrillation. [6]

Across Wellington Street, reporters stacked like cordwood in the press gallery traded rumours by text. One message pinged: *TD froze $1.1 M—source says panic in convoy Signal chat.* [7] Phone-cold thumbs hammered replies while camera lenses stared at Rideau Hall's gates, waiting for the motorcade that would prove, at last, that whispers had become policy. "He actually going to pull the trigger?" someone typed. Another answered with the gallows brevity of the trade: "Reloading."

Back in the war room, the Justice briefing reminded everyone of the legal high-wire they were about to cross. To declare a public order emergency, the Emergencies Act demanded threats "so serious as to be a national emergency," Cabinet counsel underlined the clause twice, as if ink could catch them should they slip. [8] An older minister, grey rising like frost on a fence post, recalled his father recounting the War Measures Act of 1970; *history, it seems, never quite retires—it just waits for an encore.*

The Prime Minister entered without ceremony, mask off, eyes red-veined from nights paced through corridors of classified dread. He listened more than he spoke, nodding at line items of lost shifts in Oakville, half-built pickup trucks in Dearborn, and lettuce shipments yellowing on the wrong side of Coutts. *The Guardian* headline, printout still damp from a hurried photocopier, lay on the table like a warrant: *$50m a day at stake.* [9] Someone joked—too loud, too brittle—about "just-in-time democracy." No one laughed.

When the discussion turned to the financial squeeze, Freeland laid down her play: extend anti-money-laundering rules to crowdfunding platforms and grant banks the shield to freeze accounts without a court order. [10] The room exhaled a collective "so be it," and you could almost see Samuel Johnson sharpening his quill—because, as he famously observed, *nothing concentrates the mind quite like a fortune about to be dragged into fluorescent daylight.*

By noon, *Al Jazeera's* global feed flashed the scoop—Canada to wield emergency powers for the first time in history, [11] and the phones in the gallery sang like cicadas. *Axios* quickly followed with a bulletin, noting that calls with premiers and opposition leaders had established that the threshold was met. However, no one outside the circle knew precisely who set the standard or how high it was. [12]

Downstairs, a lone civil servant lugged a banker's box stamped *Section 58 Consultations* toward the secure cabinet registry. Its contents—handwritten notes from premiers, half-legible Zoom transcripts, and the rhetorical lint of federal-provincial diplomacy—would soon become both shield and spear in the future judicial melees. The Public Order Emergency Commission would later note the "imperfect information, uncertainty, and high stakes" that stalked every hallway that day. [13] Academic commentary already collecting in SSRN's digital catacombs wondered aloud if the justification truly matched the Act's ferocious standard, or if Ottawa had mistaken noise for threat. [14]

Outside, Parliament Hill's lawn lay under a crust of trampled snow and diesel grit. A mosaic of salt stains told the week's story: trucks idling, flags fluttering, and grievance gone from carnival. Yet somewhere in the crowd, a radio crackled the rumour of bank accounts freezing like windshield fluid in February, and suddenly the hat-passed donations felt as brittle as the ice on the Rideau Canal.

At 3:41 p.m., the prime ministerial motorcade rolled to the Confederation's stone stage. Reporters surged, microphones bobbing like cattails. Trudeau's step was deliberate, jaw set; he spoke of "targeted, time-limited" measures to restore order and protect livelihoods, a phrase destined to be quoted in both the House and the courts. [15] Questions volleyed: Was this the thin edge of authoritarian ice? Why now, not earlier? Could frozen funds melt faith in the Charter? Cameras clicked; pens raced; history, dressed in a navy overcoat, took a bow.

The proclamation landed with the upholstered thud of something simultaneously historic and bureaucratic. A clerk pressed print somewhere, and Canada's first Public Order Emergency scrolled out in courier font. The Act's machinery whirred awake: expanded arrest zones, insurance suspensions, and that most modern levers—financial asphyxiation. Banks began combing ledgers for suspect transfers; one executive texted a colleague, "Feels like running antifraud during an avalanche."

Yet even as the ink dried, the counter-narrative cocked its sling. Civil liberties advocates signalled lawsuits before supper; a judge, a year, and a winter later, would call the invocation *unreasonable* and a violation of Charter rights. [16] The government pledged appeal, insisting prudence sometimes wears steel-toed boots.

Dusk settled in mauve layers over the Peace Tower, and a charged silence pooled across the nation's living rooms. On kitchen televisions flickered scrolls of new rules; on cell phones, crowdfunding links expired mid-refresh. Somewhere in a Windsor stamping plant, the line lurched back to life, but the lesson lingered like hot metal cooling too fast: supply chains and civic trust share a fragility of identical gauge.

So the day closed—gavel struck, act invoked, questions launched into the winter night like sparks from a brake drum. Tomorrow would bring parliamentary showdowns, court filings, and a public inquiry sifting through each minute of this morning. But in that pause between declaration and consequence, Canada held its breath, tasting the alloy of emergency power—sharp, metallic, unforgettable.

The green-walled chamber of the House still rang with the shout of "Yeas" when the clerks tallied the result—185 to 151, emergency affirmed—yet the echo was scarcely dead before its ripples raced the length of the country. [17] Reporters scrolling the official vote sheet on their phones watched column after column of names. The integers of parliamentary will make flesh and pixel, each soldered to a riding and a livelihood. [18] Outside, the February sky sagged like spent bellows over Wellington Street, but inside Ottawa's political lungs, the air was suddenly thin, as though the vote had burned it for fuel.

Partisanship, that dependable Canadian ice storm, crackled in every corridor. *Politico* declared the Prime Minister "had staked his minority on a single throw of the legislative dice," noting the gamble had paid off—for now. [19] *The Guardian's* London desk, wary of precedent, warned that other democracies were watching to see if Canada's velvet gloves concealed iron knuckles. [20] And before the ink on the division list dried, Ottawa found itself not merely capital but specimen, pinned beneath a magnifying glass held by the world.

Down the hill, in a borrowed boardroom at the Wellington Building, the Conservative shadow cabinet convened over cardboard cups of Tim's and a stack of polling cross-tabs that read like a cardiogram in fibrillation. "This thing is radioactive," growled a strategist, tapping the column labelled *Ontario Suburbs*. A *National Observer* headline on the table—*Emergencies Act motion passes after heated debate*—seemed to wink like a match struck in a powder room. [21] Interim leader Candice Bergen entered last, cheeks winter-red, clutching the draft text of a revocation motion signed by two dozen MPs. "We don't let them normalise this," she said, voice pitched low as gravel on an iced highway. Her evening press release, fired moments later, accused the Liberals of turning a "public-health pothole into a continental sinkhole." [22]

Yet the government's grip held—for now—thanks to New Democrats who, as one *Washington Post* piece noted, had chosen emergency pragmatism over ideological purity. [23] Across the river in the *CBC* newsroom, assignment editors pack-muling headlines onto the wire could feel the centre of gravity wobble. A fresh *NPR* bulletin, datelined Toronto, reminded readers that police still ring-fenced the parliamentary precinct "lest the engines of discontent crank alive again." [24] By midnight, the *CBC* crawl carried three verbs in rotation—*invoked, affirmed, contested*—each lighting the studio set like a traffic signal nobody knew how to obey.

Out in the country, the signal effects were measurable. An *Angus Reid* poll, taken even before the vote, showed 72 per cent of Canadians shouting "Go home" at the convoy from their living-room sofas, while 65 per cent scolded the Prime Minister for letting the crisis metastasise. [25] A *Léger* tracker layered further complexity: nearly two-thirds opposed the protest, yet a stubborn one-third insisted mandates must melt *like February sludge under spring sun*, hinting at a nation divided not by halves but by fault lines. [26]

Those fissures widened on Parliament Hill's north lawn, whereby candlelight from a grassroots vigil for *democracy undefiled* unfolded beside a barricade still fragrant with diesel. Mothers in rainbow-stitched toques lifted cardboard hearts that read *Hold the Line on Rights*, while a knot of convoy loyalists unfurled a banner warning of *bank tyrants* and *digital prisons*. The clash mainly comprised vox, very little pop, and a duel of megaphones and hymns. *National Observer* reporters, while taking notes, found that even silence showed partisanship when expressed in two competing ways. [27] Police kept the camps two lamp-posts apart—just wide enough for democracy's elbows, not wide enough for its comfort.

In the control room at *CTV*, producers stitched a tick-tock timeline that ran like a metronome from the first honk on January 29 to the flash-bang on February 19. [28] Their late-night slot featured civil-liberties lawyer Abby Deshman, cheeks ghost-white under studio lights but voice sharp as sleet, warning that frozen bank accounts could outlast the frost itself: "Emergency measures have a habit," she said, "of lingering like February salt stains on March shoes." [29] Viewers tweeted seismically—some cheering prudent caution, others crying that Ottawa had seized the national debit card.

Come Sunday, the national phone-in show *Cross Country Checkup* crackled across kitchen radios from Kitchener to Kuujjuaq. Callers talked over one another like cousins at an overly competitive cribbage table: a long-haul driver from Red Deer damned the Act as "black ice on liberty's highway"; a nurse in Montréal begged Parliament to "keep the emergency until the last Q-Tip of the pandemic is tossed." Host Ian Hanomansing, juggling experts, and anecdotes, finally sighed: "Seems the convoy's gone, but the convoy conversation's double-parked in our heads." [30]

Meanwhile, the Senate opened sober second thoughts on the far side of Centre Block's scaffolding. Debates Issue 19 reads like frost etching on vellum—senators fretting about precedent, others waving footnotes at one another like wandering lanterns. [31] Yet even here, the gravity shifted hourly; word leaked that finance officials had already thawed some seized accounts, a signal the government was easing the choke, or perhaps merely loosening a knot before the rope burned.

And so the weeks unspoiled: Bergen's revocation motion scheduled, then drowned beneath procedural tides; civil-rights litigants filing injunctions before dawn couriers collected their coffee stamps; committees setting hearings on whether the Act should sunset with a hiss or a bang. In town halls, voters pressed MPs like blacksmiths, testing sword metal for flaws. On campus quads, law students argued that proportionality was the new patriotism. In quiet bedrooms, citizens refreshed bank apps just in case a protest donation made six clicks earlier should suddenly flag them persona non grata.

By early March, talk of "sunset" coloured every scrum. Ministers spoke of off-ramps; critics warned of on-ramps to a surveillance state. The Public Order Emergency Commission, still more rumour than body, loomed like a summons in the national mailbox. And in that suspense, before fact could be adjudicated from feeling, Canada stood at its fulcrum, asking which was heavier: three weeks of occupation or the millstone of unprecedented power. Everyone agreed the story remained incomplete, but its footnotes had already grown taller than the story itself.

Canada's winter sun rose thin and judicial on 17 February 2023, the day Justice Paul Rouleau's five-volume report slid onto Parliament's desks, its 56 recommendations stacked like icicles over the rim of a nation's conscience. [32] By sundown, headlines from Vancouver to St. John's repeated his verdict that Ottawa had met the Emergencies Act's "very high threshold," though he added—like a schoolmaster pencilling regret into the margin—that the crisis was one Canada ought never to have let ferment. [33] His commission's news release, printed on frost-white paper, tallied 85,000 documents, 139 interviews and 76 sworn witnesses, reminding readers that democracy can still keep its receipts. [34]

In a drab boardroom a block from the Château Laurier, junior counsel leafed through those volumes, lips moving as though tasting iron filings in the air. Recommendation 22—rewrite the Act's definitional fuse so it no longer borrows a spark from the CSIS Act—drew a finger-tap, a scribbled *constitutional minefield*, and a sigh that fogged the glass of a half-drunk Tim's cup. [36] Down the hall, small-business owner Sonia Patel waited to testify. Her florist's shop had survived three weeks of diesel haze, only to watch a merchant account snap shut under a name-matching algorithm; the bank freeze, she said, felt "less like security and more like a silent foreclosure," a memory she delivered in a voice brittle as January ice on tulips. [37]

Across Wellington Street, the Commission chamber resembled a winter scene: clerks in muted suits, counsel in mufflers, and Rouleau's chair conspicuously empty on the dais. A senior advocate, glasses perched like icicles, quoted the report's warning that misinformation travels faster than the convoy itself—then nudged a projector to show Telegram memes of crying Mounties and burning maple leaves. [38] The gallery murmured; democracy, it seemed, was arguing not only over law but over who owned the narrative engine under its hood.

Yet the avalanche truly began nine months later. On 23 January 2024, Federal Court Justice Richard Mosley fired off 219 pages that clanged across the capital like a snowplough striking a manhole cover: the invocation of the Act had been *unreasonable* and *ultra vires*, breaching sections 2(b) and 8 of the Charter. [39] Public Safety bulletins raced MPs' inboxes within minutes, summarising the judgment in language as spare as frozen cedar: no national emergency, no statutory threshold, no Charter justification. [40] Reporters on the Hill clutched the ruling the way schoolchildren hold pop quizzes: some with glee, others in visible panic.

International desks pounced. *The Guardian* declared the Prime Minister *rebuked* by his courts, [41] while Washington think-tanks spat out primers on how a G7 democracy could stumble on its emergency brakes. Within hours, Deputy Prime Minister Chrystia Freeland—voice flat as black ice—promised an appeal, insisting the government "remains convinced" the threat had justified the remedy. [39] An *Associated Press* bulletin, datelined New York but beating like a northern wind, called the ruling a "fresh tear in Canada's reputation for measured governance," noting civil-liberties groups were polishing victory speeches. [40]

In the mahogany hush of a Bay Street firm, charter lawyers uncorked red pens. One senior partner, recalling wartime censorship cases, muttered that Mosley's opinion read like "Roncarelli v Duplessis in winter boots." Associates highlighted paragraph 297—absence of serious violence, and paragraph 369, over-breadth of financial surveillance—while a junior clerk pinned a *TheCourt.ca* explainer to the Slack channel, its headline *Ultra Vires and Unreasonable* blinking like a hazard light. [41] Orders went out to draft class-action memos; history might not pay hourly rates, but litigation surely would.

Meanwhile, politics re-entered the ring. On 18 February 2024, *CTV* splashed a banner: *Ottawa Misses Deadline to Answer Rouleau*—the response that statute demanded within a year had drifted past like a snow-covered due date. [42] The Liberals pleaded workload; Conservatives called it contempt. In Sturgeon Falls, a noon radio show caller suggested mailing Ministers alarm clocks "set to Charter standard time." That quip trended for a day, proof that even parliamentary tardiness can mint meme currency.

Backbench New Democrats, caught between civil-rights credentials and minority-government calculus, faced caucus meetings pitched somewhere between philosophy seminar and fire drill. One MP waved Rouleau's finding that police failures, not cabinet overreach, birthed necessity; another countered with Mosley's frost-sharp rebuttal. The whip finally declared, "We may have to vote twice—once for principle, once for pragmatism," a line that drew the weary laughter of those who know Ottawa's seasons.

Amid the din, the machinery of amendment rumbled to life. On 6 March 2024, Public Safety Minister Dominic LeBlanc surfaced before microphones, promising "wide consultations" on redefining threats, tightening financial tools, and deciding whether a future commission should pierce cabinet secrecy as a matter of right. [44] Reporters noted the careful tempo: consult, discuss, maybe legislate—after the appeal, after committees, perhaps after the next election. One pundit likened it to promising to shovel the driveway once the blizzard chooses a leader.

None of this stemmed the private reckonings. In a Saskatoon farmhouse kitchen, a retired dispatcher highlighted Mosley's paragraph 401—"orders disproportionate to objective"—before folding the printout beside a mug emblazoned "True North Strong." Her ICU nurse son countered with *CTV's* reminder that Rouleau still believed the threshold had been met. [43] They argued over lemon loaf until the dog whined at the door, begging for the simpler constitution of a walk.

Far from prairie woodstoves, graduate students debated a freshly posted article in the *British Journal of Canadian Studies* in a seminar room at McGill. The article, "A Convoy, an Emergencies Act, and a State of Exception," sparred with Carl Schmitt while praising Canada's layered oversight. The paper concluded that deliberative democracy, though messy, had kept the sovereign on a leash of inquiries and courts. [45] One student mused Canada had accidentally staged a constitutional stress test for world audiences eager to witness liberalism's tensile strength.

Spring crept in, melting protest chalk from the Hill's grey stones, but the questions refused to thaw. Could we tame future blockades without trampling rights? Would banks forever serve as riot control by proxy? Would intelligence agencies share faster, or merely hoard more? Committees drafted, ministries parsed, litigants sharpened. And somewhere in a federal warehouse, six pallets of Rouleau's report sat shrink-wrapped beside boxes of Mosley's reasons—the written memory of a season when Canada inhaled emergency power and felt its lungs expand and sting at once.

When tulips shouldered through Ottawa soil, the appellate clock ticked toward the Federal Court of Appeal. Regardless of the court's decision, one undeniable reality remains: no one can definitively draw the line between security and liberty. Having walked that shifting edge, Canada now teaches by example—proof that even in a cold February, the heart of constitutional debate can heat an entire country.

ENDNOTES

[1] Scherer, S., & Gordon, J. (2022, February 14). Canada's Trudeau invokes emergency powers in bid to end protests. *Reuters*. https://www.reuters.com/world/americas/canada-police-response-protests-spotlight-after-key-bridge-us-cleared-2022-02-14

[2] Transport Canada. (2022, February 17). *Economic impact of the blockades* [Briefing binder, Section 16]. Government of Canada. https://tc.canada.ca/en/binder/16-economic-impact-blockades

[3] Lindeman, T. (2022, February 9). U.S.-Canada bridge blockade risks huge economic damage. *The Guardian*. https://www.theguardian.com/world/2022/feb/09/us-auto-plants-face-shortages-shutdowns-layoffs-protesters-block-canada-bridge

[4] Privy Council Office. (2022, February 13). *Incident Response Group minutes* [Leaked cabinet record]. Canadian Civil Liberties Association. https://ccla.org/wp-content/uploads/2022/08/IRG-Minutes-February-13-2022.pdf

[5] Anderson Economic Group. (2022, February 22). *Ambassador Bridge blockade cost auto industry nearly $300 million* [Press release]. Small Business Association of Michigan. https://www.sbam.org/ambassador-bridge-blockade-cost-nearly-300m-in-auto-industry-losses/

[6] de Rugy, V. (2024, February 10). Frozen assets: Examining Canada's use of the Emergencies Act. *Cato Institute Blog*. https://www.cato.org/blog/emergencies-act-after-two-years

[7] Westerman, A. (2022, February 14). TD Bank freezes $1.1 million linked to protests. *NPR*. https://www.npr.org/2022/02/14/1080632899/bank-freezes-funds-canadian-border-protest

[8] Department of Justice Canada. (2022, February 14). *Declaration of Public Order Emergency*. https://www.justice.gc.ca/eng/csj-sjc/section58.html

[9] Moloney, P. (2022, February 14). Trudeau to invoke Emergencies Act to deal with protests. *The Guardian*.

[10] Department of Finance Canada. (2022, February 14). *Canada invokes the Emergencies Act to limit funding of illegal blockades and restore public order* [News release].

https://www.canada.ca/en/department-finance/news/2022/02/canada-invokes-the-emergencies-act-to-limit-funding-of-illegal-blockades-and-restore-public-order.html

[11] Public Order Emergency Commission. (2023). *Final report – Volume 3: Invoking the Emergencies Act.* https://publicorderemergencycommission.ca/files/documents/Final-Report/Vol-3-Report-of-the-Public-Inquiry-into-the-2022-Public-Order-Emergency.pdf

[12] Ryder, N. (2022). Invoking the Emergencies Act in response to the truckers' protest. *SSRN Working Paper 4441405.* https://doi.org/10.2139/ssrn.4136678

[13] Al-Saib, Z. (2022, February 14). Trudeau invokes emergency powers in response to trucker protests. *Al Jazeera.* https://www.aljazeera.com/news/2022/2/14/trudeau-invokes-emergency-powers-in-response-to-trucker-protests

[14] Gonzales, O. (2022, February 14). Trudeau announces Emergencies Act to address protests. *Axios.* https://www.axios.com/2022/02/14/trudeau-emergency-powers-protest

[15] Michigan Public Radio. (2022, February 15). Canadian 'Freedom Convoy' blockades cost auto industry nearly $300 million. *Michigan Radio.* https://www.michiganpublic.org/economy/2022-02-15/canadian-freedom-convoy-blockades-cost-auto-industry-nearly-300-million-report-finds

[16] Associated Press. (2024, January 23). Judge says Canada's use of Emergencies Act was unreasonable. *AP News.* https://apnews.com/article/d7e6640f817ee12410bb99840a3df41b

[17] Ljunggren, D., & Paddon, D. (2022, February 21). Canada's parliament approves Trudeau's emergency powers. *Reuters.* https://www.reuters.com/world/canadas-trudeau-calls-national-healing-after-truckers-blockade-over-covid-curbs-2022-02-21

[18] House of Commons. (2022, February 21). *Vote 32: Motion to confirm the declaration of a public order emergency* [Roll call record]. https://www.ourcommons.ca/members/en/votes/44/1/32

[19] Blatchford, A. (2022, February 21). Trudeau wins House vote on Emergencies Act. *Politico.* https://www.politico.com/news/2022/02/21/trudeau-wins-house-vote-emergencies-act-00010474

[20] Cecco, L. (2022, February 22). Canada extends emergency powers after trucker blockades ended. *The Guardian.* https://www.theguardian.com/world/2022/feb/22/canada-extends-emergency-powers-after-trucker-blockades-ended

[21] Rabson, M., Osman, L., & Taylor, S. (2022, February 22). Emergencies Act motion passes after heated House of Commons debate. *National Observer.* https://www.nationalobserver.com/2022/02/22/news/emergencies-act-motion-passes-house-commons-debate

[22] NetNewsLedger. (2022, February 21). Conservative leader Bergen says emergency is over. https://www.netnewsledger.com/2022/02/21/conservative-leader-bergen-says-emergency-is-over

[23] The Washington Post. (2022, February 22). Trudeau's Emergencies Act powers for "Freedom Convoy" affirmed amid criticism. *The Washington Post.* https://www.washingtonpost.com/world/2022/02/22/canada-trudeau-emergencies-act-freedom-convoy

24 Westerman, A. (2022, February 21). Canadian lawmakers extend emergency-powers act for truck protests. *NPR*. https://www.npr.org/2022/02/21/1082229612/canadian-lawmakers-extend-emergency-powers-act-for-truck-protests

25 Angus Reid Institute. (2022, February 14). *Blockade backlash: Three-in-four Canadians tell convoy protesters "Go home now"* [Polling report]. https://angusreid.org/wp-content/uploads/2022/02/2022.02.14_Trucker_Protest.pdf

26 Léger. (2022, February 8). *The Freedom Convoy and federal politics* [North American Tracker survey]. https://leger360.com/legers-north-american-tracker-february-8-2022

27 Rabson, M., Osman, L., & Taylor, S. (2022, February 17). Protesters hold fast as police begin crackdown near Parliament Hill. *National Observer*. https://www.nationalobserver.com/2022/02/17/news/police-crack-down-antigovernment-protest-convoy-near-parliament-hill

28 CTV News. (2022, February 24). *Timeline: Trucker convoy protest in Ottawa*. https://www.ctvnews.ca/politics/timeline-trucker-convoy-protest-in-ottawa-1.5789217

29 Alberga, H. (2022, February 17). Canadian Civil Liberties Association takes federal government to court over Emergencies Act. *CTV News Toronto*. https://toronto.ctvnews.ca/canadian-civil-liberties-association-takes-federal-government-to-court-over-emergencies-act-1.5783900

30 Cross Country Checkup. (2022, February 20). What's your reaction to the police crackdown in Ottawa? *CBC Radio* [Audio broadcast]. https://www.cbc.ca/radio/checkup

31 Senate of Canada. (2022, February 22). *Debates of the Senate, Issue 19: Motion to confirm the declaration of a public order emergency – Debate*. https://sencanada.ca/en/content/sen/chamber/441/debates/019db_2022-02-22-e

32 Public Order Emergency Commission. (2023, February 17). *Final report*. https://publicorderemergencycommission.ca/files/documents/Final-Report/Vol-1-Report-of-the-Public-Inquiry-into-the-2022-Public-Order-Emergency.pdf

33 Boutilier, A., D'Andrea, A., & Boynton, S. (2023, February 17). The Emergencies Act's "very high threshold" was met, commissioner rules in major report. *Global News*. https://globalnews.ca/news/9493106/emergencies-act-inquiry-report-ramifications

34 Public Order Emergency Commission. (2023, February 17). *Public Order Emergency Commission releases report* [News release]. https://publicorderemergencycommission.ca/news/public-order-emergency-commission-releases-report

35 Public Safety Canada. (2024). *Government of Canada response to the Public Order Emergency Commission recommendations* [Backgrounder]. https://www.publicsafety.gc.ca/cnt/trnsprnc/brfng-mtrls/prlmntry-bndrs/20240626/09-en.aspx

36 Federal Court of Canada. (2024, January 23). *Canadian Frontline Nurses v. Canada (Attorney General), 2024 FC 42* [Judgment]. https://www.fct-cf.gc.ca/Content/assets/pdf/base/2024.01.23-306-22-T-316-22-T-347-22-T-382-22.pdf

[37] Public Safety Canada. (2024, January 23). News bulletin: Public Order Emergency decision. https://www.publicsafety.gc.ca/cnt/trnsprnc/brfng-mtrls/prlmntry-bndrs/20240626/09-en.aspx

[38] Cecco, L. (2024, January 23). Judge rebukes Trudeau for "not justified" use of Emergencies Act to break convoy. *The Guardian*. https://www.theguardian.com/world/2024/jan/23/canada-trudeau-emergencies-act-trucker-protest-covid

[39] Shakil, I., & Mukherjee, P. (2024, January 23). Trudeau government to appeal ruling on use of emergency powers. *Reuters*. https://www.reuters.com/world/americas/ottawa-appeal-ruling-canadas-use-emergency-powers-was-unreasonable-2024-01-23

[40] Associated Press. (2024, January 23). Judge says Canada's use of Emergencies Act was unreasonable. *AP News*. (duplicate of #16 domain, retained)

[41] Latremouille, C. (2024, October 29). Ultra vires and unreasonable: Federal Court rules on invocation of the Emergencies Act. *TheCourt.ca*. https://www.thecourt.ca/ultra-vires-and-unreasonable-federal-court-rules-on-invocation-of-the-emergencies-act

[42] The Canadian Press. (2024, February 18). Ottawa misses deadline to respond to Emergencies Act commission findings. *CTV News*. https://www.ctvnews.ca/canada/ottawa-misses-deadline-to-respond-to-emergencies-act-commission-findings-1.6773441

[43] Aiello, R. (2023, February 17). Trudeau met threshold to invoke Emergencies Act, commission finds. *CTV News*. https://www.ctvnews.ca/politics/trudeau-met-threshold-to-invoke-emergencies-act-commission-finds-1.6281592

[44] Bronskill, J. (2024, March 6). Federal government plans to consult widely before any changes to Emergencies Act. *CityNews Halifax / The Canadian Press*. https://halifax.citynews.ca/2024/03/06/federal-government-plans-to-consult-widely-before-any-changes-to-emergencies-act

[45] Eaton, P., & Gaspard, V. (2024). A convoy, an Emergencies Act, and a state of exception: How Canada's Emergencies Act contradicts Carl Schmitt's critiques of deliberative democracy. *British Journal of Canadian Studies, 36*(2), 133–156. https://www.tandfonline.com/doi/full/10.3828/bjcs.2024.9

CHAPTER THIRTEEN:
FAULT LINES IN FEBRUARY

"A country can measure its nerves by the noise outside and the number of coffees left half-drunk in quiet kitchens. Polling won't mend a cracked windshield, but it'll sure tell you how fast the road's splitting. We learned you can freeze money, but not opinion—especially when both change direction with the wind."
~ R.G. Cruise

By the first week of February 2022, Canada felt like a room where the wallpaper had curled at the edges. Self-rated mental health had slipped almost everywhere; Statistics Canada recorded the share of adults who still called their well-being "excellent or very good" sliding from 64 per cent before the crisis to 58 per cent by the turn of the new year. [1] A *Léger/Global News* pulse-take found nearly a third of respondents confessing they were *ready to move on* and *learn to live with the virus*, while forty-three per cent counselled caution. [2]

Into that thinned-out mood rolled the hulking geometry of the Freedom Convoy. *Léger's* first full read on the protest showed its cleaving opinion: 32 per cent supportive, 62 per cent opposed, a nation split like cordwood along pandemic stress lines. [3] Saturday, 29 January, thousands of air-horns punched the brittle sky above Parliament Hill, drowning out church bells and sparrow chatter alike; [4] by dawn Sunday, *Reuters* counted the rigs by the hundred and the protesters by the thousand, noting a mood more carnival than coup—at least so far. [5]

But numbers, like diesel, travel. *Abacus Data's* quick-draw poll, taken 31 January–2 February, found 68 per cent of Canadians saying they had "very little in common" with the demonstrators' worldview, versus 32 per cent who felt kinship. [6] In boardrooms from Bay Street to Burrard, CEOs scanned that 68 like a gale warning. Meanwhile, analysts at *Angus Reid* watched their dashboards flare red: 72 per cent of Canadians were already muttering that it was "time for the protesters to go home; they have made their point." [7] *Ipsos*, crunching a separate sample, logged a more grudging signal—54 per cent believed the truckers had at least nudged governments toward loosening restrictions. Still, only 36 per cent approved of the convoy's behaviour. [8] *Nanos*, surveying for *CTV*, iced the cake: two-thirds called the protest ineffective, and barely one in eight judged it a success. [9]

In a scarred brick loft on Ottawa's Sparks Street, *Léger's* data team pored over cross-tabs while espresso hissed in the kitchenette. "Margin's two-and-a-half, but the mood swing is ten," a junior analyst murmured, tapping a cell shaded Conservative-blue. One monitor showed raw verbatim: *Enough already, Hold the line, I want groceries.* Another displayed a flashing query draft: *Do you believe honking should be limited to daylight hours?*—the sort of question that, only weeks earlier, would have belonged to satire.

Two blocks east, in the window bay of a ByWard Market café still open between supply deliveries, patrons debated over cardamom lattes. "I'm worried about my supply chain, not my civil liberties," grumbled a restaurant manager, skimming news of produce trucks stuck at the Québec border. A barista countered, "My cousin's in Moose Jaw—he says the convoy is speaking for people nobody listens to." The argument paused when a push notification blinked across both phones: the U.S. administration urging Ottawa to use federal powers before auto plants choked for parts. [10]

Across town, Rideau Centre's big glass doors clanged shut for the second day; *CTV* calculated the mall's losses at nearly CA$20 million in a week—an invisible haemorrhage that stained spreadsheets far beyond the food court. [11] A maintenance supervisor stood on the empty concourse, listening to truck horns filter through ventilation ducts. "Feels like we're living inside the world's loudest seashell," he told a reporter, half-joking, half-done.

On Sunday evening, Mayor Jim Watson declared a state of emergency, calling the occupation "the most serious in our city's history," while *Reuters* quoted him pleading for outside reinforcements. [12] That bulletin flew up the flagpole; within an hour, the hashtag *#OttawaUnderSiege* trended, and a firehose of

American Facebook accounts began pumping gasoline-scented memes into Canadian timelines—an influence surge *WIRED* would later trace to the alt-right's digital booster cables. [13] *Axios* tallied over 19 million U.S. interactions on convoy posts during the first fortnight alone, proving outrage exports travel duty-free. [14]

Meanwhile, diesel reality kept grinding. With the Ambassador Bridge blocked and automakers idling lines, *Reuters* quoted one U.S. official urging Canada to act before a CA$500-million-a-day trade artery calcified. [10] In conference rooms, risk officers scribbled "irregular supply shock" on whiteboards; grocery chains plotted lettuce triage; a Saskatchewan farmer tweeted he had grain but no trucker willing to brave downtown Ottawa.

Back in the polling trenches, cross-tabs deepened the rifts. *Léger* supported the convoy running twice as high among Canadians aged 18–34 as among those over 55, and the strongest in Alberta and Saskatchewan. [3] *Angus Reid* found Conservative voters split down the middle, Liberals, and New Democrats almost unanimously hostile. [7] *Ipsos* detected that 20 per cent of Canadians believed mandates were rolling back *because* of the truckers—an attribution scientists later called *causal confetti.* [8]

An *Abacus* analyst, presenting to a virtual classroom at Carleton, held up a doughnut chart. "This," he said, "is what polarisation looks like when it's still soft—press it now and fingerprints remain." He clicked to the next slide—word clouds swirling *freedom, selfish, honking, tyranny, supply chain.* No one in the lecture hall missed how the nouns refused to share orbit.

Street-level live streamers became accidental ethnographers. One grassroots organiser, phone perched on a dash, framed the fight as biblical: "Pharaoh's got your pay cheque, convoy's got the plagues," he quipped to 40,000 viewers. Seconds later, a super-chat popped up: *"Here's $20, buy diesel!"* Another stream showed Ottawa residents singing *'We Can't Sleep'* to the tune of *'We Shall Overcome,'* their breath ghosting in minus-21 °C air, each note a protest against sleepless nights.

Opinion hardened by the hour, even as margins of error fluttered like carnival bunting. *Nanos'* late-month survey found that 48 per cent of respondents believed protests of this kind would likely become *a new form of political expression,* as if Canada had discovered the semi-truck as a ballot box. [9] Across the river in

Gatineau, a civil-rights lawyer highlighted the *Ipsos*, finding that only one Canadian in five blamed the federal government alone; "When blame dilutes," she said, "it seeps into the groundwater."

By midnight on 10 February—twelve days into the horns—Reuters flashed another alert: U.S. cabinet secretaries had personally phoned their Canadian counterparts, hinting that patience, like microchips, was in short supply. [10] In Windsor, truck lights shimmered against the Detroit skyline, a neon Morse code spelling *billions at stake*. StatCan would later reckon Canada's GDP for the quarter shaved by tenths of a point—a decimal that felt small unless you owned the lost slice of pie.

Still, the human register told the sharper story. Inside that Sparks Street loft, a pollster read an open-ended response from Prince Edward Island: *I was clapping for truckers two years ago; now I keep earplugs on the nightstand.* Down in the ByWard café, the restaurant manager refreshed delivery trackers—avocados stuck in Buffalo, coffee beans rerouted through Chicoutimi. "I'm living the margin of error," he sighed.

On Monday morning, the first snow since the convoy's arrival sifted over Parliament's Gothic stone, softening sirens, muting horn echoes to a distant rumble. Yet, someone had already created the fissures. One could almost hear the country creak, like lake ice deciding where to crack next. Pollsters would measure those fault lines again in the weeks ahead, committees parse causality, and lawyers argue proportionality. But in the first raw fortnight of February 2022, Canadians felt the continental divide run not along the Rockies but through their living-room radios, social-media feeds, and the survey margins that flickered on nightly news. The numbers were still shifting, but the break had occurred and would prove almost impossible to repair.

By the seventh sunrise of the protest—the one that bled rose-gold across a Parliament Hill still ringed by chrome bumpers and half-masted grievances—Canada's opinion barometers were flickering like porch lights in an ice storm. An *Angus Reid* flash poll posted at dawn showed that seventy-two per cent of respondents said the truckers had "made their point" and ought to pack it in. [15] An *Ipsos* read taken the same week found forty-six per cent confessing that, though they recoiled from the air-horn cacophony, they "sympathised" with the frustration beneath it. [16] A third *Ipsos* slice, splashed across *Global News*, handed Justin

Trudeau a failing grade for crisis management—yet reminded viewers that the convoy itself fared seven points worse in public esteem. [17]

Against that seesaw backdrop, money began to vanish and reappear with carnival-booth speed. On 3 February, GoFundMe froze a haul that had swelled past ten million Canadian dollars, pinning a notice atop the campaign page that read *paused for review*. [18] Larry Boake, a long-haul driver from Slave Lake, rolled out of his sleeper at a Petro-Pass outside Arnprior, thumbed his phone, and discovered that the diesel stipend he'd counted on was drifting back toward donors. "Ten million clicks," he muttered, "and I'm still buying my own coffee." GoFundMe's subsequent promise to refund every cent within ten days deepened the dissonance. [19]

The protest's treasury, however, behaved like water seeking a new channel. Within forty-eight hours, GiveSendGo—a Delaware-based platform— was touting itself as the libertarian ark; supporters sluiced over nine million dollars through its servers, sprinkling an extra six hundred and forty thousand in tips to the site itself.[20] Ontario's attorney-general sprinted to court and secured an order to freeze access to every digital penny. [21] Still, the platform tweeted defiance even as hackers splashed donor spreadsheets across the open web. [22]

Inside a converted Legion hall west of the capital, a sixty-three-year-old veteran named Dale watched a battered laptop, refreshing a *Tallycoin* dashboard that tracked the convoy's crypto sidecar. They had met the goal of twenty-one bitcoin, just shy of a million Canadian dollars, and already parcelled fourteen-point-six BTC into envelopes for ninety truckers. [23] "Never thought I'd see the day I'd crowdfund my protest," he chuckled, printing QR codes on neon labels.

Priya, a downtown Toronto data scientist, blue light glinting off her glasses, stared at a private *EKOS Risk Monitor* feed. The polarisation index—a measure Frank Graves once likened to *stress fractures in plate glass*—had notched another decimal toward brittle. [24] Slack pings from Queen's Park staffers begged for early tabs: *Did the sympathy spike or slide?*

Answers depended on the question. *Léger's* North-American tracker still pegged support at thirty-two per cent and opposition near two-thirds, branding the convoy a *small minority of selfish Canadians*. [25] A *Nanos–CTV* probe, fielded after the first weekend of blockades, recorded two in three Canadians calling the protest *ineffective*. Even half believed such demonstrations were likely to become a permanent political style. [26] When numbers whirl that fast, strategists listen for direction, not destination.

Out on the algorithmic wind, direction came from south of the forty-ninth parallel. Researchers at the *German Marshall Fund* tallied 14,667 convoy-related Facebook posts between 22 January and 12 February—suitable for 19.3 million interactions, a volume that outran Olympic hashtags and left Canadian content creators gasping. [27] *WIRED* magazine traced much of the digital megaphone to America's alt-right commentariat, which had bolted the convoy onto a rolling culture-war chassis. [28] The result, one analyst quipped, was "a snow-fence protest with a Super Bowl signal boost."

Meanwhile, the country's brick-and-mortar arteries felt the pinch of cyber cash. Toronto Dominion Bank froze two personal accounts holding 1.4 million dollars in convoy funds, then petitioned the Superior Court for guidance on whether to forward the money or hand it back. [29] In a press scrum, a deputy minister described the situation as "monetary quantum tunnelling": assets oscillating between legality and seizure faster than agencies could draft memos.

And still the polls pulsed. Priya refreshed the *EKOS* pane again, watching a red line hop a half point after a late-night talk-radio segment. "Our numbers just spiked twelve points overnight," she messaged her team, uncertain whether to sip coffee or sound an alarm. Beyond her window, the Gardiner Expressway rumbled, indifferent to margins of error.

Thus, in the second week of February 2022, Canada measured a movement not only in decibels but in dollars and data packets—a jumble of GoFundMe refunds, bitcoin wallets, and viral posts whose trajectories foretold bigger storms. These micro-donations, fluctuating sympathy percentages, and rattling frozen bank accounts all hinted that the protest's next chapter would unfold as much in the courts and in code as in Ottawa's diesel-scented streets.

When the calendar inched toward the last week of February 2022, the national conversation no longer sounded like a two-sided shouting match but like shards of porcelain rattling in a drawer. Editorial boards that once argued over column inches now argued over existential framing: *Is it a protest or an occupation?* The question reached the *Global News* politics desk at 4 a.m. on the twenty-fourth.

Moments after fresh *Ipsos* figures showed 43 per cent of Canadians giving Justin Trudeau a failing grade for crisis management, yet still judging the convoy seven points worse. [32] At *The Washington Post*—a country away yet palpably invested— the institution's unsigned editorial concluded the truckers had "surged beyond legitimate protest into the realm of thuggery," warning of copycat campaigns poised to jam cities worldwide. [42]

Inside *Abacus Data's* quiet Ottawa loft, senior partner David Coletto scrolled through cross-tabs, showing two out of three respondents saying they had "very little in common" with convoy grievances while one in three felt kinship. [39] "These numbers don't split down left–right so much as trust–mistrust," he whispered to a junior analyst, "and mistrust is where swing voters drink their coffee." By sunrise, an internal memo titled *Pre-Writ Risk: Populist Shockwaves* was circulating among half a dozen party war rooms.

Across the algorithmic horizon, mistrust manifested as cash. On 3 February, GoFundMe iced the convoy's campaign at CA$10 million, its progress bar stuck like a fly in amber. [33] Two dawns later, the platform promised full refunds, comparing the halt to *behaviour that violates our terms.* [34] For many sympathisers, it became a galvanising grievance—proof that faceless moderators could cancel flesh-and-blood dissent with a keystroke. GiveSendGo promptly filled the vacuum, raking in more than U.S.$9 million in forty-eight hours and, thanks to auto-tipped *gifts,* another U.S.$640,000 for itself. [35] Ontario's attorney-general raced to court for an injunction, freezing every digital penny in what one Crown lawyer likened to *a quilt stitched from a thousand small bills now hanging in the evidence locker.* [36]

Freezes begot breaches. Before dawn on Valentine's Day, hackers cracked GiveSendGo's back end, dumping an Excel sheet of 92,845 donor names, postal codes, and pep-talk comments onto the open web. [22] The leak lit social feeds like dry grass, provoking Twitter threads that read like high-school gossip sheets—*Did you see Mayor So-and-So's husband chipped in fifty bucks?* Hours later, a veteran volunteer named Dale, still stewarding the protest's Bitcoin kitty from a card table in a Legion hall, glanced at the chaos and muttered, "Fiat burns; sats stay." [23]

Yet numbers alone could not map the emotional topography. In Deep River, Ontario, café owner Linda Jamieson found her tip jar morph from a chatterbox to a confession booth. Mornings began with civil talk of lattés and lockdowns; by mid-month, the air had taken on a metallic taste. "I thought we were just talking trucks—now I'm scared to share my vote," one regular whispered, scanning the room as though ballots came with bar-codes. The barista nodded toward a fresh *Ipsos* Datapoint—46 per cent "sympathise with the frustration", even if they loathe the horns. [31]—and sighed, "That explains our pie chart of pie orders: half gluten-free, half gravy, nobody touching the middle shelf."

At Queen's Park, policy aides weighed 46 per cent like dynamite. A *Swing Ridge Models* spreadsheet estimated that a shift of two points could flip the seat in thirteen ridings in 2023. One strategist pencilled a note beside the Abacus 32/68 divide: *Silent majority ≠ stable majority.* The file circulated alongside an *EKOS* draft polarisation index whose jagged red line inched up with each successive survey—Frank Graves's stress-fractured glass[31] reference via *Reuters* would later call it "pre-cracked democracy." [26]

Meanwhile, the national media wrestled with its fault lines. *Columbia Journalism Review* tallied assaults and slurs against reporters in the field, forcing some crews to peel station logos off cameras and others to hire private security. [25] In an emergency Zoom, editors from five outlets debated whether a Saturday feature should profile protest sympathisers, detractors, or both. "We platform them, we legitimise them; we ignore them, we radicalise them," argued a senior producer, paraphrasing an ethicist he'd read at 3 a.m. No decision satisfied every byline.

Beyond newsroom windows, algorithms amplified whichever narrative clicked loudest. *Axios* counted 14,667 Facebook posts about the convoy between 22 January and 12 February, harvesting 19.3 million interactions—an online roar rivalling Olympic hashtags. [29] Data showed that the three prolific pages—Ben Shapiro, Newsmax, Breitbart—were all American, ensuring that Canadian anguish arrived already draped in U.S. partisan colours. "They can flood the zone," warned *German Marshall Fund* analyst Karen Kornbluh. "When everything feels popular, nothing feels verifiable."

For ground-level actors, those abstractions translated into ringing phones. In a dusty riding office outside Red Deer, volunteer Nicole Chan flipped through message slips: thirty-seven calls since breakfast, most demanding the MP "do something before Trudeau freezes granny's grocery money." She tried to reassure one farmer that only organisers faced account seizures—her talking point cribbed from *Nanos'* finding that 65 per cent approved of freezing organisers' assets. [30]—

but the voice cut her off: "They'll come for donors next. They've got the list." When Nicole hung up, another line lit.

Focus groups captured the angst in longer strokes. At Carleton University, polling intern Ryan Kaur watched eight participants react to a grainy clip of Confederate flags fluttering beside maple leaves. One woman murmured, "I'm done with restrictions, but that's *not* my team." Another man replied, "Those numbers don't capture the silent majority's unease." The moderator's debrief later noted "ambivalence with edges sharp enough to cut."

Even institutions normally above the fray began to wobble. Internal notes in the Public Order Emergency Commission would later recount how federal ministers, meeting by phone on 17 February, grappled with the optics of asset freezes they swore aimed at organisers yet inevitably chilled small-dollar donors. [28] "The message," one aide typed into the record, "is we *can* reach into your wallet; the counter-message is Bitcoin can vanish at the speed of Wi-Fi." In cue, *Bitcoin Magazine* celebrated the crypto disbursement as proof of "permissionless rails" that no statute could barricade. [23]

By the final Sunday of February, editorial pages and polling dashboards produced a kaleidoscope rather than a barometer. Support, opposition, sympathy, fatigue—each metric looked certain until another survey refracted the light differently. What *was* certain was drift: sympathy numbers that had crested mid-month were sagging, support for emergency measures inching upward, trust in conventional institutions eroding in microscopic flakes. Even *The Washington Post's* warning of "copy-cats planning convoys to incapacitate cities elsewhere" seemed less cautionary than predictive. [27]

When Ottawa residents awoke on 28 February to a landscape of tow scars and trampled snow, the hum of trucks had faded, but the hum inside skulls remained. Linda Jamieson reopened her café to cautious customers and a new sign—*Noise-free zone, polarisation check at the door.* She glanced at a fresh *EKOS* blip: polarisation index nudged another tenth of a point. Ryan Kaur filed his focus-group transcripts; Nicole Chan updated her call log; newsroom editors finally ran *both* features, side by side. Across screens and spreadsheets, the country's fracture lines glowed like X-rays, foreshadowing the moment, now mere days away, when the federal cabinet would conclude that ordinary statutes could no longer contain extraordinary dissent. In that charged quiet before the declaration, Canadians found themselves beyond the binary of support and opposition, standing instead on splintered ground where every conversation, every donation link, and every unanswered phone call hinted at a deeper experiment: how a 155-year-old democracy negotiates dissent in a century where money moves without permission and outrage travels faster than law.

ENDNOTES

[1] Statistics Canada. (2022, June 7). *Self-rated mental health decreases after another year of the COVID-19 pandemic* [Daily release]. https://www150.statcan.gc.ca/n1/daily-quotidien/220607/dq220607e-eng.htm

[2] Couto Zuber, M. (2022, February 10). Nearly 30% of Canadians say it's time to "learn to live" with COVID-19: Poll. *Global News.* https://globalnews.ca/news/8611838/covid-19-canada-poll-leger

[3] Léger. (2022, February 7). *The Freedom Convoy and federal politics – North American tracker* [Polling report]. https://leger360.com/wp-content/uploads/2024/02/Legers-North-American-Tracker-February-7th-2022.pdf https://leger360.com/wp-content/uploads/2024/02/Legers-North-American-Tracker-February-7th-2022.pdf

[4] Lindeman, T. (2022, January 30). Thousands join protest in Canada against Covid vaccine mandates. *The Guardian.* https://www.theguardian.com/world/2022/jan/30/thousands-join-protest-in-canada-against-covid-vaccine-mandates

[5] Ljunggren, D. (2022, January 30). Thousands stage peaceful protest in Ottawa against Canada's vaccine mandates. *Reuters.* https://www.reuters.com/world/americas/ottawa-set-massive-protest-against-canadas-vaccine-mandates-2022-01-29/ https://www.reuters.com/world/americas/ottawa-set-massive-protest-against-canadas-vaccine-mandates-2022-01-29

[6] Abacus Data. (2022, February 3). *Pandemic frustration may be running high, but more don't side with the so-called "Freedom Convoy".* https://abacusdata.ca/freedom-convoy-public-reaction-february-2022

[7] Angus Reid Institute. (2022, February 14). *Blockade backlash: Three-in-four Canadians tell convoy protesters "Go home now"* [Polling report]. https://angusreid.org/wp-content/uploads/2022/02/2022.02.14_Trucker_Protest.pdf

[8] Ipsos Public Affairs. (2022, February 24). *Majority (54%) of Canadians believe trucker protests at least partially contributed to loosening of COVID-19 restrictions.* https://www.ipsos.com/en-ca/news-polls/majority-canadians-believe-trucker-protests-covid-restrictions

[9] Nanos Research. (2022, February 25). *Two in three Canadians say trucker convoy protests were not effective* [Polling report]. https://nanos.co/wp-content/uploads/2022/02/2022-2080-CTV-Feb-Populated-Report-with-Tabs.pdf

[10] Osorio, C., Holland, S., & Shakil, I. (2022, February 11). U.S. urges Canada to use federal powers to ease border protest disruption. *Reuters*. https://www.reuters.com/world/americas/us-canada-border-closures-risk-trade-more-govt-action-is-likely-2022-02-10

[11] Larocque, L. (2022, February 2). Truck convoy costs Ottawa's busiest mall millions in lost revenue. *CTV News Ottawa*. https://www.ctvnews.ca/ottawa/truck-convoy-costs-ottawas-busiest-mall-millions-in-lost-revenue-1.5764969 https://www.ctvnews.ca/ottawa/article/truck-convoy-costs-ottawas-busiest-mall-millions-in-lost-revenue

[12] Hagberg, L., & Ljunggren, D. (2022, February 6). Ottawa mayor declares state of emergency to deal with trucking blockade. *Reuters*. https://www.reuters.com/world/americas/protest-against-vaccine-mandates-paralyzing-canada-capital-mayor-says-2022-02-06

[13] O'Sullivan, D. (2022, February 8). The alt-right on Facebook is hijacking Canada's trucker blockade. *Wired*. https://www.wired.com/story/ottawa-trucker-protest-facebook-alt-right

[14] Gold, A. (2022, February 14). U.S. accounts drive Canadian convoy protest chatter. *Axios*. https://www.axios.com/2022/02/14/us-accounts-canada-convoy-protests-social-media

[15] Duplicate of #7

[16] Ipsos Public Affairs. (2022, February 11). Nearly half (46%) of Canadians say they may not agree with everything trucker convoy says or does, but the frustration is legitimate. https://www.ipsos.com/en-ca/news-polls/nearly-half-say-they-may-not-agree-with-trucker-convoy

[17] Al-Hakim, A. (2022, February 24). Trudeau's convoy response gets failing grade, but even fewer support protesters: Poll. *Global News*. https://globalnews.ca/news/8640772/ipsos-poll-trudeau-convoy-response

[18] British Broadcasting Corporation. (2022, February 3). GoFundMe pauses donations to Canada truckers. *BBC News*. https://www.bbc.com/news/world-us-canada-60239038

[19] Saminather, N. (2022, February 5). GoFundMe to refund donations to Canada trucker protest after page frozen. *Reuters*.

[20] Bergengruen, V., & Wilson, C. (2022, March 4). 'Free' crowdfunding site linked to right-wing causes generates a windfall for itself. *TIME*. https://time.com/6150317/givesendgo-trucker-convoy-canada-profits

[21] The Canadian Press. (2022, February 10). Ontario court freezes access to donations for truckers' protest from GiveSendGo. *CTV News*. https://www.ctvnews.ca/canada/ontario-court-freezes-access-to-donations-for-truckers-protest-from-givesendgo-1.5779287

[22] Whittaker, Z. (2022, February 14). Hackers leak names of "Freedom Convoy" donors after GiveSendGo breach. *TechCrunch*. https://techcrunch.com/2022/02/14/freedom-convoy-donor-leak-givesendgo

[23] Willms, J. (2022, February 22). With Freedom Convoy, Bitcoin passes fundraising test in face of financial surveillance. *Bitcoin Magazine*. https://bitcoinmagazine.com/culture/bitcoin-passes-canada-trucker-protest-test

[24] Graves, F. (2022). *Understanding the Freedom Movement: Causes, consequences, and potential responses* [Policy paper]. Public Order Emergency Commission.

[25] Duplicate of #3

[26] Duplicate of #9

[27] Duplicate of #14

[28] Stokel-Walker, C. (2022, February 8). The alt-right on Facebook are hijacking Canada's trucker blockade. *Wired.*

[29] Duplicate of #19

[30] Nanos Research. (2022, February 24). *Levels of support for actions related to the Trucker Convoy Protest* [Polling report]. https://nanos.co/wp-content/uploads/2022/02/2022-2081-Globe-Feb-Populated-report-with-tabs.pdf

[31] Duplicate of #16

[32] Duplicate of #17

[33] Allsop, J. (2022, February 15). The "Freedom Convoy" and the press. *Columbia Journalism Review.* https://www.cjr.org/the_media_today/freedom_convoy_fox_media.php

[34] Williams, N., & Paperny, A. M. (2022, August 4). In protests and politics, Canada's "Freedom Convoy" reverberates. *Reuters.* https://www.reuters.com/world/americas/protests-politics-canadas-freedom-convoy-reverberates-2022-08-04

[35] The Washington Post Editorial Board. (2022, February 10). Canadian "Freedom Convoy" surges beyond legitimate protest. *The Washington Post.* https://www.washingtonpost.com/opinions/2022/02/10/canada-truck-convoy-protest-spawns-copycats

[36] Public Order Emergency Commission. (2023). *Report of the Public Inquiry into the 2022 Public Order Emergency* (Vol. 1, pp. 96–104). https://publicorderemergencycommission.ca/files/documents/Final-Report/Vol-1-Report-of-the-Public-Inquiry-into-the-2022-Public-Order-Emergency.pdf

CHAPTER FOURTEEN:
STATUTES IN WINTERLIGHT

"Liberty and duty sat down for coffee in Ottawa and found the cream had curdled. When the law brings a scalpel to a horn fight, everyone leaves with bandages but no clean bill of health. In this country, winter always outlasts certainty, but everyone keeps arguing about who tracked the snow inside."
~ R.G. Cruise

The winter of 2022 arrived with the brittle hush of a snow-laden spruce, and Canada found itself paging through two very different manuals for peril: one bound in maple-leaf red, the other in the cool teal of a public-health PDF. The Charter of Rights and Freedoms, resplendent in Section 2's promise that Canadians may speak, assemble, and petition as freely as chickadees in a cedar crown, sat cheek-by-jowl with Section 1's stern reminder that every liberty is "subject only to such reasonable limits prescribed by law as can be demonstrably justified in a free and democratic society." [2] The Public Health Agency's 2020 *Ethics Framework* opened with a quieter sentence—*Decisions must balance individual autonomy with solidarity and reciprocity.* [1] Yet its logic cuts just as deep: circumstances might arise when duty to neighbour outranks the long-cherished right to roam.

By February, that balancing act had become a high-wire routine, and audiences from coast to coast tuned in for every wobble. On a *CBC Newsworld* panel filmed beneath studio lights, the colour of glacier melt, constitutional scholar Dr. Amaya Desrosiers traced the jurisprudential lineage from Oakes to JTI-Macdonald, arguing that the state must hone the proportionality principle, like a logger's axe, anew for each case. "Is our Charter too fragile for emergencies?" the host asked. Desrosiers smiled like one who has rehearsed catastrophe: "Fragile? No. But it is not a sledgehammer; it's a scalpel wrapped in parchment." She waved a printout of Charterpedia's latest briefing, its margins annotated in four colours to show how courts weigh salutary effects against deleterious ones. [12]

Across town, in a third-floor office that smelled of Sharpies and stale cinnamon buns, public-health ethicist Dr. Marcus Grey huddled over his laptop. The lamplight made a halo of steam around a mug that read *DUTY–CARING*. Grey was massaging a paragraph about *least restrictive means*, borrowing language from British Columbia's Decision-Making Framework [3] and Ottawa Public Health's April 2020 ethics guide [14] He jotted in his notebook: *When does duty to the many outweigh liberty of the one?*—A question destined for the morning briefing with deputy ministers.

Down the corridor on Parliament Hill, a subcommittee on national security had recessed for coffee, leaving half-drunk paper cups beside microphones that still bristled with static. The clerk's laptop displayed evidence from Meeting 14 of the House of Commons Standing Committee on Public Safety and National Security (SECU), where Ottawa's deputy police chief had testified that convoy organisers "leveraged constitutional language to mask operational illegality." [8] "We need legislative clarity on protest rights," murmured MP Sofia Kwan, leafing through Hansard from 19 February—pages where one colleague accused the Prime Minister of invoking emergency powers "to restore public trust in him, not to end the blockade." [7] Her aide, scrolling the Canadian Legal Information Institute (CanLII) commentary on the politics of Section 1, whispered, "The test was built for cigarettes and hate speech, not 18-wheelers parked on Wellington." [17]

While parliamentarians weighed doctrine, grassroots organisers met in a drafty Glebe church basement fragrant with coffee and diesel-soaked mittens. A banner read *RIGHTS ≠ WRONGS*, spray-painted in truck-stop orange. Jasmine Cardinal, a Métis nurse from Prince Albert, argued that civil disobedience must carry reciprocal obligations: "You shut a street, you open a soup kitchen," she said, citing the Shared Health Manitoba ethics sheet that lists solidarity and reciprocity beside liberty as twin pillars of just policy. [15] Across the folding table, long-haul driver Gary Peters retorted, "The Charter didn't come with a footnote saying 'void in pandemics.'" Cardinal flipped to a recent *Facets* journal piece, concluding that the pandemic exposed "the seductive appeal of absolutist liberty that ignores communal risk." [16]

Back in Ryerson University's polling lab—re-baptised for the moment as a war-room of public mood—research assistant Elias Mo opened a fresh focus-group transcript. Participant 32, a retiree from Moncton, confessed: "I'm triple-vaxxed and tired, but freezing truckers' bank accounts feels like using a sledgehammer on a snow globe." Participant 7 countered, "If they can clog my city, I can clog their wallets." Mo highlighted the line in neon green, then cross-checked it against Abacus Data's latest note, which stated that two-thirds of Canadians felt mistrust toward the convoy's objectives. At the same time, one-third felt a kinship, numbers derived from an earlier memo titled "Pre-Writ Risk: Populist Shockwaves." [39]

In legal circles, the rhetoric grew more clinical. A CanLII lecture on justifying Charter breaches reminded students that "pressing and substantial objective" is not a synonym for "something must be done." [11] At the same hour, a Justice Department drafter updated a footnote in the internal *Guide to Section 1: proportionality remains a sliding scale; slope determined by evidence.* The evidence, alas, was beginning to slope like a toboggan run. Public Health Agency trackers showed ICU occupancy plateauing. Yet, the convoy's livestream audiences ballooned beyond 300,000 devices per day—the *Guardian* traced coordination between anti-vaccine activists and neo-Nazi chatrooms, a confluence of grievance unheard of since the G20 clashes of 2010. [10]

Editorial boards noticed. *The Guardian's* Ottawa correspondent warned that the Prime Minister now held "a set of emergency powers last used in the October Crisis but without the tanks." [9] *The Globe and Mail* in Toronto wrestled with a headline—*Rights Meet Responsibility on Wellington*—before settling for softer edges. According to columnist Renée Dalton, someone engineered Canada's Charter with both freedom and restraint valves; [4]

To keep up, the public service tried its best. Inside a beige cubicle farm at Public Safety Canada, analyst Noor Patel typed bullet points for the upcoming SECU Meeting 91: *judicial review pending; four groups challenging GIC on proportionality.* [13] She attached a House of Commons Standing Committee on Finance (FINA) report detailing how police cordoned a "Secured Area" downtown and invoked special search powers [9] (17), then sighed at the irony: freedom of movement fenced in for the sake of free expression un-fenced.

Late evenings found Dr. Grey back at his desk, eyes red at the edges, sketching a triangle labelled *Liberty—Equity—Solidarity*. He pencilled a circle around *'Solidarity'* and wrote: *Most fragile in crisis*. His reference pile grew: *Ottawa's ethical duty-of-care memo for healthcare workers,*[13] a *Saskatchewan framework reminding planners that public health emergencies shift ethics from bedside to community,*[23] and a BMJ commentary noting that limitations on rights must always meet a *necessity and proportionality* threshold. [5]

Meanwhile, fresh snow muffled the rumble of approaching engines outside Grey's window. In basement chatrooms, the phrase *Honking is a free speech* trended beside Hold the Line; On the Justice servers, lawyers rehearsed tests to show why 110-decibel air horns at 2 a.m. might fail the minimal-impairment prong. The Charter and the ethics frameworks—scriptures penned in calmer seasons—were about to be dragged onto Wellington Street and asked to referee a different sort of winter game, one where duty skated against right beneath floodlights of global scrutiny. In that suspenseful hush before rubber met ice, Canada stood astride twin legacies: a constitution that sings of liberty, and an ethics code that hums of responsibility. The chorus, soon enough, would clash in a key that echoed against Parliament's stone towers and through every living-room TV from Nanaimo to Nunatsiavut.

By the midpoint of February 2022, the word *freedom* had behaved like a hall-of-mirrors slogan—its letters stretched and refracted by every partisan outlet, Telegram channel, and kitchen-table podcast from Nanaimo to Newfoundland. Right-leaning U.S. talk shows cast the convoy as a "working-class insurrection against biomedical tyranny," a framing that Politico's media tracker counted among the top-shared Facebook links for three consecutive news cycles. [18] *The Guardian's* Ottawa file warned that while many grievances were sincere, the movement's open-door rhetoric had invited "Confederate flags, QAnon placards, and darker symbols" onto Parliament's front lawn.[19] The resulting cognitive whiplash seeped into parliamentary corridors where, as one opposition aide quipped, every MP now carried two briefing binders—one labelled *Liberty* and the other *Public Order*—and prayed no journalist asked, which was heavier.

Although the temperature on Wellington Street hit minus-17 °C, people engaged in incredibly heated rhetoric. A plywood stage—cobbled from pallet scraps and framed by two upended barbecue drums—served as bullhorn central. At 10:00, convoy organiser Ben "Big Dog" Harrison revved the crowd with a riff from social media memes: *They locked our livelihoods, so we're locking their capital!* Phones tilted skyward; livestream hearts split up the screen. In a quieter cove between rigs, *Reuters* reporter Julie Gordon jotted down the confession of twenty-six-year-old trucker Mason Delaurier, whose Peterbilt now doubled as dorm: "They've taken my rights," he said, voice half-hope, half-throttle, "and if this is what it takes to get 'em back, so be it." [20]

Two blocks east, a red-brick coffee roastery offered a contrasting view. Through fogged windows, the Chowdhury family watched foot traffic thin to a trickle and tried to balance accounts now haemorrhaging seven thousand dollars a day—figures later echoed by a *CTV* segment estimating downtown losses "in the millions per week." [23] "I support protest," said Mrs. Chowdhury, chalking *We're Still Open* on a sandwich board, "but who reimburses freedom's collateral damage?"

Across the Wi-Fi nodes and antenna towers, that damage translated into fury. On Valentine's Day, the *Washington Post's* despatch quoted residents who felt "abandoned by institutions" and trapped in a siege that no headline could soften. [21] Their grievances found a courtroom echo: on February 7, Justice Hugh McLean granted a ten-day injunction silencing the incessant air-horns that had become the blockade's metronome. [22] The ruling followed an emergency Saturday hearing where downtown plaintiff Zexi Li, voice shaking under oath, described *startle-flinching* hundreds of times a day—testimony that *CityNews* later published in full. [27]

Police liaison officers—a new breed of crowd whisperers kitted in powder-blue vests—took to the streets with printed copies of the order. One, Constable L. Varga, stood atop a snowbank reading paragraph four in tones that tried for calm authority yet barely cleared the diesel grumble: "Any person who contravenes this injunction may be found in contempt of court and subject to fines or imprisonment." A heckler replied with a cowbell solo. Another livestream caption flashed: *Honk if you love liberty—just not in court.*

Inside a canvas command tent stitched with patchwork Canadian flags, Harrison fielded frantic Signal messages: *COURT SAYS NO HORNS—OPTION?, NEED LEGAL QUICK.* The organiser's thumb hovered, then tapped a reply: "We pivot to song." Minutes later, the stage amp squawked to life with a ragged chorus of *We Won't Back Down*, audible five blocks away—the acoustic loophole in an order aimed at air horns, not heartstrings.

Yet even as decibels dipped, digital decibels spiked. *WIRED*'s tech desk traced how American alt-right influencers were "hijacking a local labour protest and exporting it as pandemic populism," generating millions of interactions for hashtags like *#TruckersForFreedom.* [28] *Politico's* earlier tally showed *Fox News* segments recycling protest footage on near-hourly rotation, turning oil-patch grievances into prime-time set pieces. [18] The algorithmic amplification fed fundraising at warp speed until, on February 3, GoFundMe froze CA$10 million amid "terms-of-service concerns," a move that hardened protest resolve and birthed new rally cries—*Unlock The Money.* [23]

The fundraising river carved a new bed. GiveSendGo—a U.S. site branding itself *the place for freedom-oriented campaigns*—absorbed more than US$9 million in forty-eight hours despite a pending Ontario court order to halt distribution[35]. However, its refusal became a badge of honour; its vulnerability soon emerged. In the early hours of February 14, *TechCrunch* reported a breach that dumped nearly 93,000 donor names and pep-talk comments onto the open web. [25] *Reuters* confirmed the leak site had received the files—and that GiveSendGo, now offline for *maintenance*, insisted it was "still soliciting donations." [26] Within hours, convoy group chats buzzed with screenshots of U.S. zip codes and crypto wallet addresses. "See?" typed one admin into a Telegram channel of 42,000 members. "They fear our wallets more than our rigs."

Meanwhile, police intelligence units began swapping classified briefs flagged *BearHug 2.0.* One O.P.P. report later tabled at the Public Order Emergency Commission warned that extremist chatter sought to "embed operational support" within the convoy, including potential weapons caches. [30] Journalists glimpsed the summary line but not the attachments, fuelling speculation from Twitter blue-checks and back-lot tabloids.

At street level, the mood oscillated hourly. Noon saw families snapping selfies beside chrome bumpers; by dusk, chants of "Hold! Hold! Hold!" erupted as rumours spread of impending tow orders. A family-run stationery shop on Sparks Street logged the chaos in its daybook: February 12—sold three pens, lost two window panes to fireworks; February 13—closed early, the customer screamed *TRAITOR* through glass; February 14—siren lull, but dogs still trembled.

That same Monday, *Politico's* world desk dissected how convoy hashtags had leapfrogged oceans to inspire blockades in France, Australia, and New Zealand, where protesters ring-fenced Wellington's parliament. [24] [32] "Contagion," mused Dr. Desrosiers when asked on *CBC* to define the trend, "travels now by diesel and data in equal measure."

Data, of course, is mother's milk to policymakers. In a windowless boardroom beneath Centre Block, analysts from the Privy Council Office projected opinion graphs onto pale cream walls. *Abacus* cross-tabs showed two-thirds of Canadians mistrusting convoy aims while one-third felt kinship; [39] Ipsos charts revealed a paradox: 46 per cent sympathised with protest frustrations even as majorities opposed tactics. [31] "What happens," asked one senior clerk, "when support and opposition share the same voter?" No one answered. The meeting ended with a note to "monitor risk of radical pivot."

The asphalt already hinted at that pivot through its symbols. A black sun, *Sonnenrad* appeared spray-painted on a diesel can near the Lord Elgin; a skull-and-crossbones flag with a QR code fluttered from a crane arm; both vanished before photojournalists could snap close-ups. *The Guardian's* Leyland Cecco tweeted that such iconography, though fringe, "picks the ideological lock" of a broader movement. [24]

Tension finally cracked the afternoon of February 19 when police advanced in phalanx, pepper spray and "siren-finned stun devices", clearing a corridor toward Parliament. [24] Residents watched from balconies, filming through curtains; protesters live-streamed retreat routes while vowing to "reseed the capital come thaw." At 16:00, a tow line hooked Mason Delaurier's Peterbilt. He climbed down, patted the hood, and texted his father: *They're taking my truck but not my rights.*

By twilight, the air-horn chorus was a memory, replaced by the soft mechanical whirr of street sweepers pushing gravel into neat rows. Yet, conflict merely migrated from pavement to policy. Lawmakers weighed emergency powers, the cabinet debated financial sanctions, and editorialists dusted off section-one jurisprudence. *The Guardian* would soon report that Parliament affirmed those extraordinary measures, 185 to 151, even after most trucks had gone, [29] and pundits would argue whether liberty or duty had blinked first.

But in late February's crucial hour, they had reached no decision. Instead, a fragile hush lingered over Wellington Street: diesel stains on snow, paper injunctions flapping from lamp-posts, donation links cycling in endless refresh loops. Liberty had made its claim with chrome and horn; duty, its call with court orders and silent shopfronts. Every Canadian sensed the deferral, not the resolution, of their collision. Who knew the next chapter would determine which definition of freedom could withstand the public emergency?

The roar of air-horns had faded, but on Parliament Hill, the echoes lingered in committee rooms and coffee queues. When the House of Commons voted 185 to 151 to confirm the Emergencies Act on the night of 21 February, the division board glowed like a fault-line map—green for yeas, red for nays, and the thin amber of abstention nowhere to be found. [33] *CityNews* splashed a *Maru* poll across its homepage the next morning: two-thirds of Canadians told interviewers they backed the extraordinary powers, though half in the same breath worried they were "setting a dangerous precedent." [34] *Abacus Data* added fresh ambiguity two days later, reporting 57 per cent approval, 30 per cent opposition, and a thicket of "soft" opinions that shifted with every headline. [35]

Headlines arrived by the hour. "Immediate emergency is over," Prime Minister Justin Trudeau announced on 23 February, flicking off the Act just nine days after flicking it on; *CTV's* push alert pinged millions of phones before the podium microphones had cooled. [36] Yet in the Senate, Issue 20 of the Debates recorded a different cadence the same afternoon, as veteran parliamentarians fretted that revocation gutted their chance to vote at all: "The privilege and responsibility of reflection has been trumped by haste," one lamented. [37] *Axios* called the flip-switch "a lesson in political bandwidth—too little and you're reckless, too long and you're tyrant." [38]

Legal capacity had already clogged. On 17 February, the Canadian Civil Liberties Association filed for judicial review, arguing that the declaration failed every Oakes proportionality test prong; the *JURIST* headline captured the tone: "Civil Rights Groups to Challenge Invocation of Emergencies Act." [39] Their factum joined one from the CCLA itself, posted hours later with a promise to *defend the Charter, not the convoy.* [40] The Canadian Constitution Foundation piled on the next day, branding Ottawa's move an *unconstitutional sledgehammer* and inviting donors to bankroll the fight. [41]

By 28 February, four separate applications thickened the Federal Court dockets. Chief Justice Paul Crampton assigned the matter to Justice Richard Mosley, a former JAG with a reputation for granular cross-examination. When the parties convened for case-management in Courtroom 30A—just off a corridor that smelled of printer ink and winter boots—Mosley urged speed: "The country demands certainty; so does the law." Counsel scribbled deadlines on blue-lined pads, unaware their judge would spend the next twenty-two months marinating 27,000 pages of evidence before striking with a gavel-loud verdict. The final decision, released as *2024 FC 42*, observed dryly that the threshold for a national emergency "was not met" and labelled the Cabinet's move "unreasonable and ultra vires." [42] *The Associated Press* translated the legalese for global audiences: Ottawa had *failed to clear the bar*, freezing bank accounts and corralling citizens without sufficient cause. [43] Academics at Osgoode's *TheCourt.ca* called the ruling "the most consequential administrative-law correction in a generation." [44]

However, none of that future thunder was audible in early March 2022, when the Public Order Emergency Commission was still a concept on Privy Council letterhead. In a makeshift office on Sparks Street, staffers drafted witness lists under the fluorescent buzz of rented fixtures. Volume 3 of the eventual report would later describe their mandate as "investigating decision-making under imperfect information and high stakes," a phrase circled three times in red by junior counsel. [45] For now, they scrolled social feeds to gauge public mood: relief-emoji chains from Ottawa residents, fury-caps from convoy channels, and a growing chorus predicting that frozen funds were only the first skirmish in a wider digital war.

Outside, winter clung to the capital. In Centretown's Community Hub—typically a basketball court, recently a respite centre—activists gathered for a post-mortem town hall. A teacher named Helen clicked through a slide deck of legal milestones: cabinet order, House vote, Senate stalemate, revocation. "So did liberty win?" someone shouted from the bleachers. "Ask my shop's ledger," replied a hairstylist whose February revenues had shrunk to snowflakes. The debate tipped into midnight, punctuated by coffee refills and screenshots of the injunction Justice Hugh McLean had granted three weeks earlier—paragraph four still underlined on every printout. [47]

Across Elgin Street, the legal fraternity held its vigil. At the Copper Cup café, lawyer Daniel Brooks unfolded a copy of Mosley's freshly scheduled timeline, reading aloud to a half-circle of clients and bar-call rookies. A truck mechanic who'd donated fifty dollars via GiveSendGo leaned forward: "If they win, do I get my bank fee back?" Laughter met silence, then dissolved when Brooks quoted the Act's immunity clause. Phones lit with the *TechCrunch* link about the donor-list breach; patrons scrolled the alphabetised dump in uneasy quiet. [25]

Meanwhile, the national mood charted peaks and troughs. *Reuters* described Trudeau as "increasingly isolated" amid global reopenings and domestic fatigue, noting that provincial premiers were shedding mandates faster than cabinet could draft justifications. [36] *CityNews*, mining the same *Maru* data set, emphasised that 54 per cent still feared rights erosion even while 66 per cent backed the Act. [34] *Abacus* found trust in federal institutions down eight points since January, but trust in local police down fourteen—a divergence analysts said might haunt future campaigns. [35]

Inside the Commission's stately temporary quarters at 395 Wellington, archivists sifted citizen emails for patterns: pleas for relief from noise trauma, condemnations of *authoritarian overreach*, and a surprising batch of letters framing the fiasco as a lesson in civics. One unsigned note read, "Dear Commissioner, if the Charter is a contract, then February has taught us the fine-print matters. "Staff pinned it to a corkboard labelled *Public Reflection.*

Reflection saturated the Senate, too. During Issue 21 on February 24, Senator Leo Housakos questioned Government Representative Marc Gold about the Act's lifting before the Upper Chamber voted. "Deference is not a blank cheque," Housakos snapped, tapping the Rules of the Senate with his index finger. [46] Gallery visitors whispered that this was procedural arcana; reporters knew better—process, in Ottawa, is politics with its jacket off.

Three days later, an ad hoc reconciliation circle convened in St. Luke's church basement. Residents, tow-truck operators, and three former protesters sat knee to knee. Someone read aloud the *AP* lede declaring the government's action "unconstitutional"; another countered with the *Guardian* article stressing that Rouleau's inquiry had reached the opposite view. [41] [46] The circle concluded that certainty was a luxury the law seldom affords.

Certainty certainly eluded Ottawa's merchants. On Richmond Road, the Chowdhury family finally reopened their coffee roastery, but foot traffic lagged. Mrs. Chowdhury taped the Federal Court's docket number— *T-347-22*—beside the debit machine like a talisman, telling customers, "This file decides whether our lockdown insurance will pay." Across the street, a bookstore staged a window display of constitutional anthologies under a banner: *READ YOUR RIGHTS—AND YOUR DUTIES.*

As early March melted ice into slurry, television pundits pivoted from horns to hearings. "Watch the courts," urged *CBC's Power & Politics.* "That's where February's questions will find March's answers." Pollsters agreed. *Abacus* modelled hypothetical referenda on emergency powers, the "yes" side led by single digits, brittle as lake ice in April. [35] *CityNews* framed the split differently: 52 per cent said they now trusted courts more than Parliament to guard liberties, a seven-point jump in ten days. [34]

Yet Canadian democracy, like its weather, prizes variety. On 3 March, a Maple Ridge trucker posted, "Back to hauling lumber—won't forget February." An Ottawa nurse tweeted, "Back to sleeping through the night—won't forgive February." Algorithms filed under *Engagement.* The Public Order Emergency Commission quietly booked community forums for the fall. In an anteroom at Justice Canada, drafters opened a file titled *Emergencies Act Reform Options.*

And so, beneath a pale equinox sun, the country entered a season of reckonings. Court clerks typed schedules; commissioners annotated affidavits; citizens refreshed headlines for the next poll, the subsequent appeal, the following footnote in a story that had begun with diesel and decibels but now hinged on paragraphs and precedents. Whether future protests would meet newer laws or revived distrust remained unwritten. Still, one certainty threaded every conversation from café to courtroom: Canada's choreography of liberty and duty had moved from the street into the ledger of jurisprudence, where every step leaves a citation.

ENDNOTES

[1] Public Health Agency of Canada. (2020). *Public health ethics framework: A guide for use in response to the COVID-19 pandemic in Canada* [Guidance document]. Government of Canada. https://www.canada.ca/en/public-health/services/diseases/2019-novel-coronavirus-infection/canadas-reponse/ethics-framework-guide-use-response-covid-19-pandemic.html

[2] Department of Justice Canada. (2024, August). *Charterpedia: Section 1 – Reasonable limits*. https://www.justice.gc.ca/eng/csj-sjc/rfc-dlc/ccrf-ccdl/check/art1.html

[3] B.C. Centre for Disease Control. (2020, November). *COVID-19 ethical decision-making framework* [PDF]. https://www.bccdc.ca/Health-Professionals-Site/Documents/COVID-19_Ethical_Decision_Making_Framework.pdf

[4] National Collaborating Centre for Healthy Public Policy. (2020). *Public health ethics and COVID-19: Selected resources*. https://ccnpps-ncchpp.ca/public-health-ethics-and-covid-19-selected-resources

[5] Trotter, C. (2020). Human rights, public health and COVID-19 in Canada. *Canadian Journal of Public Health, 111*(5), 760–762. https://doi.org/10.17269/s41997-020-00421-7

[6] Canadian Legal Information Institute. (1985). *Reasonable limits under the Canadian Charter of Rights and Freedoms* [Commentary]. https://www.canlii.org/en/commentary/doc/1985CanLIIDocs138

[7] House of Commons of Canada. (2022, February 19). *Debates (Hansard), 44th Parl., 1st Sess., No. 34*. https://www.ourcommons.ca/DocumentViewer/en/44-1/house/sitting-34/hansard

[8] Standing Committee on Public Safety and National Security. (2022, February 17). *Evidence, Meeting 14*. https://www.ourcommons.ca/DocumentViewer/en/44-1/SECU/meeting-14/evidence

[9] Cecco, L. (2022, February 14). Trudeau invokes rare emergency powers in attempt to quell protests. *The Guardian*. https://www.theguardian.com/world/2022/feb/14/canada-protests-justin-trudeau-use-rare-emergency-powers

[10] Cecco, L. (2022, February 8). How conspiracy theorists steered Canada's anti-vaccine trucker protest. *The Guardian*. https://www.theguardian.com/world/2022/feb/08/canada-ottawa-trucker-protest-extremist-qanon-neo-nazi

[11] Sharpe, R. J. (2000). Justifying breaches of Charter rights and freedoms. *CanLII Commentary*. https://www.canlii.org/en/commentary/doc/2000CanLIIDocs86

[12] Department of Justice Canada. (2024, August). *Charterpedia: General principles for the interpretation and application of the Charter*. https://www.justice.gc.ca/eng/csj-sjc/rfc-dlc/ccrf-ccdl/check/principles-principes.html

[13] Standing Committee on Public Safety and National Security. (2023). *Evidence, Meeting 91*. https://www.ourcommons.ca/DocumentViewer/en/44-1/SECU/meeting-91/evidence

[14] Ottawa Public Health. (2020, April 24). *Ethical framework for pandemic response* [PDF]. https://www.santepubliqueottawa.ca/en/professionals-and-partners/resources/Documents/Ethical-Framework-for-Pandemic-Response-April-24-2020-.pdf

[15] Shared Health Manitoba. (2020). *COVID-19 ethics framework: Information for providers* [PDF]. https://sharedhealthmb.ca/files/covid-19-shared-health-ethics-framework.pdf

[16] Eaton, P., & Gaspard, V. (2020). Reconciling civil liberties and public health in the response to COVID-19. *FACETS, 5*(1), 172–178. https://doi.org/10.1139/facets-2020-0070

[17] Hogg, P., & Thornton, W. (1986). The politics of judging: Section 1 of the Charter of Rights. *CanLII Commentary.* https://www.canlii.org/en/commentary/doc/1986CanLIIDocs469

[18] Fitzpatrick, A., et al. (2022, February 6). Ottawa truckers' convoy galvanizes far-right worldwide. *Politico.* https://www.politico.com/news/2022/02/06/ottawa-truckers-convoy-galvanizes-far-right-worldwide-00006080

[19] Cecco, L. (2022, February 13). Freedom convoys: Legitimate Covid protest or vehicle for darker beliefs? *The Guardian.* https://www.theguardian.com/world/2022/feb/13/freedom-convoys-legitimate-covid-protest-or-vehicle-for-darker-beliefs

[20] Gordon, J. (2022, February 3). Ottawans fed up with trucker blockade, blame police for inaction. *Reuters.* https://www.reuters.com/world/americas/ottawans-fed-up-with-trucker-blockade-blame-police-inaction-2022-02-03

[21] Coletta, A. (2022, February 14). Beleaguered Ottawans losing faith in leaders, want 'siege' to end. *The Washington Post.* https://www.washingtonpost.com/world/2022/02/14/canada-freedom-convoy-ottawa-counterprotest

[22] Ranger, M. (2022, February 7). Judge grants injunction against honking in downtown Ottawa. *CityNews Toronto.* https://toronto.citynews.ca/2022/02/07/ottawa-residents-protest-horn-honking-court

[23] CTV News Ottawa. (2022, February 12). Some businesses losing millions of dollars per week due to protest in downtown Ottawa. *CTVNews.ca.* https://www.ctvnews.ca/ottawa/some-businesses-losing-millions-of-dollars-per-week-due-to-protest-in-downtown-ottawa-1.5768991

[24] Cecco, L. (2022, February 19). Ottawa: Police use pepper spray and stun grenades to clear trucker protest. *The Guardian.* https://www.theguardian.com/world/2022/feb/19/ottawa-police-pepper-spray-stun-grenades-trucker-protest

[25] Whittaker, Z. (2022, February 14). Hackers leak names of "Freedom Convoy" donors after GiveSendGo breach. *TechCrunch.* https://techcrunch.com/2022/02/14/freedom-convoy-donor-leak-givesendgo

[26] Das, A. (2022, February 14). Names of Canada truck convoy donors leaked after reported hack. *Reuters.* https://www.reuters.com/world/us/leak-site-says-it-has-been-given-list-canada-truck-convoy-donors-after-reported-2022-02-14

27 CityNews Staff. (2022, February 5). Injunction hearing to stop convoy protesters honking downtown adjourned until Monday. *Ottawa CityNews.* https://ottawa.citynews.ca/2022/02/05/injunction-hearing-to-stop-convoy-protesters-honking-downtown-5032383

28 Stokel-Walker, C. (2022, February 8). The alt-right on Facebook are hijacking Canada's trucker blockade. *Wired.* https://www.wired.com/story/ottawa-trucker-protest-facebook-alt-right

29 Cecco, L. (2022, February 22). Canada maintains emergency powers after trucker blockades ended. *The Guardian.* https://www.theguardian.com/world/2022/feb/22/canada-extends-emergency-powers-after-trucker-blockades-ended

30 Ontario Provincial Police. (2022, February 15). *Freedom Convoy 2022 – Operation BearHug 2.0* [Intelligence report, POEC Exhibit OPP00002179]. Public Order Emergency Commission. https://publicorderemergencycommission.ca/files/exhibits/OPP00002179.pdf

31 Patrick, R. (2023, January 27). A year after the "Freedom Convoy," Ottawa residents say recovery is slow. *Global News.* https://globalnews.ca/news/9438127/freedom-convoy-one-year-anniversary-ottawa

32 Pollard, N. (2022, February 11). New Zealand protesters occupy parliament grounds for fourth day, inspired by Canada convoy. *Reuters.* https://www.reuters.com/world/asia-pacific/new-zealand-protesters-occupy-parliament-grounds-fourth-day-2022-02-11

33 Ljunggren, D., & Paddon, D. (2022, February 21). Canada's parliament approves Trudeau's emergency powers. *Reuters.* https://www.reuters.com/world/canadas-trudeau-calls-national-healing-after-truckers-blockade-over-covid-curbs-2022-02-21

34 CityNews Toronto. (2022, February 17). Two-thirds support Trudeau's use of Emergencies Act against protesters: Poll. https://toronto.citynews.ca/2022/02/17/trudeau-emergencies-act-poll

35 Anderson, B., & Coletto, D. (2022, February 24). Emergency measures: Government approval holds as Liberals and Conservatives deadlocked. *Abacus Data.* https://abacusdata.ca/canadian-politics-emegencies-act-feb-2022

36 Turnbull, S. (2022, February 23). 'Immediate emergency situation is over': PM Trudeau revokes Emergencies Act. *CTV News.* https://guelph.ctvnews.ca/politics/immediate-emergency-situation-is-over-pm-trudeau-revokes-emergencies-act-1.5790374

37 Senate of Canada. (2022, February 23). *Debates of the Senate, Issue 20.* https://sencanada.ca/en/content/sen/chamber/441/debates/020db_2022-02-23-e

38 Allen-Ebaugh, H. (2022, February 23). Trudeau ends emergency powers invoked to quell trucker protest. *Axios.* https://www.axios.com/2022/02/23/trudeau-emergency-powers-trucker-revoke

39 Canadian Civil Liberties Association. (2022). *Emergencies Act – Major case file.* https://ccla.org/major-cases-and-reports/emergencies-act

[40] Canadian Civil Liberties Association. (2022, February 17). *CCLA launch of judicial review* [Press release]. https://ccla.org/fundamental-freedoms/emergencies-act-challenge-ccla-in-court-today-to-defend-historic-victory

[41] Canadian Constitution Foundation. (2022). *Emergencies Act challenge case page.* https://theccf.ca/?case=emergencies-act-challenge

[42] Federal Court of Canada. (2024, January 23). *Canadian Frontline Nurses v. Canada (Attorney General), 2024 FC 42* [Judgment]. https://www.fct-cf.gc.ca/Content/assets/pdf/base/2024.01.23-306-22-T-316-22-T-347-22-T-382-22.pdf

[43] Gillies, R. (2024, January 23). Judge says Canada's use of Emergencies Act was unreasonable. *AP News.* https://apnews.com/article/d7e6640f817ee12410bb99840a3df41b

[44] Latremouille, C. (2024, October 29). Ultra vires and unreasonable: Federal Court rules on invocation of the Emergencies Act. *TheCourt.ca.* https://www.thecourt.ca/ultra-vires-and-unreasonable-federal-court-rules-on-invocation-of-the-emergencies-act

[45] Public Order Emergency Commission. (2023). *Final report – Volume 3: Invoking the Emergencies Act.* https://publicorderemergencycommission.ca/files/documents/Final-Report/Vol-3-Report-of-the-2022-Public-Order-Emergency.pdf

[46] The Guardian. (2024, January 23). Judge rebukes Trudeau for "not justified" use of Emergencies Act. *The Guardian.* https://www.theguardian.com/world/2024/jan/23/canada-trudeau-emergencies-act-trucker-protest-covid

[47] Duplicate of #22

CHAPTER FIFTEEN:
REBELLIONS AND THE BIRTH OF DISSENT

"A man who cannot pay his rent soon learns the price of freedom is never listed in wheat or coin. Governments reach for the sledgehammer when the petition gets too noisy, but the noise always finds a new drum. Every Canadian winter, someone tests the ice between order and justice, and every spring, the river carries away the evidence—until next time."
~ R.G. Cruise

The wind that swept down the St. Lawrence in November 1837 carried more than ice crystals; it whistled through half-shuttered storefronts and *seigneurial* barns like a summons, rattling census-thin pocketbooks and the brittle authority of London alike. Grain prices had collapsed, credit was choking on a trans-Atlantic recession, and the *seigneurial* rents that habitants once paid in wheat now came due in hard cash they did not possess. [1] In the cafés of Montréal and the taverns of York, printers ran off pamphlets in both languages excoriating aristocratic Family Compacts and *Château Clique* monopolies; republican maxims leaked northward from New York papers, meeting the radical fires of the French July Revolution and the memory of 1830 Chartist rallies in a volatile alchemy. [2] "If Westminster will not hear us," Louis-Joseph Papineau told the packed wooden pews of *Notre-Dame-de-Bonne-Nouvelle*, "we must rattle its gates with the clamour of a people awakened." His words cracked like musket-shot across the nave, earning cheers from weavers who had seen looms repossessed and from Irish labourers laid off when canal contracts dried up. [3]

South-east along the Richelieu, Saint-Denis lay under a crust of hoarfrost the colour of pewter. In the Nelson surgery, barrels of liniment vied for floor space with crates of fowling-pieces smuggled upriver in potato sacks. [4] Wolfred Nelson, thick-set and matter-of-fact, blew on his spectacles while dictating a coded inventory to a clerk who doubled as his apothecary: "Forty quinine phials, sixty Brown Bess, two kegs of powder, and God help the tally should the Crown come calling." Outside, under a lantern gutting in the wind, a knot of *Patriote* couriers passed a bottle of spruce beer and argued whether the tricolour they had dyed green for hope, white for purity, red for the blood already pledged—needed starch to keep it flying stiff against British grapeshot. [5]

Not far away in a draught-riddled farmhouse, schoolmaster Pierre Cherrier explained Lord Durham's rumoured plan to merge the colonies: "A marriage where one partner devours the other," he scoffed, dropping a black bean on the table each time he named a new grievance—ruined harvests, an unelected council, Protestant school boards in Catholic parishes. [6] His teenage daughter traced the beans into the shape of a guillotine and whispered that Paris had settled such disputes a generation earlier. This indiscretion made her mother slap the candle, sending tallow spattering like buckshot across the ledger.

By dawn on 23 November, British infantry in mud-crusted greatcoats trudged from Sorel toward Saint-Denis through knee-deep slush the locals called *neige pourrie*—rotten snow that swallowed wheels and chilled ankles to the bone. [7] Lieutenant-Colonel Charles Gore's column rehearsed volleys behind hedgerows of naked maples, their bayonets flashing like icicles in the brief sun breaks. In the village, Nelson posted pickets at every lane and converted *Madame Saintes's* parlour into a field hospital. "Remember," he told the shoemaker-turned-sharpshooter beside him, "aim low in this weather; cold fingers jerk high." When the first cannon boomed, its echo ricocheted along the Richelieu cliffs and set geese honking in frantic assent.

The battle of Saint-Denis that followed lasted seven wheezing hours—houses splintered, a barn burned like a straw comet, and snowdrifts steamed where hot lead met frozen earth. Nelson's men, firing from loopholes cut in stone walls, repelled assault after assault, the acrid scent of spent powder mingling with boiling horseflesh from a shattered limber. [8] A drummer boy from the 24th Regiment fell face-first into a trough and froze there, his sticks still crossed on the rim. At dusk, the British withdrew, leaving the *Patriotes* their lone outright victory—a triumph as dazzling as a tallow-wick and just as brief.

Word of the win galloped upriver on foaming horses. In Saint-Charles, Thomas Storrow Brown rallied three companies of volunteers behind a hastily fortified manor whose cedar shakes clattered like dice cups in the storm. [9] Villagers fashioned breastworks from flax bales and upended sleighs, while kitchen kettles became makeshift caissons filled with nails. Yet Brown's muster rolls listed barely two hundred muskets—many without flints—and only fifty rifles worth the powder. Against them marched Lieutenant-Colonel George Wetherall's disciplined column, field guns in tow, their scarlet coats an arrogant bloom against the dun December hills. [10]

On 25 November, the guns opened at Saint-Charles, tearing gaps through the *Patriote* palisade wider than a church door. Brown's men fired once, twice, then scattered when the grapeshot rang like sleigh bells on frozen boards. A priest trying to rescue the parish silver slipped on bloody ice and slid beneath a cannon wheel; his cassock fluttered a moment before silence took him. By nightfall, British soldiers stacked captured flags in the snow and burned them for warmth, the green-white-red silk sighing into smoke. When the char reek reached Wolfred Nelson, he crushed his pipe in a gloved fist and muttered, "The fire's not out; it's just under the ashes." [11]

Upper Canada, meanwhile, hummed with its discontents. In taverns along Yonge Street, William Lyon Mackenzie sketched battle plans on ale-stained tables, railing that oligarchs treated the colony as a "wheat-to-water conveyor for London bankers." In one tavern, a wag pinned up a notice: "Meeting of Patriots tonight— bring courage, leave caution at home. Pitchforks are acceptable legal tender." A farmer from Etobicoke boasted he could field fifty men but confessed he possessed only twelve serviceable locks; another offered hay-forks "sharpened on both ends to save turning." Their insurgency congealed in the chill of early December as they converged on Montgomery's Tavern, an inn that smelled of smoke, wet wool, and the raw conceit of amateurs. [12]

The government's reply was as brisk as a bayonet prod. On 7 December, regulars, and militia under James FitzGibbon advanced in two loose ranks, pressed through snow-clotted cedar scrub, and opened with grapeshot that blew mugs off window ledges and shattered fiddle-backs left in the corner for evening reels.

Rebel volleys cracked high; quail scattered; then an artillery round punched through the dining-room wall, fanning embers across split-pine floorboards. The entire structure went up like kindling tossed on Advent fire; Mackenzie's dreams with it. By sundown, smoke muddied the sky above Toronto, and loyalist volunteers toasted the Queen with mulled whisky as embers snowed on their shoulders like orange confetti. A grinning sergeant declared, "That's the last time a Scotsman calls himself king of Yonge." [13]

Across the colonies, magistrates read proclamations beneath portraits of a newly crowned Victoria, declaring traitors subject to death or transportation "beyond the seas." The phrase chilled spines, for everyone, knew "beyond" meant Van Diemen's Land or Bermuda—colonial purgatories where winter came in letters, not weather. Wolfred Nelson, captured after a cabbage-crate chase through snow-blind orchards, would feel the iron echo across his wrists on a July afternoon in Montréal Gaol before boarding the transport that carried him toward Atlantic fog and penal oubliette. [14]

When the snows melted in April 1838, the Richelieu valley lay quiet, but its silence was that of a banked hearth. *Habitant* children gathered *Minié-balls* like marbles; charred palings marked where farmsteads had stood; a widow in Saint-Eustache still kept a mousetrap baited with gun-flint "to remind the rodents," she said, "that even vermin meet resistance." Lord Durham arrived amid that uneasy calm, writing in his diary that Lower Canada was "two nations warring in the bosom of a single state"—a diagnosis that sparked outrage for its frankness and admiration for its clairvoyance. [15] His remedy—union of the Canadas and the concession of responsible government—would bruise French hearts yet plant the seed of modern federalism.

Mark Twain once quipped that a cat, once burned, forever fears a cold stove; so, too, Canada would glance over its shoulder at each future protest. The musket-cracks of 1837 echoed in the put-upon shouts of conscripts in 1917 and 1944, in the kettle-drum chants outside Winnipeg's Union Station in 1919, and in the flaring of fuse wire beneath Montréal mailboxes in 1970. The rebellion failed in arms yet prevailed in memory, carving a covenant that dissent was no foreign contagion but a domestic birthright. By spring's first thaw, the Richelieu carried melted snow and the ashes of flag-silk alike, sweeping them toward the Atlantic and the wider world that had lent both its republican spark and its cautionary smoke. And if the river's current whispered anything as it passed under thaw-loosened ice, it was a promise that each generation would test anew the thin ice between order and justice before the century was out.

The first summer of 1917 found Canada's grain bins half-empty and its recruiting halls emptier; Sir Robert Borden's pledge to keep a full Canadian Corps on the Western Front no longer squared with casualty lists that read like unrolled funeral scrolls. [16] Imperial cables warned London needed fresh divisions for the coming Flanders drive, and London's impatience echoed across Parliament's maple-panelled benches until Parliament made it law: the Military Service Act, passed on 29 August, bound every British subject aged twenty to forty-five to serve when called. [17]

In Montréal that August, a recruiting officer fanned himself with a ledger while a queue shuffled past posters of Vimy Ridge. "You'll be in khaki by harvest," he promised a Métis farmhand, who replied in French that wheat would not reap itself. A grey-haired matron thrust forward her son's exemption for "essential work" and hissed, "Mon fils ne mourra pas pour Londres." ➤ *My son will not die for London.* Behind her, Father Bruchési's circular lay folded in parishioners' pockets, counselling obedience to civil law but warning that forced service "must not offend conscience or the harmony of this dominion." [18]

The counting of beans, not ballots, shattered the harmony around Québec kitchen tables. On one sweltering evening in Sainte-Foy, a black-robed *curé* set down Cardinal Bégin's pastoral letter and told his flock, "A mother may not tithe her sons twice"—a sentiment answered by the village notary, who pointed to Ottawa's *alouette*-plumed publications and said, "The Crown now keeps receipts, not promises." [19]

By winter, the ledgers had turned to arrest warrants. Dominion Police hauled a draft-exempt apprentice through Québec City's snow-slick streets on Holy Thursday, 1918; within hours, 200 townsfolk surrounded the station, shattering the windows with fist-sized ice. The riot escalated to fifteen thousand people over Easter. People looted hardware stores for rifles, and soldiers fired on crowds amidst the burning registry offices' sulfurous glare, resulting in the deaths of four civilians. [20]

Labour halls from Trois-Rivières to Moose Jaw seized the moment. The Trades and Labour Congress denounced *blood conscription without bread conscription,* demanding a levy on war profits equal to the levy on flesh. [21] Yet in English Canada, ribboned parades of Gold Star mothers urged "every man a soldier, every home a battalion," and Borden's Unionist coalition swept the December election, while losing Québec by landslide. The Military Service Act pulled 99,651 conscripts into uniform, but fewer than half would ever cross the Atlantic before Armistice embers cooled. [17]

The quarrel slept uneasily for twenty-five years. By September 1944, the Scheldt estuary churned red with Canadian blood, infantry graves outpacing volunteers by a margin cabinet statisticians called "catastrophic." In Ottawa's Centre Block, Mackenzie King repeated his talismanic phrase—*conscription if necessary, but not necessarily conscription*—even as telegrams from General Crerar begged for 16,000 replacements. [22]

Far from Parliament, Camp Dundurn baked under prairie dust. Corporal Jim Cardinal, an NRMA "Zombie," scuffed at tumbleweeds along the rifle range while a sergeant barked, "Sign the overseas form or keep guarding grain elevators." Cardinal muttered, "I'll guard the prairie—it's the prairie that fed me," and stacked his Ross rifle butt-down in defiance. [23] That night, a bootleg radio crackled news of mutinous marches on the Pacific coast; Prince Albert's papers warned of "home-defence soldiers blowing off steam—no damage, yet." [24]

In Toronto, a different storm brewed. Union leaders of the Electrical Workers met under a haze of cigar smoke, plotting to link workforce shortages with wage-cap grievances. "If King breaks faith with Québec, he breaks faith with labour," declared president Alphonse Ouimet, brandishing a Trades and Labour Congress of Canada (TLC) resolution that still called for a "conscription of wealth" before bodies. [21] Their telegram to Ottawa offered conditional support: endorse post-war collective bargaining, and the shop floors would be quiet.

The cabinet cracked first. Defence Minister J. L. Ralston slammed his portfolio on King's desk, and Angus Macdonald hovered by the door like a sharpened hatchet. That evening, diary ink recorded the prime minister's dread of a "general's revolt." [22] Three futile weeks of voluntary appeals produced only a few hundred infantrymen. On 22 November, King signed Order-in-Council 1003, issuing overseas service for 16,000 NRMA men; by dawn, his slogan lay as tattered as autumn leaves on the Rideau. [25]

At Dundurn, the order spread faster than a prairie fire. Some conscripts penned resigned lines—"Tell Ma they're shipping us east, pray for calm seas"— others broke barracks windows with kit boxes. Yet most boarded troop trains silently, their breath frosting the carriage panes as miles of wheat stubble blurred into the night. [23] Only 2,463 would reach frontline units before VE-Day, but their departure shook a nation more than their arrival in Europe. [26]

Across from Parliament, union emissaries secured modest pledges on post-war industrial councils; their telegram back read, "Support offered—keep word." In Notre-Dame Basilica, Archbishop Charbonneau preached that citizenship "carries duties set by God and ratified by men," yet paused long enough to add, "No duty is greater than the charity that binds a people together." [18]

When the guns fell silent in May 1945, French-English fissures still yawned beneath victory parades. The dual conscription crises had branded dissent as both peril and privilege, proving that loyalty to liberty often meant resisting the laws written to defend it. From the Easter blood on Rue Saint-Joseph to the dust of Dundurn's siding, Canadians learned that compulsory service could win wars but wound nations, and that every generation would inherit not only the medals of the last but also the hairline cracks that run between conscience and command.

The guns of 1918 had scarcely cooled before Canada stared down a different muzzle—prices ran wild, wages crawled, and a global fever of labour unrest drifted home with demobilised soldiers and Russian-tinged pamphlets. A federal cost-of-living survey showed the index had almost doubled between 1916 and 1919, while basic pay packets lagged far behind, fuelling shop-floor talk of "owners' profiteering and workers' penury." [28]

At Winnipeg's Market Square, 15 May 1919, the 11:00 strike whistle snapped store doors shut "as cleanly as an artillery ripple," according to an entry in Mayor Charles F. Gray's diary now preserved in the University of Calgary digital archive. [29] Carpenter R. B. Russell, standing on the City Hall portico, read a telegram from Brandon sympathisers—*Hold fast. The wheat-belt walks out at noon.* His words carried above church bells and the fretful cough of police horses in their traces. Across Portage Avenue, the Citizens' Committee of One Thousand—stockbrokers in stiff collars who feared "Bolshevism dressed in boot-grease"—telephoned Ottawa, while Labour Temple secretaries calmly logged milk deliveries approved for hospitals, proving the walk-out's discipline and defiance. [31]

Inside a pine-panelled hall on Rupert Street, stenographers recorded minutes while a baker proposed a silent procession "to show even silence has a roar." The motion carried, but on 17 June, federal officers swept through the night, arresting strike leaders under seditious-conspiracy warrants, and L. B. Foote's courtroom photographs were stamped exhibits 995–1000 for the upcoming trials. [32]

"Bloody Saturday," 21 June, brought fifteen thousand marchers and two detachments of the Royal North-West Mounted Police. Marchers tipped and burned a streetcar, and Foote's lens caught the sparks mingling with tear-gas plumes. [33] Later inquiries disagreed on whether the Act or the rifle butts broke the strike, but all concurred that constitutional order stood ready to trample mass dissent. Labour veterans sowed those seeds: within five years, they held seats in Parliament, and decades later, Medicare and collective bargaining statutes reflected the strike's impact. "Winnipeg taught us the price of silence," historian Nolan Reilly told a centenary symposium, "but it also gave us the vocabulary of rights we speak today." [35]

If 1919 framed class struggle in the open air, 1970 recast dissent in the shuttered duplexes of Montréal. The *Front de libération du Québec* (FLQ) had seasoned its radical nationalism with TNT for years; its manifesto, read over *CBC* radio on 8 October, declared *We are the insurgent people* and demanded a socialist Québec free of "Anglo-Saxon capitalism." [36] Five days earlier, the FLQ had kidnapped British trade commissioner James Cross; on 10 October, another cell seized Québec Labour Minister Pierre Laporte. In Ottawa's Langevin Block, the cabinet met almost without adjournment. Cornered by reporters, Prime Minister Pierre Trudeau flicked an ash and said, "Well, just watch me." [37]

At 04:00 on October 16, the government proclaimed the War Measures Act. That evening, Trudeau's televised address warned that democracy "must root out the cancer of armed revolution." [38] Code-named *Operation Essay*, eight thousand soldiers deployed to Montréal and Ottawa—a show of force intended more for psychology than firefights. [39] Parliament convulsed: New Democratic

Party leader Tommy Douglas rose amid jeers to protest "a sledgehammer cracking a peanut;" [40] columnist Peter Gzowski lamented the next day that Douglas's voice "broke like a plywood oar against a tide of fear," yet polls registered over eighty per-cent public approval for the crackdown. [41]

Inside the FLQ hideout, the tone soured. Laporte, restless and under-fed, played paper football with his captors until they strangled him on 17 October and abandoned his body in a green Chevrolet at Saint-Hubert airport. Cross survived fifty-nine days; he recalled the kidnappers growing "as frightened of their revolution as of the soldiers outside." Historian Reg Whitaker later wrote that the state's response "recalibrated the boundary between order and liberty for a generation," proof that Ottawa would again reach for emergency law when confronted by perceived insurrection. [42]

From Market Square's overturned streetcar to the armoured personnel carriers on Sherbrooke, the through-line is simple: Canadian governments opt for extraordinary power when collective grievance spills beyond polite petition. Citizens learn new synonyms for fear. Yet each flash point leaves democratic sediment—labour codes, language rights, constitutional debates—widening the riverbed even as they roil its waters. This uneasy covenant—that dissent be punished immediately and honoured later—revives itself; this pattern reappeared in the 2022 horn-blare convoys and will reappear whenever conscience challenges authority.

ENDNOTES

[1] Greer, A. (1993). *The Patriots and the People: The Rebellion of 1837 in Rural Lower Canada*. University of Toronto Press. https://www.jstor.org/stable/10.3138/j.ctt1287v96

[2] UCL Press. (2020). The Canadian civil wars of 1837–1838. *London Journal of Canadian Studies, 35*(1), 1–16. https://journals.uclpress.co.uk/ljcs/article/id/492

[3] Sinclair, P. (1967). The economic background of the rebellions of eighteen thirty-seven. *Canadian Historical Review, 48*(4), 327–352. https://www.jstor.org/stable/136890

[4] The Canadian Encyclopedia. (2008). *Battle of Saint-Denis*. Historica Canada. https://www.thecanadianencyclopedia.ca/en/article/battle-of-st-denis

[5] CRW Flags. (2019, May). *Patriote flag before 1900 (Québec)*. https://www.crwflags.com/fotw/flags/ca-qc%7D18.html

[6] The Canadian Encyclopedia. (2024). *Durham Report (plain-language summary)*. Historica Canada. https://www.thecanadianencyclopedia.ca/en/article/durham-report-plain-language-summary

[7] DeCelles, A. D. (1906/2009). *The "Patriotes" of '37: A Chronicle of the Lower Canada Rebellion* [Project Gutenberg e-text #29973]. https://www.gutenberg.org/files/29973/29973-h/29973-h.htm

[8] Anonymous. (ca. 1900/2023 scan). *The Rebellions of 1837 in Upper and Lower Canada* [Digitized book PDF]. https://archive.org/download/rebellionsof183700unse/rebellionsof183700unse.pdf

[9] OpenTextBC. (2015). 11.10 Rebellions, 1837-38. In *Canadian History: Pre-Confederation*. https://opentextbc.ca/preconfederation/chapter/11-10-rebellions-1837-38

[10] Taylor, J. (2024). The new history of the Canadian Rebellion, 1837-38: New directions. *RANAM, 57*(1), 23-38. https://journals.openedition.org/ranam/1363

[11] Morin, J. (2018). *Markets for rebellions? The rebellions of 1837-38 in Lower Canada* (SSRN Working Paper #3235561). https://papers.ssrn.com/abstract=3235561

[12] The Canadian Encyclopedia. (2017). *Montgomery's Tavern*. Historica Canada. https://www.thecanadianencyclopedia.ca/en/article/montgomerys-tavern

[13] Henderson, A. (2018). Banishment to Bermuda: Gender, race, empire, independence. In *Open History Seminar: Canadian History* (Interpretation 1). https://openhistoryseminar.com/canadianhistory/chapter/interpretation-1-henderson-banishment-to-bermuda-gender-race-empire-independence

[14] Durham, J. L. G. (1839). *Report on the affairs of British North America* [Parliamentary paper]. https://archive.org/download/lorddurhamsrepor01durhiala/lorddurhamsrepor01durhiala.pdf

[15] OpenTextBC. (2015). 11.6 Republicanism in Canada. In *Canadian History: Pre-Confederation*. https://opentextbc.ca/preconfederation/chapter/11-6-republicanism-in-canada

[16] Parliament of Canada. (1917). *Military Service Act, 1917 (7-8 Geo. V, c. 19)*. https://archive.org/details/MilitaryServiceAct1917canada

[17] Canadian War Museum. (n.d.). *Conscription, 1917*. https://www.warmuseum.ca/firstworldwar/history/life-at-home-during-the-war/recruitment-and-conscription/conscription-1917

[18] Vimy Foundation. (n.d.). *The Québec City Conscription Riots, 28 March – 1 April 1918*. https://vimyfoundation.ca/battles/the-quebec-city-conscription-riots

[19] St Croix, B. (2018). Labour movements, trade unions and strikes (Canada). *1914-1918-online*. https://encyclopedia.1914-1918-online.net/article/labour_movements_trade_unions_and_strikes_canada

[20] Auger, M. F. (2008). On the brink of civil war: The Canadian government and the suppression of the 1918 Quebec Easter Riots. *Canadian Historical Review, 89*(4), 503-540. https://doi.org/10.3138/chr.89.4.503

[21] Pellerin, R. D. (2019, October 25). Not enough trained infantrymen: The 1944 conscription crisis. *ActiveHistory.ca*. https://activehistory.ca/blog/2019/10/25/not-enough-trained-infantrymen-the-1944-conscription-crisis

[22] Canadian War Museum. (n.d.). *Politics & Government: Conscription.* https://www.warmuseum.ca/cwm/exhibitions/newspapers/canadawar/conscription_e.html

[23] Henderson, T. S. (2004). Angus L. Macdonald and the Conscription Crisis of 1944. *Acadiensis, 33*(1), 1-20. https://journals.lib.unb.ca/index.php/Acadiensis/article/download/10858/11691

[24] *Prince Albert Daily Herald.* (1944, November 27). *Allies grinding out new gains* [PDF facsimile]. https://princealbertlibrary.ca/padh/1944/November/Nov%2027%2C1944.pdf

[25] Saskatchewan Virtual War Memorial. (n.d.). *Camp Dundurn.* https://svwm.ca/camp-dundurn

[26] Canadian War Museum. (n.d.). *Chronology of Canadian military history – Conscription 1944.* https://www.warmuseum.ca/cwm/exhibitions/chrono/1931conscription_e.html

[27] Davidson, M. (2019). *For God, King, and Country: The Canadian Churches and the Great War, 1914-1918* (Doctoral dissertation, University of Ottawa). https://ruor.uottawa.ca/server/api/core/bitstreams/4f67da9e-d51c-4889-a46c-9bf69d262989/content

[28] Labour Gazette. (1919). Inflation and wage statistics, 1916-1919 (reprinted in *Labour/Le Travail* 86 Appendix). https://lltjournal.ca/index.php/llt/article/download/2600/3003

[29] University of Calgary News. (2019, May 13). 100th anniversary of Winnipeg General Strike: UCalgary archive now online. https://ucalgary.ca/news/100th-anniversary-winnipeg-general-strike-ucalgary-makes-archive-former-winnipeg-mayor-available-online

[30] University of Manitoba. (n.d.). *1919 Winnipeg General Strike – Digital resources.* https://1919strike.lib.umanitoba.ca/index.php/resources

[31] Archives of Manitoba. (n.d.). *Photographs entered as exhibits in the Winnipeg General Strike trials.* https://www.gov.mb.ca/chc/archives/exhibits/index.html

[32] Archives of Manitoba. (n.d.). *Exhibits 995–1000: Strike trial photographs.* https://pam.minisisinc.com/scripts/mwimain.dll/144/LISTINGS_IMAGES/LISTINGS_DET_IMAGES/SISN%201133853

[33] University of Manitoba. (n.d.). *Newspapers and the Strike.* https://1919strike.lib.umanitoba.ca/index.php/who-media

[34] Reilly, N. (2020). Remembering 1919: The Winnipeg General Strike. *Labour/Le Travail, 86,* 7-10. https://www.jstor.org/stable/26976181

[35] Canadian Museum for Human Rights. (2019, May 13). *The Winnipeg General Strike: Demanding rights for the working class.* https://humanrights.ca/story/winnipeg-general-strike

[36] Front de libération du Québec. (1970). *FLQ Manifesto* (English trans.). Marianopolis College. https://faculty.marianopolis.edu/c.belanger/quebechistory/docs/october/FLQmanifesto.html

[37] Gruending, D. (2020, October 9). Pierre Trudeau, October Crisis 1970. *Great Canadian Speeches.* https://greatcanadianspeeches.ca/2020/10/09/pierre-trudeau-october-crisis-1970

[38] Trudeau, P. E. (1970, October 16). *Televised statement on the War Measures Act* [Transcript]. HistoryOfRights.ca. https://historyofrights.ca/wp-content/uploads/documents/OC_Trudeau_TV.pdf

[39] Cotton, R. (2005). *Canadian Army domestic operations plans (Operation Essay)* [Master's thesis, Canadian Forces College]. https://www.cfc.forces.gc.ca/259/290/291/286/cotton.pdf

[40] Gruending, D. (2020, October 14). Tommy Douglas, October Crisis 1970. *Great Canadian Speeches.* https://greatcanadianspeeches.ca/2020/10/14/tommy-douglas-october-crisis-1970

[41] Taras, D. (2000). The terrorists' best ally: Quebec media coverage of the FLQ. *Canadian Journal of Communication, 25*(2), 255-272. https://doi.org/10.22230/cjc.2000v25n2a1154

[42] Whitaker, R. (2009). Inside Canada's "first war on terror," 1968-1970. *Journal of the Canadian Historical Association, 20*(1), 215-248. https://www.erudit.org/en/journals/jcha/2009-v20-n1-jcha3851/039786ar.pdf

CHAPTER SIXTEEN:
THE SPREAD OF MISINFORMATION

"In a world where a lie can circle the earth before the facts have even left the driveway, outrage is currency and patience is spare change. Each new algorithm promises light but mostly sells us heat; the trick is not to mistake the bonfire for sunrise. If truth moves slow, give it sturdy boots and teach your children how to tie the laces."
~ R.G. Cruise

A thin winter sun rose over a Canada already glazed with pandemic fatigue and algorithmic glare, and two years of doom-scrolling had made every thumb a divining rod, dipping for truth in newsfeeds designed to value heat over light. Global trust in governments and media had slipped into what Edelman's 2022 barometer called a "vicious cycle of distrust," the steepest slide in modern polling. [1] Into that crevasse poured platforms whose ranking code—optimised for *meaningful social interactions*—super-charges posts that trigger anger or awe; controlled field experiments on Facebook and Instagram have shown that such architecture steers users toward more extreme content within days. [2] A complementary modelling study found that the 2018 tweak boosting comment-weighted engagement measurably deepened ideological polarisation in Italy, illustrating a broader law: the louder the emotional signal, the longer the platform spotlight. [3] Researchers mapping 208 million U.S. accounts likewise observed "asymmetric segregation," with right-leaning users five times likelier to inhabit news silos than their left-leaning peers. [4] Even attempts to blunt the harm, such as zero-rating the *angry* reaction after vaccine hoaxes spiked, proved half-measures that still left falsehoods circulating faster than corrections. [5]

In that super-heated environment, the nascent Freedom Convoy was tinder in search of a spark. Disinformation scholar Caroline Orr Bueno later noted that foreign extremist networks had been amplifying convoy hashtags weeks before a single air horn sounded on the Prairies, framing the protest as a righteous uprising against "medical tyranny." [6] Their posts blended seamlessly with cottage-industry conspiracy pages already primed by QAnon to distrust vaccines, journalists, and any institution wearing a crest.

At 05:47 on 28 January, Troy Laidlaw—a long-haul owner-operator idling at a truck stop outside Swift Current—rubbed sleep from his eyes and thumbed open Instagram. The first tile showed a clip of a rig crawling past the Alberta-Saskatchewan line in blowing snow; the soundtrack was a remix of *We're Not Gonna Take It* inter-cut with thunderclaps. He tapped *like*. The algorithm, sensing engagement, served a second tile: a meme of Prime Minister Trudeau Photoshopped in Mao's uniform. Another swipe and up popped a Q-flag collage promising *Nuremberg 2.0* for public-health *criminals,* cross-posted from an American alt-right account tagged *#WWG1WGA*. *WIRED* would later document how U.S. influencers, including Ben Shapiro and Donald Trump Jr., drove millions of impressions toward convoy content, distorting its Canadian scale while flooding feeds with culture-war tropes. [8]

By breakfast, Laidlaw's phone lit with a Telegram link titled *CONVOY GPS—LIVE!* He joined and found 11,000 members trading geotagged pins of overpasses where *patriots* planned banner drops. A pinned message claimed Ottawa police were "50 per cent resigned, refusing to enforce mandates"; *Reuters* would debunk the rumour within hours, citing official payroll numbers that showed zero mass resignations. [7] The correction never entered the convoy chat; the falsehood remained, accruing exclamation marks and fist-pump emojis as evidence of a collapsing regime.

Two blocks from Parliament Hill, *CBC* reporter Maya Singh stared at an anonymous email with the subject line *Media won't show THIS*. Inside was a JPEG of flaming bio-waste boxes stamped with the Pfizer logo under the caption "Ottawa burns unused vax doses!" The sender stated that the photo depicted the scene "outside a secret incinerator, Feb 2, 2022." Singh forwarded it to the newsroom's verification desk. Reverse-image tools traced the picture to a 2018 *Reuters* wire of a Kenyan medical-waste plant; nothing about Ottawa or vaccines.

In the next hour, the doctored image appeared on twenty-three Facebook groups and a half-dozen subreddits—all citing *CBC sources* that did not exist. Singh drafted a fact-check but sighed, knowing the correction would travel on foot while the lie rode shotgun in a Peterbilt.

Meanwhile, the Citizens for Freedom Telegram super-channel—population 140,000 and climbing—nested sub-chats with names like *Supply Chain Truthers* and *Disabled Vet Convoy*. In one, an admin dropped a Google Drive folder labelled *Intel: Hotspots*, featuring an aerial map of downtown Ottawa shaded in traffic-light colours. The legend marked radio frequencies, police staging lanes, and "weak points" in concrete barriers. Arushi Ganguly, writing for the Australian Institute of International Affairs, later reported that nearly identical maps surfaced in Melbourne and Brussels convoy spinoffs within forty-eight hours, evidence of a fast-mutating memeplex that leapt borders faster than omicron. [9] *Washington Post* reporters likewise traced D.C. convoy planning groups that copied Canadian road-block diagrams pixel for pixel. [10]

Yet the chats were more than logistics; they were echo chambers of grievance. *VICE* journalists lurking in a convoy room captured screenshots of users fantasising about egging counter-protesters in Oakland and "shipping leftists to China." [11] Other channels lionised Romana Didulo, the self-styled "QAnon Queen of Canada," whose followers believed she held divine authority to sign "royal decrees" nullifying vaccine mandates. [15] Her videos, shot in an RV trailing the convoy, stitched sovereign-citizen rhetoric to apocalyptic scripture, then blasted outward across TikTok, where the platform's sound-tracking feature let users remix her monologues into viral chant-loops.

Mainstream amplification arrived on cue. *Fox News* Chyroned *Revolt in Canada* while images of bouncy castles and pancake grills suggested a winter carnival rather than a siege. TV anchor Tucker Carlson cited "verified intel" that federal agents had planted Confederate flags to smear protesters—a claim with no sourcing beyond a single tweet. The next morning, Carlson's monologue trended on YouTube Canada's homepage, racking 600,000 views before any Canadian broadcaster rebutted it. Nature's modelling of misinformation would later show how even modest influencer boosts can make false narratives "super-critical," tipping them into epidemic-style take-off within hours. [13]

Attempts at platform interventions landed unevenly. Facebook attached generic COVID-19 banners to convoy live-streams but left donation links untouched. *Harvard's Misinformation Review* has found that nearly half of U.S. adults recall seeing such disclaimer labels, yet fewer than one-in-ten trust them to be effective. [14] Twitter briefly suspended one organiser for urging a "truck blockade of every provincial legislature," only to reinstate the account after appeals, citing *public interest exceptions*. Each zigzag fed a persecution narrative already coursing through right-wing channels: "They fear our truth," posted Pat King, a chief convoy strategist later convicted of mischief for horn-blasting downtown residents. [12]

By 1 February, drone footage of Parliament Hill resembled an over-wintering army: trailers serried like Lego bricks, diesel fumes hanging in the minus-20 °C air. Journalists on the ground struggled to separate staged shots from organic scenes; one viral clip of *Ottawa police surrendering coffee to truckers* was filmed outside Perth, Ontario, three days earlier. *WIRED* analysts traced its journey: uploaded to a fringe video site, screen-recorded onto Telegram, then reposted to Facebook, where algorithmic cross-promotion with *anger* reactions quadrupled its reach in two hours. [8] Facebook's research, leaked months later, admitted that angry-react content garnered the highest average watch time, leading engineers to label it *bad for brand but good for metrics*.

Inside Ottawa's press gallery, Maya Singh, and colleagues built a shared spreadsheet of convoy claims—each new rumour, from *UN troops massing in Québec* to *Trudeau fled to Davos*, received a row with sourcing, debunk trail, and spread velocity. The list hit 137 entries by Candlemas. One persistent fiction alleged that pharmaceutical CEOs had patented *permanent immunity serums* for themselves, citing a non-existent *British Medical Journal* article. Science editors at *BMJ* published a public rebuttal, but Telegram channels screenshot the headline and added *Editor ADMITS cover-up*, turning the denial into a fresh proof of conspiracy.

Against this cacophony, academic efforts to create early-warning dashboards felt Sisyphean. A *Science Advances* study testing real-time down-ranking of angry posts found only marginal reductions in misinformation, as users adapted by substituting *wow* or *haha* reactions, proving the cat-and-mouse game between platform tweaks and content strategists. [5] Scholars at MIT's Senseable City Lab suggested external *middleware* systems that let users reorder feeds chronologically, but the idea collided with proprietary walls and dwindling patience.

The convoy's digital mayhem also served as a cover for a grift. A crowdfunding link purporting to buy diesel for truckers routed donations through a Florida-registered LLC with no Canadian directors. International banking data flagged by FINTRAC (later revealed at the Emergencies Act hearings) showed that nearly 40 per cent of contributions originated from U.S. zip codes, many pinging from the same Kansas server farm used by QAnon storefronts. Journalists who tweeted the statistic faced instant brigades accusing them of *foreign collusion*. As one veteran reporter quipped, "In the disinfo age, revealing the ledger just gets you accused of forging the irlk."

By the first Sunday in February, Ottawa's downtown boardwalk was a patchwork of contradictory realities. To convince live-streamers, the scene was *Woodstock for the working class*, all hot cocoa and drum circles. To residents kept awake by ceaseless horns, it was psychological warfare. We can quantify this divergence: an alt-tech video tagged #Honkhonk amassed 1.2 million views on Rumble. The same clip cross-posted to CBC's site drew 60,000—proof of what scholars call the *misinformation engagement premium*, where false or incendiary content outperforms factual reportage by an order of magnitude. [13]

When Maya Singh filed her Sunday feature, she opened not with riot scenes but with the vertigo of data voids: "The harder we fact-check, the faster the horizon recedes," she wrote, paraphrasing a senior producer. Her editor kept the line. By press time, the convoy chats were already repurposing it as an inadvertent confession that *legacy media admits defeat*. Singh closed her laptop and watched snow swirl past the window, recalling the old proverb that falsehood can race halfway around the world before truth has even laced its boots, and pondering how Canada's stories seldom finish with spectacle alone but with the quiet consequences that follow.

Those consequences were gathering like storm clouds: foreign amplification networks eyeing an exportable template, federal ministers drafting new digital-harms legislation, and law-enforcement agencies debating whether encrypted-chat rumours justified kinetic counter-measures. The convoy, still idling beneath fairy-lights strung from cab to cab, had become less a protest than a prism, refracting a million individual anxieties into a single blinding beam. In that glare, facts, and fictions melted together until the asphalt beneath Parliament seemed to ripple, and the country's shared sense of reality buckled like ice in an early thaw.

Digital Canada entered Valentine's week tangled in a web of transcontinental packet traffic: WhatsApp links tucked inside Signal groups, Facebook Reels clipped into Telegram "megachats," and Rumble rants ricocheting off TikTok duets. Scholars tracing pandemic-era media habits had already shown how encrypted messaging apps such as Telegram, WhatsApp, and Signal leapt from niche to mainstream once public-health mistrust peaked, giving conspiracy brokers a friction-free switchboard for cross-border mobilisation. [16] Diaspora fact-checkers warned the same closed channels let rumours outrun rebuttals in languages regulators scarcely monitored. [17] while a behavioural study of convoy Facebook pages documented how comment-weighted algorithms herded like-minded users into ideological bunkers where dissenting posts died on arrival. [18]

The convoy's hashtags, already crackling with domestic grievance, were soon goose-stepped by overseas actors. A Foreign Interference Commission briefing circulated inside Public Safety Canada described Russian-affiliated extremist networks pumping convoy clips through proxy Telegram accounts linked to *Atomwaffen* and the *Russian Imperial Movement.* [19] *Politico's* scraping of 4Chan and white-supremacist Telegram channels counted at least twenty-five reposts of the convoy's GoFundMe link in a single week, each tagged "global uprising." [20] The result was a feedback loop in which every diesel-soaked selfie from Wellington Street was captioned in Cyrillic, Spanish, or Bahasa within hours, divorced from Canadian context but freighted with transnational rage.

One node in this lattice sat in a two-car garage outside Waco, Texas, where alt-right streamer "Rusty Ranger" (birth name Darren Coil) propped an iPhone against a gun safe and re-broadcast Ottawa TikToks to 300,000 followers on Rumble. "Look at our northern brothers draw the line," he said, overlaying convoy B-roll with a Chyron that screamed *COMMIE CASTRO JUNIOR PANICS.* His show lifted the trucker audio, then stitched on instructions for viewers to "siege state capitols, peaceful-like." *WIRED* analysts later found that Coil's channel quadrupled its subscriber count during convoy week, ranking among Rumble's top ten political streams. [21] *VICE* reporters traced Coil's PayPal tip jar to a Florida-registered LLC that deposited funds directly to Bitcoin wallets advertised on extremist Gab groups, [22]. A *Reuters* investigation revealed that allied U.S. Republicans rode the same outrage to accuse GoFundMe of "fraud" when it froze convoy donations. [23]

Coil swapped the day's Ottawa drone shots each night for a Stars-and-Bars backdrop, telling his chat, "In Texas, we'd park 'em sideways on Congress Avenue." By dawn, his clip had migrated into Canadian Telegram rooms. It offered proof that *America's watching*—a self-fulfilling prophecy since Canadian users reposted it back to U.S. feeds in ever-louder loops. The empirical assessment prepared for the Public Order Emergency Commission would later chart six distinct cross-platform cascades where a single Ranger video seeded content on Facebook, Twitter, TikTok, and three major Telegram hubs within fourteen hours. [24]

Six thousand kilometres east, in Oradea, Romania, ultranationalist vlogger Radu-Ioan Tănase scrolled the same footage and fired up his own Telegram cast. "*Acești camionagii sunt legiunea noastră*," he told 12,000 subscribers—"These truckers are our legion." He overdubbed English slogans into Romanian, swapped maple leaves for the blue-yellow-red tricolour, and packaged the memes for planned protests in Bucharest. When Telegram's founder boasted, he had refused Western requests to "silence conservative voices in Romania," analysts suspected Tănase's channels were among those protected. [25] *Politico's* data later showed Romanian-run Facebook groups reposting the convoy GoFundMe from Vietnamese IP addresses, suggesting a cottage industry of content mills chasing ad revenue with rage clicks. [20]

European uptake spread faster than a prairie grass fire: Finnish Soldiers of Odin pages swapped snow machines for semis; French *Convoi de la Liberté* admins cloned Canadian route graphics pixel for pixel; and a Swedish disinformation study mapped antisemitic symbols embedded in convoy GIFs circulating from Calgary to Kraków within forty-eight hours. [30] Academic reviewers would later argue that Canada's protest supplied a ready-made mythos—working-class authenticity, big-rig spectacle, and a soundtrack of air horns—that European far-right groups could localise without translation. [31]

While influencers and translators fanned the flames, the convoy's encrypted back-channels functioned as its logistical nervous system. A Media Engagement study of political messaging apps found that 60 per cent of convoy strategising occurred on Telegram and Zello push-to-talk streams, bypassing the public feeds where platform moderation could intervene. [22] Harvard researchers tracking diaspora WhatsApp circles observed identical Ottawa-shot clips captioned in Punjabi, Tagalog, and Arabic, then repurposed to attack mandates in Brampton, Dubai, and Manila. [28] The speed of translation outpaced traditional fact-checking so much that misinformation escaped linguistic silos before debunkers could draft a headline.

Inside Ottawa's Sir John A. Macdonald Building on 22 February, the Public Order Emergency Commission convened a closed-door panel of digital-security experts. According to meeting minutes later released with redactions, cyber-analyst Dr Shreya Dhillon projected a network graph showing 1.1 million unique accounts interacting with convoy hashtags, 36 per cent located outside Canada. [17] A second slide highlighted *bridge nodes*—Texas influencers like Coil, Romanian translators like Tănase, and a cluster of bot-amplified Russian accounts flagged by CSIS threat briefs. [27] Dhillon warned the mesh made de-platforming *whack-a-mole with hydras*, as each banned account re-emerged under fresh handles within minutes. Commission counsel asked whether existing criminal law could tackle foreign-funded digital incitement; Dhillon's reply, "Not without new treaty frameworks," went unredacted.

A supplementary expert report, "Canada Is No Exception," argued that the convoy's network typified identity-driven protest across the West: horizontally organised, algorithmically incentivised, and culturally portable. [29] Another study comparing Canadian and Swedish COVID-protest Telegram channels found shared memes invoking the "Great Replacement" theme, demonstrating how fringe ethno-nationalist narratives piggybacked on public-health discontent. [30] These findings landed on policy desks as the cabinet debated whether the Emergencies Act's financial-control tools could throttle cross-border crypto donations. Treasury Board officials cited *Reuters* data that U.S. donors comprised the plurality of frozen contributions, [24] while cybersecurity staff warned that Bitcoin tumblers already masked newer transfers.

Rusty Ranger opened his February 17 stream in Waco by reading Ottawa's new fines for idling heavy vehicles downtown. Then, he urged viewers to "honk digitally" by posting air-horn emojis under every *CBC* tweet. The stunt trended overnight, hijacking national broadcasters' comment sections. A POEC-commissioned empirical analysis later confirmed that emoji-spam campaigns could quadruple the apparent engagement on targeted posts, triggering platform promotion algorithms that inadvertently magnified protest messaging. [19]

On 18 February, Commission counsel grilled federal tech officers on whether Canada should join an emerging U.S.–EU task force to synchronise de-platforming protocols. One deputy minister cautioned that heavy-handed takedowns in February had already fed martyr mythology; *TechPolicy.press* commentators had made the same point in a podcast titled *Networked Activism and Extremism*, noting that platform bans often escalate rather than dampen mobilisation. [21] Staff from the Communications Security Establishment countered that leaving extremist bridge nodes intact allowed foreign adversaries to piggyback on legitimate protest, echoing warnings in the foreign-interference memo. [16]

By the month's midpoint, the convoy narrative existed less on pavement than in packets: 80 per cent of all mentions occurred outside Canada, yet every spike in U.S. or European traffic fed morale in Wellington Street camper-vans. Researchers from the Institute for Strategic Dialogue told commissioners that "perception of momentum" kept trucks parked long after diesel stipends ran dry, a psychological subsidy delivered free by algorithms and overseas amplifiers. [20] Deputy Prime Minister Chrystia Freeland would later cite those findings when justifying emergency financial freezes, framing them to cut the digital oxygen fuelling physical occupation. [27]

The week closed with snowfall, burying downtown signs. Online engagement soared, a paradox noted in sage-green font on the CSIS situation board: *Street shrinkage inversely correlated with hashtag reach.* In today's fibre-optic world, a rumour doesn't need legs to circle the globe—it travels at the speed of light—and Canada must still decide exactly where open debate ends and authority begins. Ahead awaited the reckoning: a government wielding unprecedented statutes, tech firms tightening API spigots, and civil-rights lawyers readying challenges—all of them groping for the off-switch in a machine designed to stay on.

The convoy's horns had barely faded when another noise filled the vacuum: the brittle crack of public trust splintering under the weight of half-believed claims. Edelman's 2022 Trust Barometer recorded Canada's sharpest twelve-month slide, warning of a "cycle of distrust" fuelled by what respondents called an "info-demic" of lies and half-truths. [32] That erosion collided head-on with a federal government suddenly governing by emergency decree; even as Finance Minister Chrystia Freeland unveiled powers to freeze protester bank accounts, *Reuters* noted critics whispered about *financial martial law* while supporters called the move overdue. [33]

Inside R.C.M.P. headquarters, an electric kettle hissed over stale coffee while Corporal Amina Khoury raced a progress bar on her dual-screen rig. A thirty-second TikTok—purporting to show an officer kneeling in solidarity with protesters moments before "going missing"—had racked up 2 million views since dawn. Khoury's open-source toolkit flagged GPS metadata from Edmonton, not Ottawa, and a reverse-image crawl matched the clip to 2019 footage of a Yellow Vest rally, a fact she slid into the morning brief marked URGENT—Ministerial Eyes Only. The final POEC report later confirmed that R.C.M.P. analysts debunked dozens of such viral hoaxes between 22 and 25 February, but often *after narrative uptake was already irreversible.* [36]

"Every myth we kill spawns two more," Khoury muttered, reading the following alert: a claim that federal agents were setting fire to seized trucks. The POEC-commissioned paper on mis-, dis- and mal-information would quote her anonymous frustration—that the Mounties were "trapped in a contest of upload speeds, not evidence." [35] By 26 February, the unit's dashboards tracked 18 million convoy-related engagements originating outside Canada—traffic intelligence later linked to foreign extremist amplifiers, prompting a classified warning that the occupation was now *a transnational spectacle as much as a local threat.* [43]

While Khoury punched facts into spreadsheets, Ottawa's Sir John A. Macdonald Building staged a different theatre. Meta's public-policy director appeared under subpoena before the Public Order Emergency Commission and, under oath, conceded that encrypted WhatsApp "density" made real-time sharing with law enforcement "operationally unworkable." Twitter's counsel followed, arguing that Canada lacked "legal clarity" for compelled data disclosure, prompting Commissioner Paul Rouleau to quip, "We have clarity in abundance— just not alignment." A chuckle rippled through the press gallery; the transcript would later record *laughter* in brackets, rare comic relief in a fortnight of lawyerly grind. [39]

Across town, a high-school social studies class in Calgary wrestled with the same digital mire. Ms Janelle Wyatt wheeled a projector to the front of Room 214 and queued a convoy meme of a masked Mountie torching vaccine vials. "Real or fake?" she asked. Twenty-three hands voted "real." Wyatt unfolded MediaSmarts' Break the Fake checklist—source, date, evidence—and guided students through lateral-reading drills. By the bell, the class had traced the image to a 2015 *Reuters* photo of a pharmaceutical waste incinerator in Nairobi. "Facts are slow," Wyatt told them, "so we have to make them sticky." Her lesson plan, posted later on the staff portal, drew on a teacher toolkit that *MediaSmarts* published during the occupation to help educators counter convoy disinformation. [40] [41]

In Ottawa, consequences arrived faster. On 28 February, the House finance committee asked FINTRAC executives why they had frozen only CA$7.8 million in convoy funds under emergency regulations. Director Barry MacKillop explained that FINTRAC's mandate had not expanded; only its client list had, adding crowdfunding portals and crypto exchanges to the roster. "We follow the money," he said, "but the law stops at foreign servers." Committee minutes show the exchange ended with MPs mulling new cross-border data treaties. [37]

Outside Parliament, interim Ottawa Police Chief Steve Bell briefed media on the occupation's endgame. "The Emergencies Act was a turning point," he said, but warned that future protests would unfold first on screens, not streets. [37] Two days later, Prime Minister Justin Trudeau revoked the declaration—"the situation is no longer an emergency"—yet banks remained authorised to unfreeze accounts only at their discretion, a hangover *Reuters* called *a governance headache in search of Tylenol.* [34]

Law enforcement after-action reviews echoed Bell's concern. In March 2024, a leaked internal R.C.M.P. report revealed to *CityNews* that frontline officers had not been shown the online death threats circulating in convoy chats, leaving them "blind to digital precursors of physical risk." The review urged a permanent open-source task force and faster clearance for *digital plain-clothes* operations. [44]

Platform executives, however, remained wary. At a POEC policy round-table on 17 November, Treasury Board Secretary Michael Sabia argued that financial measures "helped end the occupation in as peaceful a way as possible," while Google's regional counsel countered that blanket freezes risked pushing activists onto "dark-forest" platforms beyond regulatory reach. [42] The tension underscored a legal grey zone: Canada could compel data, but not guarantee cooperation, and every enforcement spike seemed to fortify the narrative of censorship among convoy sympathisers.

In the classroom, Wyatt's students drafted reflection journals. One grade-eleven wrote, "When the government froze money, my uncle said it proved the conspiracy. The fact-check proved him wrong, but he said it was staged." Wyatt circled the sentence and scribbled, "How do we measure success—changing minds or planting doubt?" Weeks later, she shared the journals at a provincial PD day, where educators swapped tactics for inoculating teens against future disinformation waves. Academic evaluations would show that such pilots improved lateral-reading scores by 25 per cent, but researchers cautioned that "skills beat single myths, not the system that manufactures them."

Back in Ottawa, the R.C.M.P.'s Khoury closed yet another tab. A new rumour claimed that UN armoured vehicles were massing in Saskatchewan. She geolocated the image to a Kansas rail yard and drafted a tweet-length debunk—only to wonder whether posting it would amplify the lie. She thought of Wyatt's class and the students sitting between two imperfect choices: algorithms that reward outrage and institutions that respond too slowly.

By 4 March, the convoy site had emptied, but the hashtag *#NextConvoy* trended in cyberspace—proof that narratives neither die nor sleep, they migrate. Cabinet instructed Justice officials to draft *online harms* legislation for autumn; civil-liberties groups readied challenges. Platform lawyers braced for a Canadian version of Europe's *Digital Services Act*. And somewhere in Texas, "Rusty Ranger" teased a new episode: *Ottawa Part 2—They Can't Silence Us*.

Pierre Berton once wrote that Canada's history is "a quest for order against the tug of liberty." The digital convoy made that quest recursive: every clampdown birthed a fresh grievance, every fact-check a fresh suspicion. As Khoury shut down her workstation, she wondered whether the next emergency declaration would concern capacity, not downtown streets. And in a Calgary classroom, Wyatt rolled up the projector screen, telling her students that the truth may still lace its boots—but in their hands lay the shoelaces.

ENDNOTES

[1] Edelman. (2022, January). 2022 Edelman Trust Barometer: Cycle of Distrust [Global report]. https://www.edelman.com/sites/g/files/aatuss191/files/2022-01/2022%20Edelman%20Trust%20Barometer%20Global%20Report_Final.pdf

[2] Mosleh, M., Guess, A. M., Nyhan, B., Pennycook, G., Lyons, B., & Lazer, D. (2023). How social media feed algorithms affect attitudes and behavior in an election campaign. Science, 380(6648), 119–127. https://doi.org/10.1126/science.abp9364

[3] Cinelli, M., Brugnoli, E., Quattrociocchi, W., & Schmidt, A. L. (2022, August). Facebook's "Meaningful Social Interactions" update increases polarization (SSRN Working Paper #4238756). https://ssrn.com/abstract=4238756

[4] Bak-Coleman, J. B., Guess, A., Lyons, B., Reifler, J., Nyhan, B., & Lazer, D. (2023). Asymmetric ideological segregation in exposure to political news on Facebook. Science, 380(6648), 144–150. https://doi.org/10.1126/science.ade7138

[5] Kreis, J., Narea, C., Maier, J., Stier, S., & de Vreese, C. (2023). The efficacy of Facebook's vaccine misinformation policies. Science Advances, 9(12), eadh2132. https://doi.org/10.1126/sciadv.adh2132

[6] Orr Bueno, C. (2023, February 8). "The feelings are still there": A disinformation expert on the legacy of the Freedom Convoy. TVO Today. https://www.tvo.org/article/the-feelings-are-still-there-a-disinformation-expert-on-the-legacy-of-the-freedom-convoy

[7] Reuters Fact Check. (2022, January 31). No truth to online rumours that 50 % of Ottawa's police force resigned. Reuters. https://www.reuters.com/article/fact-check/no-truth-to-online-rumors-that-50-of-ottawas-police-force-resigned-idUSL1N2UJ1TF

[8] Barrett, B. (2022, February 6). The alt-right on Facebook are hijacking Canada's trucker blockade. Wired. https://www.wired.com/story/ottawa-trucker-protest-facebook-alt-right

[9] Ganguly, A. (2022, March 3). Freedom convoys: The spread of misinformation across borders. Australian Institute of International Affairs. https://www.internationalaffairs.org.au/australianoutlook/freedom-convoys-spread-misinformation-across-borders

[10] Hermann, P. (2022, February 22). As "Freedom Convoy" spinoffs pop up on social media, D.C. region prepares. The Washington Post. https://www.washingtonpost.com/dc-md-va/2022/02/22/dc-freedom-convoy-protest-plans

[11] Macklam, B. (2022, February 10). The anti-vax trucker convoy made a crucial error in messing with Oakland. Vice News. https://www.vice.com/en/article/k7bh7m/the-anti-vax-trucker-convoy-made-one-crucial-error-in-messing-with-oakland

[12] Gillies, R. (2023, November 20). Prominent figure from Canada's trucker protests found guilty. Associated Press. https://apnews.com/article/canada-truck-protests-freedom-convoy-ottawa-guilty-3975bb6bbd0c089e0c56cebbe9187fd2

[13] Pacheco, D., Cuevas, A., & Spiro, E. S. (2024). Real-time fake news detection in online social networks. Scientific Reports, 14, 76102. https://doi.org/10.1038/s41598-024-76102-9

[14] Guess, A. M., & Lyons, B. (2021). Misinformation interventions are common, divisive, and poorly understood. Harvard Kennedy School Misinformation Review, 1(8). https://misinforeview.hks.harvard.edu/article/misinformation-interventions-are-common-divisive-and-poorly-understood

[15] Lamoureux, M. (2022, April 14). Inside the QAnon Queen's cult: "The abuse was non-stop". Vice News. https://www.vice.com/en/article/g5qgzq/qanon-queen-romana-didulo-cult-convoy-canada

[16] Center for Future Intelligence. (2023). Russia's role in the far-right truck convoy: An analytical briefing (POEC Exhibit COM0000197). https://foreigninterferencecommission.ca/fileadmin/foreign_interference_commission/Documents/Exhibits_and_Presentations/Exhibits/COM0000197.pdf

[17] Public Order Emergency Commission. (2023). Report of the Public Inquiry into the 2022 Public Order Emergency (Vol. 3). https://publicorderemergencycommission.ca/files/documents/Final-Report/Vol-3-Report-of-the-Public-Inquiry-into-the-2022-Public-Order-Emergency.pdf

[18] Hennebry, J. (2024). The polarized "naturalizations" of the 2022 Freedom Convoy. Digital Society, 3(2). https://doi.org/10.1007/s44282-024-00107-y

[19] Poirier, C. (2022). An empirical assessment of the convoy protest on six online sites (POEC Exhibit COM00000864). https://publicorderemergencycommission.ca/files/exhibits/COM00000864.pdf

[20] Scott, M. (2022, February 6). Ottawa truckers' convoy galvanizes far-right worldwide. Politico. https://www.politico.com/news/2022/02/06/ottawa-truckers-convoy-galvanizes-far-right-worldwide-00006080

[21] Donovan, J., & Amarasingam, A. (2022, February 9). Canada's trucker protests: Online and offline. TechPolicy.Press. https://techpolicy.press/canadas-trucker-protests-online-and-offline

[22] Woolley, S. C. (2023). Encrypted messaging applications and political messaging (Center for Media Engagement Report). https://mediaengagement.org/wp-content/uploads/2023/06/CME-Encrypted-Messaging-Report.pdf

[23] Reuters. (2025, May 18). Telegram founder says he rejected request to silence conservative voices in Romania. Reuters. https://www.reuters.com/world/europe/telegram-founder-says-he-rejects-request-silence-conservative-voices-romania-2025-05-18

[24] Shepardson, D. (2022, February 5). U.S. Republicans vow to probe GoFundMe decision halting Canada trucker donations. Reuters. https://www.reuters.com/world/florida-governor-investigate-gofundme-over-canada-trucker-donations-2022-02-05

[25] Owen, T. (2022, February 15). Everything we know about the U.S. "Freedom Convoy." Vice News. https://www.vice.com/en/article/z3nd9w/us-freedom-convoy

[26] Barrett, B. (2022, February 6). Duplicate of #8 for in-text superscripts—citation identical.

[27] Public Safety Canada. (2024). Government response to the Public Order Emergency Commission recommendations. https://www.publicsafety.gc.ca/cnt/rsrcs/pblctns/2024-pblc-rdr-mrgncy-rcmmndtns/index-en.aspx

[28] Eldorado Misinformation Review. (2023). Taking the power back: How diaspora organizations fight misinfo on encrypted apps. https://misinforeview.hks.harvard.edu/article/taking-the-power-back-how-diaspora-community-organizations-are-fighting-misinformation-spread-on-encrypted-messaging-apps

[29] Gillies, J., Raynauld, V., & Wisniewski, A. (2023). Canada is no exception: Political entanglement and identity-driven protest. American Behavioral Scientist. https://journals.sagepub.com/doi/full/10.1177/00027642231166885

[30] Ekman, M. (2024). Far-right extremist narratives in Canadian and Swedish COVID-19 protests. Journal of Deradicalization, 28, 45-70. https://doi.org/10.1080/19434472.2024.2340492

[31] Dick, H. (2023). Americanized discourses of religious freedom during the Ottawa trucker convoy. Studies in Religion/Sciences Religieuses, 52(4), 513-534. https://doi.org/10.1177/00084298241243084

[32] Duplicate of #1

[33] Ljunggren, D. (2022, February 14). Canada invokes emergency powers in bid to end protests. Reuters. https://www.reuters.com/world/americas/canada-s-trudeau-invokes-emergency-powers-in-bid-to-end-protests-idUSKBN2KJ27N

[34] Ljunggren, D. (2022, February 23). Canada ends emergency powers invoked to tackle trucker protests. Reuters. https://www.reuters.com/world/americas/canada-ends-emergency-powers-invoked-tackle-truckers-protests-pm-trudeau-2022-02-23

[35] Laidlaw, K. (2022). Mis-, dis- and mal-information and the convoy (POEC Policy Paper). https://publicorderemergencycommission.ca/files/documents/Policy-Papers/Mis-Dis-and-Mal-Information-and-the-Convoy-Laidlaw.pdf

[36] Public Order Emergency Commission. (2023). Final report (Vol. 2, pp. 134-140). https://publicorderemergencycommission.ca/files/documents/Final-Report/Vol-2-Report-of-the-Public-Inquiry-into-the-2022-Public-Order-Emergency.pdf

[37] House of Commons Standing Committee on Finance. (2022). Invocation of the Emergencies Act and related measures (Report 5). https://www.ourcommons.ca/Content/Committee/441/FINA/Reports/RP11697507/finarp05/finarp05-e.pdf

[38] Lee, M., & Cousins, B. (2022, February 15). Emergencies Act a "turning point" to end trucker occupation: Ottawa interim police chief. CTV News. https://www.ctvnews.ca/canada/emergencies-act-a-turning-point-to-end-trucker-occupation-ottawa-interim-police-chief-1.5776246

[39] Public Order Emergency Commission. (2022, November 2). Public hearings transcript (Vol. 15: Meta & Twitter testimony).

https://publicorderemergencycommission.ca/files/documents/Transcripts/POEC-Public-Hearings-Volume-15-November-2-2022.pdf

[40] Paul, W. (2022, October 13). Lessons on critical thinking: Kicking the tires of the "Freedom" Convoy. Education Action Toronto. https://educationactiontoronto.com/articles/lessons-on-critical-thinking-kicking-the-tires-of-the-freedom-convoy

[41] MediaSmarts. (2022). Break the fake: Critical thinking vs. disinformation (Teacher tip sheet). https://mediasmarts.ca/sites/default/files/tipsheet/break-fake-teacher-tip-sheet.pdf

[42] Public Order Emergency Commission. (2022, November 17). Public hearings transcript (Vol. 25: Financial measures panel). https://publicorderemergencycommission.ca/files/documents/Transcripts/POEC-Public-Hearings-Volume-25-November-17-2022.pdf

[43] Duplicate of #16

[44] Canadian Press. (2024, March 9). Officers weren't told of threats to harm police, says RCMP "Freedom Convoy" report. CTV News. https://vancouverisland.ctvnews.ca/politics/officers-werent-told-of-threats-to-harm-police-says-rcmp-freedom-convoy-report-1.6783792

CHAPTER SEVENTEEN:

POPULIST SOLIDARITY IN CANADA'S CAPITAL

"Freedom crossed borders faster than trucks and left tolls in every currency but caution. When a protest outlives its echo, the reckoning arrives with lawyers, accountants, and a neighbour who can't remember why you argued in the first place. Ultimately, not the horns or hashtags linger, but the uneasy quiet when the dust settles and everyone checks the bill."
~ *R. G. Cruise*

Authorities pushed the convoy encampments off Wellington Street, but in the first week of March, the reverberations only grew louder, as though the diesel thrum had migrated from pavement to broadband. Pollsters were the first to quantify the mood: Edelman's 2022 Trust Barometer warned that Canada, like much of the world, had slipped into a "vicious cycle of distrust," with faith in government and media collapsing faster than ever since the index began. [1] That vacuum proved a perfect resonance space for the grievance language sweeping three continents. *Politico's* data journalists traced over forty Telegram "mirror channels" that lifted Canadian convoy clips, overdubbed them in half a dozen languages, and stitched them into a broader narrative of a righteous "people" besieged by an arrogant "elite." [2] From Paris to Wellington, the slogans now sounded interchangeable—a chorus of air horns, flag-draped tailgates, and hashtags that insisted freedom travelled by truck.

Ellen Francis of the *Washington Post* captured the geography of that surge, noting how marches in Paris, Canberra, and Jerusalem all paraded placards that read, in English, *Hold the Line*—a phrase born on an Ottawa livestream three weeks earlier. [3] When the Paris police prefecture pre-emptively banned a planned *convoi de la liberté* and threatened €7,500 fines, French activists livestreamed the order back to Canadian channels to prove that "elites fear the people." [4] The borderless relay worked in reverse, too: video of a thousand American rigs circling the Washington Beltway on 6 March under the banner of the *People's Convoy* flooded Canadian feeds within minutes, persuading hold-outs in Alberta that "the fight has gone continental." [5]

If algorithms supplied the transport, U.S. conservative media supplied the fuel. *The Associated Press* counted dozens of syndicated talk-radio segments that replayed Ottawa speeches verbatim, usually with a soundtrack of martial snare drums. [6] One afternoon, Ben Shapiro clipped organiser Tamara Lich's phrase "We're done being pushed around" and looped it between ad reads for survival gear; by nightfall, TikTok compilations had set the quote to trap beats and posted it under the hashtag *#WorldFreedomConvoy*. *WIRED* analysts later showed how such U.S. influencer boosts could treble a convoy video's reach inside twelve hours, essentially relocating the protest's centre of gravity from Parliament Hill to the Florida server farms where Meta stored North America traffic. [7]

Ezra Kane, a convoy digital-strategy volunteer hunched over a folding table in a Kanata basement, noticed those numbers. Between gulps of lukewarm Tim Horton's coffee, he refreshed his Restream dashboard, watching concurrent viewers spike whenever a *Fox* or *Salem Radio* host picked up their feed. "Texas is beating Toronto two-to-one," he muttered, jotting a note to schedule speeches for U.S. drive-time slots. A *Reuters* feature that summer would confirm what his spreadsheet implied: the convoy's most ardent online audience now lived south of the 49th parallel, a fact later weaponised by Conservative leadership hopeful Pierre Poilievre, who pledged to "make Canada the freest country on Earth" while courting the same follow-ship. [8]

In Toronto, veteran columnist Marsha Kingston walked past Queen's Park and heard a chant she had last reported on the Champs-Élysées in 2019: *On est chez nous!* ➤ "We are in our own house!" The slogan, signature of France's Yellow Vest insurgency, now bounced off the Ontario legislature's sandstone façade. Over lunch on *Newsworld*, Kingston told viewers the sound gave her "the same chill as tear-gas season in Paris," proof that grievances, like viruses, "mutate yet keep the spike protein that latches onto anger." Canadian Twitter featured her segment for an hour—until clips of Tucker Carlson accusing Ottawa of deploying *globalist shock troops* overwhelmed it. [9]

Ottawa itself remained a theatre of contested narratives. On 2 March, the House of Commons opposition benches demanded whether Russian state media had magnified convoy streams for geopolitical gain. Government members cited CSIS briefs; Conservatives accused Liberals of deflecting from inflation. The Hansard transcript preserves the cacophony: "Is this a grassroots revolt," one MP bellowed, "or a Kremlin co-production?" [10] Across the street, the Standing Committee on Public Safety hauled GoFundMe executives into a televised grilling about foreign donations; Juan Benitez conceded that of the first CA$10 million raised, roughly 45 per cent hailed from U.S. ZIP codes. [11]

Not everyone saw puppet strings. On Parliament's front lawn, plumber-turned-truck-driver Dave Gervais insisted the movement was "pure maple." Still, he admitted that someone filled the convoy's Discord server with Portuguese subtitles and a banner reading *Liberdade para o Povo* ➤ "freedom for the people," overnight. He shrugged. He said, "Freedom sounds good in any language," and then, climbing onto a flatbed, livestreamed a speech that a Missouri AM station would rebroadcast within hours, sandwiched between segments on fuel prices.

Back in the Commons, debate sharpened. New Democrats warned of "dark-money megaphones" distorting weary Canadians' anxieties; Bloc Québécois members fretted about federal overreach; Conservatives waved print-outs of inflation charts. When a Liberal MP branded the convoy "foreign-inspired discord," opposition benches erupted, and the Speaker's gavel thundered until microphones cut out. The uproar fed evening newscasts, supplying split-screen drama that algorithmic editors found irresistible—a pattern later documented by ACLED (the Armed Conflict Location & Event Data Project) researchers as a feedback loop between parliamentary flashpoints and surges in social-media engagement. [12]

While politicians sparred, scholars mapped the deeper currents. An International Studies Quarterly paper used network analysis to show that Canadian populist pages had become central *bridge-nodes* connecting European anti-establishment groups to U.S. militia forums, effectively turning Ottawa into a hub of transatlantic grievance traffic. [13] Political-science bloggers at *The Loop* argued that the convoy moment sped up a home-grown populist turn—membership in Maxime Bernier's People's Party doubled over six weeks, and even mainstream parties dabbled in "elite versus everyday" rhetoric. [14] The diagnosis:

Canada's story was no outlier; it was Chapter Next in a populist anthology penned from Budapest to Brasília.

Outside the bubble of analysis, Ottawa residents craved sleep. On 4 March, interim Police Chief Steve Bell told *CTV* that invoking the Emergencies Act had been "the turning point." However, he cautioned that digital solidarity could resurrect blockades in hours if new sparks found dry kindling. [15] His warning landed just as a *Guardian* despatch reported that Parliament had voted to keep certain emergency powers in reserve, lest future caravans roll toward the capital. [16]

That safeguard, however, stoked another wave of solidarity narratives. A Montana podcaster described the vote as *Ottawa's Patriot Act.* When asked why they cared about a distant protest, a Czech moderator replied, "Because your fight is our rehearsal."

Marsha Kingston watched the ripples from her Toronto studio with both fatigue and fascination. "I hear Paris in Ottawa's chants and Ottawa in Prague's," she said on-air, "as though appeals to the people have become a single, borderless anthem." Ezra Kane clipped the quote, added a guitar riff, and pushed it to TikTok. The video clocked 120,000 views in an afternoon, most comments from users who had never heard of Kingston but loved the tagline: *Borderless anthem.*

On 7 March, Question Period reopened the theatre. A Conservative MP brandished a chart of YouTube analytics to argue the protest was evidence of *organic outrage,* and a Liberal rose to accuse the Tories of *clickbaiting insurrection.* When the Speaker called for order, MPs shouted, "Whose side are you on?" The question seemed larger than partisan taunts; it was the very riddle of the populist age—whether governments served citizens or algorithms, whether sovereignty lay in ballots or viral reach.

By sunset, the flag-draped semis were long gone, yet their digital exhaust hung over continents like contrails that refused to dissipate. Analysts at CSIS would later admit that the real frontline was no longer Rideau Street but the invisible highways of attention where a Toronto pundit, a Texas radio host, and a Romanian live translator could form a choir without ever sharing a time zone. In that choir, the word *freedom* flexed to fit each grievance, sung in accents as varied as the emojis beneath live streams.

The stage is now set for a mid-March showdown where these transnational harmonies will collide with the cold arithmetic of municipal by-laws and riot shields. Whether the anthem crescendos or fractures will depend not just on trucks or tweets, but on the fragile seam between solidarity and opportunism— between a people's earnest cry and the echo chambers that sell it wholesale, in that seam, Canada will discover whether it can host a protest without importing every anger on Earth. The world will learn whether Ottawa was prelude or prologue to the next populist refrain.

Mid-March opened on a note of *déjà vu.* headlines from *The Guardian* warned that talks to clear downtown Ottawa were "teetering" while skirmishes flared where concrete barricades met back alleys. [16] *Reuters* push-alerts minutes later relayed that protesters near the U.S. border at Windsor had already ignored one injunction and might ignore another. [17] The world watched the livestream counter climb: 3.2 million cumulative views by the time the sun hit the Peace Tower's copper roof, proof that the convoy's occupation, though physically diminished, still pulsed on every screen that trafficked in outrage.

Under the Ambassador Bridge overpass, Corporal Nadia D'Souza of the R.C.M.P.'s Crisis Negotiation Unit flicked her pen cap in rhythm with a diesel engine idling nearby. "Your trucks won't move until we have tow capacity and safe egress," she said, voice partly swallowed by exhaust. Across the folding table sat convoy marshal Brad Kernohan, thumbs flying over his phone as legal counsel texted screenshots of a fresh cease-and-desist letter from the Ontario Superior Court. *They can't fine an idea,* he muttered, then raised his head: "Show me the contract for that tow company—every driver's already been doxxed." *Project NATTERJACK's* later after-action report would confirm that at least three firms quit after their operators received death threats. [20]

Before the meeting, Ottawa's deputy mayor circulated an email—subject line *REMOVE HEAVY EQUIPMENT NOW*—to federal and provincial partners, attaching a draft by-law order that cited blocked fire routes and *demonstrable risk to life safety.* The message, preserved in the Public Order Emergency Commission's timeline, [22] landed in D'Souza's inbox mid-conversation; she slid her phone across to Kernohan, who scanned the PDF, scoffed, and typed *"tell them to rescind mandates first."* Above them, the bridge vibrated with north-bound semis, each thrum punctuated by a horn blast that echoed down Huron Church Road like a civic heartbeat out of rhythm.

Back downtown, Sergeant Luc Tremblay of the Ottawa Police manoeuvred through a corridor of rigs on Kent Street, the air flavoured by burnt coffee dripping from a toppled thermos and the metallic tang of idling exhaust. He handed a printed notice— *Vehicles must vacate by 1800 hrs or face seizure under federal emergency powers*—to a driver warming his hands over a propane heater. The man folded it into an origami aeroplane, launched it, and grinned. A *Guardian* stringer captured the scene; her caption later anchored a cost-analysis piece showing Ottawa had already spent more than CA$36 million policing the occupation. [18]

Analytics volunteer Ezra Kane refreshed Restream in a converted campaign bus on Queen Street. A Syndicaster scrape showed that three U.S. talk-radio shows had just replayed his speech word-for-word; two nights prior, he had given a fifteen-minute speech punctuated by intermittent shouts over the rumble of a generator. "Louisville numbers up sixty per cent," he told co-organiser Tamara Lich via Signal. Lich replied with a single emoji: a flexed bicep. *Associated Press* auditors would later count over forty American media segments airing convoy audio that week alone. [21]

Negotiators weren't the only ones drafting documents. City Hall couriers delivered a hard-copy letter signed by Deputy Mayor Laura Dudas requesting that organisers move fifteen trucks off residential side streets to a designated lot—a deal hashed out the month before but never honoured. Moments later, protester Rachel Lapierre read the letter aloud to an independent videographer: "They say it's for school-bus access," she scoffed to the camera, "but they just want us out of sight." The clip hit TikTok's *For You* feed within an hour, algorithmically adjacent to a February video in which protesters installed saunas on Wellington Street, still unfazed by threats of police escalation. [19]

At 14:07, a pickup backfired outside the Château Laurier, its bang mistaken for a flash-bang by jittery livestream viewers. Twitter rumours of *tear gas on Sparks Street* surged; R.C.M.P. analyst D'Souza, now back at the downtown fusion centre, scrambled to verify. A push notification from the City Auditor General's just-released report flashed across her second screen, citing *fragmented command structures* and warning that misinformation could outpace official updates. [21] She phoned the field commander: negative on gas, just a busted tail-pipe. Still, hashtags *#GasinOttawa* and *#Tyranny* trended within minutes, underscoring the audit's point.

Inside Parliament, MPs jousted across the aisle. A Conservative member waved a print-out of YouTube analytics, claiming 1.2 million unique Canadian viewers of convoy streams in the past 48 hours. "That's not Russian bots, that's real Canadians," he thundered. Public Safety Minister Marco Mendicino countered with a CSIS memo noting foreign amplification networks and warning that the occupation was "no longer purely domestic." [24] Hansard captured the cacophony: shouted accusations of "selling out to Klaus Schwab" versus "cheering on sedition."

Back under the bridge, talks stalled. Kernohan's phone buzzed: a Reuters alert quoting Prime Minister Trudeau—"All options, including the Emergencies Act, remain on the table if negotiations fail." [25] He tossed the handset onto the dash. D'Souza watched two toddlers chalk hearts on the pavement beside a truck tire taller than them; their giggles rose above the diesel haze. "We can still do this easily," she said softly. Kernohan exhaled. Somewhere above, an eagle circled against a gun-metal sky.

By dusk, neither side had budged. City ploughs lined Bronson Avenue, engines idling like elephants waiting to charge. Two still-willing contracts sat unsigned on a clerk's clipboard; R.C.M.P. had requested military flatbeds as backup, a detail later confirmed in POEC testimony. [26] D'Souza filed her end-of-shift notes: "Negotiations respectful but unproductive; legal escalation likely." She added one personal line: "Tempers cool, engines hot."

That evening, *The Hill Times* quoted Ottawa's deputy mayor calling the police operation "managing the unmanageable," lamenting residents as collateral damage. [27] Across social media, convoy supporters posted drone footage of the bridge encampment over a mash-up of *We're Not Gonna Take It* and bagpipe reels—the digital campfire around which global populists warmed their hands.

Yet cracks appeared. A leak of cease-and-desist letters reached a pro-convoy Discord; some drivers, spooked by potential five-year impound holds under the Emergencies Act, quietly moved rigs out of bus lanes after midnight. City CCTV logged the exits; nothing on Telegram acknowledged the retreat. The illusion of unity held—barely. Academic observers later called the night "the hinge," when momentum could still swing either direction. [28]

In a final message to Public Safety, the R.C.M.P. fusion cell warned that social-media engagement spikes now coincided with every rumour of police action—digital adrenaline priming physical confrontation. The memo ended with a stark line: *If Act invoked, expect instantaneous framing as global tyranny.* At 23:59, D'Souza signed off, stepped into the cold, and inhaled air still laced with diesel and the faint aroma of funnel cakes from a charity stand.

Overhead, Parliament's Centre Block clock struck midnight. The sound of the bells echoed across empty intersections, where melting snow smeared the chalk hearts. Tomorrow, the government would decide whether rhetoric would harden into regulation, the whirr of tow winches and the clank of cuffs would replace the sound of horns. And somewhere on a Missouri talk-radio loop, Ezra Kane's speech began again, riding AM waves toward a dawn audience already bracing for the next battle in a war where every street corner doubled as a stage and every smartphone as a loudspeaker.

Canada woke to an unaccustomed hush the morning after Parliament revoked the Emergencies Act: no horns, no diesel haze, just a collective intake of breath as front pages pivoted from siege imagery to sober examinations of civil liberty, economic scars, and the country's tarnished international standing. [29] Conservative think-pieces abroad spoke of Ottawa's *first-resort reflex*, warning that a G7 state had reached for financial choke-holds faster than diplomats could reach for talking points. [30] In the capital, a freshly struck Special Joint Committee began sifting cabinet minutes and tow-truck invoices for proof that the February emergency had met the statute's high bar. [31]

Yet the balance sheet told a different story: plant shutdowns at Ontario auto lines, a billion-dollar trade hit tallied by border economists, and supply-chain whiplash *Axios* likened to "a week-long snow day for Detroit." [32] *Fortune* pegged industry losses near U.S. $1 billion in the auto sector alone, a figure that spooked premiers eyeing tax receipts. [33] Ottawa's comptroller counted CA$30 million in overtime, barricades, and hotel vouchers to keep downtown semi-functional. [34]

Inside a brick walk-up off Metcalfe Street, lawyer Cara Ouellette skimmed affidavits beneath a desk lamp that hummed like fluorescent doubt. The

Canadian Civil Liberties Association's challenge to the Act was due in federal court in forty-eight hours, and her binder bristled with precedents about "clear and present danger" and "least intrusive means." [35] A ping on her phone brought late-breaking news: Justice Richard Mosley had, months later, found the invocation unreasonable, an omen Ouellette highlighted for oral argument. [36] She paused at a Privy Council Office memo leaked to *The Globe and Mail*, margin-noted *REPUTATIONAL RISK—FRAME AS NECESSARY, PROPORTIONATE*. The word *proportionate* felt suddenly elastic.

A kilometre north, veteran MP Bernard Duheme paced the Centre Block colonnade, mouthing lines of a speech he would deliver once the Question Period opened. He would accuse the government of "pocket-dialling martial law," cite a 24 March petition demanding an end to all mandates, then pivot to economic peril. [37] Down the hall, a Liberal aide tapped out contingency tweets—*#StrongInstitutions keep us safe*—ready to deploy should Duheme's clip trend. Another aide scrolled Hansard from February 20 to resurrect the minister's earlier promise that rights remained *sacrosanct*. [38]

Beyond the marble, ByWard Market tried for normalcy. In a hastily arranged town hall at a craft-beer pub, shopkeepers whose February revenues had flat-lined faced former convoy donors who now wondered whether they had bankrupted the neighbourhood they claimed to champion. "Your horns cost me two months of payroll," said florist Rana Mansour, voice quivering. "Your frozen account cost me my mortgage pre-approval," countered trucker Mike Dwyer. A *CBC* stringer recorded the exchange; the clip would run at six, framed as *Canada's rift in miniature*. University researchers later cite that meeting to show how economic grievance and civil-rights backlash intersected on the same bar stool. [39]

Outside, sandwich-boards offered *Convoy Specials* half in jest. A poster listed a city-sponsored counselling hotline for residents experiencing *post-horn stress*. The Auditor General's preliminary audit—"fragmented command structures, misinformation, outpacing briefings"—landed with a thud in council chambers. [40] Councillors passed a motion to seek provincial funds; downtown merchants applauded, then googled "business-interruption insurance."

On Parliament Hill, debate rippled like pennants in the March wind. Government benches referenced CSIS testimony that foreign extremist channels had latched onto the protest, citing evidence compiled for the SECU committee.

[41] Opposition MPs replied that CSIS had found *no* actionable plot, waving the interim joint-committee report and accusing ministers of conflating *loud* with *dangerous*. [42] Reporters filed sidebars on rhetorical *freedom inflation*, noting how every party now invoked liberty, though seldom the exact definition.

Down Rideau Street, coffee steam fogged the windows of a legal-aid office where paralegal Shay Lumsden helped low-income residents unfreeze accounts netted during the emergency order. Some had merely PayPaled twenty dollars to a convoy GoFundMe before the bank flags tripped. "Collateral damage," she muttered, filling out Release Form P-6. Think tanks from Cato to CCLA now cite such stories as proof that financial data-sharing posed systemic risks. [43]

Economic reckonings piled up: the Canadian Chamber of Commerce unveiled a trade-tracker showing billions in delayed goods and a warning that *investor confidence comes on foot, leaves on horseback*. [44] *Bloomberg* graphed currency jitters against convoy chronology; the loonie dipped each time a border closed. [45] A *Fortune* op-ed mused that *rule-of-law premiums* might now shadow Canadian bonds. *Fraser Institute* editorials fretted that Ottawa had traded economic stability for a quick political fix.

Even police introspection went public. *Project NATTERJACK's* after-action draft leaked online—PDF pages stamped *CONTROLLED* yet viral by lunchtime—detailing blurred command chains and a plea for *digital plain-clothes* capacity. [46] Columnists quipped the Mounties needed TikTok analysts more than riot shields. The same day, a Senate interim review critiqued "policy fog" around threshold definitions of national emergency. [47]

By the last Friday of March, the House rose for a constituency break, but the reckoning travelled with every MP. In rural ridings, town-halls split between applause for bank-account freezes and fury at "Trudeau's tyranny." In Toronto's 905 belt, polling hinted that swing voters liked restored quiet but feared precedent. Strategists predicted the issue would surface in Ontario's June election and Alberta's sovereignty-tinged race the following spring.

Internationally, headlines shifted from *Ottawa occupied* to legal post-mortems. The *BBC* led with the federal court ruling that the Act had been unreasonable, noting Ottawa's intent to appeal. [36] Cato labelled the decision *a cautionary tale for liberal democracies*, reprising its earlier critique of financial overreach. [43] Human-rights NGOs filed amicus briefs; the United Nations Special Rapporteur on assembly requested a briefing.

Late on 31 March, a staffer texted the Privy Council Office: *Draft narrative: Act saved economy & democracy—insert poll numbers.* Meanwhile, civil-liberties lawyers rehearsed oral arguments set for April, Parliament Hill security installed new bollards, and ByWard Market vendors debated whether to hang *Welcome Back* banners for Tulip Festival tourists. In a sense, the protest had ended; in another, it had merely dispersed into courthouses, committee rooms, and the small, sceptical conversations between neighbours.

Irwin Cotler once warned, "Liberty must be defended vigorously if it is to endure," and as March drew to a close, the ledger of lessons remained open— costs tallied but consequences still compounding. Ahead lay hearings, ballots, and the global echo chamber poised to remix Ottawa's cautionary tale into its next chorus.

ENDNOTES

[1] Edelman. (2022, January). *2022 Edelman Trust Barometer: Cycle of distrust* [Global report].
https://www.edelman.com/sites/g/files/aatuss191/files/2022-
01/2022%20Edelman%20Trust%20Barometer%20Global%20Report_Final.pdf

[2] Scott, M. (2022, February 6). Ottawa truckers' convoy galvanizes far-right worldwide. *Politico.*
https://www.politico.com/news/2022/02/06/ottawa-truckers-convoy-galvanizes-far-right-
worldwide-00006080

[3] Francis, E., & Timsit, A. (2022, February 9). 'Freedom Convoy' in Canada inspires protests from France
to New Zealand. *The Washington Post.*
https://www.washingtonpost.com/world/2022/02/09/freedom-convoy-protests-australia-
new-zealand-europe

[4] Willsher, K. (2022, February 10). Paris police ban 'freedom convoy' protests over Covid rules. *The
Guardian.* https://www.theguardian.com/world/2022/feb/10/paris-police-authority-bans-
freedom-convoy-covid-protests

[5] Chavez, J.-C. (2022, March 6). 'People's Convoy' circles Washington in protest of pandemic rules. *Reuters.*
https://www.reuters.com/world/us/peoples-convoy-truck-protest-drives-laps-around-
washington-2022-03-06

[6] Associated Press. (2022, February 11). U.S. conservative media figures cheer on Canadian trucker
protest. *AP News.* https://apnews.com/article/coronavirus-pandemic-sean-hannity-business-
health-ottawa-6ced8d978d2b2e36d4c1f40261bb0d6a

[7] Barrett, B. (2022, February 6). Alt-right on Facebook hijacking Canada's trucker blockade. *Wired*. https://www.wired.com/story/ottawa-trucker-protest-facebook-alt-right

[8] Thomson, N. (2022, August 4). Protests and politics: Canada's 'Freedom Convoy' reverberates. *Reuters*. https://www.reuters.com/world/americas/protests-politics-canadas-freedom-convoy-reverberates-2022-08-04

[9] Canada. House of Commons. Standing Committee on Public Safety and National Security. (2022, March 3). *Evidence, Meeting 12 – GoFundMe testimony* [Transcript]. https://www.ourcommons.ca/DocumentViewer/en/44-1/SECU/meeting-12/evidence

[10] Canada. House of Commons. (2022, March 2). *Debates (Hansard), 44th Parl., 1st Sess., No. 39*. https://www.ourcommons.ca/Content/House/441/Debates/039/HAN039-E.PDF

[11] Lee, M., & Cousins, B. (2022, February 15). Emergencies Act a "turning point" to end trucker occupation, says Ottawa interim police chief. *CTV News*. https://www.ctvnews.ca/canada/emergencies-act-a-turning-point-to-end-trucker-occupation-ottawa-interim-police-chief-1.5776246

[12] Armed Conflict Location & Event Data Project. (2022, March 17). *Regional overview: United States and Canada, 5–11 March 2022*. https://acleddata.com/2022/03/17/regional-overview-united-states-and-canada-5-11-march-2022

[13] Tran, K. H. (2024). Transnationalism and populist networks in a digital era: Canada's Freedom Convoy in comparative perspective. *International Studies Quarterly, 68*(4), Article sqae131. https://academic.oup.com/isq/article/68/4/sqae131/7815709

[14] Harcourt, L. (2024, August 10). The rising tide of populism in Canada since the Freedom Convoy. *The Loop* (ECPR blog). https://theloop.ecpr.eu/the-rising-tide-of-populism-in-canada-since-the-freedom-convoy

[15] Helmore, E. (2022, February 22). Canada extends emergency powers after trucker blockades end. *The Guardian*. https://www.theguardian.com/world/2022/feb/22/canada-extends-emergency-powers-after-trucker-blockades-ended

[16] Cecco, L. (2022, February 15). Saunas, haircuts, hot meals: Ottawa protesters set up for the long haul. *The Guardian*. https://www.theguardian.com/world/2022/feb/15/ottawa-truck-convoy-protesters-unfazed-by-emergencies-act

[17] Reuters. (2022, February 12). Protesters defy injunction order, continue to occupy key U.S.–Canada trade corridor. *Reuters*. https://www.reuters.com/world/americas/canada-protests-enter-third-week-sophisticated-demonstrators-dig-2022-02-11

[18] Cecco, L. (2022, March 18). Ottawa truck convoy cost the city more than C$36 million. *The Guardian*. https://www.theguardian.com/discover-cool-canada/2022/mar/18/ottawa-truck-convey-cost-c36m-police

[19] Duplicate of #16

[20] Royal Canadian Mounted Police. (2023). *Project NATTERJACK: National after-action review into the RCMP response to the Freedom Convoy 2022*. https://rcmp.ca/sites/default/files/doc/project-natterjack-national-after-action-review.pdf

[21] Office of the Auditor General of Ottawa. (2023). *Audit of the City of Ottawa's response to the convoy protest.* https://www.oagottawa.ca/media/tklagr1h/final-audit-report-audit-of-the-city-of-ottawa-s-response-to-the-convoy-protest-1-final-ua.pdf

[22] Public Order Emergency Commission. (2022). *Timeline overview – City of Ottawa events (OTT.IR.00000002).* https://publicorderemergencycommission.ca/files/overview-reports/OTT.IR.00000002.pdf

[23] Hatzipanagos, R. (2022, February 4). U.S. anti-vaccine mandate campaigners aim to mimic Canadian convoy. *The Guardian.* https://www.theguardian.com/us-news/2022/feb/04/us-anti-vaccine-mandate-convoy-canada

[24] Center for Future Intelligence. (2023). *Russia's role in the far-right truck convoy: Analytical briefing* (POEC Exhibit COM0000197). https://foreigninterferencecommission.ca/fileadmin/foreign_interference_commission/Documents/Exhibits_and_Presentations/Exhibits/COM0000197.pdf

[25] Cecco, L. (2022, February 4). 'Lawlessness must end': Canada police pledge tougher action on truck protests. *The Guardian.* https://www.theguardian.com/world/2022/feb/04/canada-ottawa-protests-trucks-police

[26] Public Order Emergency Commission. (2023). *Report of the Public Inquiry into the 2022 Public Order Emergency* (Vol. 1). https://publicorderemergencycommission.ca/files/documents/Final-Report/Vol-1-Report-of-the-Public-Inquiry-into-the-2022-Public-Order-Emergency.pdf

[27] Ryckewaert, L. (2022, February 11). Ottawa Police Service 'managing the unmanageable,' says city's deputy mayor. *The Hill Times.* https://www.hilltimes.com/story/2022/02/11/ottawa-police-service-managing-the-unmanageable-says-citys-deputy-mayor/229975

[28] Maguire, E. (2024). Codification, confusion and crisis: Police-government relations when Ottawa became unmanageable. *Policing & Society.* https://doi.org/10.1080/10439463.2024.2389926

[29] Duplicate of #15

[30] McTeague, J. (2022, February 24). Emergencies Act another blow to Canada's international reputation. *Fraser Institute Insights.* https://www.fraserinstitute.org/commentary/emergencies-act-another-blow-canadas-international-reputation

[31] Special Joint Committee on the Declaration of Emergency. (2022, March 3). *Interim report.* https://www.parl.ca/DocumentViewer/en/13098381

[32] Axios. (2022, February 11). Canadian protests lead to auto factories shutting down. https://www.axios.com/2022/02/11/canadian-protests-auto-factories-shutting-down

[33] Fortune staff. (2022, February 14). Here's how much the "Freedom Convoy" has cost the U.S. and Canada. *Fortune.* https://fortune.com/2022/02/14/freedom-convoy-protest-cost-us-canada

[34] Blanchfield, M. (2022, March 16). "Freedom Convoy" cost city of Ottawa C$30 million: City manager. *CTV News.* https://www.ctvnews.ca/ottawa/freedom-convoy-cost-city-of-ottawa-30-million-city-manager-1.5819624

[35] Canadian Civil Liberties Association. (2022). *Emergencies Act—CCLA court challenge.* https://ccla.org/major-cases-and-reports/emergencies-act

[36] Associated Press. (2024, January 23). Judge says Canada's use of Emergencies Act was unreasonable. *AP News.* https://apnews.com/article/d7e6640f817ee12410bb99840a3df41b

[37] Canada. House of Commons. (2022, March 24). *Debates (Hansard) No. 45.* https://www.ourcommons.ca/Content/House/441/Debates/045/HAN045-E.PDF

[38] Canada. House of Commons. (2022, February 20). *Debates (Hansard) No. 35.* https://www.ourcommons.ca/DocumentViewer/en/44-1/house/sitting-35/hansard

[39] Stone, K. (2022, March 17). Downtown Ottawa businesses recuperate following convoy occupation. *The Charlatan.* https://charlatan.ca/downtown-ottawa-businesses-recuperate-following-convoy-occupation

[40] Duplicate of #21

[41] Canada. House of Commons. Standing Committee on Public Safety and National Security. (2023). *Evidence, Meeting 91.* https://www.ourcommons.ca/DocumentViewer/en/44-1/SECU/meeting-91/evidence

[42] Canadian Security Intelligence Service. (2024). *Special Joint Committee on the Declaration of Emergency – CSIS submission.* https://www.canada.ca/en/security-intelligence-service/corporate/transparency/special-joint-committee-on-the-declaration-of-emergency.html

[43] de Rugy, V. (2023, February 14). Frozen assets: Examining Canada's use of the Emergencies Act. *Cato Institute Blog.* https://www.cato.org/blog/emergencies-act-after-two-years

[44] Canadian Chamber of Commerce. (2022). *Cost of Canada-U.S. trade disruption tracker.* https://chamber.ca/news/the-cost-of-canada-u-s-trade-disruption-on-full-display-with-new-trade-tracker

[45] Bloomberg News. (2022, February 10). How trucker protests shut the Canadian border and rocked the economy. *Bloomberg.* https://www.bloomberg.com/news/articles/2022-02-10/how-trucker-protests-shut-the-canadian-border-and-rocked-the-economy

[46] Duplicate of #20

[47] Senate of Canada. (2022). *Review of the exercise of powers pursuant to the declaration of emergency (Interim report).* https://publications.gc.ca/collections/collection_2024/sen/yc3/YC3-441-0-1-3-eng.pdf

CHAPTER EIGHTEEN:
DIESEL DOMINOES ACROSS THE MERIDIAN

"A protest that began with horns and diesel soon learned that a rumour travels faster than any rig and lingers longer than any exhaust. Don't be surprised if the banner changes when your movement becomes everyone's movement, but the bill will still arrive in your name. The world's new engine runs on outrage, and the road is always slick."
~ R. G. Cruise

The diesel drone that had rattled Canada's capital did not so much fade as refract, ricocheting along fibre optics and motorways until the early-February air over half a dozen Western capitals thrummed with borrowed outrage. Pollsters could still point to fatigue after two winters of lockdowns, but a deeper current— years of populist ferment that had lifted hard-right parties from Helsinki to Madrid—had primed the ground for what came next. [1] [2] When Ottawa's occupation hit global feeds, it offered a made-for-export kit: big rigs as barricades, horns as hymnals, a ready-made slogan of "freedom" broad enough to fit every grievance. From Washington talk-radio studios to Polish meme pages, influencers spliced Canadian dash-cam clips with their jeremiads, creating a montage of grievance that travelled faster than any convoy could. [1]

By dawn on 11 February, the effect was visible in Paris, where a salt crust of old road grit crackled beneath tyres circling the *Place du Trocadéro*. Two veterans of the 2018 *gilets jaunes*—Élodie, a former forklift driver, and Marc, once a coachman for tourist barges on the Seine—leaned on the fender of a dented Peugeot Boxer and scrolled through WhatsApp. "Irish lads say border checks are light at Cherbourg—roll tomorrow," Marc read aloud, translating a voice note thick with Dublin consonants. Above them, the Eiffel Tower's lattice glimmered like a tuning fork for discontent. Police sirens Doppler'd in the distance, announcing the roadblocks President Emmanuel Macron had ordered to keep the *Convoi de la liberté* out of the city. Yet by mid-morning, dozens of vehicles broke through, snarling traffic around the Arc de Triomphe as squads in riot gear loosed tear-gas volleys. [3] [4] Over the shouting rose a chant in accented French: *On roule pour la liberté!* ➤ We ride for freedom.

The metallic cough of camper vans fills the roundabouts surrounding Brussels' European Quarter hundreds of kilometres to the north-east. A Flemish carpenter named Pieter hoisted a bedsheet banner spray-painted *MAPLE LEAF SOLIDARITY* and taped beneath it a photocopied manifesto attributed to a Canadian organiser: *Block the arteries of tyranny, and the heart will capitulate.* Police rings diverted the column to a rest-area car park, but protesters continued on foot, winding past EU glass façades while a lone fiddler sawed out *Frère Jacques* in minor key. [5] [6] [7] The symbolism was not lost on journalists: Canada's domestic standoff had mutated into a rolling critique of supranational governance, aimed at Brussels as much as Ottawa.

Across oceans and seasons, a Melbourne suburb provided the movement's antipodal mirror. A podiatrist on pandemic leave jabbed at her phone in a sun-bleached café, smelling of eucalyptus and diesel exhaust. "Two hundred bucks to the boys in Ottawa," she announced, tapping *Donate* on a GiveSendGo page already awash in kangaroo emojis and red-and-white maple leaves. Beside her, a tradesperson refreshed a Telegram channel, beaming voice messages directly from Parliament Hill: "Fuel funds low—tell Aussie mates we stand with them." Australian media later confirmed that leaked donor lists showed hundreds of contributors from every state, funnelling money through Canadian accounts even after GoFundMe froze its Canadian convoy page. [8] [1] [5] Outside, cars plastered with *Convoy to Canberra* decals honked down Sydney Road, accelerating toward the nation's capital just as their northern counterparts had toward Wellington. [9]

Indeed, New Zealand's Beehive soon rang with the same klaxon chorus. On 8 February, Wellington streets filled with trucks and utes, many flying silver fern and maple leaf flags. Protesters chanted *Hold the line!* In improvised *haka* rhythms, while police in high-vis tried to pry camping chairs from the parliamentary lawn. [10] Three days in, over fifty arrests had done little to thin the crowd. A Māori elder, leaning on a carved walking stick, muttered that the commotion felt "less warrior, more imported carnival."

That phrase—*imported carnival*—echoed through op-ed pages as analysts scrambled to map the new geography of dissent. One columnist dubbed the global freedom movement *a rolling carnival of crank and conspiracy*, noting how QAnon slogans and sovereign-citizen legalisms travelled side-by-side with the trucks. [11] Researchers at *WIRED* traced surges of Facebook engagement: 88,000 convoy-related posts generating over sixteen million interactions in just two weeks, many seeded by American alt-right influencers who smelled culture-war profit in Canadian diesel fumes. [12] The Institute for Strategic Dialogue went further, charting Telegram graphs where French, German, and English channels braided together in real time, sharing route maps, legal disclaimers, and playlists heavy on Johnny Cash and AC/D.C.. [13] In this network, the Canadian flag became both brand and passport—proof of authenticity for any would-be convoy, whether rolled on asphalt or scrolled on screens.

Extremist actors were quick to seize the opportunity. A GNET study of convoy-themed subreddits found Holocaust metaphors, Nazi salutes rendered in emojis, and calls to *finish what January 6 started*. [14] An extremist newsletter in Central Europe praised the Canadian model as *the logistics template of the Fourth Political Theory*—proof, it argued, that infrastructure, not ideology, was the ultimate chokepoint. Even fund-raising glitches served the narrative: when GoFundMe yanked the original Canadian campaign and promised automatic refunds, Florida's governor thundered about theft of patriotic dollars, inadvertently steering traffic to less-regulated platforms where transparency was optional and transaction fees discreetly higher. [15]

Amid the smoke of flare guns and the static of livestreams, smaller moments hinted at how easily real-world and digital arenas now overlapped. In Paris, Élodie filmed a quick tutorial—*Mask your plates; buy prepaid SIMs*—and uploaded it to a Dutch Telegram group before police confiscated her phone. In Brussels, Pieter's Maple Leaf banner trended on Twitter for six hours, far longer than it flapped in the actual wind before officers folded it into an evidence bag. And in Melbourne, the podiatrist's $200 donation appeared on a public ledger milliseconds after she pressed send, her initials nested among Kansas retirees and Finnish crypto-miners.

By mid-February, open-source analysts compiled heat maps where convoy hashtags glowed like constellations: *#ConvoyEU* over Antwerp, *#KonvoiSuomi* over Helsinki port roads, *#TruckYeah* under the Texan sun. The patterns resembled a cold-front radar, or perhaps the diesel spill across an uneven pavement, one spark away from ignition. Next would come the acceleration online and the shadowy money trails. For now, though, the world watched an atlas of protest being redrawn in real time, every horn blast in Paris answered by a motorcycle rev in Brisbane, every Canadian flag abroad reminding Ottawa that its domestic drama had achieved the dubious honour of going global.

The convoy's second act began not on snow-packed highways but inside a million bright rectangles. By 11 February, the tag *#FreedomConvoy* had already burst its Canadian banks; a torrent of 4.8 million tweets, peaking at 171,848 in a single day, sluiced through phones from Alberta to Auckland. [16] Every refresh felt like a drumroll: Facebook groups for *truck-riding liberty* doubled their membership overnight while *CrowdTangle* graphs skied upward in a blue-bar frenzy. [17] Algorithms, feeding on rage and repetition, pulled the protest into every feed the way winter winds pull smoke up a chimney; American influencers supplied the draft, supplying 19.3 million of the first 25 million Facebook interactions despite never smelling diesel on Wellington Street. [18]

It was the perfect storm for echo chambers—a "stickier than snow-chains" pipeline of Facebook pages, Telegram social media loops and right-wing broadcasters turned fringe despatches into a prime-time spectacle, *The Verge* warned, [17]. At the same time, *WIRED* logged the alt-right's gleeful hijack of convoy memes, Confederate flags photoshopped behind maple leaves. [19] Behind the façade, security analysts at ISD (the Institute for Strategic Dialogue, a London-based *think and do* tank dedicated to understanding and innovating real-world responses to extremism, hate, and disinformation) traced dozens of mega-groups to Bangladesh, Vietnam, and Bulgaria—profit farms slapping Canadian banners on clickbait so loud it rattled ad servers. [20]

The money rolled in. When hackers cracked GiveSendGo on Valentine's Eve, 92,845 donor names spilt into the open; the database showed 56 per cent U.S. zip codes, 39 per cent Canadian, a river of small bills mirroring anti-mandate hashtags across the border. [21] Screens erupted with celebratory pings—*cha-ching* GIFs spinning beside avatars of cartoon big-rigs.

In a dim Oregon attic smelling of burnt coffee and solder, a QAnon streamer who called himself *PatriotSkies* punched the *Go Live* icon. His Discord den, wallpapered in 8-K monitors, crackled as he piped Ottawa drone footage across half a dozen channels. *Retweet the meme, fam—we're topping seven figures tonight,* he drawled, dropping a new template: a chrome semi smashing chains beneath block letters *REV THE PEOPLE.* The sidebar counters spun upward; each thock of a new subscriber sounded like a lug-nut dropping into a steel tray. Behind him, a second screen flashed the *Axios* chart showing U.S. Facebook pages out-engaging Canadian ones three-to-one. [18]

His co-host read aloud a *Guardian* headline about extremist cross-pollination—"vehicle for darker beliefs," she chuckled, adding, "Yeah, that's the engine mod." [26] In the chat, emojis of smokestacks and red pill capsules scrolled faster than Oregon rain. Links to GoFundMe clones, Monero wallets, and a rumour that Elon Musk would bankroll diesel vouchers filled the right margin. Somebody pasted the fresh GiveSendGo leak—*Siebel dropped 90k!*—and the room howled in approval. [21]

Thirty-seven hundred miles east, the February sun lifted through pewter clouds over Warsaw. On a cracked concrete lot behind the *Stadion Narodowy,* four Polish ultranationalists huddled around a tablet displaying a Telegram thread titled *Konwój Wolności–Bruksela.* "Two-to-one Yanks over Canucks in donors—respect," one muttered, tapping the data screenshot. "We do better," another replied, unfurling a home-printed banner that mashed together the maple leaf and the crowned Polish eagle. The thread's pinned message forwarded *Politico's* tip about a pan-European convoy rendezvous on Valentine's Day; [24] next to it, a *Euronews* alert warned Parisian drivers of prison time for blocking the *Périphérique.* [23]

Plans ricocheted between Polish, English, and a scatter of emoji. Somebody dropped Google-Map pins for fuel stops west of Łódź. Another bragged of finding a sympathetic mechanic in Łask willing to disable emission sensors gratis. Over every line hovered the question of money; one user shared *VICE* screenshots claiming Canadian organisers now faced "martial-law bank freezes," sparking a volley of flame icons and "let them try here" replies. [22]

Meanwhile, a flurry of Slack pings rattled the moderation war room of a U.S. social-media giant. A whistle-blower email, later leaked to investigative reporters, showed compliance lawyers agonising over whether convoy content met the threshold for *Coordinated Harmful Activity*. "We have never seen cross-border amplification at this velocity outside election misinfo," one staffer wrote, pointing to the *German Marshall Fund* graph of 14,667 convoy posts in three weeks. [18] Another warned that scammers were already cloning groups. *Reuters* would confirm a day later that Meta had nuked dozens of convoy pages run from Vietnam. [20] [30] The final line of the memo, reproduced in the leak, read like a sigh: *Either we throttle the hashtag or it drives the evening news—there is no neutral gear.*

By mid-month, the convoy's digital heat signature glowed like forge-iron. *The Washington Post's* live tracker of Ambassador Bridge blockades generated millions of clicks even after police cleared the lanes, [27] and *Guardian* photographers in Ottawa caught the sting of pepper spray drifting between trucks. Tweets tagged *#HoldTheLine* broke another hundred-thousand ceiling. [28] *Axios* christened the moment *populism's new inferno*, noting copycat rigs revving from California to Canberra. [29] Homeland-security analysts echoed the metaphor in a bulletin warning U.S. law enforcement that Super Bowl traffic might be the next target. [25]

Inside the convoy channels, the air buzzed with tactical fantasies: screenshots of interactive *Freedom Maps* stitched from Google Sheets; colour-coded spreadsheets of border crossings rated for media optics; a parody flight-radar map where truck icons replaced aeroplanes. The Simon Fraser University (SFU) dataset logged 81,242 distinct hashtags by 15 February, [16] each a breadcrumb in what one disinformation scholar called "a choose-your-own-revolution board game."

And yet cracks appeared. After a platform purge, someone took PatriotSkies' Discord feed offline. This purge also removed a Missouri woman's hacked account that had quietly administered five of the largest Facebook convoy groups. [17] [30] Warsaw organisers fumed when Belgian police banned their Brussels finale; [24] their Telegram poll pivoted to *Plan B: block the Łazienkowski Bridge*. Donations wobbled as banks flagged wire transfers; a moderator read Vice's leak aloud in Oregon—names, ZIP codes, passport scans—and one user typed,

"They're doxing the fuel lines." Participants argued whether to shift to privacy coins or lean on diaspora churches.

Still, the current ran. Screens continued to blaze pewter light on sleepless faces. In basements, cabs, and cafés, keyboards clacked like distant woodpeckers, matching the tattoo of air-horns half a world away. The atlas of protest was no longer measured in miles but in retweets per minute, in the rate at which a slogan could peregrinate from Winnipeg to Warsaw before breakfast. A data-visualisation graduate student plotted the exponential curve and realised the y-axis had room for state actors, darknet wallets, and things beyond grassroots horsepower.

From the sky, the network looked like an arterial system flooding with dye: red-gold nodes pulsing in Montréal, Tacoma, Melbourne, Antwerp. The dye kept spreading into ever-darkening channels, where geopolitics lay in wait, ready to hitch a ride.

It was the winter fortnight when diesel politics met digital geopolitics. On the surface, late February 2022 looked like a newsreel stuck on repeat—horns in Ottawa, tractors in Paris, roadblocks in California—but a colder war was warming behind the drifts. Russian armour massed on Ukraine's border; Western agencies whispered about "hybrid playbooks"; and every television crawl from *Fox* to *RT* looped the same Canadian truck clips, stripped of context and draped in whatever flag best served the hour's narrative. Canadian police listening posts heard it first: an R.C.M.P. after-action note, stamped *Project NATTERJACK*, logged that Kremlin-branded Telegram channels had injected *Freedom Convoy* hashtags into Ukraine disinformation streams within forty-eight hours of one another. [31]

Analysts hunched over scrolling code points in a fluorescent briefing room at National Headquarters. One monitor showed an English-language *RT* segment praising "grass-roots truckers defying tyranny," another a Cyrillic meme casting the same trucks as proof that NATO capitals were imploding. An intelligence officer traced the memes' hopscotch route—St. Petersburg bot farm to a Florida QAnon chat to a Winnipeg Facebook page with 120,000 followers—and muttered that the map looked "less like traffic and more like plumbing." What clogged those pipes, an ISD researcher had warned days earlier, were hundreds of "conspiracy clickbait groups" run from Vietnam, Bangladesh and—tellingly—Saint Petersburg, all repackaging convoy videos for ad revenue while amplifying anti-NATO tropes. [32]

The Foreign Interference Commission would later label the pattern *opportunistic co-branding*. A classified exhibit laid out the mechanics: Russian state media clipped Canadian livestreams, overlaid them with Kremlin talking points about a *failing liberal order*, then pushed the package back into Western feeds via shell Telegram channels and romance-scam Facebook accounts. [33] The tactic cost Moscow almost nothing, yet bought a global billboard to scrawl doubt about democratic resolve.

Meanwhile, mainstream airwaves reflected the distortion. *RT* devoted entire evening blocks to the blockade, portraying truckers as proletarian kin resisting *sanitary authoritarianism*. When EU regulators finally yanked the network off satellite, *RT* doubled down online, seeding mirrors reachable through VPNs that mixed convoy footage with pre-invasion Ukraine talking points. [34] On the opposite ideological pole—but often in eerie synch—Fox News anchors cut live to Wellington Street, punctuating monologues about *medical apartheid* with the lower-thirds of the screen that read *FREE SPEECH UNDER SEIGE*, a *National Observer* media study later showed dozens of *Fox* segments re-using tropes first surfaced on Russian channels. [34]

Not everyone in the Murdoch newsroom felt comfortable at 02:00 on 24 February—a scant hour before Russia's tanks crossed the Ukrainian frontier—producers locked in a sixth straight convoy package. One junior editor slid a compliance memo across the table: *Multiple intel partners flag foreign-state amplification. Are we abetting psy-ops?* A senior producer exhaled, pinched the bridge of her nose and replied, "We run the pictures; we can't fact-check the internet at 180 decibels." Similar debates flickered in New York boardrooms and London control rooms, proof that echo chambers were now big enough to make executives sweat.

In Ottawa, the Public Order Emergency Commission felt the tremor. During late-February hearings, a cybersecurity witness told commissioners: "We monitored coordinated fundraising appeals routed through Russian proxy sites. Seventeen of the top fifty crypto wallets hitting convoy accounts were seeded out of Moscow time-zone IPs." The room fell silent as counsel scrolled the spreadsheet of wallet addresses—strings of hexadecimal that looked like harmless snowflakes to the untrained eye. [38]

Those data trails mattered because money was the movement's oxygen. On 13 February, hackers dumped GiveSendGo's back-end, exposing 92,845 donors—55 per cent American, but also a sprinkle of names traced to Eastern European ISPs and one wallet tied to a St. Petersburg exchange. [39] *VICE* reporters noticed that several ruble-friendly wallets stopped transacting within hours of Western sanctions on Russian banks, suggesting a nervous hand on the tap. *PBS* would calculate that of the nearly $10 million raised in the first GoFundMe wave, roughly 44 per cent originated south of the 49th parallel, a figure pundits weaponised on both sides of the border. [42]

While investigators followed the money, code warriors traced packet routes. In late February, a Cybersecurity and Infrastructure Security Agency (CISA) bulletin warned North American logistics firms that GRU Unit 26165 had expanded its target set to include *entities facilitating COVID-protest supply chains*, a phrase widely read as convoy fuel depots and sympathetic trucking co-ops. [41] One R.C.M.P. analyst dryly observed that after years of ransomware, the Kremlin had discovered a cheaper weapon: convince truckers to park their rigs.

Yet disinformation is a hydra—lop one head, two sprout. When Meta axed hundreds of fake convoy pages run from Hanoi click-farms, fringe influencers cried censorship and migrated to alt-video platforms where Russian state outlets still lurked unfiltered; *Guardian* columnist Arwa Mahdawi quipped that the "siege of Ottawa" had become "a carnival ride for the algorithm." [40] *Reuters* photographers caught the carnival's other face: at the Ambassador Bridge, Maple Leaf signs fluttered beside banners reading *We Stand With Russia*—a juxtaposition that made Detroit auto execs blanch. [44]

Inside Parliament, the Emergencies Act froze accounts faster than an Ottawa February. A leaked R.C.M.P. ledger showed dozens of domestic accounts flagged for suspected foreign pass-throughs—some transactions routed via a Seychelles crypto-mixing service famed for laundering ransomware proceeds. [31] Civil-liberties lawyers gasped; bankers complied; convoy chat rooms lit up with tutorials on converting diesel money into Monero. By the month's end, National Finance officials briefing the Commission conceded that the freeze had "snagged a non-trivial volume of offshore dark money." Still, they refused to quantify it, citing ongoing probes. [38]

All the while, hashtags metastasised. *#RussianWinter* trended for a day after *RT* framed the blockade as a harbinger of EU energy revolts. *#TruckersForPeace* trended next, a DFRLab scrape showing its earliest boosters were English-language accounts previously hawking anti-NATO memes. In Michigan, the self-styled *People's Convoy* organisers boasted to *Reuters* that they had cribbed their entire logistics plan from Telegram playbooks shared by anonymous users posting Moscow-time emojis. [43]

By the first week of March, Canada had cleared most rigs from Wellington Street, but the engines still idled online. Someone refitted the once-rolling protest convoy into a ghost fleet—its chrome silhouettes projected across thousands of avatars, its slogans ready for redeployment in whatever culture war came next. Hybrid-war tacticians could scarcely design a neater tool: low overhead, high yield, and deniable from every direction.

Somewhere behind a firewall, a Russian operative logged the analytics: Western news channels recycling RT sound bites, cryptocurrency drips bypassing sanctions, Ottawa, and Washington bickering over emergency powers. *Mission cost: negligible. Mission effect: to be determined.*

So the diesel fog lifted to reveal a deeper haze—the one that seeps through modems, not exhaust stacks, and turns every grievance into a global broadcast. That haze will settle into culture, trade, and even family dinner tables, forcing democracies to decide whether truth can still find traction on roads slick with algorithmic oil.

ENDNOTES

[1] Scott, M. (2022, February 6). Ottawa truckers' convoy galvanizes far-right worldwide. *Politico.* https://www.politico.com/news/2022/02/06/ottawa-truckers-convoy-galvanizes-far-right-worldwide-00006080

[2] Aktas, M. (2024). The rise of populist radical right parties in Europe. *International Sociology, 39*(6), 591-605. https://doi.org/10.1177/02685809241297547

[3] Associated Press. (2022, February 12). Protests against Covid restrictions held in France and Netherlands. *The Guardian.* https://www.theguardian.com/world/2022/feb/12/covid-pass-protesters-convoy-paris-police

4 Paone, A., & Thomas, L. (2022, February 13). French COVID protest convoy defies Paris stay-away order. *Reuters*. https://www.reuters.com/world/europe/police-stop-50-vehicles-heading-paris-protest-convoy-2022-02-12

5 Willsher, K. (2022, February 14). Belgian police prevent French 'freedom convoy' from entering Brussels. *The Guardian*. https://www.theguardian.com/world/2022/feb/14/french-covid-freedom-convoy-heads-for-brussels-despite-police-warning

6 The Guardian. (2022, February 14). Covid-pass protest arrives in Brussels – live blog. https://www.theguardian.com/world/live/2022/feb/14/covid-news-live-england-delays-plan-to-vaccinate-children-aged-5-11-hong-kong-overwhelmed-by-fifth-covid-wave

7 Reuters Pictures. (2022, February 14). 'Freedom Convoy' inspires protests beyond Canada [Photo package]. *Reuters*. https://www.reuters.com/news/picture/freedom-convoy-inspires-protests-beyond-idUSRTS5H6JX

8 Roy, T. (2022, February 16). Leaked data reveals hundreds of Australian donors to Canadian convoy fundraiser. *ABC News (Australia)*. https://www.abc.net.au/news/2022-02-16/australians-donate-to-canadian-convoy-givesendgo-fundraiser/100832928

9 Butler, J. (2022, February 4). 'Occupy Canberra': Behind the anti-vaccine protests at Parliament House. *The Guardian (Australia)*. https://www.theguardian.com/australia-news/2022/feb/04/occupy-canberra-behind-the-anti-vaccine-protests-at-parliament-house

10 ABC News. (2022, February 10). Clashes at New Zealand parliament as protests inspired by Canada's "Freedom Convoy" continue for third day. https://www.abc.net.au/news/2022-02-10/new-zealand-parliament-protests-covid-canada-convoy/100818610

11 Badham, V. (2022, February 11). The global 'freedom movement' is a carnival of crank and conspiracy—and very dangerous. *The Guardian (Comment)*. https://www.theguardian.com/commentisfree/2022/feb/12/the-global-freedom-movement-is-a-carnival-of-crank-and-conspiracy-and-very-dangerous

12 Stokel-Walker, C. (2022, February 8). The alt-right on Facebook are hijacking Canada's trucker blockade. *Wired*. https://www.wired.com/story/ottawa-trucker-protest-facebook-alt-right

13 Institute for Strategic Dialogue. (2022, February 21). *Jan 6 series: The new face of transnational extremism* [Brief]. https://www.isdglobal.org/digital_dispatches/jan-6-series-the-new-face-of-transnational-extremism

14 Molas, B. (2022, March 14). "Victims of the Holocaust": The 'Freedom Convoy' subreddits as spaces for antisemitism and far-right radicalisation. *GNET Insight*. https://gnet-research.org/2022/03/14/victims-of-the-holocaust-the-freedom-convoy-subreddits-as-spaces-for-antisemitism-and-far-right-radicalisation

15 Reuters. (2022, February 5). GoFundMe removes donation page for Canadian trucker protest. *The Guardian* (syndicated). https://www.theguardian.com/world/2022/feb/05/gofundme-removes-donation-page-for-canadian-truckers-protest

[16] Al-Rawi, A. (2022). *An empirical assessment of the convoy protest on six online sites* [Research report]. Simon Fraser University. https://publicorderemergencycommission.ca/files/exhibits/COM00000864.pdf

[17] Broderick, R. (2022, February 19). How Facebook twisted Canada's trucker convoy into an international movement. *The Verge*. https://www.theverge.com/2022/2/19/22941291/facebook-canada-trucker-convoy-gofundme-groups-viral-sharing

[18] Gold, A. (2022, February 14). U.S. accounts drive Canadian convoy protest chatter. *Axios*. https://www.axios.com/2022/02/14/us-accounts-canada-convoy-protests-social-media

[19] Duplicate of #12

[20] Thomas, E. (2022, February 24). Fake "Freedom Convoy" Facebook groups are being run by foreign networks for profit. *Institute for Strategic Dialogue (Blog)*. https://www.isdglobal.org/digital_dispatches/fake-freedom-convoy-facebook-groups-are-being-run-by-foreign-networks-for-profit

[21] Gilbert, D. (2022, February 14). Hackers just leaked the names of 92,000 "Freedom Convoy" donors. *Vice News*. https://www.vice.com/en/article/freedom-convoy-givesendgo-donors-leaked

[22] Lamoureux, M. (2022, February 15). "Freedom Convoy" conspiracy theorists are losing it over Trudeau's Emergencies Act. *Vice News*. https://www.vice.com/en/article/freedom-convoy-conspiracy-theorists-are-losing-it-over-trudeaus-emergencies-act

[23] Euronews. (2022, February 10). Paris police ban Canada-style "Freedom Convoy" protest against French COVID restrictions. https://www.euronews.com/2022/02/10/paris-police-ban-canada-style-freedom-convoy-protest-against-french-covid-restrictions

[24] Busvine, D. (2022, February 11). *Pandemic Passport* newsletter: Truckers' revolt; the EU's useless travel app; England ends isolation. *Politico Europe*. https://www.politico.eu/newsletter/pandemic-passport/truckers-revolt-the-eus-useless-travel-app-england-ends-isolation

[25] Axios Staff. (2022, February 10). U.S. warns protest convoys could hit Super Bowl. *Axios*. https://www.axios.com/2022/02/10/us-warns-protest-convoys-could-hit-super-bowl

[26] Rankin, J. (2022, February 13). Freedom convoys: Legitimate Covid protest or vehicle for darker beliefs? *The Guardian*. https://www.theguardian.com/world/2022/feb/13/freedom-convoys-legitimate-covid-protest-or-vehicle-for-darker-beliefs

[27] Bearak, M. (2022, February 13). Canada's Ambassador Bridge reopens after blockade by "Freedom Convoy". *The Washington Post*. https://www.washingtonpost.com/world/2022/02/13/canada-freedom-convoy-border-blockades-truckers

[28] Cecco, L. (2022, February 19). Ottawa: Police use pepper spray and stun grenades to clear trucker protest. *The Guardian*. https://www.theguardian.com/world/2022/feb/19/ottawa-police-pepper-spray-stun-grenades-trucker-protest

[29] Muller, J. (2022, February 11). Populism's new inferno. *Axios*. https://www.axios.com/2022/02/11/canadian-truck-protests-bridge-shutdown

[30] Culliford, E. (2022, February 8). Meta says it removed scammers' Canada convoy Facebook groups. *Reuters*. https://www.reuters.com/technology/meta-says-it-removed-scammers-canada-convoy-facebook-groups-2022-02-08

[31] Royal Canadian Mounted Police. (2024). *Project NATTERJACK: National after-action review into the RCMP's response to the 2022 Freedom Convoy* [Government report]. https://rcmp.ca/en/corporate-information/publications-and-manuals/project-natterjack-national-after-action-review

[32] Duplicate of #20

[33] Foreign Interference Commission. (2023). *Russia's role in the far-right truck convoy: An analysis of Russian amplification strategies* (Exhibit COM0000197). https://foreigninterferencecommission.ca/fileadmin/foreign_interference_commission/Documents/Exhibits_and_Presentations/Exhibits/COM0000197.pdf

[34] Boynton, S. (2023, February 13). 'Freedom Convoy' picked up by Russian propaganda, then Fox News. *National Observer*. https://www.nationalobserver.com/2023/02/13/analysis/fox-news-freedom-convoy-russian-propaganda

[35] RT News. (2022, February 12). Freedom Convoy movement spreads across the globe. https://www.rt.com/news/548545-freedom-convoy-protests-spread

[36] Colton, E. (2022, January 30). Canadian news host slammed for suggesting Russia behind massive "Freedom Convoy" protest. *Fox News*. https://www.foxnews.com/world/cbc-canada-russia-freedom-convoy-vaccine-protest-criticisms

[37] Lewis, D. (2022, February 12). 'Freedom Convoy' inspires protests beyond Canada. *Reuters* [Photo package]. https://www.reuters.com/news/picture/freedom-convoy-inspires-protests-beyond-idUSRTS5H6JX

[38] Public Order Emergency Commission. (2022, November 28). *Public hearings transcript* (Vol. 32: Financial Governance Panel, pp. 145-146). https://publicorderemergencycommission.ca/files/documents/Transcripts/POEC-Public-Hearings-Volume-32-November-28-2022.pdf

[39] Duplicate of #21

[40] Mahdawi, A. (2022, February 8). The whole world should be worried by the 'siege of Ottawa'. *The Guardian (Opinion)*. https://www.theguardian.com/commentisfree/2022/feb/08/ottawa-truckers-protest-anti-vaxx-canada

[41] Cybersecurity & Infrastructure Security Agency. (2025, May 21). *AA25-141A: Russian GRU targeting Western logistics entities and influence operations* [Cybersecurity advisory]. https://www.cisa.gov/news-events/cybersecurity-advisories/aa25-141a

[42] Associated Press & PBS NewsHour. (2022, February 18). How American right-wing funding for Canadian trucker protests could sway U.S. politics. https://www.pbs.org/newshour/world/how-american-right-wing-funding-for-canadian-trucker-protests-could-sway-u-s-politics

[43] Sullivan, L. (2022, February 11). U.S.-based groups plan convoys in support of Canadian truckers. *Reuters*. https://www.reuters.com/world/americas/us-organizers-plan-convoys-support-canadian-truckers-2022-02-11

[44] Kassam, A., & Greve, J. (2022, February 11). U.S. urges Canada to end trucker border blockade as mayor warns of force. *The Guardian*. https://www.theguardian.com/us-news/2022/feb/11/us-urges-canada-to-end-trucker-border-blockade-as-mayor-says-protesters-could-be-removed-by-force

CHAPTER NINETEEN:
IRON HORSES BEFORE DAWN

*"A man will brag about shifting gears on black ice and call it
freedom, but it takes a village to fix the ruts his rig leaves behind.
When horns become policy and diesel becomes debate, the real
cost is measured in sleepless nights and salt on the curb. However,
the loudest stories still have to share the road with everyone
else—no matter how many axles they ride in on."*
~ R.G. Cruise

The tractor-trailer has never been just a box on wheels; since the gas-shock 1970s, it has rumbled through North American imagination as a testosterone-gauged proving ground where asphalt replaces prairie grass and a 600-horse Cummins becomes the last honest measure of man. [1] In December 1973, when independent hauliers throttled interstates to protest the newly imposed 55 mph limit, newspapers called them "diesel cowboys," and a young nation, weary of OPEC lines, briefly decided that the renegade trucker was a folk hero rather than a freight contractor. [2] Pop culture stoked the myth: C. W. McCall's novelty single "Convoy" rocketed to the top of both pop and country charts in January 1976, selling two million copies while immortalising CB slang—"10-4, good buddy," "rubber duck," "bear in the air." [3] Movie studios followed with Smokey and the Bandit, White Line Fever, and a Kris Kristofferson flick titled Convoy, all of them reinforcing the script: the rig as rolling saloon, the driver as self-reliant outlaw. [4]

Advertising departments were already lacing the steel with testosterone. A 1990s run of Chevrolet spots—later dissected by media scholars as "phallic mythmaking on eighteen wheels"—shot chrome grilles from ankle height and synced ignition roars with heartbeats, selling torque as virility. [5] Content analyses of truck commercials between 2000 and 2020 confirm a near-monopoly of white, square-jawed actors whose denim sleeves rise just enough to show forearm veins, an aesthetic researchers label hegemonic masculinity. [6] On Canada's prairies, that aesthetic bled into daily life: a 2011 *Winnipeg Free Press* market survey found Manitobans bought trucks over cars at a two-to-one ratio, citing "work ethic" and "winter dominance" as emotional drivers. [7] By 2023, opinion essays in The Manitoban dismissed many of those purchases as "vanity pickups"—symbolic armour against cultural change. [8] Political theorist Cara Daggett has another term: petro-masculinity, the fusion of fossil-fuel attachment and threatened male identity that produces grievances loud enough to drown out climate warnings. [9]

When COVID mandates tightened cross-border logistics, that grievance finally found a horn. Posts in Telegram channels curated by memes of rolling-coal dodge duallys lamented that *real men don't scan QR codes* and that diesel smoke was the *smell of freedom*. A *Simon Fraser University* scrape of six major platforms clocked a 312 per cent spike in convoy-related content during the first two weeks of February 2022; most high-engagement posts hailed from U.S. zip codes—a foreign chorus cheering a Canadian plot. [10] Analysts could trace each surge, like aftershocks from an unseen detonation: first mid-January when GoFundMe topped $5 million, again on 10 February when Ontario declared a state of emergency, and peaking in the pre-dawn hours of Valentine's Day when the final western rigs rolled toward Ottawa.

Sixty-one kilometres west of Parliament Hill, on a gravel pull-out beside Highway 7, a sodium bulb buzzed against the prairie dark. Six Peterbilts and one battered Freightliner idled nose-to-tail; exhaust curled upward and mingled with Orion. Inside a converted chip wagon—grease film on the windows, coffee refills a loonie with your mug—drivers lounged on duct-taped stools beneath a hand-painted sign: *DIESEL IN MY VEINS / FREEDOM IN MY HEART*. Storytelling commenced the moment the air brakes hissed.

> *"Remember Rogers Pass '95? Ice fog so thick you could smell it."*
> *"Ha! Ran that with a busted turbo. Cops said park it, I said buy me a new block heater."*

> *"Brother, I hauled calves through the Wyoming Red Desert with the clutch cable snapped—shifted by rev sound alone."*

Folklorists call it ritual braggadocio: narrative rounds that reaffirm the group's claim to antifragility. [11] The cadence matched any locker room but swapped quarterback glory for axle weights and grade percentages. Lawrence Ouellet had chronicled the rhythm decades earlier—how CB legends stitched together men otherwise alone for ten-hour stretches of crop stubble and static. [12] Tonight, every punch-line landed on the refrain because somebody had to get it done, and the laughter shook pie tins on the warmer.

The digital layer overlapped the analogue. Between tales, a driver opened TikTok: a loop of a lifted Ford Super Duty burning coal while Merle Haggard's "Are the Good Times Really Over" played under a caption—*Rolling to free my kids*. Likes climbed past eighty-thousand while coffee steamed. Outside, a driver named Vince "Lone Wapiti" Benoit crouched by his 389 Pete, polishing the chrome eagle affixed to his bumper, the wingspan riveted into sheet metal like a war medal. "Hold steady, old girl," he whispered—then flipped open a spiral notebook wedged above the visor.

Load Manifest:

> *Pallets—Non-perishable*
> *Destination—OTTAWA, ONT. HOLD UNTIL MANDATES FALL*
> *Right to roam. Right to wrench. Right to refuse.*

Cultural geographers studying *cab iconography* argue that talismans perform sovereignty: a private constitution restored each dawn with key-turn and air-pressure build. [13] Vince slid a battered cassette—Red Sovine's Greatest Hits—into the deck. No Bluetooth here; the truck itself was vintage 1997, mechanical pump, pre-DEF, immune to electronic governors. "Old school like me," he liked to say. In policy circles, that elegantly tuned non-compliance—vaccine refusal paired with pre-emissions motors would soon stand trial as a proxy war over modernity.

At 03:57, the CB crackled: "Breaker one-nine, Tango-Romeo rolls at oh-five-hundred. Watch your mirrors for O.P.P. hedgehogs." Someone replied in a smoky alto, "Copy that, boys. Hammer down." Women now constitute 13.7 per cent of North American long-haul drivers, according to the 2022 Women in

Trucking Index,[14] and statistically exceed men in logbook compliance, yet on the airwaves, many still darken their tone, protective camouflage against cat-calls

A clipboard circulated bearing Prairie Star Logistics letterhead:

OPERATIONAL ADVISORY – OTTAWA
Maintain nose-to-tail column; dashcams must run.
Record all law-enforcement contacts.
Refuelling rendezvous Renfrew Esso 0500-0600.
Company counsel on call 24/7.

Legal caution draped in convoy bravado: an accountant's spine behind a bar-room swagger. One veteran skimmed the note, tapped line three with a stubby finger, and muttered, "Interference? They ever drop forty tons through ice fog at minus forty?" He grinned, but a tremor lived behind the joke; everyone knew the Emergencies Act briefing downtown could freeze more than bank accounts.

Engines fired sequentially—first a choked cough, then a harmonic rumble that vibrated the aluminium trailer walls. A helicopter pilot filming for the morning newscast would later describe the spectacle as "a steel river waking up," tail-lights stretching east in red constellations. Vince felt the surge in his throat as turbo pressure hit 20 PSI. Mirrors reflected plumes of exhaust silvered by moonlight. CB chatter spooled like jazz:

"Keep 'er tight, shovel-head."
"Gumball machine sittin' at mile-post 18."
"Solid copy. We ain't here to start fights—just end 'em."

Anthropologist Emily Scharrer calls that dialect *fraternal positionality*, code that recasts state authority—DOT officers, weigh-scale clerks—as trickster adversaries, elevating the driver's defiance to moral cause[6]. Later on Wellington Street, it would matter where by-law officers were renamed *blue shirts* and horns became *truth cannons*.

Digital sociologist Ahmed Al-Rawi traced the same theatre online. Between 02:00 and 05:00 EST on 14 February, his scraper captured 15,482 convoy-tagged posts, the largest 180-minute spike in the dataset; top geolocations were Texas, Florida, and Alberta, in that order[10]. Roughly one-third used the muscle-arm emoji bracketed by twin smokestacks—a meme that, Daggett notes, "compresses fossil fuel, whiteness, and patriarchy into a single glyph." [9] By sunrise, the hashtag #ConvoyValentine was trending above the Super Bowl recap on U.S. Twitter.

Inside each cab, dawn emerged first as a blue-black smear over snowdrifts. Vince downshifted to hold at 90 kph—column integrity. He sipped thermos coffee, tasting diesel in the foam. A folded letter from his daughter sat on the passenger seat: "Bring freedom home, Dad." He'd laminated it against spilt coffee; the plastic gleamed in the dashboard light. For a man who had grown up measuring self-worth by odometer clicks, the note felt heavier than the 30,000 lbs of canned goods behind him.

At 05:27, the column merged with Highway 417 proper. City light domes glowed ahead like false dawn. Ottawa Police cruisers waited at on-ramps, windows fogged; an officer texted her partner that the sound felt "like thunder rolling on diesel." A *Reuters* stringer, staged on an overpass, framed the rigs against pre-dawn sky and typed that they appeared "chrome-armoured and testosterone-fuelled." [8] Downtown hoteliers, still half-haunted by January sleeplessness, fitted earplugs into welcome packets.

In the ByWard Market, barista Mallory Kim flicked on espresso boilers at 05:45 and felt cups rattle as the first horn blast ricocheted off brick façades. She cursed softly, remembering how last month's gridlock had cut tip revenue in half. A graduate student livestreamed the oncoming lights upstairs, telling TikTok followers how truck culture "queues a nostalgia that borders on cosplay." He closed the window against fumes and turned to finish an abstract on labour precarity.

However, on Highway 417, the myth still outran such footnotes. Vince nudged the wheel as ruts grabbed at the steer tires. He glanced at the eagle ornament and recalled a childhood road trip when his father, also a trucker, had pointed to the Trans-Canada sign and said, "That's the only arrow you need in life." The story tasted sweeter than coffee. The convoy behind him—dozens, maybe hundreds by now—echoed that arrow. Each rig is a neuron, each driver a synapse carrying the old gospel: mobility equals merit, horsepower equals dignity.

A gust shuddered the cab. Vince feathered the throttle; the trailer swayed like a sail. Near the middle of the column, the lone female voice returned: "Heads up, fellas—saw a cruiser tuck in at Carp Road."[14] tonight, that vigilance guarded the brothers who often doubted them. A driver replied, "Copy, sister. You got the angel watch." In that one sentence, the myth bent, if only slightly, to accommodate new actors.

Downtown, the Peace Tower clock ticked toward six. Aides inside the Prime Minister's Office refreshed social feeds—the digital hum of a distant convoy already inside the building. An elder civil servant muttered that he'd heard this before during the grain-price riots of 1974, "except back then the horns stayed west of Renfrew." Producers debated lower-thirds in a basement media room at *CTV: HAULING FREEDOM?* versus *PETRO-MASCULINE BACKLASH?* Editorial friction mirrored axle friction.

Back on the highway, the column crested the final rise. City lights sprawled beneath like circuitry, the Parliament silhouette a dark tuning fork in the middle. Vince felt an ache in his wrists—adrenaline or dawn chill, hard to tell. He keyed the CB:

"Boys and girls, Ottawa off the bow. Let's show 'em how the west rolls."

A chorus of mic clicks answered, a sound like distant applause. The rigs poured downhill, exhaust brakes gabbling as speed limits dropped. Suppose a historian had paused the scene here. In that case, he might note the converging arcs: half-century of diesel lore, decades of ad-driven masculinity, two years of pandemic fatigue, ten thousand terabytes of meme agitation—all compressed into forty tonnes of chrome and conviction. What came next would test by-laws, bank regulations, marriage vows, and national patience. But in this heartbeat, before the first badge flagged the first tail-light, the convoy occupied the purest form of its legend: iron horses galloping unchallenged toward the capital dawn.

The collision course pitted horsepower against the heritage district, highway myth against urban livelihood, and petro-masculine reverie against the messy pluralism of a city still half asleep. The engines carried forward, pistons hot with nostalgia. Ottawa would wake whether or not it wished to.

The instant the first grey wash of Valentine's Day crept over Ottawa's eaves, it revealed a capital whose centre of gravity had shifted from stone façades to idling steel. Trucks squatted on carriageways like siege towers, turn signals clicking in the half-light, each flash a small declaration that public space now answered to air horns, not by-laws. Residents who once choreographed their commutes around bike lanes faced the blunt arithmetic of blockade physics: a single tandem-axle on Kent Street erased two bus routes and three crosswalks, reallocating freedom from feet to fourteen-ply rubber. Lawyers in a Centretown class-action would later call the transformation "unbearable torment," citing horn blasts clocked at 105 dB and strangers banging on apartment doors at midnight. [16] The convoy's champions spoke of liberty; the insomnia crowd whose windows rattled under diesel idling knew it as expropriation by noise.

At 07:00, Jules Bouchard stepped from his brick walk-up on Arlington and froze. A burgundy Peterbilt blocked the curb so completely that its chrome air cleaner hovered over his hydrangea bed. The cab was high enough that the driver, leaning out the window, seemed to address him from a balcony. "Smile for freedom, snowflake!" the man barked, throttling the engine so the exhaust stack coughed soot across Jules's winter coat. Startled, Jules fumbled for his phone— only to feel the tremor of another rig bowling past, mud flaps flicking slush onto the sidewalk. Later, civil filings would catalogue dozens of such exchanges, where the word snowflake morphed from political jab to street-level taunt, shorthand for anyone claiming the right to quiet enjoyment of property. [17] Jules watched the rig inch forward, tires grinding salt crystals like broken glass. His day job at the archives would start in twenty minutes, but the bus stop was gone, replaced by a row of Alberta licence plates angled nose-in like battering rams.

Eight blocks north, where the convoy's ring road met Sparks Street, an Innu elder named Mathieu Neeposh tapped a carved maple cane against ice-rutted pavement. He had travelled from Maliotenam for a medical consult, expecting civic neutrality from a city that still bills itself as unceded Algonquin territory. Instead, he found a barricade of F-350s festooned with "Don't Tread on Me" flags. Three men in hi-vis bibs lounged against the tailgate, swigging from thermoses that smelled faintly of spiced rum. "Move it, grandpa—freedom lane," one jeered when Mathieu tried to slip by. Another unfurled a banner daubed with a maple leaf embedded in a skull. Mathieu steadied himself, voice low: "Your wheels sit on our people's bones." The retort came fast and foul—*wagon-burner*, followed by a bark of laughter. Before the insult could harden into assault, a teenager in a Raiders hoodie stepped from the shadows, phone raised. "You want to go viral for that?" he asked, thumb poised over the record button. The tension drained, replaced by performative shrugs; the bibbed men parted just wide enough for Mathieu to pass. Downtown charities would later warn that Indigenous clients reported a "high-level anxiety and increased fear" when venturing past convoy checkpoints, citing shouted slurs and blocked doorways. [18]

By 08:30, the convoy's acoustics dominated every frequency range: sub-bass diesel rattle, mid-range horn blasts, treble cowbells clanged by protest kids perched on tailgates. A homeless-shelter PA cracked an emergency code when another cluster of protesters stormed the soup kitchen line, demanding breakfast. Staff at Shepherds of Good Hope tweeted that volunteers had been harassed, a security guard threatened with racial epithets, and a shelter resident assaulted. [19] Across downtown, paramedics radioed despatch to report rocks hurled at an ambulance and anti-Asian slurs screamed at a medic while he checked damage to the windshield. [20] One Ottawa Paramedic Association spokesman said crews were "leaning on out-of-town units" because convoy gridlock added precious minutes to every response, turning lower-Townsend addresses into logistical outposts[22].

Nine o'clock found city traffic control war-rooming detours on digital maps that looked increasingly like Pac-Man mazes. An injunction against horn honking—granted a week earlier after a Superior Court judge declared "tooting a horn is not an idea"—proved unenforceable amid hundreds of rigs whose very presence advertised lawlessness. [21] At City Hall, a staffer cracked the window for air and recoiled; diesel fumes rolled in, carrying the faint scent of propane grills someone had set up on the median. The Council chamber's glass façade mirrored a tableau of flags, some upside-down Canadian banners, others Confederate or bearing slogans against "globalists." The mirror image felt metaphorical: democratic transparency now reflecting its siege.

Dr. Hanna Lu drafted an email to Ontario's Chief Medical Officer within a beige clinic in Somerset. "Road access between Bronson and Kent remains impassable. Two oncology patients missed infusion windows; home-care nurses report verbal threats at convoy checkpoints. Please advise if provincial resources can clear medical corridors." Though the note would surface months later in a federal inquiry, its urgency echoed testimony from health-care workers who said jammed bridges and street blockades forced staff to sleep in hospital call rooms or book hotel rooms on personal credit[17]. Epidemiologists warned that missed treatments risked compounding the health burden the convoy claimed to fight.

Just before 10:00, a phalanx of bicycles—locals too stubborn to surrender asphalt—attempted a rolling barricade on Bank Street. They rang bells in counterpoint to air horns, a clangour that ricocheted off storefronts already shuttered after weekend vandalism. Through café glass, a barista watched the scene and muttered that the city had become "a grand experiment in acoustic warfare." An Armed Conflict Location & Event Data Project (ACLED) fact-sheet later chronicled similar micro-clashes: cyclists jostled, journalists shoved, shelter staff mocked with Nazi salutes. [24] The report concluded that convoy spaces functioned as "pop-up zones of patriarchal entitlement," where the threat of noise or intimidation maintained territorial control.

Meanwhile, a junior policy analyst across Laurier Avenue stared at the municipal audit draft open on her laptop. The document, eventually 214 pages long, would fault City leadership for ceding downtown to "unlawful occupation," noting that transit paralysis stranded essential workers and syphoned police resources from domestic-violence calls. [25] She highlighted a paragraph on gendered impacts: women reported avoiding night shifts, while LGBTQ cafés logged a spike in vandalism. Her cursor hovered, then she added a citation to an independent community report outlining "hate incidents and misogynist slogans" etched into convoy signage. [26]

At eleven, the sun cleared low clouds, warming chrome and melting yesterday's flurries into oily slush. Water pooled against curb snowbanks that now served as impromptu urinals; the smell drew flocks of frustrated downtown residents banging pots in protest, their kitchenware chorus clashing with diesel percussion. Over a bullhorn, a convoy speaker dismissed them as "government drones," prompting a howl from a landlord whose tenants were threatening to break leases. NPR would broadcast his quote that evening: *Freedom to blast a horn can't trump freedom to sleep.* [21]

Inside Queen Street's warren of media trucks, producers argued over lower-thirds. One favoured *SIEGE ON THE CAPITAL*, another *WORKING-CLASS REVOLT*. The debate underscored a city-wide confusion: whose streets, whose story? A jurist blog noted that the horn-injunction lawsuit framed the dispute as a private-nuisance tort rather than a clash of ideologies, a legal pivot that let residents seek damages for trauma without litigating pandemic policy. [23] Everywhere discourse fractured along those lines—decibel readings versus charter rights, neighbourhood welfare versus national myth.

Just past noon, the convoy thickened on Wellington as new arrivals merged from side streets that had served as overnight truck berths. Drivers were cleared of residential zones only after internal marshals waved them forward, mindful of a fragile truce Mayor Watson had negotiated to keep heavy rigs off narrower arteries. Yet the morning's gendered theatre had already imprinted itself on the city's psyche: a ritual display of machine dominance met by civilian recoil and bureaucratic triage. The trucks idled before the Peace Tower like statues of a parallel republic governed by compression ratios and horn chords. Behind Parliament's Gothic stone, staffers drafted talking points for an afternoon press conference about "maintaining public order while respecting peaceful protest." Outside, a resident chalked onto the pavement: Our kids hear your freedom fifteen hours daily.

As light glittered off the Rideau Canal—a surface too thin for skating, too thick for runoff—the convoy's lead organiser climbed atop a flatbed and shouted through a PA that "the people have taken back their streets." The declaration rang half-true: public space had certainly been repossessed, but by whose title deed was a question now ricocheting through council inboxes, clinic emails, court dockets and private living-room arguments. By evening, those arguments would reach the House of Commons, but for now, late morning belonged to engines and those determined—or compelled—to navigate around them.

By late afternoon, the convoy's steel spectacle had mutated into political litmus: every TV crawl, every Question Period volley now asked which version of the country deserved the highway—chrome-plated manhood or the quieter majority who kept their engines off. National Observer columnists argued the occupation had weaponised "white-supremacist and patriarchal fantasies of the 'real Canadian' frontier," warning that trucks were merely "props in a cultural passion play about who gets to belong." [27] *Teen Vogue's* unexpected explainer agreed, noting the hard hats and lifted pickups functioned as costumes in a drama "less about liberty than about whose bodies set the national tempo." [28] The phrase *real Canadian* began trending minutes later, a proxy duel fought in hashtags while, on Wellington Street, the actual duel was measured in decibels.

At 16:00, the marble foyer outside the House of Commons smelled of coffee, printer toner, and diesel residue blown in through revolving doors. Reporters pressed record buttons as a back-bench MP from rural Saskatchewan strode to the microphones, eyes glittering with the day's talking-points memo. "This government sneers at hardworking Canadians who build and fix," she said, emphasising hard and working as though calibrating a torque gun. "Out there"— she thumbed toward the windows where jackknifed trailers formed a metallic picket—"are fathers and mothers who keep shelves stocked while ivory-tower elites sip lattes." The phrase ivory tower landed with practised force; aides nodded. A correspondent asked if she condemned the harassment of shelter staff reported over the weekend. She pivoted: "Let's not be delicate snowflakes. You can't fight tyranny with inside voices." Phones vibrated with push alerts; one thread reminded colleagues that snowflake had become convoy shorthand for feminised weakness since the first insult hurled at pedestrians that morning. When the MP ducked into the caucus room, a colleague murmured, "Careful—your base loves it when you crack that whip, but centrists smell leather." No retort—just the hiss of the door and a sudden hush heavy with calculation. Hours later, *CTV* would reveal caucus emails fretting that over-engaging the convoy's harder edges could spook suburban women voters. [39]

By 17:30, mahogany panels in the Senate's Human Rights committee chamber glowed under LED sconces as the day's final witness took the lectern: Dr. Saira Qureshi, director of the Institute for Gender-Based Justice. Her prepared brief trembled slightly in her grip. "Honourable senators," she began, "the streets outside your doors illustrate how misogyny and racism travel in convoy with anti-government outrage." She cited ACLED figures logging over forty documented incidents of harassment or intimidation within the protest's first fortnight. [37] A senator shifted in his seat; another tapped a stylus against a tablet displaying tweets layered with fist-pump emojis and horn icons. Dr. Qureshi's cadence sharpened. "When a woman in scrubs is told to 'go back to the kitchen' or an Indigenous elder is labelled 'wagon-burner,' that is not free speech—it is a shock tactic policing who belongs." She referenced House security testimony warning that ideologically motivated violent extremists (IMVE) had primed the protests as recruitment fairs, [33] and pointed to a Commons report detailing how women in extremist finance networks remain invisible labour. [32] Notes scribbled around the horseshoe suggested unease: "If gender frame sticks, comms plan needed";

"Check data on female trucker participation." When the chair thanked her, a convoy horn bled faintly through double-glazed panes—distant yet impossible to ignore.

While senators mulled definitions of public order, the Prime Minister prepared to invoke extraordinary law. At 16:45, Reuters flashed its banner: "Trudeau activates rarely used Emergencies Act." [29] The measure, last deployed in a different statute half a century prior, would freeze protest funds, compel tow-truck operators, and bar minors from the occupation. Within minutes, three provincial premiers blasted the move as federal overreach; [36] a columnist quipped that the Fathers of Confederation never imagined babysitting clauses. Yet on social feeds, the announcement collided with testosterone memes: Come and Take It under a clip of an excavator yanking jersey barriers aside. *BBC's* world desk summarised the mood: "Most demonstrators remain peaceful, but reports of harassment, Nazi slogans, and relentless horn noise stain the freedom brand." [30]

At 19:00, in the climate-controlled hush of the *Globe and Mail* city bureau, senior columnist Valérie Tremblay stared at a blank Word doc—deadline in forty. Headline debate thrummed over *Slack: Freedom or Fear?* vs. *Noise and Nationhood*. She sipped burnt coffee, recalling an *Independent* piece about soup-kitchen volunteers berated as "communists" by hungry convoyers. [31] Somewhere outside, a horn chord rose, fell, then rose again—call-and-response with her thinning patience. She typed:

> *"If occupation is the metric of patriotism, whose homeland counts—the man with the air-horn or the nurse with earplugs?"*

Footnote needed. She clicked open an open letter from 1,300 health-care workers declaring "we will not hide out of fear" after weeks of threats. She blocked hospital routes, [34] amplified by *Global News* coverage of physicians shifting from heroes to hated status. [35] The sentence firmed, the cursor marched. Her cubicle neighbour muttered about the decibel spikes logged by engineering professors who likened the horns to "a pneumatic drill at bedroom distance," data now tabled in the class-action suit. [38] Tremblay added another para: "Ottawa's gendered soundscape teaches that the line between protest and patriarchal coercion can be measured in hertz." Save. Send. Coffee cup down.

Parliament's Gothic arches flickered amber under sodium lamps outside her window, reflecting in puddles streaked by diesel rainbow. On the steps of West Block, MPs in winter coats huddled for scrum number three. A cabinet minister invoked "public order" while a reporter shouted a question about white-supremacist flags. Earlier National Observer analysis had already warned that the media frame risked normalising those symbols by over-focusing on gas prices rather than hate speech. [27] An aide whispered that *Teen Vogue's* piece was trending internationally, framing Canada's crisis as a lesson in racial power at scale. [28] Image management, once an afterthought in snowbound Ottawa, now felt like a national security file.

By 20:00, Senate cameras captured a Conservative member praising the convoy as a "dance party of patriots," lamenting "chattering-class demonisation." Fact-checkers pulled the transcript, noting her claim she'd "never felt safer walking home at night" because rigs blocked usual bar crowds. [37] Twitter answered with photos of women holding "My street, my sleep" placards, children's earmuffs strapped over toques. Under the hashtag #UnequalFreedom, clips of racialised residents recounting slurs reached six-figure views; *Yahoo News* aggregated survivor stories of "sexual harassment and intimidation" along the route. [40]

Valérie hit refresh on convoy livestreams inside the newsroom: engines idling against a copper-pink sky, flags snapping, silhouettes of men dancing on flatbeds to a boombox version of *Convoy*. She typed her kicker: "As the day dims, the question hardens: when roar becomes governance, whose silence becomes law?" Send a copy forty seconds before the embargo.

Police scanner chatter crackled across open office space: new roadblocks near Booth Street, call for additional perimeter units. Lights on the Peace Tower blinked eight. A page was flipped in the Auditor General's draft audit, already calling the occupation "a governance failure that magnified existing inequities." [25] Dr. Qureshi's earlier testimony resurfaced on a Senate live blog: "Patriarchy rarely arrives alone; it drives a diesel." One senator annotated the line with a shaky pen stroke—exclamation or question mark, impossible to tell.

Streetlamps hummed. Diesel plumes mingled with the first whiff of river fog. In apartment windows, kettles clicked for evening tea, doors double-latched, phone screens glowed with the push alert: *EMERGENCIES ACT INVOKED: WHAT IT MEANS FOR YOU*. The national debate about belonging had moved from op-ed columns into statutory code. Tomorrow's committees would parse legality; residents still parsed the bass throb beneath their floorboards tonight.

Yet within that vibration lived the next chapter: conversations about who can claim public roads, civic quiet, and patriotic myth. The convoy forced the nation to question whether citizenship stemmed from chrome or community resilience. As dusk deepened, horns tested their echo against Gothic stone, and the city answered not with silence, but with the low murmur of people deciding what freedoms they would no longer cede. Canada's future tense took shape in that negotiation—the hiss of air brakes across cracked pavement, the scratch of pens across committee documents.

ENDNOTES

[1] History.com Editors. (2018, January 2). *When truckers shut down America to protest oil prices—and became folk heroes.* History. https://www.history.com/articles/oil-crisis-1973-truck-strike

[2] McGinty, P. (2024, October 12). *"A long way to go and a short time to get there": How truckers became 1970s folk heroes.* Bunk History. https://www.bunkhistory.org/resources/a-long-way-to-go-and-a-short-time-to-get-there

[3] Rolling Stone Australia Staff. (2024, March 3). *C. W. McCall, "Convoy".* Rolling Stone Australia. https://au.rollingstone.com/music/music-lists/-60414/c-w-mccall-convoy-60509

[4] AllMusic. (n.d.). *Kris Kristofferson – Biography* (notes *Convoy* film, para. 11). Retrieved May 22, 2025, from https://www.allmusic.com/artist/kris-kristofferson-mn0000774588

[5] [Author unknown]. (2014). *Like a rock: The phallic mythology of trucks* [White paper]. Academia.edu. https://www.academia.edu/11432210/Like_a_Rock_The_Phallic_Mythology_of_Trucks

[6] Scharrer, E., Kang, Y., Zhou, Y., Durrani, A. A., Suren, N., & Butterworth, E. (2022). Tough guys and trucks: Early adolescents' critical analysis of masculinity in a TV commercial. *International Journal of Communication, 16*, 1585-1607. https://ijoc.org/index.php/ijoc/article/view/18604

[7] Hossack, P. (2011, February 2). Manitoba is truck country, survey finds. *Winnipeg Free Press.* https://www.winnipegfreepress.com/business/2011/02/02/manitoba-is-truck-country-survey

[8] Brown, G. (2023, January 17). Vanity pickup trucks are a blight on Manitoba society. *The Manitoban.* https://themanitoban.com/2023/01/vanity-pickup-trucks-are-a-blight-on-manitoba-society/44406

[9] Daggett, C. (2019). Petro-masculinity: Fossil fuels and authoritarian desire. *Millennium: Journal of International Studies, 47*(1), 25-44. https://doi.org/10.1177/0305829818775817

[10] Al-Rawi, A. (2022). *An empirical assessment of the convoy protest on six online sites* [Research report]. Public Order Emergency Commission (Exhibit COM00000864). https://publicorderemergencycommission.ca/files/exhibits/COM00000864.pdf

[11] Ouellet, L. (1994). *Pedal to the metal: The work life of truckers.* Temple University Press.

[12] Scherrer, K. (2020). *Identity and mobility in the United States trucking industry* (Doctoral dissertation, University of Kentucky). https://uknowledge.uky.edu/geography_etds/20

[13] Sicard, S. (2012). Female truck drivers: Negotiating identity in a male-dominated environment. *McNair Scholars Journal, 4*(1), 17-29. https://digitalcommons.cedarville.edu/cgi/viewcontent.cgi?article=1020&context=as_masters

[14] Heavy Duty Trucking. (2023). *WIT Index shows women drivers at 13.7 percent in 2022* [Industry fact sheet]. https://www.truckinginfo.com/10179472/hdt-fact-book-2022-driver-turnover-slows-except-for-private-fleets

[15] Scherer, S., Lewis, J., & Porter, D. (2022, February 14). Canada's Trudeau invokes emergency powers in bid to end protests. *Reuters.* https://www.reuters.com/world/americas/canada-police-response-protests-spotlight-after-key-bridge-us-cleared-2022-02-14

[16] CityNews Staff. (2022, February 22). Trucker convoy lawsuit going ahead; lead plaintiff says residents "tortured by sound." *CityNews Toronto.* https://toronto.citynews.ca/2022/02/22/ottawa-protest-class-action-lawsuit

[17] CTV News Ottawa Staff. (2022, January 30). Ottawa homeless shelter staff harassed by convoy protesters demanding food. *CTV News Ottawa.* https://www.ctvnews.ca/ottawa/ottawa-homeless-shelter-staff-harassed-by-convoy-protesters-demanding-food-1.5761654

[18] Al Jazeera English. (2022, February 4). Ottawa residents decry anti-vaccine trucker "occupation." *Al Jazeera.* https://www.aljazeera.com/news/2022/2/4/ottawa-residents-decry-anti-vaccine-trucker-occupation

[19] The Independent. (2022, January 30). Soup kitchen says Freedom Convoy truckers "harassing" staff for meals. *The Independent.* https://www.independent.co.uk/news/world/americas/convoy-truckers-canada-soup-kitchen-b2003765.html

[20] CityNews Ottawa Staff. (2022, February 1). Ottawa paramedics leaning on out-of-town support as convoy protest continues. *CityNews Ottawa.* https://ottawa.citynews.ca/2022/02/01/ottawa-paramedics-leaning-on-out-of-town-support-as-convoy-protest-continues-5015469

[21] CityNews / Canadian Press. (2022, February 7). Judge grants injunction against honking in downtown Ottawa. *CityNews Toronto.* https://toronto.citynews.ca/2022/02/07/ottawa-residents-protest-horn-honking-court

[22] Hernandez, J. (2022, February 7). Ottawa declares state of emergency over truckers' growing anti-government protests. *NPR.* https://www.npr.org/2022/02/07/1078861392/ottawa-protest-state-of-emergency

[23] JURIST Staff. (2022, February 5). Honking truckers face Ottawa residents' class-action lawsuit seeking injunction, damages for "unbearable torment." *JURIST.*

https://www.jurist.org/news/2022/02/canada-dispatch-honking-truckers-face-ottawa-residents-class-action-lawsuit-seeking-injunction-damages-for-unbearable-torment

[24] Armed Conflict Location & Event Data Project. (2022, February 25). *Fact sheet: "Freedom convoys" and anti-vaccine demonstrations in Canada.* https://acleddata.com/2022/02/25/fact-sheet-freedom-convoys-and-anti-vaccine-demonstrations-in-canada

[25] Office of the Auditor General of Ottawa. (2023). *Audit of the City of Ottawa's response to the convoy protest.* https://www.oagottawa.ca/media/tklagr1h/final-audit-report-audit-of-the-city-of-ottawa-s-response-to-the-convoy-protest-1-final-ua.pdf

[26] The Link Newspaper Staff. (2022, February). Marginalized communities are bearing the brunt of the "Freedom Convoy." *The Link.* https://thelinknewspaper.ca/article/feature/marginalized-communities-are-bearing-the-brunt-of-the-freedom-convoy

[27] Badham, V. (2022, February 12). The white-supremacy convoy can leave—but it will be back. *National Observer.* https://www.nationalobserver.com/2022/02/12/opinion/white-supremacy-convoy-can-leave-it-will-be-back

[28] Boulianne, M. (2022, February 9). Canada's "Freedom Convoy" protests aren't about freedom. *Teen Vogue.* https://www.teenvogue.com/story/canada-freedom-convoy-oped

[29] Ljunggren, D. (2022, February 14). Canada's Trudeau invokes emergency powers in bid to end protests. *Reuters.* https://www.reuters.com/world/americas/canada-police-response-protests-spotlight-after-key-bridge-us-cleared-2022-02-14

[30] BBC News. (2022, February 7). Judge grants injunction to stop horn honking in Ottawa. *BBC News.* https://www.bbc.com/news/world-us-canada-60293407

[31] Jamieson, A. (2022, January 30). Soup kitchen staff harassed by Freedom Convoy truckers demanding food. *The Independent.* https://www.independent.co.uk/news/world/americas/convoy-truckers-canada-soup-kitchen-b2003765.html

[32] Canada. House of Commons. Standing Committee on Public Safety and National Security. (2022). *Evidence, Meeting 16: IMVE and online financing.* https://www.ourcommons.ca/DocumentViewer/en/44-1/SECU/meeting-16/evidence

[33] Grundberg, F. (2022, February 8). "We will not hide out of fear": Open letter from health-care workers. *HealthyDebate.* https://healthydebate.ca/2022/02/topic/open-letter-speaks-out-against-harassment

[34] Gilmore, R. (2022, February 7). From heroes to hated: Health-care workers sign open letter slamming abuse. *Global News.* https://globalnews.ca/news/8600964/covid-healthcare-harassment-hate-misinformation

[35] Ljunggren, D. (2022, February 14). Premiers oppose Ottawa's emergency measures. *Reuters.* https://www.reuters.com/world/americas/health-coronavirus-canada-truckers-provi-idINL4N2UP3SP

[36] Senate of Canada. (2022, February 22). *Debates, Issue 19: Motion to confirm declaration of emergency.* https://sencanada.ca/en/content/sen/chamber/441/debates/019db_2022-02-22-e

[37] Armed Conflict Location & Event Data Project. (2022, February 25). *Fact sheet: "Freedom convoys" and anti-vaccine demonstrations in Canada.* https://acleddata.com/2022/02/25/fact-sheet-freedom-convoys-and-anti-vaccine-demonstrations-in-canada

[38] The Canadian Press. (2022, November 24). Candice Bergen privately acknowledged concerns about engaging Freedom Convoy protesters. *CTV News.* https://www.ctvnews.ca/politics/candice-bergen-privately-acknowledged-concerns-about-engaging-freedom-convoy-protesters-pmo-staff-1.6165650

[39] Yahoo News Staff. (2022, February 14). Residents describe violent occupation marked by racism and misogyny. *Yahoo News Canada.* https://ca.news.yahoo.com/freedom-convoy-violent-occupation-areas-185109053.html

CHAPTER TWENTY:

WINTER JUDGMENTS

"Justice does not come by horn blast or gavel alone, but by the slow work of shovels and red pens in the cold. You can park a rig in the middle of Parliament, but sooner or later, someone will tow it and send you the bill, usually with interest. In this country, freedom means arguing until the snow melts and then arguing some more—because every winter leaves a little more to plough."
~ R.G. Cruise

Canada's long legal winter began with the low-throated rumble of diesel engines still echoing in the collective ear and ended, at least for now, with a gavel-crack that sounded like spring unclenching. Between lay a season of reckonings, each argument, and affidavit reminding the country that rights and responsibilities must share the same shovel when the snowdrifts of protest pile higher than Parliament Hill. From the moment Prime Minister Justin Trudeau reached for the Emergencies Act on 14 February 2022, an unbroken chain of court challenges coiled around federal power like barbed wire—first the injunctions, then the judicial reviews, and finally the criminal trials that would decide whether the convoy's loudest voices were patriots, pests, or a little of both. [1] In January 2024, that tension snapped: Federal Court Justice Richard Mosley declared the government's emergency proclamation "unreasonable," a word that landed with the cold precision of an ice-fisher's auger and re-opened every dinner-table debate from St. John's to Sooke. [2] The ruling's Charter analysis, echoed by legal commentators from Osgoode Hall to Yorkton coffee shops, insisted that the cabinet's fear of *unknown unknowns* could not trump clear statutory thresholds. [3] Academic bloggers parsed Mosley's language the way scribes once dissected papal bulls, concluding that executive deference ends where the plain text of a statute begins. [4] Pollsters found the country almost perfectly bifurcated—46 per cent cheered the rebuke, 44 per cent warned it hobbled future crisis responses. The rest wondered why politicians could not simply shovel the streets themselves. [5]

Against that national backdrop, the Ontario Court of Justice prepared to render its verdict on the convoy's figureheads. The calendar read 3 April 2025, but the mood inside courtroom 36 felt older, as though the ghosts of the 1970s October Crisis had slipped between the pews. Justice Heather Perkins-McVey entered a hush broken only by the staccato rustle of reporters' notepads. Tamara Lich sat ramrod straight, her Métis sash folded on her lap like a question that had outlived its answer; Chris Barber, jaw set, tapped a boot heel to an inaudible metronome. The judge's voice never rose above conversational warmth. Yet, each syllable drew the gallery forward: guilty of mischief for both defendants, plus counselling mischief for Barber, not guilty on intimidation and obstruction. [6] Cameras were banned, but pens proved sharper: "Freedom, it turns out, is not an air-horn blast at two in the morning," one columnist muttered, scribbling as the clerk recorded the convictions. Outside, *CTV* microphones caught Barber's lawyer vowing an appeal even as the Crown hinted it would seek a two-year sentence. The click of camera shutters and the sigh of cold April rain on courthouse steps replaced the truck horns that were once the soundtrack of downtown gridlock. *Land Line Media*—an industry outlet more accustomed to axle weights than legal briefs—summed it up with prairie understatement: *Protest organisers await sentencing.* [8] *The Associated Press*, connected to a thousand international newsrooms, told distant readers that the paralysis of Ottawa's streets had been long enough to prompt the federal cabinet to consider an emergency law for the first time. [9]

If Lich and Barber's verdict was a controlled burn, Pat King's trial six months earlier had been a grease fire. The self-styled livestream evangelist of the convoy strode into an Ottawa courtroom on 22 November 2024 wearing a suit one size too defiant. Prosecutors salted the record with King's videos—*Hold the line!*—while defence counsel argued the clips were mere puffery. Internet chest-thumping never meant for real-world ignition. The judge disagreed: guilty of mischief, counselling mischief, counselling obstruction, and two counts of disobeying court orders. [10] *BBC* headlines bounced from London to Lagos within minutes, presenting King as the movement's first fallen domino. [11] Sentencing came on 19 February 2025: three months of house arrest, a year of probation, and a geographical ban from Ottawa except for future court dates. [12] King declared the outcome "a badge of honour" on a post-verdict livestream, but the badge came riveted with an ankle monitor. His followers flooded comment threads with maple-leaf emojis and Old Testament verses; his critics replied with noise-meter charts and sleepless-night tallies.

While individual fates turned on criminal codes, an even larger fight brewed in civil court, inside a fluorescent boardroom near Bank Street on 6 February 2024, weary downtown merchants huddled over styrofoam coffee and a 72-page draft pleading. The lead plaintiff, data analyst Zexi Li, read aloud paragraph 1: "The Plaintiffs, on behalf of the classes described herein, claim … general damages for private and public nuisance in the amount of $60 million." [13] The numbers climbed like a runaway odometer—$70 million for business losses, $150 million for lost wages, $10 million in punitive damages—and somewhere near the margin, a café owner whispered, "That's more zeroes than my annual revenue." Two days later, defence counsel fired back with an anti-SLAPP (Strategic Lawsuit Against Public Participation) motion—a quick-dismissal remedy created to stop lawsuits whose real purpose is to silence or intimidate speech on matters of public interest—branding the class action an assault on free expression; Superior Court Justice Calum MacLeod was unmoved. "I am not persuaded," he wrote, dismissing the motion and describing the residents' evidence of sleepless nights, diesel fog, and blocked doorways as "meritorious." [14] Legal firms tracking the case updated their websites: class certification inching closer, freezing orders on cryptocurrency donations still in force.[15] One boutique litigation shop warned donors they could find themselves defendants under newly added representative categories for truck owners and small-sum contributors. [16]

Through it all, the broader constitutional conversation kept circling back to Justice Mosley's ruling. Scholars at Osgoode's *The Court* blog noted that Mosley's reasoning signalled an end to *trust-us* executive security arguments: statutes bind, even in febrile times. [17] At kitchen tables, the analysis distilled into Will Rogers–style quips: "If Ottawa couldn't meet the threshold this time," an uncle in Medicine Hat asked, "what's the Act for?" Surveyors from the Angus Reid Institute tracked the pulse and found political identity the best predictor of one's answer, the same cleavage that the convoy had widened two winters earlier. [5] On talk radio, callers demanded Parliament rewrite the Act before the next crisis; constitutional lawyers countered that such surgery might replace a flawed shield with a rubber one.

Yet for all the high rhetoric, the lived texture of the courtroom winter remained stubbornly human. On verdict day, a grandmother who had dodged honking rigs to reach the pharmacy in February 2022 slipped into the back row to watch Justice Perkins-McVey speak. She clutched a folded newspaper article documenting how convoy air-horns had reached 105 decibels outside her apartment; when the guilty finding came, she allowed herself one silent tear before disappearing into the hallway's fluorescent hum. In a downtown co-working space, Lich's supporters gathered around a laptop streaming reaction panels; one man punched the air when a pundit called the convictions *a political trial,* even as the feed cut to legal experts explaining mischief's century-old common-law roots. Meanwhile, outside the Federal Court on Wellington Street, a protest sign from Mosley's January ruling leaned against a lamppost: *Charter > Cabinet.* The cardboard was soggy now, its marker bleeding, but the exclamation point aimed straight at the Peace Tower.

No ruling resolved every grievance; no sentence restored the lost sales of a February day when foot traffic vanished under truck bumpers. Even the class action's swollen numbers carried more symbolism than certainty—experienced litigators quietly predicted years before any cheque changed hands. In the pubs around Elgin Street, staff serving late-winter stout joked that Ottawa's next tourist season might offer guided *Courtroom Crawl* tours: criminal at 10:00, civil at 12:00, constitutional at 15:00. When someone suggested adding a stop at Bank Street to see the statue of Terry Fox still bearing convoy graffiti scars under its restored bronze, conversation faltered; nobody wanted to laugh at that.

Yet something undeniably shifted when the gavel met hardwood in April 2025. Across the country, municipalities amended their by-laws to add decibel limits for vehicle horns. Even convoy-sympathetic MPs conceded that, whatever one thought of vaccines, a line existed beyond which civil disobedience curdled into civil harm. Justice Perkins-McVey had phrased it more gently: "Freedom is always a dialogue," she said from the bench, "but conversations end when only one voice is amplified." [6]

Spring eventually arrived, as it always does, pushing slush into the gutters outside Ottawa's courthouses. But Canadians understood intuitively how farmers knew blackfly season follows the thaw and that more legal tempests loom. They will docket an appeal of Mosley's ruling for autumn. The winter judgments are opening gambits, the first precise brushstrokes on what promises to become a national triptych of jurisprudence, politics, and memory. The story carries into the scathing Emergencies Act appellate arguments, where Parliament's stone walls may yet reverberate with questions sharper than any air-horn blast.

The blast reached the nation the instant the docket number lit up on laptops: Federal Court Justice Richard Mosley had ruled that the Trudeau cabinet's 2022 invocation of the Emergencies Act was "unreasonable, ultra vires, and unconstitutional." [18] Before the afternoon sun finished glazing the Rideau Canal, the phrase was ricocheting through talk-radio switchboards, Slack channels, and supper-hour kitchens from Nanaimo to Notre-Dame-de-l'Île-Perrot. Cable Chyrons competed for superlatives—*historic rebuke, government overreach exposed*—while opposition strategists ordered fresh pots of coffee and government lawyers scanned PDFs for appeal angles. Canada, which prides itself on quiet incrementalism, suddenly felt like a snow globe whipped off a shelf: *shake once and watch the flakes swirl.*

The mood was icicle-sharp inside Courtroom 36 on Wellington Street, 23 January 2024. Mosley's black robes swept past counsel tables as if he were parting bilingual seas, and the hush that followed carried an audible crackle of static from live-blogging phones. Beginning not with bombast but with a schoolmaster's calm, he recited section-by-section faults: the government misread the statutory threshold for a "public order emergency," conflated "economic harm" with "threats to national security," and relied on CSIS assessments that never claimed the bar was met. [19] As the judge spoke, Crown counsel shuffled binders like gamblers re-sorting unlucky cards; defence lawyers for civil-liberties groups exchanged glances that said, wordlessly, *we just drew four aces.* When Mosley pronounced the measures "disproportionate to the reasonably foreseeable harms," a lone gasp escaped the gallery and reporters scrawled furiously, ink blotting like snowmelt. [20]

Outside, microphones bristled. Finance Minister Chrystia Freeland, flanked by Public Safety Minister Dominic LeBlanc and Justice Minister Arif

Virani, declared the government would "immediately appeal to defend Canadians' safety and our democratic institutions." [21] The scrum's floodlights etched her breath into the sub-zero air; one bystander muttered she looked like a locomotive in reverse, whistling while rolling back into the station. Across the street, Conservative leader Pierre Poilievre's staffers distributed printed excerpts of the ruling and a terse statement: "Justin Trudeau broke the law." [22] New Democratic Party MPs offered a softer chord—relief that civil-rights protections held, coupled with worry that future crises might now lack practical tools. The Bloc Québécois, ever mindful of October 1970, reminded cameras that Québecers knew the sting of emergency laws better than most.

The following morning—24 January 2024—Parliament Hill thrummed like a boiler room. Behind oak-panelled caucus doors, Liberals debated appeal strategy, one backbencher quipping that *"reasonable grounds" now felt as elusive as the last seat on the Trillium Line at rush hour.* In the Conservative suite, aides pored over the judgment's footnotes, highlighting every reference to Charter breaches in yellow as if painting caution lines on election asphalt. A Justice Department analyst slid briefing binders down the hall under closed doors; through the transom, someone could hear Virani intone, "Judicial review does not equal judicial supremacy." A Page darted past, clutching a fresh printout of polling cross-tabs—*Angus Reid's* overnight flash survey showing 46 per cent calling the ruling "correct," 44 per cent "dangerous," and 10 per cent "not sure, but tired." [23] Even the cafeteria smelled different, reporters swore later, as though the steam from split-pea soup carried a hint of constitutional sulphur.

Across town, the *Ottawa Herald's* pressroom vibrated at 03:00 Veteran bureau chief Delia Ward hunched over a desktop, piercing her front-page narrative like a quilt: direct quotes from paragraph 355 of Mosley's reasons, a phone interview with Osgoode Hall's Dr. Sujit Choudhry comparing the decision to *Vavilov's* reset of administrative-law standards, and a sidebar on how the freeze-and-seize bank-account orders flunked proportionality. [24] Her copy editor, running on burnt espresso, trimmed a metaphor about "legal frost heave" and inserted a late-breaking *Reuters* line Freeland had already filed the notice of appeal. [21] Beside them, the ancient Linotype clanked, spitting molten lead slugs that hissed in a tray of water—industrial punctuation marking the moment Canada's emergency-powers narrative slipped a gear.

Newsrooms nationwide echoed the hum. In Halifax, a *CityNews* producer spliced archival footage of the convoy's air-horn din with B-roll of Mosley's solemn face, titling the package *From Chaos to Courtroom*. [25] In Vancouver, the *North Shore Courier* mapped each of the judgment's 415 paragraphs onto an interactive timeline for phone readers, drawing more taps than their Stanley Cup coverage had managed in a month. Talk-radio lines in Winnipeg jammed as callers recycled folk wisdom: one retired trucker said you can't plough a street with a statute book; a nurse countered that you can't sleep through sirens of *freedom* at 03:00.

Legal scholars, meanwhile, sharpened scalpels. The Osgoode-based blog *The Court* dissected Mosley's approach to "reasonableness" review post- *Vavilov*, praising his insistence on "justification, transparency, and intelligibility." [26] The Alberta Civil Liberties Research Centre hailed the decision as a "re-anchoring of executive discretion to constitutional bedrock," warning against appeal arguments that would "normalise extraordinary measures." [27] Even libertarian think-tank Cato tweeted a thread noting that asset-freezing powers mirrored U.S. debates under the International Emergency Economic Powers Act—which, they observed, Congress now eyes with suspicion. [28]

For the Trudeau government, the blow was two-edged: on the one hand, an immediate political migraine; on the other, a rhetorical gift on democratic accountability—"Courts work, challenges succeed, institutions endure," Virani told caucus, echo picked up by corridor microphones. In private, senior aides worried aloud that a lost appeal could neuter the Emergencies Act for decades. "We might need a successor statute," one policy adviser whispered, "something between pepper spray and martial law." Another muttered that rewriting emergency legislation in a minority Parliament was like repairing skates mid-game.

Citizens, of course, processed the saga in texture, not theory. In Sudbury, a family dinner dissolved into raised voices: Grandpa slammed the table—"They froze honest men's accounts!"—while his daughter shot back that diesel fog had triggered her asthmatic son. In Charlottetown, a Grade 10 civics teacher scrapped the day's lesson on the Meech Lake Accord and asked students to diagram Mosley's reasoning instead; half the class sided with the judge, the other half with Freeland's appeal. Meme-makers on TikTok mashed courtroom stills with convoy horn audio; one viral clip ended with Mosley's gavel synced to the beat drop of a remix called *Ultra Vires Vibes.*

By week's end, pundits spoke of *the Mosley Aftershocks. The Hill Times* ran a 25 January analysis arguing that Liberals could no longer paint Conservative scepticism of the Act as extremist without risking blowback. [29] A 30 January follow-up piece suggested that despite victory laps, Tories would keep message discipline on affordability rather than civil-liberties grandstanding. [30] In Montréal, *La Presse* editorialised that Québec's homegrown memory of the War Measures Act made the ruling feel *comme un rappel d'histoireó* ➤ "As a reminder of history". Pollsters charted new fault lines: support for invoking the Act in any future protest scenario fell nine points among suburban women, yet rose five points among Prairie men who feared blockades at grain terminals. [23]

Justice Mosley maintained monk-like silence through it all, but his prose did the touring for him. Paragraph 403—"A judiciary that defers in the face of indeterminate threat abandons its office"—surfaced in almost every op-ed, sometimes trimmed, sometimes tattooed on principle. When a law student opened the mic in Toronto, debating the line, an audience member joked Mosley had achieved what every professor craved: making *administrative law* go viral. The joke landed because it felt true; even cab drivers knew the phrase *standard of review* that week.

Yet, a deeper tremor lay beneath headlines and hashtags: Canadians had perceived the fragility of the rights architecture when connected to undefined emergencies. If the invocation two winters earlier had felt like thick ice cracking, Mosley's ruling sounded more like a corrective chisel—loud, precise, and potentially fragmenting old political alignments. Already, civil-society coalitions were drafting white papers for a parliamentary review of the Act's definitions; premiers in Edmonton and Halifax grumbled. Any rewrite must respect provincial sovereignty; banks quietly asked regulators whether future account freezes would come with indemnity.

As January slipped into February, Ottawa's street-side snowbanks hardened to grey crusts, but the constitutional debate stayed molten. Appeals would fly, committees would summon witnesses, and the Public Order Emergency Commission's recommendations—because of land on ministers' desks by spring—promised dilemmas on surveillance thresholds, supply-chain safeguards, and digital-currency choke points. Those deliberations belong to the following pages. For now, the country stands at a drafting table scattered with rewritten clauses and coffee-stained polling cross-tabs, a national rulebook midway through revision. Descending into that workshop, where legislators and lobbyists spar over commas that could decide how Canada responds to its next roar of diesel and discontent.

Canada's constitutional weather shifted the moment Justice Paul Rouleau dropped five thick volumes on the clerk's desk at 09:32, on 17 February 2023, each page still warm from the printer and all of them stamped with the same refrain—"Public Order Emergency Commission" and "56 recommendations." [31] By sundown, analysts called the report a national MRI; it confirmed the Emergencies Act threshold was met, yet it also revealed fractures in policing, intelligence sharing, and political coordination that were impossible to ignore. Prime Minister Justin Trudeau, standing before a bank of microphones in the West Block foyer, tried to claim vindication—"the very high threshold was met," he said—but his eyes betrayed the weight of a verdict that was equal parts licence and warning.[33] The report reads like a winter road-safety manual: yes, you may hit the brakes in an emergency, but next time, rotate the tires, clean the windshield, and tell your passengers why you're swerving. [34]

For twenty-three days of televised hearings leading up to that publication, Commissioner Rouleau had conducted what one MP dubbed "the country's longest civics class." Witnesses arrived by the dozen: an Ottawa police chief admitting his force "lost the operational narrative," a CSIS director conceding analytic silos, an Alberta mayor describing supply routes strangled by big-rig barricades. Rouleau never asked barbed questions; instead, he asked insistent ones, and counsel learned to fear when his fountain pen paused mid-sentence— a sure sign he'd found a major logical flaw. Each afternoon, the hearing room pulsed with competing aromas: printer toner, wool coats thawing by space heaters, and coffee strong enough to float a wrench. Gallery benches overflowed with neighbourhood residents clutching decibel charts, truckers in ball caps muttering into earbuds, and constitutional scholars live-tweeting paragraphs before stenographers could certify them.

Volume III of the final report mapped those testimonies onto a lattice of failure so dense it looked structural. Policing organisations talked past one another; provincial officials waited for Ottawa's lead while Ottawa waited for provincial consent; federal intelligence flagged rising extremism but never quantified engine-brake volume at curbside. Hence, Recommendation 12: *create a permanent national coordinator for protest intelligence.* Recommendation 27: *compel social-media platforms to preserve data during declared emergencies.* Recommendation 41: *Legislate a graduated toolbox of financial measures before vaulting straight to mass account freezes.* [34] The document's true thunderclap, however, sounded in Recommendation 55: *amend the Emergencies Act itself, clarifying that future declarations must pass the same proportionality test already demanded by the Charter.*

The ruling Liberals received that thunderclap in a cabinet room thick with March slush and political unease. On the morning of 6 March 2024, Public Safety Minister Dominic LeBlanc slid a blue binder labelled *Government Response—POEC* onto the oval table while staff closed the blinds against telephoto lenses across Wellington Street. [36] Justice Minister Arif Virani began reading passages aloud— commitments to stronger parliamentary review, a statutory definition of *economic emergency*, and a promise to table a draft Emergency Oversight Act within twelve months. Foreign Affairs Minister Mélanie Joly winced at a clause on cryptocurrency choke points ("We cannot spook the FinTech sector into Delaware," she whispered). Finance Minister Chrystia Freeland underlined a line about indemnifying banks during future freezes. No one touched the pastries.

The response, released to the public that afternoon, adopted all 56 recommendations in principle and 42 outright, pledging new inter-agency fusion centres and a biennial joint exercise code-named *Maple Shield.* [37] The technical annex specified the written documentation, time stamping, and immediate tabling in the House of Commons (upon declaration) required for consultation with the provinces. [38] Reporters seized on footnote 57, which hinted at amendments to Section 63 of the Act that would give civil-liberties groups standing to request expedited judicial review. LeBlanc insisted to cameras, "This is about transparency," yet veteran scribes noted the subtext: head off another Mosley-style shellacking before it reaches the Court of Appeal.

Across the Ottawa River in a rented Gatineau conference suite, a coalition of rights advocates welcomed the news with cautious fists-in-pockets. The Canadian Constitution Foundation's Christine Van Geyn clicked through slides quoting Mosley's January ruling, *no national emergency*, *ultra vires*, and announced fresh filings to preserve that precedent against any watering-down on appeal. [39] Beside her, the Canadian Civil Liberties Association's Cara Zwibel sketched a flowchart linking class-action plaintiffs to prospective charter applications, warning that partial compliance on recommendation counts was *a win on paper, a maybe in practice*. [40] Amnesty International Canada's Ketty Nivyabandi dialled in from Montréal to argue the reforms must bar algorithmic surveillance of peaceful dissenters, citing global patterns of emergency creep. [41] The room nodded, then quarrelled over whether to back a private member's bill or wait for government draft language. Someone proposed simultaneous strategies: one inside the committee room, another in the court of public TikTok.

Academics weighed in from all corners. A blog post titled *Ultra Vires and Unreasonable—Again?* published by York University's *The Court* warned that any new law must survive the same post-*Vavilov* reasonableness microscope that humbled the cabinet in January. [42] Public Safety's briefing binder admitted as much: federal drafters were already benchmarking word counts against recent Supreme Court clarity tests. [43] Parliamentary committee clerks, anticipating marathon clause-by-clause sessions, bulk-ordered highlighter refills and gluten-free snacks.

Beyond Parliament Hill, the conversation seeped into daily life. Credit-union managers in Moose Jaw drafted contingency memos to freeze convoy-style crowdfunding without snaring farmers' equipment loans. City councils from Windsor to Whitehorse introduced by-laws, limiting stationary industrial vehicles to eight consecutive hours downtown. One Halifax librarian curated a display titled *From War Measures to Emergencies: Canada's Crises in Statute and Story,* and was surprised to find teenagers checking out dusty volumes on the FLQ. Talk-show hosts asked callers whether they'd trade an eight-hour workday for eight days of frozen pay cheques; opinion lines crackled like woodstoves in January.

By April 2024, the coalition's strategy papers had coalesced into a draft Civil Liberties Safeguard Act: automatic sunset clauses on financial prohibitions, mandatory judicial authorisation for asset freezes, and an ombudsman empowered to audit data-sharing during emergencies. The text borrowed phrasing from Amnesty's *Protect the Protest* campaign and Rouleau's Volume IV footnotes.[41] Lawyers haggled over verbs—should ministers "may" or "must" disclose consultation records? Social-media teams debated whether a hashtag could survive five syllables of legalese. Robins nested in a Stop sign outside the window, perhaps unaware it would soon feature in the campaign's logo.

Meanwhile, federal drafters hammered out their bill. Early leaks suggested Ottawa might create a two-track declaration system: *alert* and *emergency,* each with escalating powers but descending durations. Cabinet hawks liked the flexibility; doves feared a slippery slope. Civil servants compared Australian bushfire statutes, New Zealand's pandemic orders, and Germany's *Grundgesetz* emergency provisions, seeking a Goldilocks clause for a country that boasts the world's longest undefended border and winters that turn diesel into jelly. The Treasury Board quietly costed a permanent Emergency Oversight Secretariat—sixty analysts, two database architects, and disposable pop-up offices ready for any city square that needed a royal commission in a hurry.

Opposition parties found fresh talking points: Conservatives framed the reforms as proof of the Act's misuse. Backbench Liberals braced for constituency town halls where questions would ping-pong between housing prices and horn volumes. One MP joked that door-knock scripts now needed a checkbox for "Diesel Discontent."

The litigation landscape grew busier, too. Civil-liberties charities filed materials resisting the Crown's cross-appeal in *Canadian Frontline Nurses.* This procedural thicket turned on standing, clean hands, and whether peaceful assembly rights end at 105 decibels.[44] Reuters flashed an alert each time the Attorney-General lodged a factum, reminding global investors that Canada, usually placid, was still calibrating the legal speed bumps of protest. [45] Law students filled moot-court galleries to argue whether digital wallets count as "property" under Section 8 of the Charter. Professors delighted in the pedagogical irony: a convoy that began as a protest against mandates had produced the most vibrant mandate for public-law reform in a generation.

Rouleau's closing words echoed through it all: "Democracy's durability lies in its capacity for self-correction." [31] Canada was now deep in that corrective cycle, redrafting statutes, retraining police, and re-teaching citizens that emergency is not a synonym for shortcut. Snow piles melted on Wellington Street, revealing yellow lane stripes scarred by tire chains; soon, landscapers would paint over the last vestiges of protest slogans. But within committee rooms and coalition Zoom calls, the work of rule-making continued. Every comma weighed like ballast in a ship designed for storms not yet on the horizon.

Come summer, legislators would table bills, lawyers would argue appeals, and trainers would replace screenshots of blocked border bridges with flowcharts of accountability in training manuals. Anyone's guess was whether those pages would hold fast in the next gale. Rouleau had implied that the act of writing them together mattered—government, courts, and citizens all wielding red pens. The ultimate test will arrive with the next convoy, cyber-siege, or climate-driven flood. That test—citizen-level, ground-truth, and weather-beaten, awaits.

ENDNOTES

[1] Ljunggren, D. (2022, February 14). *Canada's Trudeau invokes emergency powers in bid to end protests.* Reuters. https://www.reuters.com/world/americas/canada-police-response-protests-spotlight-after-key-bridge-us-cleared-2022-02-14

[2] Cecco, L. (2024, January 23). *Judge rebukes Trudeau for "not justified" use of Emergencies Act. The Guardian.* https://www.theguardian.com/world/2024/jan/23/canada-trudeau-emergencies-act-trucker-protest-covid

[3] Alberta Civil Liberties Research Centre. (2024, January 24). *Federal Court declares Emergencies Act invocation unreasonable.* ACLRC Blog. https://www.aclrc.com/blog/federal-court-rules-that-the-governments-invocation-of-the-emergencies-act-on-february-14-2022-was-unreasonable-and-not-justified

[4] Alberta Civil Liberties Research Centre. (2024). *Judicial review in the Federal Courts: The Emergencies Act* (Working paper No. 24-01). SSRN. https://papers.ssrn.com/sol3/Delivery.cfm/SSRN_ID4802382_code2512502.pdf

[5] Angus Reid Institute. (2024, January 30). *Emergencies Act court ruling revives political fault lines.* https://angusreid.org/emergencies-act-federal-court-trudeau-poilievre-convoy-protest-compromise

[6] Cryderman, K. (2025, April 3). "Freedom Convoy" organizers Lich, Barber found guilty of mischief. *National Observer.* https://www.nationalobserver.com/2025/04/03/news/guilty-verdict-freedom-convoy-organizers-lich-barber-mischief-trial

[7] The Canadian Press. (2025, April 17). "Freedom Convoy" organizer asks for stay after guilty verdict. *CTV News.* https://www.ctvnews.ca/canada/freedom-convoy-organizer-asks-for-stay-of-proceedings-after-guilty-verdict-1.6852182

[8] Land Line Media. (2025, April 9). *Protest organizers await sentencing after being found guilty of mischief.* https://landline.media/protest-organizers-await-sentencing-after-being-found-guilty-of-mischief

[9] Associated Press. (2025, April 3). *Canada trucker protest organizers found guilty of mischief.* AP News. https://apnews.com/article/a45b9c16148a1453f290b86350fea795

[10] Calvinho, D. (2024, November 22). Pat King found guilty of mischief for role in "Freedom Convoy." *CP24.* https://www.cp24.com/news/pat-king-found-guilty-of-mischief-for-role-in-freedom-convoy-1.6665323

[11] BBC News. (2024, November 22). *Pat King: Canada "Freedom Convoy" organiser found guilty of mischief.* https://www.bbc.com/news/articles/cx25nkx7plyo

[12] Dolski, A. (2025, February 19). Pat King sentenced to three months of house arrest in convoy case. *Global News.* https://globalnews.ca/news/11024887/pat-king-sentence-freedom-convoy-case

[13] Li v. Barber et al., Court File CV-22-00088514-00CP (Ontario S.C.J. Mar. 14, 2023) (Further fresh as amended statement of claim). https://ottawaconvoyclassaction.ca/docs/pleadings/23-03-14%20-%20Further%20Fresh%20Amended%20Claim.pdf

[14] Helmer, A. (2024, February 6). Judge tosses motion to dismiss proposed class-action lawsuit against convoy participants. *Ottawa Citizen.* https://stillcoviding.ca/en/news/judge-tosses-motion-to-dismiss-proposed-class-action-lawsuit-against-convoy-participants

[15] CFM Lawyers LLP. (2025). *Ottawa Convoy Class Action* [Overview page]. https://www.cfmlawyers.ca/class-action/ottawa-convoy-class-action

[16] Ottawa Convoy Class Action. (n.d.). *About the lawsuit and recent developments.* Retrieved May 22, 2025, from https://ottawaconvoyclassaction.ca

[17] Zhang, S. J. (2024, November 12). *Ultra vires and unreasonable: Federal Court rules on invocation of the Emergencies Act. The Court* (Osgoode Hall Law School). https://www.yorku.ca/osgoode/thecourt/2024/11/12/ultra-vires-and-unreasonable-federal-court-rules-on-invocation-of-the-emergencies-act

[18] Federal Court of Canada. (2024, January 23). *News bulletin: Public Order Emergency.* https://www.fct-cf.ca/Content/assets/pdf/base/2024-01-23-News-Bulletin-Public-Order-Emergency.pdf

[19] Associated Press. (2024, January 23). *Judge says Canada's use of Emergencies Act was unreasonable.* AP News. https://apnews.com/article/d7e6640f817ee12410bb99840a3df41b

[20] Cecco, L. (2024, January 23). Judge rebukes Trudeau for "not justified" use of Emergencies Act to break convoy. *The Guardian.* https://www.theguardian.com/world/2024/jan/23/canada-trudeau-emergencies-act-trucker-protest-covid

[21] Lewis, J. (2024, January 23). Ottawa to appeal ruling that Emergencies Act use was unreasonable, Freeland says. Reuters. https://www.reuters.com/world/americas/ottawa-appeal-ruling-canadas-use-emergency-powers-was-unreasonable-2024-01-23

[22] CityNews Halifax (The Canadian Press). (2024, January 23). *How key players reacted to the Federal Court's Emergencies Act decision.* https://halifax.citynews.ca/2024/01/23/heres-how-key-players-reacted-to-the-federal-courts-decision-on-the-emergencies-act

[23] Angus Reid Institute. (2024, January 30). *Emergencies Act court ruling revives political fault lines.* https://angusreid.org/emergencies-act-federal-court-trudeau-poilievre-convoy-protest-compromise

[24] National Observer Staff. (2024, January 24). Emergencies Act court ruling opens old emotional wounds. *National Observer.* https://www.nationalobserver.com/2024/01/24/news/emergencies-act-court-ruling-emotional-wounds

[25] CBC News. (2024, January 23). *Federal judge rules Emergencies Act wasn't needed* [YouTube video]. https://www.youtube.com/watch?v=YCX5tXIw_V4

[26] Duplicate of #17

[27] Duplicate of #3

[28] Anthony, N. (2024, February 14). *Frozen assets: Examining Canada's use of the Emergencies Act on its two-year anniversary.* Cato Institute Blog. https://www.cato.org/blog/emergencies-act-after-two-years

[29] Campbell, I. (2024, January 25). Federal Court decision may blunt a key Liberal attack against Poilievre: Pollster. *The Hill Times.* https://www.hilltimes.com/story/2024/01/25/federal-court-decision-on-emergency-act-may-blunt-a-key-liberal-attack-against-poilievre-pollster/409296

[30] Benson, S. (2024, January 30). Despite Emergencies Act vindication, Conservatives shouldn't deviate from message discipline, say politicos. *The Hill Times.* https://www.hilltimes.com/story/2024/01/30/despite-emergencies-act-vindication-conservatives-shouldnt-deviate-from-message-discipline-say-politicos/409817

[31] Public Order Emergency Commission. (2023, February 17). *Final report of the Public Inquiry into the 2022 Public Order Emergency.* https://publicorderemergencycommission.ca/final-report/

[32] Associated Press. (2023, February 17). *Judge: Canada met high threshold to invoke Emergencies Act in truck protest.* AP News. https://apnews.com/article/9c1e37aa86d4315703e69f7794637e7f

[33] Prime Minister of Canada. (2023, February 17). *Statement on the report of the Public Order Emergency Commission.* https://www.pm.gc.ca/en/news/statements/2023/02/17/statement-prime-minister-report-public-order-emergency-commission

[34] Public Order Emergency Commission. (2023, February 17). *News release: Commission makes 56 recommendations.* https://publicorderemergencycommission.ca/news/public-order-emergency-commission-releases-report

[35] Parliament of Canada. (2023). *Special Joint Committee on the Declaration of Emergency: Report No. 2.* https://www.parl.ca/DocumentViewer/en/13098381

[36] Public Safety Canada. (2024, March 6). *Government response to the Public Order Emergency Commission's final report.* https://www.publicsafety.gc.ca/cnt/trnsprnc/brfng-mtrls/prlmntry-bndrs/20240719/41-en.aspx

[37] Public Safety Canada. (2024, March 6). *Statement from Minister LeBlanc.* https://www.canada.ca/en/public-safety-canada/news/2024/03/statement-from-minister-leblanc0.html

[38] Public Safety Canada. (2024). *Briefing binder: Public Order Emergency Commission follow-up.* https://www.publicsafety.gc.ca/cnt/trnsprnc/brfng-mtrls/prlmntry-bndrs/20240626/08-en.aspx

[39] Canadian Constitution Foundation. (2024, July). *Government is still fighting against civil liberties.* https://theccf.ca/government-is-still-fighting-against-civil-liberties

[40] Canadian Civil Liberties Association. (2025, February). *Emergencies Act challenge: CCLA in court to defend historic victory.* https://ccla.org/fundamental-freedoms/emergencies-act-challenge-ccla-in-court-today-to-defend-historic-victory

[41] Amnesty International Canada. (2022). *Statement on Emergencies Act inquiry.* https://amnesty.ca/human-rights-news/amnesty-statement-on-emergencies-act-inquiry

[42] Duplicate of #17

[43] Public Safety Canada. (2024, January 23). *Briefing note: Federal Court ruling on the invocation of the Emergencies Act and next steps.* https://www.publicsafety.gc.ca/cnt/trnsprnc/brfng-mtrls/prlmntry-bndrs/20240626/09-en.aspx

[44] Canadian Civil Liberties Association, Canadian Constitution Foundation, & Alberta Civil Liberties Research Centre. (2024, November 8). *Attorney General's factum on cross-appeal* (Federal Court of Appeal File A-42-24). https://ccla.org/wp-content/uploads/2025/01/2024-11-08-AGCs-factum-on-cross-appeal.pdf

[45] Reuters Staff. (2024, January 23). Canada to appeal ruling that Emergencies Act use was unreasonable. Reuters. https://www.reuters.com/world/americas/ottawa-appeal-ruling-canadas-use-emergency-powers-was-unreasonable-2024-01-23

CHAPTER TWENTY-ONE:
THE HORNS OUT-SHOUTED THE HEARTBEAT

"A truck horn will not make you a citizen, but it can make you a neighbour nobody wants. Diesel does not care about pronouns, borders, or soup kitchens—it settles in your clothes and lungs and refuses to leave. In Ottawa, we learned you can blockade a street with grievance, but you can't unblock a heart with noise."
~ *R.G. Cruise*

Diesel was the hour's perfume. From the Peace Tower's carillon down to the corrugated cul-de-sacs of the ByWard Market, dusk on 2 February 2022 vibrated with a bass line of truck horns that did not so much echo as occupy, the sound squatting in alleyways and vestibules like a tenant who would never pay rent. [1] The convoy had come advertised as a rolling referendum on vaccine mandates, yet by its sixth night, the protest had mutated into a civic MRI, lighting up every pre-existing fracture over gender, sexuality, and who counts as "real" Canadian citizenry. [2]

People at street level felt the fractures before debating them. Morgan and Riley—partners, food-spattered aprons still bundled under one arm from a late Valentine's prep shift—emerged from a bistro on Clarence Street thinking only of tiramisu leftovers and sleep. The momentary hush that lives between restaurant clatter and outdoor bustle lasted precisely three steps; then a rig's high-beams cleaved the dark, and an amplified voice leaned on their names like a crowbar: "Hey, sweethearts, how about a smile—get those masks off so we know what you are!" The truck's grill loomed close enough that they could make out a decal reading *"No Mandates, No Genders"*—the slogan of the day among convoy

Telegram channels. [3] Riley's laugh died in her throat while Morgan's free hand found hers; together they retreated into the lee of a convenience-store doorway until the horn barrage faded. Later, they would tell a *CBC* stringer that the incident felt "less like politics, more like curfew for people like us," their pronouns a provocation in that makeshift cantonment. [4]

Confederation Park was the occupation's gastrointestinal tract. Propane tanks, jerry cans, and pallets moved in relay as volunteers erected a plywood canteen—locals nicknamed *the Cookshack of Discontent*—within sight of the National War Memorial. By early evening, ladles clanged against stockpots and the smell of chilli mingled with gasoline. Over the doorway, someone had repurposed an old anti-trans placard so the hand-painted words *"NO MANDATES, NO GENDERS"* bled through the new lettering advertising *"Free Meals for Freedom Lovers."* City inspectors would later describe the kitchen as a fire hazard and a flashpoint for harassment complaints. [5] One volunteer—Dana, a Two-Spirit Métis paramedic on furlough—kept a tally on her phone: two slurs per ladle served, three leers per garbage bag emptied. She and a small circle of LGBTQ2S+ counter-volunteers devised a watch system: one stirring, one scouting, one walking anyone who felt unsafe back across Elgin Street, their hearts drumming in sync with diesel idling.

Inside the canteen, a portable speaker barked out country anthems between megaphone sermons. A bearded Albertan preached that "gender theory is the government's next virus," earning whoops that rattled prayer flags strung between cedars. Dana flicked her penlight across the crowd, noting half-finished beers, no police, and a teenager distributing "People's Media Badges" that granted the wearer license to shove cell phones in faces without consent. The Office of Ottawa's Auditor General would later catalogue over six hundred resident complaints of intimidation or hate speech within five downtown census tracts during the first week of the occupation. [6]

Further south, on Laurier near the University of Ottawa, staff at the women-and-gender-diverse shelter switched to lockdown protocol when a convoy pickup parked against their accessible ramp, the driver shouting, "Show us your papers—prove you're not government plants!" ACLED analysts would classify such encounters as "micro-siege events," brief but cumulative shocks to community safety. [7] The shelter's porch lights flickered; inside, crisis-line phones blinked like aural seismographs.

Midnight came, and Eva Nguyen's shift ended at the Civic Hospital. Eva—an ICU nurse who measured her days in millilitres of vasopressors and her nights in decibels of truck horns—consulted the memo taped beside the staff-entrance door: *Consider buddy system when walking to transit; avoid scrubs or ID in convoy zones.* Transit had become a board game of blocked squares, so she opted for foot travel. Her route traced the narrow service lane behind Gloucester, where rig bumpers jutted out like fortified balconies. The lane lighting was down to phone-flash quality because, as one protestor told the Ottawa People's Commission inquiry months later, "We unscrewed the bulbs—light pollution, you know, the city should thank us." [8]

Eva kept her ID badge inside her coat, the lanyard still imprinted on her neck. Halfway home, she met a checkpoint of two men in Carhartt overalls who asked if she was "with the jab Nazis." She side-stepped them, heart sprinting, and clocked the path ahead: five rigs, one alley exit, no visible police tape. *Reuters* later quoted an O.P.S. officer who conceded that by-laws against harassment existed, but "enforcement was complicated by the blockade's urban setting and the presence of children." [9] Eva reached her apartment to find someone had sketched a needle crossed out by an X on her lobby door—public-health graffiti turned private threat.

Horns paused at 03:00 for a driver-coordinated "moment of silent resolve," then resumed with what activists on Twitter christened *the Rooster Reveille.* The Guardian tallied noise complaints peaking at ninety-eight decibels—louder than a lawn mower, painful enough to make toddlers cry in their sleep. [10] Local hardware stores sold out of industrial ear protection; one clerk joked Ottawans were about to achieve the highest per capita rate of tinnitus in North America.

Even the movement's internal narrators could not agree on its script. *Truck News* columnist James Menzies argued genuine hauliers had been *duped* by culture-war opportunists, writing on 30 January that the convoy was never about border mandates. [11] On 2 February, *The Tyee* dissected how federal Conservative leadership hopefuls were already monetising the occupation's social-media virality, shaping a *truck-stop populism* that folded anti-gender ideology into an all-purpose grievance burrito. [12] *Teen Vogue*, reaching readers an ocean away from Parliament Hill, warned that white-supremacist and anti-LGBTQ2S+ motifs were bleeding from Canadian streets into global screens, a pattern familiar from January 6th footage but now sporting maple-leaf flair. [13]

By 04:00, when night should be deepest and quietest, Eva flicked on the radio only to find talk shows celebrating the Cookshack as proof of convoy self-reliance. *CTV News* would shortly air footage of that same *community kitchen*, its plywood joints still dripping with nocturnal sleet, framed by half-burned tiki torches and stacked propane tanks—a tableau that one fire marshal described, off-record, as *Fyre Festival meets Trailer Park Boys*. [14]

Yet dawn blushed, indifferent. In that murky pre-dawn light, Morgan and Riley brewed coffee on their balcony, the steam mixing with the cold diesel haze. Beneath them, a woman in an orange safety vest—later identified as a city sanitation supervisor—approached a protest pickup to request its removal from a fire route. The driver revved in reply, thrusting his thumb toward a cardboard sign that read *Hold the Line*. *Reuters* would recall similar testimonies during the Rouleau Commission's hearings a year later, where city staff spoke of *feeling harassed just for wearing an ID lanyard*. [15]

The horn crescendo returned at sunrise, brassier this time, as if determined to stamp a copyright on the day. And so the convoy's seventh morning began much like its sixth night had ended: with engines drowning conversation, with sidewalks re-purposed into ideological customs posts, and with every queer laugh or nurse's nametag subject to inspection by self-appointed border guards of belonging. The sound carried across the Rideau Canal and up Wellington Street until even the Peace Tower bells seemed to ring a half-note flatter. Later chapters of inquiry would ask how a dispute over public-health regulations spiralled into a referendum on social inclusion; the answer, like a truck horn at 03:00. People could not ignore the dispute once they heard it. For now, Ottawa's women and gender-diverse residents learned to breathe between honks and to watch the darkness lift, wary of what daylight might demand to see next.

Morning rode in on a stalled horn blast and never left. By dawn of 3 February 2022, the Freedom Convoy no longer felt like a protest that was in Ottawa; it felt like the protest had annexd Ottawa, a miniature city-state of chromed exhaust pipes, home-made sovereignty proclamations and diesel-powered border crossings that ring-fenced whole blocks in the capital's core. [16] What many white-collar commentators still described as a carnival of *patriots* looked, from the vantage of racialised and immigrant neighbourhoods, like a siege manned by strangers who had deputised themselves to decide who could move, speak or pray—a revelation less about vaccine rules than about the elastic boundaries of Canadian belonging. [17] In patchy police radio chatter, the area south of Wellington Street was now the "red zone," but apartment dwellers along Somerset and Gladstone used an older label whispered in foyer echoes: *the outside.*

Just after 09:00, a dozen community organisers filed through the glass doors of the Multifaith Housing Initiative (MHI) hall on Laurier Avenue, each carrying notes for a panel on pandemic-relief micro-grants. Imam Farah Abdi kept a folded spreadsheet of halal-kitchen deliveries; Reverend Deborah Brown gripped a USB stick packed with eviction-prevention stats; entrepreneur Kareem Mensah wore a suit jacket that still smelled faintly of the jollof he had cooked before sunrise for his mother's caregiving co-op. None made it ten metres before a barricade of rigs snarled the curb lane. Men in camo hoodies jumped down, and demands rang out: "Let's see your papers—show us the stamp that lets you lecture Canadians!" The words tasted imported, part checkpoint, part internet meme, but the menace was local, vibrating between laughter and assault. Someone mistook Abdi's pocket Qur'an for a vaccination card. The group retreated indoors, pallets jammed against the doors while camera phones recorded the plate numbers. Later that week, an Ottawa People's Commission witness would recall that MHI session as *the morning sanctuary became a Kafka turnstile.* [18] Amnesty International, monitoring reports of racial intimidation, cited "demands for identification directed almost exclusively at Black and Muslim residents" as evidence of discriminatory harassment patterns. [19]

Across town, Confederation Park simmered beneath its snow crust like a pot left unattended. Someone had planted a Confederate flag in the snowbank beside the volunteer soup line; someone else balanced a poster on a lawn chair that showed a cartoon imam holding a syringe above the text *Make Canada Muslim-Free. BBC* cameras, roaming for noon-hour colour, captured the tableau even as a City of Ottawa by-law van idled fifty metres away with the engine still running. [20] Just beyond the lens, Anishinaabe elder Asha Migizi stood at the corner of Elgin and Laurier, waiting for two youth volunteers who had promised to help her collect medicines for a ceremony at the Human Rights Monument. Instead, she met three convoy partisans arrayed like goalies across the crosswalk, arms folded, eyes laughing. They called her "shaman granny," accused her of owning "liberal crystals," and mimed drumming while chanting an off-key pastiche of pow-wow vocals. When she stepped forward, they shuffled sideways to block the walk light. Migizi, eighty-two winters and one silver walking pole, inhaled the diesel and remembered the 1969 protests against the White Paper—only the slogans had aged, not the contempt. An *APTN News* headline later distilled her verdict: *'Interlopers need to go,' Algonquin elder warns.* [21] The day's notebook entry in the ACLED fact sheet would list *verbal racial harassment (Indigenous), obstruction of movement (critical infrastructure)* occurring at 10:47 a.m. [22]

Back at MHI, the panel resumed on folding chairs inside a storage alcove that smelled of mop buckets because the main hall's windows rattled each time a jake-brake barked outside. Reverend Brown rewrote her opening line on a yellow sticky: *If charity begins at home, how do we fund a home that no longer feels charitable?* Her question never reached the mic; the Zoom link froze when a protester pointed a Bluetooth speaker at the façade, flooding the bandwidth with country rock and horn feedback. Afterwards, sociologist Darnell Thompson told the National Observer that the convoy "performed citizenship checks on racialised bodies while claiming to resist state surveillance—a paradox only if you assume the state watches everyone equally." [23] The same afternoon, *WIRED* traced thirty-eight convoy Facebook groups sharing memes of border guards demanding passports from masked Black toddlers. [24]

Around 13:30, the temperature dipped to minus-14°C, but the cultural thermostat swung hotter. A man in a fur trapper hat cornered Kareem Mensah outside as he sought fresh air, introducing himself as "Border Patrol." The man pressed a laminated flyer to Mensah's chest: *No Jabs, No Jobs, No Foreign Mobs.* Kareem's accent—Ottawa-raised, Ghanaian cadence—became provocation enough; the flyer fluttered to the slush with a wet *slap* as the self-appointed patrol barked, "Time you queued up for the next flight out." A journalism student from *The Link* newspaper, live-streaming across the street, caught the exchange before a second protester tried to yank her press badge off-camera. Her story later quoted Mensah's quiet coda: "This morning I brought housing stats; by lunch I felt stateless." [25]

When the horns paused for a hymn at 15:00—a makeshift choir belting out "O Canada" with a stanza swapped to "True North Strong and Pure"—shelter outreach worker Dr. Lillian Reyes studied her phone like a general scanning weather reports. Reyes supervised disability supports at an emergency shelter on Queen Street, where several residents used mobility scooters; diesel haze had seeped into the vents overnight, triggering asthma attacks. She left the Somerset Annex pushing a trolley stacked with inhalers, adult diapers and tactile-signage kits, but found Kent Street clogged by nose-to-bumper pickups, engines left on to keep the cab heaters roaring. A volunteer advised her to try the alley parallel to Bank Street; she discovered a wheelchair user spinning futilely in the ice because convoyers had lined plastic fuel jugs across the asphalt "as art," one told her, "showing how the government gasses us." Reyes moved the jugs, guided the chair through, and felt a hand clap her shoulder—too friendly, too firm. "Mask off, sweetheart," a voice said. "Let us see you smile." She kept walking, pulse drumming triple-time, and texted her colleague: *clients terrified to leave shelter; horns causing sensory overload; call O.P.S.* Later, the Ottawa People's Commission filed testimony from a mobility-restricted resident whose wheelchair a similar taunt had seized. [26] *Charlatan* columnist Jaya Kaur put it simpler: "The convoy re-invented Jim Crow as a street party and asked marginalised neighbours to bring the snacks." [27]

By sunset, diesel droplets condensed into a yellow film on apartment windows; residents traced it with fingers the way bored students outline hearts in bus-stop frost. Rabble's early-evening push notification summarised the People's Commission presser: *Harassment, assaults, hate symbols—occupation meets threshold for state failure.* [28] In the Centretown Community Health Centre foyer, volunteers printed flyers reading *Hate Crime Hotline: 613-236-1222, ext 5015,* replicating an Ottawa Police tweet about a new reporting line launched after a surge of race-based complaints. [29] Yet many who dialled heard only hold music, the system jammed by crank callers quoting the convoy anthem about *the tyrant Justin.* Elder Migizi, resting at home after her thwarted ceremony, watched the hotline glitch scroll by on *CP24* and muttered an Ojibwe proverb: *The wolves chase loudest when the moon is thin.*

Night returned, though *returned* felt euphemistic; it had hardly left. The MHI hall dimmed its lights to avoid drawing another impromptu audition from Border Patrol, and Kareem Mensah emailed his keynote slides to an inbox labelled

Archive-For-After. Imam Abdi led a whispered Maghrib prayer beneath a stairwell, the hum of fluorescent ballast mingling with distant foghorns. In Confederation Park, convoyers stacked pallets for a bonfire, sparks rising like rebel confetti against the gothic silhouette of the Château Laurier. ACLED's live-mapping software pinned four new icons for *intimidation of service workers, obstruction of emergency route, hate-speech incident, unauthorised pyrotechnics.* [30]

Close to 21:00, the horns executed what protesters on Telegram called the *Freedom Crank:* three long, two short, three long—Morse for SOS repurposed as a victory salute. Apartment balconies shook. Somewhere between the final blare and the return of silence, a child in a top-floor unit of Bay Street Tower pressed a hand-drawn sign to the glass: *Let us sleep. Reuters* later quoted the child's father saying, "My seven-year-old now asks if rights come from honking or voting." [31]

The day ended as it began with a city counting honks like aftershocks. But amid the noise, a separate tally had begun—one kept in spiral notebooks, shelter logs, hotline transcripts and witness affidavits. Each shouted slur, each blocked wheelchair ramp, each "papers please" demand added ink to a ledger that civil-rights lawyers would soon carry into court and that commissioners would thump upon parliamentary desks. By the end of February, those pages would become calls for an inquiry, demands that policing mandates be rewritten, and petitions insisting that any future protest permit should include an audit identifying those most at risk of losing their city when the trucks arrive. For racialised Ottawans, the memory of 3 February was already proof that freedom too often arrives on selective invitation; the question hovering over the diesel haze was whether lawmakers would bother to RSVP.

Daylight on 4 February rose into a city already hollowed out by crisis budgets and pandemic attrition, then found the hollows clogged with chrome. By its second Friday, what had begun as a border-mandate tantrum was a civic siege: trucks welded together by snowdrifts barred ambulance lanes, diesel haze fogged traffic lights, and the word *occupation* replaced *protest* in morning newscasts. [32] Before dawn, the Centretown food-bank coordinator dialled neighbouring charities to ask who still had bread racks; every line gave the same answer—a tired whistle between clenched teeth—because suppliers could not snake past the rolling barricades or dared not try after a week of horn assaults. [33]

Inside Shepherds of Good Hope, the city's main soup kitchen, overnight staff stacked eight-litre stew pots by flashlight; generators had guzzled their final jerry cans while convoy engines idled outside, as if taunting the shelter with spare fuel. At 06:05, the first volunteer arrived to find tractor-trailers wedged across Murray Street, drivers pounding on plexiglass and hollering for "breakfast on the house." One slapped the window with a fistful of Canadian Tire vouchers, another filmed on his phone while barking, "We fed you with taxes, now you feed us." A security guard's attempt at de-escalation earned a shoulder shove and a racial epithet recorded on CCTV. [34] By the time police cruisers threaded through, staff had barred the doors and ushered fifty bleary shelter residents into the chapel for safety. Hours later, the charity's Twitter plea spawned a wave of $10 e-transfers that would swell into CA$750,000 within a week, [35] a paradoxical windfall read by one board member as "evidence that Ottawans will crowd-source dignity when government supply chains collapse."

Across Rideau Street, a mobile outreach van nosed toward an encampment under the Queensway flyover, quilt bundles, and thermoses rattling in its cargo bay. Nurse-driver Arielle Daoust had patched frost-bitten toes there nightly since December without incident, but today a phalanx of pickups boxed her in beneath the overpass murals. Tailpipes coughed exhaust into the sliding door as men in camo ball caps demanded she explain *why the homeless get free needles, but the working man gets mandates.* An engine back-fired; someone yelled *standoff!*, Daoust's clients—three rough-sleepers hunched beside shopping carts—watched their coffee steam cancel against the fumes. GPS logs later submitted to the Ottawa People's Commission showed the van immobilised for fourteen minutes; Daoust's recording captures her voice modulating from calm instruction to a cracked whisper: "Gentlemen, I am literally the medic." [36] In testimony, months later, she would describe the moment as "the inverse of triage—healthy bodies barricading sick ones." Commissioners folded her story into a 294-page indictment of systemic policing failure. [37]

Mid-morning sirens tried to compete with air horns as municipal crews attempted a garbage pickup on Sussex Drive; they retreated after buckets of snowball-packed litter flew from truck cabs. Farm tractors hemmed *Guardian* correspondents, roaming on foot in, tallied at least five Confederate bumper flags and a portable sauna under construction beside East Block, "hardly the optics of a weekend rally," their notebook read. [38] Ottawa Police, stung by days of criticism, promised a crackdown on "an increasingly dangerous demonstration" at a noon press briefing; residents noted the language was notably tardy, considering paramedic routes had been breached since day one. [39] While senior officers listed forthcoming enforcement steps, the city's emergency operations centre fielded sixty-one calls about blocked disability ramps and unserviced fire hydrants, triple the usual count for a winter weekday. [40] Internally, an excerpt later unearthed by the Public Order Emergency Commission recorded a planner's blunt margin note: "Essential services sabotaged by inertia, not ignorance." [41]

At 13:45, a funeral contingent of two dozen gathered at the National War Memorial for a wreath-laying, mostly septuagenarian veterans in dress coats. They found the plaza choked with eighteen-wheelers whose drivers blasted *La Cucaracha* horns between chants of *Hold the Line*, one veteran's reading of the Act of Remembrance dissolved as the refrain "We will remember them" drowned beneath diesel revs. Video posted to TikTok, later scrubbed but archived by hate-incident researchers, captures a protester straddling the Tomb railing to wave a *Make Canada Great Again* flag. [42] When a legionnaire asked for quiet, a truck's PA answered with Macarena beats that bounced off the granite like rubber bullets. Moments after someone ripped down and tossed the fencing erected days earlier to protect the monument onto a salt pile, *CTV* cameras arrived. [43] Neither police nor by-law officers intervened. Later that night, an anonymous veteran began drafting a petition demanding federal guardianship of memorial sites during national protests; within forty-eight hours, it reached 25,000 signatures.

Meanwhile, the city's class-action lawyer filed new affidavits for downtown residents whose windows rattled at 100-decibel horn blasts; the suit, lodged the previous afternoon, named thirty additional licence plates and claimed damages past CA$9.8 million. [44] *Reuters'* explainer reminded foreign readers that only a minority of Canadian truckers opposed vaccination rules, underscoring how quickly a niche grievance had metastasised into an all-purpose choke-point on civil space. [45]

Back at Shepherds, the lunch service proceeded behind locked doors: peanut-butter sandwiches slid through a vestibule hatch one at a time to avoid stampedes. Word of the morning, the blockade had already migrated across Signal groups; donors from Halifax to Haida Gwaii queued digital transfers faster than the accountant could issue receipts. When *CBC's* evening newscast aired a

CA$750k donation surge segment, shelter CEO Deirdre Freiheit reframed the money as community self-defence: "Ottawa wrote itself the cheque officials wouldn't sign." [46]

Sunset arrived muted—clouds thick with exhaust—but the convoy's improvised fairground came alive: wood-burning stoves ticked, saunas hissed, and a karaoke machine near the Château Laurier belted *Life Is a Highway* while adjacent speakers pulsed conspiracy podcasts. ACLED's live feed logged five fresh icons for *service obstruction* between 17:00 and 18:00, colour-coded crimson for *escalating risk*. [47] In the alley behind Lisgar Street's family shelter, Arielle Daoust finally delivered her blankets four hours late; two of her clients had already wandered off into minus-16°C darkness in search of heat vents and were later found by outreach volunteers with early frostnip.

As horns mounted their nightly crescendo, municipal Twitter asked residents to report hate incidents to a hotline that still looped a busy signal. Downtown councillors pleaded for federal intervention; cabinet ministers spoke of *tools on the table*. By the time headlights painted the Parliament façade in restless sweeps, pundits were sketching the outlines of an inevitable inquiry: not just into emergency powers or police command, but into how a nation so proud of its social safety net had left the net unguarded. Ottawa's unhoused and their caregivers carried the answer in chapped hands and diesel-clogged lungs: the convoy had merely exposed the seams already splitting. Until those seams were stitched, every future protest—whatever the cause—would find the same easy leverage: starve the aid lines, flood the memorial steps, drown silence in horns, then wait for the hunger-line hangfire to catch.

ENDNOTES

[1] *Washington Blade*. (2022, February 8). COVID protests in Canadian capital get violent and homo/transphobic. https://www.washingtonblade.com/2022/02/08/covid-protests-in-canadian-capital-get-violent-homo-transphobic

[2] Jones, S. (2022, February 9). Canada's "Freedom Convoy" protests aren't about freedom. *Teen Vogue*. https://www.teenvogue.com/story/canada-freedom-convoy-oped

[3] Morrow, A. (2023, April 5). Poilievre's big bet on convoy-loving politics. *The Tyee*. https://thetyee.ca/Analysis/2023/04/05/Poilievre-Convoy-Loving-Politics

[4] CBC News/Yahoo News. (2023, January 31). Residents abandoned to a violent occupation during "Freedom Convoy," areas report. https://ca.news.yahoo.com/freedom-convoy-violent-occupation-areas-185109053.html

[5] Pringle, J. (2022, February 3). Protesters build wooden structure in downtown Ottawa park. *CTV News*. https://www.ctvnews.ca/ottawa/protesters-build-wooden-structure-in-downtown-ottawa-park-1.5765787

[6] Office of the Auditor General of Ottawa. (2024). Audit of the City of Ottawa's response to the convoy protest (Report). https://www.oagottawa.ca/media/tklagr1h/final-audit-report-audit-of-the-city-of-ottawa-s-response-to-the-convoy-protest-1-final-ua.pdf

[7] Armed Conflict Location & Event Data Project. (2022, February 25). Fact sheet: "Freedom Convoys" and anti-vaccine demonstrations in Canada. https://acleddata.com/2022/02/25/fact-sheet-freedom-convoys-and-anti-vaccine-demonstrations-in-canada

[8] Ottawa People's Commission. (2023). What we heard (Part I report). https://www.opc-cpo.ca/wp-content/uploads/2023/02/OPC-Report-Part-I-What-We-Heard.pdf

[9] Paperny, A. M. (2022, February 9). Explainer: Ottawa protests—What you need to know about the anti-mandate movement. *Reuters*. https://www.reuters.com/world/americas/how-ottawas-anti-vaccine-mandate-protests-are-spreading-globally-2022-02-09

[10] Cecco, L. (2022, February 22). Canada extends emergency powers after trucker blockades ended. *The Guardian*. https://www.theguardian.com/world/2022/feb/22/canada-extends-emergency-powers-after-trucker-blockades-ended

[11] Menzies, J. (2022, January 30). The so-called Freedom Convoy was never about truckers. *Truck News*. https://www.trucknews.com/blogs/the-so-called-freedom-convoy-was-never-about-truckers

[12] Duplicate of #2

[13] Duplicate of #2

[14] Duplicate of #5

[15] Paperny, A. M. (2023, February 17). Canada's use of emergency powers during "Freedom Convoy" met threshold: Commissioner. *Reuters*. https://www.reuters.com/world/americas/canadas-use-emergency-powers-met-threshold-commissioner-2023-02-17

[16] Gable, B. (2022, February 3). Ottawans fed up with trucker blockade blame police inaction. *Reuters*. https://www.reuters.com/world/americas/ottawans-fed-up-with-trucker-blockade-blame-police-inaction-2022-02-03

[17] Kestler-D'Amours, J. (2022, March 19). What the truckers' convoy revealed about policing in Canada. *Al Jazeera*. https://www.aljazeera.com/news/2022/3/19/what-truckers-convoy-revealed-about-policing-in-canada

[18] Ottawa People's Commission. (2023). Part II – After the occupation: Change (Report). https://www.opc-cpo.ca/wp-content/uploads/2023/04/Part-II-After-The-Occupation-Change.pdf

[19] Amnesty International Canada. (2022, February 7). Stop violence and harassment at Ottawa protests [Statement]. https://amnesty.ca/human-rights-news/ottawa-protests-freedom-convoy-statement

[20] BBC News. (2022, February 8). Canada trucker protest: Ottawa declares emergency. https://www.bbc.com/news/world-us-canada-60281088

[21] Forester, B. (2022, February 3). Algonquin elder says "interlopers need to go" as Ottawa braces for convoy protest surge. *APTN News.* https://www.aptnnews.ca/national-news/algonquin-elder-says-interlopers-need-to-go-as-ottawa-braces-for-convoy-protest-surge

[22] Duplicate of #7

[23] Wilson, L. (2022, February 11). Expert warns of convoy backlash and racist tokenism. *National Observer.* https://www.nationalobserver.com/2022/02/11/news/expert-warns-tokenizing-racialized-supporters-ottawa-convoy-backlash-hate

[24] O'Sullivan, D. (2022, February 5). The alt-right on Facebook is hijacking Canada's trucker blockade. *Wired.* https://www.wired.com/story/ottawa-trucker-protest-facebook-alt-right

[25] Dore, M. (2022, February 10). Marginalized communities bear the brunt of the Freedom Convoy. *The Link.* https://thelinknewspaper.ca/article/feature/marginalized-communities-are-bearing-the-brunt-of-the-freedom-convoy

[26] Duplicate of #2

[27] Kaur, J. (2022, February 12). Opinion: The convoy shows Canada's tolerance of white supremacy. *The Charlatan.* https://charlatan.ca/opinion-the-trucker-convoy-demonstrates-canadians-tolerance-of-white-supremacy

[28] Trick, S. (2023, April 4). Commission concludes Ottawa convoy was an occupation. *Rabble.ca.* https://rabble.ca/politics/canadian-politics/commission-concludes-ottawa-freedom-convoy-was-an-occupation

[29] Ottawa People's Commission. (2023). Part I – What we heard. https://www.opc-cpo.ca/wp-content/uploads/2023/02/OPC-Report-Part-I-What-We-Heard.pdf

[30] Kim, S. (2022, February 1). Ottawa police set up hate-crime hotline amid protest violence. *Axios.* https://www.axios.com/2022/02/01/canada-ottawa-police-hate-crime-hotline-anti-vax-protest

[31] Gable, B. (2022, February 5). Residents furious at nonstop horn blaring fear no end in sight. *Reuters.* https://www.reuters.com/world/americas/canadas-ottawa-residents-furious-nonstop-trucker-horn-blaring-2022-02-05

[32] Kestler-D'Amours, J. (2022, February 4). Ottawa residents decry anti-vaccine trucker "occupation". *Al Jazeera.* https://www.aljazeera.com/news/2022/2/4/ottawa-residents-decry-anti-vaccine-trucker-occupation

[33] Identical to #16

[34] Raymond, T. (2022, January 30). Ottawa homeless shelter staff harassed by convoy protesters demanding food. *CTV News*. https://www.ctvnews.ca/ottawa/ottawa-homeless-shelter-staff-harassed-by-convoy-protesters-demanding-food-1.5757225

[35] Dubé, D-E. (2022, February 10). Community raises $750 K for Shepherds of Good Hope since run-in with truck convoy protesters. *Ottawa CityNews*. https://ottawa.citynews.ca/2022/02/10/community-raises-750k-for-shepherds-of-good-hope-since-run-in-with-truck-convoy-protesters-5048933

[36] Armed Conflict Location & Event Data Project. (2022, February 10). Regional overview: United States and Canada, 29 Jan – 4 Feb 2022. https://acleddata.com/2022/02/10/regional-overview-united-states-and-canada-29-january-4-february-2022

[37] Ottawa People's Commission. (2023). What we heard (Report, p. 68). https://www.opc-cpo.ca/wp-content/uploads/2023/02/OPC-Report-Part-I-What-We-Heard.pdf

[38] Mahdawi, A. (2022, February 8). The whole world should be worried by the "siege of Ottawa." *The Guardian*. https://www.theguardian.com/commentisfree/2022/feb/08/ottawa-truckers-protest-anti-vaxx-canada

[39] Ljunggren, D. (2022, February 4). Ottawa police vow crackdown on "dangerous" trucker protest. *Reuters*. https://www.reuters.com/world/americas/ottawa-police-promise-tougher-action-against-blockading-truckers-2022-02-04

[40] Panetta, N. (2022, February 7). Ottawa declares state of emergency over trucker convoy COVID-19 protests. *NPR*. https://www.npr.org/2022/02/07/1078861392/ottawa-protest-state-of-emergency

[41] Public Order Emergency Commission. (2023). Final report, Vol 2, § 5.1. https://publicorderemergencycommission.ca/files/documents/Final-Report/Vol-2-Report-of-the-Public-Inquiry-into-the-2022-Public-Order-Emergency.pdf

[42] Duplicate of #36

[43] Pringle, J. (2022, February 12). Protesters tear down fencing around the National War Memorial. *CTV News*. https://www.ctvnews.ca/ottawa/protesters-tear-down-fencing-around-the-national-war-memorial-1.5771231

[44] Reuters Staff. (2022, February 19). Key events in Canada's trucker protests against COVID curbs. *Reuters*. https://www.reuters.com/world/americas/key-events-canadas-trucker-protests-against-covid-curbs-2022-02-19

[45] Ljunggren, D. (2022, February 9). Explainer: How Ottawa's anti-mandate protests spread globally. *Reuters*. https://www.reuters.com/world/americas/how-ottawas-anti-vaccine-mandate-protests-are-spreading-globally-2022-02-09

[46] CBC News. (2022, February 10). Ottawa shelter "blown away" by donations after harassment. https://www.cbc.ca/news/canada/ottawa/ottawa-shelter-donations-convoy-protest-1.6345974

CHAPTER TWENTY-TWO:
DAWN TRADES QUIET FOR QUESTIONS

"Freedom left with the trucks, but the arguments stayed to haunt the kitchen tables. A horn blast can clear a street faster than law, but only silence will teach us what we lost in the noise. In Ottawa, we measured democracy in decibels and learned the real repairs begin when the talking gets quiet."
~ R. G. Cruise

Night's last blue charcoal still clung to the Peace Tower when the first commuter trains rattled over the Rideau Canal, their windows catching the glow of traffic lights that had blinked red, unchallenged, for the better part of a fortnight. What met those dawn-bound riders was not silence so much as the negative image of silence: the sudden absence of a sonic wall that had made every kitchen cabinet jitter like crockery in a passing freight car. Across the country, radios filled the vacuum with post-mortems. All at once, the talk shows sounded less like call-in weather reports and more like a civics class taught at the volume of disbelief.

Pollsters were already tallying the mood. An *Angus Reid* snapshot, taken while diesel soot still floated above Wellington Street, found three out of four Canadians telling the convoys to *go home now,* a rebuke so lopsided that even veteran strategists blinked twice at the cross-tabs. [1] Editors flung the numbers into headlines that asked whether the episode would reset the calculus of protest or only harden it. Pundits on one station wondered aloud if the weekend's brief, jubilant horn blasts marking the blockade's retreat would age into a folk memory of triumph or Exhibit A in the next handbook on radicalisation. On another, callers swapped stories of cancelled shifts, supply snags, and a strange new allergy to the word *freedom.*

Ottawa's political class felt the tremor before most. In a windowless corridor behind the Prime Minister's Office, senior adviser Léonie Tran advanced toward the secure briefing room, tablet bobbing against a mug gone lukewarm two crises ago. Her screen glowed with polling cross-tabs, Bank of Canada flash estimates, and a bullet-point marked *upstream litigation risks.* Tran's task between sunrise and Question Period was to sand any jagged data into talking points sturdy enough for an emergency Commons session to gavel in by noon. She moved like a paramedic rolling a gurney: swift, economical, eyes already parsing the prognosis.

She rehearsed the choreography. First, reassure skittish backbenchers that public opinion had snapped in the government's favour — the *Angus Reid* numbers made that plausible. Second, frame the occupation as an economic haemorrhage, not a culture-war carnival. Bank Street merchants had lost more revenue in two weeks of gridlock than during full pandemic lockdowns, a downtown BIA director told *City News.* [2] Third, douse talk of overreach with the language of proportionality. Opposition MPs in the last emergency debate's House Hansard still vehemently criticized the scene outside as "bouncy castles and noisy truckers," implying that sound levels could measure constitutional limits. [6] Tran would counter with invoices: policing overtime, snow-clearing reroutes, hotel cancellations—an eerily methodical ledger of disruption.

Across the canal, in a family-run café wedged between two souvenir shops, Nico, and Marta Gagliano watched the milk steamer hiss while the cash drawer yawned empty. The blockades had shrunk their usually busy weekday mornings to a trickle, embarrassingly small. They had tried counting blessings— no smashed windows, no looting—but relief curdled when the insurance adjuster hinted that business-interruption clauses rarely pay out without *direct physical loss.* The civil disobedience of parked Peterbilts did not, on paper, qualify as physical. [4] Rumour said Ottawa's smallest shops might be in line for federal relief grants of up to $10,000, but the application portal would not open for weeks, and Mira's textbooks for her first year at Carleton were due next Monday. [5]

Between pouring cappuccinos, Nico reopened security footage from the blockade's loudest night. At 02:07, a convoy driver had leaned through the service window, demanding espresso for *patriots*; when told the machine was off, he revved his engine so fiercely the patio umbrellas pirouetted in their iron stands. The café now smelled faintly of ghost diesel, the way a rural train crossing holds phantom whistles long after the caboose has passed. Marta traced the insurance policy's fine print with a fingernail, whispering clauses to herself like penance.

South of them, where Centretown row houses meet the skeletal shadows of office towers, community organiser Farah Bellegarde zipped her parka and set out with a clipboard that still bore grease smears from peace-bond paperwork signed at 03:00 the previous night. Farah had become, by accident, a hinge between worlds: the volunteers who cooked stews for stranded truckers, the local councillor scrambling to reopen bus routes, and the police liaison officers blinking under their riot helmets. She had shuttled ceasefire text messages when air horns drowned out phone calls; she had mapped an evacuation lane wide enough for ambulances yet narrow enough to keep negotiators from bolting.

One sergeant, two lead drivers, a mediator from the local mosque, and Farah sealed the final withdrawal not in a boardroom but on a slush-slick street outside St. Patrick's Basilica. Patrick's Basilica: all circled a pickup's tailgate that served as both desk and diplomatic buffet. They bartered over parking tickets, fuel-reimbursement rumours, and a half-whispered promise that operators who exited before dawn might avoid licence suspensions. Such mercy proved fleeting. Within forty-eight hours, Ontario ordered a dozen commercial plate holders out of service, an administrative guillotine that landed with paperwork's quiet thud. [10]

Farah recorded every concession in shorthand, barely keeping pace with the snowfall. She watched gloved signatures bleed ink in the cold and thought of how easily signatures could bleed intentions once microphones appeared. But the drivers rolled out, exhaust plumes curling like question marks in the mica-bright streetlamps. When the last cab rattled over Laurier Avenue, Farah's radio crackled with a police dispatcher announcing the *clear for sanitation* route—the coded benediction of municipal relief.

Elsewhere, architects of order prepared their after-action reports. A draft audit from Ottawa's Office of the Auditor General would later accuse city management of *conceptual drift*, its polite euphemism for misjudging a rally's half-life. [9] The Public-Order Emergency Commission, struck months later, would devote paragraphs to the weekend of February 5, calling it the hinge where provincial sympathy rallies fanned out to Victoria, Edmonton, and Québec City, illuminating jurisdictional grey zones in neon hazard yellow. [8]

But none of that hindsight glowed yet at the dawn of February. What Ottawa felt instead was the uncanny hush after a carnival folds its tents: the plywood tacked onto hot-tub frames, the footprints thawing into slush, the quick recalibration of GPS apps that had learned to detour around the "red zone" as instinctively as salmon dodge a dam. Radio hosts parsed the difference between civil disobedience, aimed at laws, and civil disruption, aimed at life itself. A *BBC* reporter, voice hoarse from cold air interviews, admitted that locals' patience had "run paper thin," a phrase that stuck to windshield chatter like frost. [2]

Inside East Block, Léonie Tran finally ducked into the briefing room, coffee sloshing over a sheaf of annotated headlines. Ministers would arrive in seven minutes. Her phone pinged with a fresh advisory from the Privy Council: hold firm on *proportionate response*, flag upcoming provincial legislation that could embed "critical infrastructure zones," and expect pushback from civil-liberties groups already drafting op-eds warning of a slippery slope. Down on Sparks Street, a maintenance crew scraped neon-green spray-paint off the War Memorial's granite base and wondered whether the next protest would bother with trucks.

Dawn brightened into the tawny haze of a city overdue for snowmelt. Even though no one was seated, the Gaglianos reopened their patio heaters; Farah texted her volunteers to meet at the community centre for a debrief; Tran exhaled as the Question Period began with fewer jeers than forecast. Yet a riddle hovered over the skyline, a riddle no poll could qualify: where did freedom end and order begin once authorities had towed, ticketed, and turned them into campaign slogans? Canada was now balanced on that edge, and the air was too brittle to decide which way to tip.

> *"The nation has doused the last camp-stove, yet every kitchen table still smoulders with argument. When truck horns fade, talk takes their place, louder for being wordless so long."*

By 7 February, the convoy's smoke had drifted into print, and the front pages looked like duelling editorials. *The Globe* warned emergency powers risked becoming "policy by bullhorn," while *Le Devoir* countered that *laissez-faire* policing had already mortgaged public trust. Across the aisle, the House of Commons extended the Emergencies Act measures 185–151, a tally that read less like arithmetic than a national Rorschach: order to some, over-reach to others. [11] Online petitions flowered in opposite directions. One Change.org drive urged Ottawa police to *evict* the rigs, clearing 38,000 signatures in four days, and its comments section was a wall of sleepless frustration. [12] Another, branding convoy figure Pat King a *political prisoner*, logged thousands of endorsements from voters convinced civil disobedience had been re-priced as sedition. [13] A third petition demanded King's immediate release, its rhetoric equal parts Magna Carta and message-board sarcasm. [14]

Pollsters noted a fresh wrinkle: not just polarisation, but polarisation about polarisation. The Public Policy Forum's *Far and Widening* study rushed to policy staffers in PDF form and warned of *affective sorting* so strong that disagreement now felt like trespass. The report's authors mapped 1,600 young adults, ten researchers and a constellation of listening circles—data points that glowed like storm cells on the civic Doppler. [15]

Kingston was the first to test the weather. Grant Hall's limestone arches rarely host capacity crowds at noon, yet by Ash Wednesday, even the upper gallery was elbow-locked. Queen's University had advertised its town hall as *a civil conversation on an uncivil month*, the room answered with the tension of a drawn bow. Student ushers handed out colour-coded mics—red for those wanting to challenge, blue for those wanting to "build"—an innovation that looked suspiciously like camp counsellor psychology until the questions began. Halfway through, professor-moderator Elaine Wu read aloud from Sean Richmond's essay, *What Every Canadian Should Remember About the 'Freedom Convoy' Crisis*. "Our rights are not blank cheques; a truck may possess horsepower, but it owns no constitutional standing." [16] The line landed like gravel on a windshield—small, decisive, impossible to ignore. A bakery owner replied his storefront had become a checkpoint; a commerce student shot back that checkpoints sometimes mark the front lines of liberty. Overhead lights flickered as if to remind everyone the grid, at least, remained impartial.

Two time zones west, Vancouver's Chinatown filled a different room with a quieter electricity. Elder May-Louie Song, whose grey braid carried the authority of eighty-three remembered springs, arranged the chairs in a cedar-scented circle inside the Dr Sun Yat-Sen Garden annex. She opened with the geotaxes woo-wop protocol: speak briefly, then listen for long. Around her sat a second-generation restaurateur, a Syrian newcomer whose first Canadian memory was a flag-draped truck, two non-binary art students, and a retired R.C.M.P. sergeant who kept his badge in a coat pocket "to remind me I'm not that uniform anymore." They passed a quartz talking stone, each voice layering story on story until the circle resembled a woven basket—flexible, load-bearing. When the restaurateur confessed he no longer flew the Maple Leaf for fear customers would assume an anti-vax agenda, the elder nodded toward the koi pond outside: "Symbols swim. We decide whether the water is fresh." The Public Policy Forum's roundtables also revealed young adults describing polarisation not as poison, but as noise, something that could be engineered down by redesigning the room. [15]

If Kingston crackled and Vancouver murmured, Halifax crackled, murmured, then howled—all inside the bandwidth of a single *CBC* frequency. On 20 February, the late-night edition of *Cross Country Checkup* opened its lines with host Ian Hanomansing asking, "What's your reaction to the police crackdown in Ottawa? Where do we go from here?" The answer arrived in 127 calls, two dropped f-bombs, three on-air apologies, and a cross-section of the country seldom heard in a single sitting: Mi'kmaw fishers disputing marine checkpoints, a Cape Breton trucker still idling in Sudbury for lack of freight, an international grad student timing his comments between shifts at a Halifax ICU.[17] One rural caller quoted his grandfather—"A government that freezes bank accounts is a bank that governs"—and hung up before the screener could thank him. Minutes later, a downtown millennial retorted that her rent payment had bounced because of blocked streets, "so whose account got frozen first?"

Whenever the Charter was invoked, producers behind the studio glass watched the waveform spike; Listeners vented about foreign cash sluicing through GiveSendGo; *The Guardian* had traced more than half the leaked donations to U.S. zip codes, a statistic callers bandied like stock tips. [20] Others fretted over early reports of extremist crossover: Diagolon patches, Confederate flags, a meme of Pierre Poilievre shaking hands with a podcast demagogue. Canada's public safety minister was already warning of links between Coutts suspects and Ottawa organisers. [19] The switchboard flashed until 02:00, finally collapsing under a backlog that resembled—if you squinted—a nation determined to talk itself whole.

As February tilted toward March, elected officials tried to choreograph the dialogue they had once begged to mute. Parliamentary emails sprouted invitations to *citizen roundtables* and *digital town halls*, phrased in the polite urgency of evacuation notices. A Liberal backbencher proposed a cross-party working group on protest thresholds; a Bloc MP demanded a sunset clause on asset freezes; the New Democrats filed a motion for a national summit on algorithmic disinformation. One draft briefing note warned that ignoring grassroots forums now "risks ceding narrative to actors with louder trucks." Senior staff pencilled arrows from petitions to polling graphs—cause, effect, effect, cause—until the arrows tangled like highway detours.

Meanwhile, the digital petitions kept metastasising. A single weekend yielded a motion to rename Wellington Street "Peacekeepers Way," a counter-motion to rename it "Truckers' Way," and an irreverent third petition—2,000 signatures strong—to pave it as a pedestrian plaza so nobody could blockade anything on wheels ever again. The algorithms treated each initiative equally enthusiastically, amplifying fury and farce in alternating scrolls. Opinion writers joked Ottawa had invented a perpetual-motion machine fuelled by civic indignation.

Yet amid the din, glimmers of synthesis appeared. After the Queen's town hall, students organised a *forum of forums* mapping points where libertarian protest and social-justice advocacy overlapped: corporate concentration, precarious labour, institutional opacity. In Vancouver, Elder Song's circle birthed a weekly potluck whose first agenda item was *flags without baggage*—participants stitched miniature cloth banners bearing both the Maple Leaf and an embroidered eye, to say *we are watching over, not taking over*. *CBC* producers turned the most civil Halifax call-ins into a podcast segment titled *Peacemaking in Real Time*, soon shortlisted for an industry award. [17]

Political aides took note. Cabinet's March agenda suddenly featured consultations on critical-infrastructure buffer zones, while the Privy Council ordered fresh research into emergency-powers sunset triggers. Leaked memos suggested a forthcoming "National Dialogue Act," a bill to underwrite citizen assemblies the way Canada funds elections—an idea once relegated to civics textbooks. Rumours reached the convoy alum chatrooms, triggering debates over whether taxpayer-sponsored listening circles were dialogue or dilution.

On 1 March, the air felt transitional: winter's ragged breath backing away, budget season ahead, and somewhere between the two a constitutional middle ground Canadians had not yet invented. Newspapers swapped war metaphors for medical ones—"healing," "triage," "recovery plan"—but the headlines still pulsed with doubt. Opinion polls steadied, then twitched whenever a new video surfaced of frozen bank accounts thawing or rigs refitted for spring planting.

That night, in a last echo of February's cacophony, someone played an air-horn recording through a portable speaker outside the shuttered gates of Parliament Hill. The blast bounced off sandstone and died quickly, like a skipped stone. A passer-by muttered, "Wrong month." Maybe so. Or perhaps it was the audio bookmark of a chapter Canada had only begun to annotate—one that would soon move from campus podiums and cedar-scented circles into committee rooms where the sentences could shape statutes. For now, the country lingered in the anteroom of reform, ears still ringing, hearts calibrated to both thunder and hush.

> *"Laws were ink on vellum until a horn's blast proved how brittle ink can be. Now Parliament patches the parchment while seamstresses of protocol mend a flag frayed by too many meanings."*

March arrived like a legislative fire drill. The freedom convoy's exhaust had barely cleared when the House resumed, every party leader wielding new catch-phrases: *'civic literacy deficit,' 'symbolic security,' 'crowdfunding contagion.'* Opposition critics flourished, drafting bills promising compulsory civics modules in every high school. Government benches countered with a vow to fold online-funding platforms into Canada's anti-money-laundering regime. Their rhetoric took on the crackle of sheet metal in the sun as committee rooms overflowed. On 3 March, the Public Safety committee summoned GoFundMe, PayPal, and Stripe executives; Juan Benitez's Zoom-fed apology framed the platform's January disbursement as "a unique anomaly" that now justified tighter KYC thresholds. [21] *CTV* cut the feed into a split-screen Chyron—*86% of donors Canadian, exec says*—and suddenly, kitchen radios nationwide debated the difference between patriotism and payment processing. [22]

Reporters leaving West Block needed only to cross the courtyard to locate the next flash-point: a pop-up podium for Sergeant-at-Arms staff unveiling draft *Respectful Display* guidelines. The day's handouts quoted both a *Guardian* cost tally—Ottawa's policing and cleanup bill had climbed past CA$36 million, [25] and a *Reuters* brief in which senior officers conceded they had "under-scoped" the occupation, fearing escalation if they acted too soon. [23] "Symbols mobilised faster than our intel," one aide admitted, tapping a chart that paired Confederate pennants with spikes in encrypted-chat traffic. Therefore, a new directive was issued: only flags pre-approved by the Protocol Office could be displayed on federal sites. Drafters still quarrelled over *unsanctioned* versus *unauthorised*, their laptops glowing against half-empty coffee urns. They cited Mississauga's freshly updated municipal policy as precedent [26]. They cross-checked the phrasing against Canadian Heritage etiquette sheets that reminded them the maple leaf must hang "with the upper point of the leaf to the observer's left." [27]

Far from the Hill's oak-panelled fervour, a civics reboot took flesh in the drywall scent of Room 214 at Daniel McIntyre Collegiate in Winnipeg. Ms Rizwan's Grade 10 history pilot opened with a role-play: students argued whether blockading a downtown artery counted as peaceful assembly or public-order offence, each side required to ground claims in Sections 1 and 2 of the Charter. Chalk dust swirled under the ceiling fans as Anika, the shy goalie from girls' hockey, raised her hand to ask whether freezing bank accounts might breach Section 7 liberty guarantees; the class gasped—someone had finally named the most challenging question. The smart board flashed a *Policy Options* headline calling the convoy *a wake-up call for citizenship education*, its April dateline close enough to feel prophetic. [28] On an adjacent tab, Ms Rizwan queued the Ontario Civics course parent guide—proof, she explained, that constitutional literacy was already mandatory east of the Red River, just not always memorable. [31] When the bell rang, desks were littered with stick-note "rights tests" students had drafted for homework: *May I honk if my neighbour is sick? Does a meme count as assembly?*

Ottawa's Government Conference Centre, a *Beaux-Arts* maze reborn as a spill-over war room during the blockade, became the site of another first: a cross-departmental workshop on flags. Legal advisers from Justice, protocol clerks from Heritage and a backbench MP's staffer who once designed scout badges huddled around a parchment-coloured seating chart. Their task was to replace decades-old custom with enforceable language. Pages rustled like restless pigeons: Should the definition of "flag" exclude banners affixed to hockey sticks? Could a by-law compel removal after dusk? Past midnight, the group argued, statistical sidebars from the Public Policy Forum's *Far and Widening* report projected on the wall—

bar graphs showing trust plummeted whenever citizens felt their symbols hijacked. [29] Someone suggested mandatory QR-coded permits; another retorted that bureaucracy could turn patriotism into parking enforcement. The only consensus was caffeine: espresso machines and legal dictionaries steamed in tandem.

Mid-month, Treasury Board President Mona Fortier fronted a press gaggle to launch the Downtown Ottawa Business Relief Fund—$20 million for storefronts that had become collateral to protest theatre. [24] Behind her stood Nico and Marta Gagliano, the café owners, last seen staring at empty till drawers. Marta, voice quivering, recounted how insurance adjusters had called a three-week horn barrage a "non-physical loss." Reporters scribbled while economists from Public Policy Forum sketched a slide deck on transparency rules for platform donations, citing the same House testimony that found 1,346 convoy contributions had evaded geographic tagging. [21] One analyst drew applause by likening un-traced micro-donations to *political dark matter—unseen but shaping orbits.*

The grassroots circles that formed in February now disseminated their findings in policy memos. Elder May-Louie Song's Vancouver cohort submitted a brief urging that any new flag code allow cultural banners of welcome at Chinatown celebrations; staff working the inbox at Heritage noticed the phrase 'inclusive patriotism' cropping up hourly. Podcasters in Halifax repurposed *CBC* call-in audio into a mini-series titled *How To Argue Without Air-Horns,* downloaded 90,000 times in three weeks. *The Charlatan,* a Carleton University paper, chronicled how downtown merchants were "trying to stand on their feet again". City planners floated the idea of pedestrianising part of Wellington to prevent future gridlocks. [30]

On 22 March, the Commons erupted in its most theatrical exchange of the session. A Bloc Québécois MP waved a pocket Constitution and called the proposed civics mandate a *paternalistic cram-down.* The education minister riposted that ignorance was the true paternalism, quoting polling that 41 per cent of Canadians could not name a single Charter right. [29] As heckles ricocheted off stained-glass crests, a young page whispered to the Clerk: "They're arguing civics—maybe the lesson plan's already working."

By month-end, the first tranche of reforms finished their gestation. Draft regulations extending FINTRAC oversight to crowdfunding intermediaries circulated for pre-publication comment, buoyed by testimony that platforms already ran sanction-screening algorithms but needed statutory clarity. [21] Pilot civics modules shipped to ten school boards, embedding scenario-based assessments where students must balance free-expression claims against municipal noise by-laws. Heritage circulated a 37-page "Interim Flag Display Framework" that would, for the first time, empower site managers to order the removal of any banner "whose messaging contravenes public-order statutes," a phrase slimmed to placate constitutional lawyers but broad enough to catch next season's rogue slogans. Review copies bore tracked-change battles over unsanctioned and unauthorised words, as though semantics alone could keep cloth from catching fire.

Outside, spring pressed its palm against the Library of Parliament's iron lattice; scaffolds left by winter maintenance came down, revealing stone cleaned of protest graffiti. Yet the forecourt still bristled with questions. Could a civics quiz inoculate against conspiracy? Would stricter KYC checks dam the flash flood of rage-funding? Could they restore a flag, once used to express grievance, to its neutral red and white? Canada stood at the threshold of answers, pens clicking, sewing machines purring, the hush before new rules test their seams.

ENDNOTES

[1] Angus Reid Institute. (2022, February 14). *Blockade backlash: Three-in-four Canadians tell convoy protesters "go home now."* https://angusreid.org/trudeau-convoy-trucker-protest-vaccine-mandates-covid-19

[2] BBC News. (2022, February 7). *Canada truckers' protest: Patience running thin among local people.* https://www.bbc.com/news/world-us-canada-60297364

[3] CityNews Ottawa. (2022, February 12). *Businesses are being devastated by ongoing convoy protest: Bank Street BIA.* https://ottawa.citynews.ca/2022/02/12/businesses-are-being-devastated-by-ongoing-convoy-protest-bank-street-bia-5058317

[4] Canadian Underwriter. (2022, February 9). *Are businesses covered for damage caused by the Freedom Convoy?* https://www.canadianunderwriter.ca/claims/are-businesses-covered-for-damage-caused-by-the-freedom-convoy-1004217240

[5] Tayeb, Z. (2022, February 20). *Canada offers $20 million to local businesses affected by trucker protests. Business Insider.* https://www.businessinsider.com/canada-grants-20m-local-businesses-affected-trucker-protests-freedom-convoy-2022-2

[6] House of Commons of Canada. (2022, February 20). *Debates (Hansard), 44-1, No. 35.* https://www.ourcommons.ca/DocumentViewer/en/44-1/house/sitting-35/hansard

[7] Cecco, L. (2022, February 22). *Canada maintains emergency powers after trucker blockades ended.* The *Guardian.* https://www.theguardian.com/world/2022/feb/22/canada-extends-emergency-powers-after-trucker-blockades-ended

[8] Public Order Emergency Commission. (2023). *Report of the Public Inquiry into the 2022 Public Order Emergency* (Vol. 1). Commission of Inquiry. https://publicorderemergencycommission.ca/files/documents/Final-Report/Vol-1-Report-of-the-Public-Inquiry-into-the-2022-Public-Order-Emergency.pdf

[9] Office of the Auditor General of Ottawa. (2024). *Audit of the City of Ottawa's response to the convoy protest.* https://www.oagottawa.ca/media/tklagr1h/final-audit-report-audit-of-the-city-of-ottawa-s-response-to-the-convoy-protest-1-final-ua.pdf

[10] Miller, N. (2022, February 23). *Ontario orders 12 truck operators out of service over Freedom Convoy protest.* *FreightWaves.* https://www.freightwaves.com/news/ontario-orders-12-truck-operators-out-of-service-over-freedom-convoy-protest

[11] Duplicate of #7

[12] CTV News. (2022, February 11). *Online petition calling on Ottawa police to evict Freedom Convoy tops 38,000 signatures.* https://www.ctvnews.ca/canada/article/ottawa-protesters-vow-to-stay-in-face-of-mounting-opposition-from-city-businesses

[13] Change.org. (2022, February 1). *Ottawa Police must evict Freedom Convoy* [Petition]. https://www.change.org/p/ottawa-police-department-ottawa-police-must-evict-freedom-convoy

[14] Change.org. (2022). *Do you feel that Pat King is a political prisoner?* [Petition]. https://www.change.org/p/do-you-feel-that-pat-king-is-a-political-prisoner

[15] Public Policy Forum. (2023). *Far and widening: The rise of polarization in Canada.* https://ppforum.ca/wp-content/uploads/2023/08/TheRiseOfPolarizationInCanada-PPF-AUG2023-EN2.pdf

[16] Richmond, S. (2022, March 21). *What every Canadian should remember about the 'Freedom Convoy' crisis.* The *Conversation.* https://newsroom.carleton.ca/story/freedom-convoy-crisis

[17] Cross Country Checkup. (2022, February 20). *What's your reaction to the police crackdown in Ottawa?* [Radio broadcast]. *CBC Radio.* https://muckrack.com/podcast/cross-country-checkup-from-cbc-radio/episodes

[18] New York Festivals. (2023). *Cross Country Checkup: "Freedom Convoy 2022" protest in Ottawa* [Audio award finalist]. https://radio.newyorkfestivals.com/Winners/WinnerDetailsNew/d60acf32-4bdd-4c17-a527-a428b9f05a51

[19] Mendick, R. (2022, February 16). *Ottawa blockade: 'Strong ties' between some occupiers and far-right extremists, says minister.* The Guardian. https://www.theguardian.com/world/2022/feb/16/ottawa-blockade-strong-ties-extremists

[20] Lindeman, T. (2022, February 14). *Foreign money funding 'extremism' in Canada, says hacker.* The *Guardian.* https://www.theguardian.com/world/2022/feb/14/foreign-money-funding-extremism-in-canada-says-hacker

[21] House of Commons Standing Committee on Public Safety and National Security. (2022, March 3). *Evidence, Meeting No. 12, 44-1.* https://www.ourcommons.ca/DocumentViewer/en/44-1/SECU/meeting-12/evidence

[22] Turnbull, S. (2022, March 3). *GoFundMe head testifies over Freedom Convoy fundraising, says most donors were Canadian. CTV News.* https://www.ctvnews.ca/politics/article/gofundme-head-testifies-over-freedom-convoy-fundraising-says-most-donors-were-canadian

[23] Williams, N. (2022, March 3). *Ottawa police misjudged protesters who besieged Canada's capital, testimony shows. Reuters.* https://www.reuters.com/world/americas/ottawa-police-misjudged-protesters-who-besieged-canadas-capital-testimony-2022-03-03

[24] Federal Economic Development Agency for Southern Ontario. (2022, March 9). *Downtown Ottawa businesses impacted by demonstrations can apply for Government of Canada support as of March 15* [News release]. https://www.canada.ca/en/economic-development-southern-ontario/news/2022/03/downtown-ottawa-businesses-impacted-by-demonstrations-can-apply-for-government-of-canada-support-as-of-march-15.html

[25] Cecco, L. (2022, March 18). *Ottawa truck convoy cost the city more than C$36 million, police say. The Guardian.* https://www.theguardian.com/discover-cool-canada/2022/mar/18/ottawa-truck-convey-cost-c36m-police

[26] City of Mississauga. (2022, March 17). *Flag protocol at city facilities* (Policy 06-04-03). https://www.mississauga.ca/wp-content/uploads/2022/03/17142430/06-04-03-Flag-Protocol-at-City-Facilities-Policy.pdf

[27] Canadian Heritage. (n.d.). *Rules for flying the national flag of Canada.* https://www.canada.ca/en/canadian-heritage/services/flag-canada-etiquette/flying-rules.html

[28] O'Neill, M. A. (2022, April 11). *The trucker protests and the blatant failure of citizenship education. Policy Options.* https://policyoptions.irpp.org/magazines/april-2022/citizenship-education-failure

[29] Duplicate of #15

[30] Adwan, A. (2022, March 17). *Downtown Ottawa businesses recuperate following convoy occupation. The Charlatan.* https://charlatan.ca/downtown-ottawa-businesses-recuperate-following-convoy-occupation

[31] Ontario Ministry of Education. (n.d.). *Civics and citizenship, CHV2O: A guide for parents.* https://www.dcp.edu.gov.on.ca/en/chv2o-parent-guide

CHAPTER TWENTY-THREE:
WHEN THE GAVEL DROWNED THE DIESEL

"A judge's ruling can silence more horns than a convoy of tow trucks. Laws may be printed on fine paper, but the only ink that lasts is the kind you can see from the street. When the engines stop and the ballots settle, a country discovers if it trusts its own quiet."
~ R.G. Cruise

The verdict sounded first in parchment, not a piston. On 23 January 2024, under the ribbed stone of the Federal Court's Courtroom 36, Justice Richard Mosley read aloud a sharp ruling that seemed to part the winter air. The jurist's baritone declared the Trudeau cabinet's 2022 declaration of a Public Order Emergency "unreasonable" and, in the antique Latin, that makes the law feel like masonry, *ultra vires*—beyond the powers Parliament had granted. [1] [2] [3] The judge's criticism of ministers for mistaking political gridlock for national peril caused reporters in the gallery to stop scribbling and listen. Outside, cameras waited for quotes; inside, constitutional scholars traded eye-glints that said a decade of law-school syllabi had just rewritten itself.

In the marble-floored corridor that funnels litigants toward the main atrium, veteran advocate Sheila Hart muttered that the judgment would "sing like a truck horn across the prairies." Her junior, lugging a stack of Hansards, replied that horns had notes; silence echoed here—Ottawa's first calm after two years of procedural thunder. Tourists peered at the pair through security glass, sensing drama without knowing why. Hart pointed to the library skylight where ghostly snowflakes drifted between panes, reminding them that rule-of-law stories always begin with atmosphere: a nation must *see* its checks and balances before it trusts them. [1] [2] [3]

Two blocks south, the Ontario Court of Justice staged a subtler theatre. The criminal trial of Tamara Lich and Chris Barber, convoy celebrities-turned-defendants, had dragged through autumn cross-examinations and January *voir-dires* until only the sentencing phase remained. On a late-February morning, the pews filled before sunrise: long-haul drivers in sponsor caps, retirees clutching Charter pocketbooks, a half-dozen TikTok streamers banned from filming yet filming anyway through memory. Lich sat forward, spine military-straight; Barber rolled a wedding band between thumb and index finger, knuckles whitening whenever Crown counsel cited residents who had fled Centretown for sleep. Justice Perkins-McVey rapped once for order, and the room fell into a hush dense enough to press against the walls. Barber's last glance traced the courtroom clock, then the window sliver beyond which his Peterbilt—wrapped in February slush like a forgotten totem—waited in a side street no longer blocked by protest. [4]

The afternoon's submissions unfurled like opposing weather fronts. Defence counsel pleaded for non-custodial sentences, invoking convoys as "civil disobedience with air brakes." Crown prosecutors recited decibels and diesel particulates, mapping each hour of horn blasts to a spreadsheet of insomnia claims. When the gavel rose for recess, murmurs pulsed like aftershocks; one freelancer whispered Canada was finally learning whether peace, order, and good government could survive amplifier trucks. Barber rubbed his temples. Lich closed her eyes, perhaps hearing again the crowd's 14 February cheers that now sounded uncomfortably like evidence. [4]

Consumer confidence does not linger in courtrooms, and by early February, it had migrated into the dimly lit boardroom of an Elgin Street litigation boutique. Twelve Ottawa merchants—baristas, florists, a Thai-fusion restaurateur who still winced at the memory of pepper spray in her ventilation system—assembled around a scarred walnut table to sign a new raft of affidavits. On the screen behind them glowed Justice Calum MacLeod's fresh-ink ruling: anti-SLAPP defences dismissed, the proposed $300 million class action free to rumble forward like a low-gear Kenworth. [5] Paper coffee cups clinked as Champ & Associates's lead counsel outlined next steps: updated loss estimates, a Mareva order for crypto wallets, expert testimony on "ambient intimidation." One shopkeeper stammered through numbers: 17 days closed, $92,440 lost, one dishwasher quit after panic attacks. When another asked whether any cheque would ever balance that ledger, the lawyer exhaled into the bitter steam and replied that sometimes a judgment's *symbolic* weight settles accounts the market cannot.

March blew in with a promise of audits rather than sirens. Commissioner Paul Rouleau—whose 2023 report had concluded *invocation justified but caution advised*—strode into Public Safety Canada's Situation Room clutching a slide deck titled "Inter-Agency Gaps & the Persistence of MDM" (mis-, dis-, and mal-information). Someone dimmed half the ceiling lights because of the projector glare. At Q&A, a junior analyst asked whether the Federal Court decision meant the next emergency bar had moved higher. Rouleau's reply—"Higher or clearer? Clarity avoids altitude sickness"—earned a ripple of nervous laughter. Another aide leaned over to whisper that Telegram chatter, already spiking, framed Mosley's ruling as proof Ottawa's "deep-state concession" was imminent. [6]

Public Safety's Departmental Results Report quantified those whispers a week later when it landed in MPs' inboxes. Buried in Annex C lay the stark line: "The digital threat environment includes mis- and disinformation—a pervasive hazard to community safety—on which the Department will convene a national summit this fiscal year." [7] The phrase "pervasive hazard" reverberated through policy blogs faster than any statutory citation. Academics chimed in: a January issue of *Canadian Review of Sociology* had already traced how narratives around the 2022 convoy were *naturalised* into partisan identity kits circulating on Facebook clones and far-right podcasts. [8] The study's network graphs, vibrant constellations of meme-nodes, spooked civil servants unfamiliar with eigenvector centrality; one analyst joked that Canada finally had its aurora borealis of epistemic fracture.

By equinox's approach, the city where klaxons once ruled found itself ruled, instead, by footnotes. Judges, commissioners, and plaintiffs quarrelled in the polite ink of precedent: *What makes up an emergency? When does peaceful protest decay into a public nuisance? Can a honk be both political speech and actionable harm?* The answers, drafted in chambers and boardrooms, no longer smelled of diesel but recycled paper and stale conference coffee. Yet every paragraph carried the vibration of idling engines just outside memory, reminding Canadians that the line between friction and fracture lies in how a nation writes its following paragraph.

Ottawa's tulips had not yet broken the soil the morning the federal cabinet rolled out its long-trailed White Paper on "Patriotism and Public Order." Still, inside the National Press Theatre, the mood was already summer-sticky. A deputy minister drew the curtains, snapping daylight across a bank of television lenses, and quoted the paper's first sentence—"Citizenship without civility is a republic of horns"—before handing the lectern to Public Safety Minister Dominic LeBlanc. His remarks braided the Emergencies Act fallout with fresh promises: classroom toolkits on civic symbols, a new oversight commissioner, and an "emergency-powers sunset clock" visible to Parliament and public alike. Two floors above, analysts from the Privy Council compared the draft to the April 8 Defence Policy Update, noting how both framed loyalty as infrastructure: something that could buckle if inspection lagged. [9] [10]

Provinces digested the document like mismatched stomachs. In Québec City, Education Minister Bernard Drainville—already flanked by reporters after a late-April committee grilling on strike recovery—shrugged that the charter of classrooms was full enough without "Ottawa's maple-leaf flash cards," and hinted his ministry would carve its own civics supplement. [11] Down the 401 in Queen's Park, Ontario's NDP justice critic Kristyn Wong-Tam pounced from the opposite flank, accusing the Trudeau government of "militarising morale" while Doug Ford's Tories spent money on jail beds instead of judges; patriotism, the critic told the press gallery, "isn't plywood you bolt over due-process leaks." [12] The duelling sound bites travelled coast-to-coast before the printers finished the White Paper's executive summary.

Ten days later, a Listening Circle convened under a pop-up canopy beside the basketball courts in Toronto's Regent Park. Folding chairs traced a loose spiral around a cedar smudge bowl; an Anishinaabe elder began with the story of her grandfather's treaty-era oath, then passed the talking stick to teens who still carried suspensions for refusing vaccine-mandate detentions in 2022. One youth confessed he trusted TikTok more than government PDFs, prompting community-organiser Layla Hussein to unroll the White Paper draft like a treasure map missing half its icons. A mural of the convoy's red-and-blue rigs, spray-painted months earlier, peeked through budding branches. The elder's final hymn rose above the streets where the city's Social Development Plan once promised cohesion and still fought to fund it. [13]

Officials from Canadian Heritage stood at the back, collecting Post-it notes that read like mini-manifestos: *'Honk-proof our mental health,' 'Patriotism ≠ obedience,' 'Teach treaties before anthems.'* One policy aide whispered every circle added twenty more clauses to wrangle; another replied that spare clauses were cheaper than spare riot squads. Outside the park, the 506 streetcar clanged east, carrying a QR-coded flyer for next month's Saskatchewan forums.

June arrived in a shiver of wheat-field wind. At the Elks hall outside North Battleford, pickup trucks formed a dusty ellipse around tractors decked with Red River Métis flags. Inside, metal chairs squeaked across pine flooring as the Rural Emergency-Powers Oversight draft slid onto tables beside chipped coffee mugs. A rancher in oil-stained denim asked why Ottawa's clock should govern a prairie gridlock; a Métis councillor countered clocks were polite only until someone silenced them. When a Public Safety lawyer cited Saskatchewan's Emergency Management Organisation handbook—"threshold is when order breaks and freedom can't be secured"—the hall rumbled with boot-heel taps, like thunder deciding whether to stay. [14]

Conversation swung from diesel taxes to data leaks. A widow whose internet arrived by satellite described scam texts claiming the White Paper banned rifle raffles; two rows over, a fifteen-year-old coder volunteered to fact-check Ottawa's PDF metadata for deep-fake implants. By dusk, the group had pencilled a compromise clause: any future federal declaration must file a public-health impact statement within seventy-two hours or lose gasoline levy authority. It read like legislative origami—delicate folds, sharp enough to slice.

July, however, belonged to academics. On a rain-mirrored morning at the University of British Columbia's Forest Sciences auditorium, political scientists unboxed survey dashboards that glowed neon against cedar panelling. Professor Mei-Ling Carter opened with bar graphs showing civic literacy pilots in six provinces; within minutes, demographer Kris Pierre pulled the thread toward disinformation, mapping meme clusters that repurposed the maple leaf into a skull, one algorithmic filter at a time. Conference chairs waved time flags while graduate scribes scratched furiously. In the lobby, the CASCA anthropologists from Kelowna pinned ethnographic sketches of "convoy cosplay" beside voting-age heat maps, arguing that ritual and algorithm now danced the same jittery two-step. [15] [16]

During lunch break, a McMaster sociologist passed around an op-ed titled "Rising Patriotism and Who Gets to Belong," warning that demographic tides could drown nuance if the curriculum confused cheerleading for citizenship. [17] A doctoral candidate asked whether the Listening Circles had produced measurable empathy scores; another replied that empathy wasn't Wi-Fi—you felt it more when reception was bad. In a corner alcove, Public Safety staff logged panel quotes into a live document tagged "Cabinet-Summer-Read-Ahead."

By the time shadows stretched across Burrard Inlet, the symposium's keynote speaker—an Elder-in-Residence named Kendra Smoke—rounded the dialogue back to treaties. She told the delegates that no document, regardless of colour, could constrain the relationships already established, and that laws created out of fear aged more quickly than those born of curiosity. Her voice, neither podium-loud nor microphone-thin, carried a cadenced calm that made even the projector fan pause. The following applause felt less like a triumph than alignment: a pulse settling after a year-long palpitation.

Far away, on Parliament Hill's south lawn, tent stakes marked the footprint of August's policy retreat. Inside Centre Block renovation trailers, junior clerks compiled spring circle notes, prairie amendments, and UBC slide decks into a binder thick enough to raise monitors. The binder's spine read *Patriotism WP— Community Draft v.3,* but someone had scribbled an arrow to a sticky note: *V.4 Friday?–Cabinet wants plain-language examples.* The sticky flapped in the air-conditioned breeze, a tiny semaphore signalling the subsequent chase into autumn chambers and winter statutes—where ideals must squeeze through bill numbers and budget lines. For now, Canada's civic season balanced on a solstice edge: one foot in thawed earth, the other on legislative ice, listening for the next horn that might become a heartbeat or an alarm.

Parliament Hill's lawn still shimmered with the last heat of August when the Patriotism and Public Order Act returned for a second reading, but the air inside West Block already carried the chill of trench warfare. On 26 September 2024, Hansard caught the moment the Speaker's gavel fell; Minister Dominic LeBlanc rose first, comparing the bill's "sun-settable guardrails" to winter tires— "annoying to buy, indispensable when black ice hits democracy." [18] Across the aisle, Bloc Québécois whip Claude DeBellefeuille answered that no tire could grip a constitution if Ottawa kept "driving over provincial toes." New Democrats waved copies of the Mosley decision, such as parking tickets; Conservatives brandished a pocket edition of the Charter, and corners dog-eared from last year's committee marathons. The Speaker called the order three times before the cameras tilted up to the public gallery, where convoy veterans in red flannel held silent placards that read *I Honked, Therefore I Am.*

Reporters stepping into the marble foyer flipped instantly to another page of their briefs: five days earlier, Bill C-71—an unrelated but symbolically loaded Citizenship Act amendment—had survived raucous second-reading debate, reminding MPs that the year's legislative traffic jam involved more than horn clauses. [19] The Order Paper's ink was still damp when government House leaders whispered that *Pat-P.O.A.*—as staffers had nicknamed the *Patriotism Act*—would face a time-allocation motion before Thanksgiving. Outside, a swirl of orange maple leaves made the Commons' south steps look like a slow-motion flag-burning, suitably theatrical for evening newscasts.

The bill crawled into committee in November, and by 17 December, MPs had logged debates thick enough to clog the digital Hansard feed. [20] Question Period that day opened with Liberal back-benchers invoking the Emergencies Act fallout; Tory critic Dane Lloyd shot back that teaching schoolchildren new verses of "O Canada" would not erase "a $300-million class action and a Federal Court rebuke." Somewhere between those volleys, Speaker Greg Fergus sighed into his mic, the weariness audible even through closed-captioning: "Order… the House must remember that decibels do not equal persuasiveness." The line trended on X within the hour.

While elected voices traded jet streams of rhetoric, the appointed Senate warmed its engines. On 5 December, the Social Affairs, Science, and Technology Committee convened in a committee room whose walnut panelling smelled faintly of history and sanitiser. Leather-bound binders thudded on felt desktops as Clerk Maxime Charette distributed the 187-page briefing on the bill's reconciliation clause. Senator Michèle Audette opened with a Mi'kmaq land acknowledgement before reading, in sonorous French, a paragraph obliging Ottawa to consult Indigenous nations before declaring any future public-order emergency. Her reading slowed at the words free, prior, and informed, as if weighing each syllable with decades of broken consultation promises. The gallery's scribes glanced up only when Senator Ratna Omidvar asked Justice Department counsel whether the new oversight commissioner could survive a Supreme Court reference; the lawyer's reply—a half-audible "charter-proofed as far as is humanly possible"—sent a rustle of pens across notepads like small gusts of wind. [21] That séance was streamed live on *CPAC* two evenings later, the network's Chyron boiling the complexity down to *SENATORS EYE HONK CLAUSE.* [22]

Across the corridor, a sub-panel of the same committee gathered for an off-camera technical briefing on clause 14: the emergency-powers expiry clock. A Public Safety deputy admitted that coordinating real-time federal-provincial data flows remained "aspirational"; projected in dim light, his slide deck showed a three-colour Gantt chart that looked suspiciously like last spring's version. [23] Senators exchanged knowing looks, like watching a dog chase its tail but cheering the cardio benefits.

Yet legislation does not necessarily die solely in Ottawa's stone corridors. In mid-November, a civics classroom at Vancouver's Britannia Secondary traded its usual buzz for near-library hush as Grade 12 students delivered final projects titled "Freedom and Responsibility." Infographics twirled on screen: horns versus human rights, Snapchat polls on trust in federal power, TikTok montages of convoy footage captioned "democracy, season two." Their teacher, Ms. Nguyen, had built the semester around Elections Canada's newly released secondary-school resources, modules designed to marry inquiry with media literacy. [24] When one student parsed the bill's "patriotism curriculum" clause, her classmate countered with data from the Civic Literacy Youth Network, showing how participatory simulations improved confidence but not polarisation thresholds—a reminder that comprehension and consensus are uneasy bedfellows. [25]

The discussion peaked when a quiet student named Omar read aloud his essay: "I came here at nine, learned two languages, learned to follow rules; now Parliament wants to teach me love of country in PowerPoint slides. Loving a place is not remembering a verse—trusting that place to remember you." His classmates, usually allergic to silence, let the words settle like fresh snow. Ms. Nguyen wiped a tear, then scribbled, "Publish?" on her attendance sheet.

December's last week shifted the spotlight eastward again. Inside Toronto's historic Carlu ballroom, the Canadian Civil Liberties Association hosted its year-end gala under a banner that read *Guardrails > Gas Pedals*. The chandeliers glittered like curling ice while activists clinked glasses of Ontario VQA sparkling wine in honour of the campaign they'd launched mid-month to "Save Our Charter" from over-easy amendments and the creeping normalisation of Section 33. [26] Executive director Abby Deshman, fresh in the role, toasted volunteers who had live-tweeted every committee hearing since April. On stage, a journalist duo from *The Narwhal* accepted an award for explanatory reporting on the Federal Court decision microphones caught one of them quipping, "Civic literacy broke its training wheels this year." A hush fell when MC John Lorinc introduced the night's surprise guest: former convoy spokesperson Benjamin Dichter, tieless and palpably nervous. In a brief interview, he conceded that "a horn is no substitute for a ballot," adding that his reading of Mosley's ruling had taught him "due process can out-shout diesel." Phones blinked skyward like a thousand tiny satellites beaming the confession into national consciousness.

Outside, a swirl of early snowflakes tattooed the limousines' windshields. Inside, talk turned to the next steps: pro-bono litigators plotting a watchlist for provincial uses of the notwithstanding clause, educators swapping lesson-plan links, and data journalists proposing a cross-platform disinformation tracker. The hum of networking sounded almost like optimism, though an elder civil-rights lawyer at the coat check whispered that optimism ages better when paired with vigilance.

By New Year's Eve, Freedom House analysts had quietly upgraded Canada's *participatory governance* sub-score, noting that 2024's debates had "clarified emergency thresholds and widened civic space." [27] The report landed softly—overshadowed by year-end top-ten lists—but its footnote on the Patriotism Act echoed Justice Mosley: extraordinary powers demand extraordinary caution. Meanwhile, the CCLA posted a year-end digest under the simple header "Still Watching" and a link promising livestreams of regulatory consultations in early 2025. [28]

As Parliament's Gothic turrets vanished beneath a January snowfall, the Patriotism, and Public Order Act sat on the Governor General's desk awaiting royal assent, pages crisp from winter air and fingerprints of every ideology. Half-frozen and half-restless Canada stood at a crossroads forged by courtroom gavels, listening-circle drums, Senate parchment, and teenage slide decks. Whether the nation's next chapter would be written in diesel or dialogue remained unwritten— but the ink, at least, had been tested against the cold.

ENDNOTES

[1] Cecco, L. (2024, January 23). *Judge rebukes Trudeau for "not justified" use of Emergencies Act to break convoy.* The Guardian. https://www.theguardian.com/world/2024/jan/23/canada-trudeau-emergencies-act-trucker-protest-covid

[2] Associated Press. (2024, January 23). *Judge says Canada's use of Emergencies Act to quell truckers' protests over COVID was unreasonable.* AP News. https://apnews.com/article/d7e6640f817ee12410bb99840a3df41b

[3] Federal Court of Canada. (2024, January 23). *News bulletin: Public Order Emergency—Summary of decision* (Court Files T-306-22 et al.). https://www.fct-cf.gc.ca/Content/assets/pdf/base/2024-01-23-News-Bulletin-Public-Order-Emergency.pdf

[4] Osman, L. (2024, January 30). *Protester's overturned acquittal could have impact on "Freedom Convoy" case: Expert.* Ottawa CityNews. https://ottawa.citynews.ca/2024/01/30/protesters-overturned-acquittal-could-have-impact-on-freedom-convoy-case-expert

[5] Helmer, A. (2024, February 6). *Judge tosses motion to dismiss proposed class-action lawsuit against convoy participants.* Ottawa Citizen. https://ottawacitizen.com/news/local-news/judge-tosses-motion-to-dismiss-proposed-class-action-lawsuit-against-convoy-participants

[6] Public Safety Canada. (2024, March 6). *Statement from Minister LeBlanc on Emergencies Act review follow-up.* Government of Canada. https://www.canada.ca/en/public-safety-canada/news/2024/03/statement-from-minister-leblanc0.html

[7] Public Safety Canada. (2024). *Departmental results report, 2022-23.* Government of Canada. https://www.publicsafety.gc.ca/cnt/rsrcs/pblctns/dprtmntl-rslts-rprt-2022-23/index-en.aspx

[8] Brinkmann, M., & Bilodeau, C. (2024). The polarized "naturalizations" of the 2022 Freedom Convoy. *Canadian Review of Sociology, 61*(1), 23-45. https://doi.org/10.1007/s44282-024-00107-y

[9] Department of National Defence. (2024, April 8). *Release of Canada's Defence Policy Update* [News release]. Government of Canada. https://www.canada.ca/en/department-national-defence/news/2024/04/release-of-canadas-defence-policy-update.html

[10] Department of Finance Canada. (2024). *Budget 2024: Chapter 7—Protecting Canadians and defending democracy.* Government of Canada. https://budget.canada.ca/2024/report-rapport/chap7-en.html

[11] The Canadian Press. (2024, April 24). Education: True impact of teachers' strikes won't be known until 2025, says Drainville. *CityNews Montreal.* https://montreal.citynews.ca/2024/04/24/education-strike-impacts

[12] Global News. (2024, November 30). *Ontario's plan to add 1,000-plus new jail beds draws criticism from NDP justice critic.* https://globalnews.ca/news/10837421/ontario-jail-bed-increase-strategy

[13] City of Toronto. (2025, January 15). *Regent Park Social Development Plan: Key accomplishments 2019-2024* [Briefing document]. https://www.toronto.ca/legdocs/mmis/2025/bu/comm/communicationfile-186817.pdf

[14] Canadian Nuclear Safety Commission. (2024). *Canada's sixth national report under the Joint Convention on the Safety of Spent Fuel Management and on the Safety of Radioactive Waste Management.* https://www.cnsc-ccsn.gc.ca/eng/resources/publications/reports/jointconvention/sixth-report

[15] House of Commons of Canada. (2024, September 26). *Debates (Hansard)*, 44th Parl., 1st Sess., No. 344. https://www.ourcommons.ca/DocumentViewer/en/13282229

[16] OpenParliament. (2024, September 17). *Debates of the House of Commons—Bill C-71, Citizenship Act (second reading).* https://openparliament.ca/debates/2024/9/17/?page=6

[17] House of Commons of Canada. (2024, December 17). *Debates (Hansard)*, 44th Parl., 1st Sess., No. 391. https://www.ourcommons.ca/documentviewer/en/house/latest/hansard

[18] Senate of Canada. (2024, December 5). *Debates*, Issue 246. https://sencanada.ca/en/content/sen/chamber/441/debates/246db_2024-12-05-e

[19] Cable Public Affairs Channel. (2024, December 2). *Human Rights—In Committee from the Senate of Canada* [Video]. https://www.cpac.ca/in-committee-from-the-senate-of-canada/episode/human-rights--december-2-2024?id=539462fe-d4ba-48ff-9254-3e796033041f

[20] Senate of Canada. (2024). *Standing Senate Committee on Social Affairs, Science and Technology (SOCI).* https://sencanada.ca/en/committees/soci/44-1

[21] Elections Canada. (2025, March 27). *Backgrounder: New civic education resources for secondary students.* https://www.elections.ca/content.aspx?dir=bkg&document=bkg_civic&lang=e&section=med

[22] Civic Literacy Youth Network. (2024). *Program overview and registration.* https://ccrl-clrc.ca/clyn/

[23] Smith, D. (2024, December 10). Concern for the future of the Charter. *CBA National Magazine.* https://nationalmagazine.ca/en-ca/articles/law/hot-topics-in-law/2024/worries-about-the-future-of-the-charter

[24] Freedom House. (2024). *Freedom in the World 2024: Canada.* https://freedomhouse.org/country/canada/freedom-world/2024

[25] Canadian Civil Liberties Association. (2024). *Our work.* https://ccla.org

[26] Public Safety Canada. (2024, January 23). *Briefing note: Federal Court ruling on invocation of the Emergencies Act and next steps.* Government of Canada.

https://www.publicsafety.gc.ca/cnt/trnsprnc/brfng-mtrls/prlmntry-bndrs/20240626/09-en.aspx

[27] Canadian Civil Liberties Association, et al. (2024, November 8). *Attorney-General's factum on cross-appeal* (Fed. Ct. App. File A-319-23 et al.). https://ccla.org/wp-content/uploads/2025/01/2024-11-08-AGCs-factum-on-cross-appeal.pdf

[28] Reuters. (2024, January 23). *Canada to appeal ruling that Emergencies Act use was unreasonable.* https://www.reuters.com/world/americas/ottawa-appeal-ruling-canadas-use-emergency-powers-was-unreasonable-2024-01-23

EPILOGUE:

FROSTED RECKONINGS

"A verdict may end a case, but the noise takes its time leaving the walls. It's easy to freeze a bank account, harder to thaw the memory of horns at midnight. A country is built less on its victories than on the questions it still argues after the engines stall."
~ R.G. Cruise

The morning after Justice Charles Hackland pronounced a three-month conditional sentence on Pat King, the gothic pillars of Ottawa's Elgin Street courthouse shone like frozen bayonets in the February sun, every fleck of hoarfrost seeming to underline the judgment in cold ink. [1] Inside, where steam still curled from styrofoam cups and reporters' notebooks lay open like half-plucked wings, Crown counsel puzzled over how nine months of pre-trial custody, nine days of testimony, and 200 gigabytes of social-media exhibits had distilled into 180 measured seconds of oral reasons. One clerk whispered Hackland had "buried the lead," yet the lead strode out the front doors grinning—King trading shackles for a nicotine-flavoured hug as supporters whooped beneath a banner that read, with aching irony, "Let Freedom Roam." [2]

Across Canada, the wires crackled. *Global* ran with "House Arrest for Highway Hero or Hazard?"; community stations in Red Deer looped the same B-roll of King in his black ball cap; and by noon, the exchange-rate ticker on *Business News Network* had folded a faint "protest-premium" back into trucking-sector equities. "Conditional," analysts mouthed, "but not contagious." In Edmonton, a mid-tier carrier's CFO allowed himself a coffee-spoon drumroll before unfreezing a fleet-expansion line of credit, deciding that Ottawa's ice sheet of uncertainty had finally thinned. Back east, however, downtown merchants thumbed their calculators and found only red: for them, the convoy's diesel-scented winter lingered like smoke in upholstery.

Inside Happy Goat Coffee on Laurel Street, the hiss of the espresso wand could not drown a 5 March meeting that felt part bond-hearing, part group-therapy. Owner Talia Pacheco read aloud her ledger—forty-one delivery invoices bounced, nine staff shifts lost, and an unquantifiable number of regulars who had "just stopped coming because they couldn't stand the horns." Around the table, a dozen grocers, gallery-keepers, and hot-yoga instructors nodded. Lawyer Paul Champ clicked a slide: *Li v. Barber et al., Proposed Class-Action, Claim: $289,700,000.* The sum drew a collective exhale—the sound of debt masquerading as hope. Champ's plan was blunt: argue private nuisance, economic loss, and "negligent orchestration of urban gridlock," then let discovery thaw every encrypted chat. "Certification is the crossing," he said. "Once on the bridge, we drive the convoy in reverse." Heads bowed, laptops hummed, and a single spoon pinged the ceramic lip of a demitasse like a metronome of resolve. [8]

Beyond that café window, Justice Heather Perkins-McVey's docket pressed forward. On 3 April, her name would re-enter headlines beside two more famous ones: Tamara Lich and Chris Barber. But the story had already leaked in fragments by late March: leaked not from court but from sidewalks, where protesters argued over whether King's sentence foretold leniency or was, in fact, a velvet cuff. When the verdict finally landed—guilty of mischief for both organisers—the oxygen in every national newsroom seemed to tumble into the same steel barrel. "One word," Perkins-McVey wrote, "reverberated longest downtown: noise." [3] The judge's 108-page reasons noted horn-blasts tracked at 85 decibels fifteen hours a day; she cited TikTok videos in which Barber urged "replace any truck the cops tow." Reporters latched onto that line like a hook in a lip. The *BBC* called the ruling "a rare criminal blueprint for civic cacophony." [5] *The Associated Press*, filing through OPB, reminded American stations that Canada's polite myth had "splintered on a windshield of air-horn steel." [4] Even Vermont's *WCAX* led its evening newscast with stills of chrome grills and the caption "Truckers Tried, Truckers Guilty." [6]

Yet the gallery on verdict day felt nothing like the thunder outside. When Perkins-McVey reached the word "mischief," a single pen rattled to the floor; Barber's shoulders sagged; Lich stared ahead, jaw set as if bracing for an unseen pothole. Crown Moiz Karimjee barely looked up from his binder; he had lived with this file so long the pages felt like skin. Defence counsel Diane Magas jotted two words—*appeal ASAP*—then leaned sideways to whisper Charter angles. By the time journalists sprinted for the rotunda, MAGAs were already phoning Calgary, booking an April 10 slot in the Alberta Court of Appeal's electronic queue. She spoke in what sounded like code: *S-2, farm-team precedents, section 2(b) throttle.* A clerk's red stamp would echo down those marble halls less than a week later, the ink still wet when social-media feeds splashed "Lich to challenge mischief ruling, cites free-expression choke." [7]

While lawyers armoured up, civil litigants sharpened spreadsheets. On March 6, the Ontario Court of Appeal had refused to snuff the merchants' $290-million action, tossing the defendants' anti-SLAPP gambit onto the scrap heap. Justice David Brown's ruling read like a snowplough message: "Political motive is not a plough for private harm." Ottawa's business district, upon reading paragraph 47, erupted in Slack emojis of clapping hands. [8] One restaurateur printed the judgment, pinned it above the dishwasher, and told staff, "There: proof the clatter mattered." Meanwhile, the Justice Centre for Constitutional Freedoms vowed to press on, issuing a March 10 release that likened Brown's decision to "punishing donors for spilt coffee they never sipped." [9]

Amid the paper-storm, King spent his sentence's first Sunday staring at the prairie sky from a porch near Red Deer, ankle monitor blinking every thirty seconds. Local station *RDNewsNOW* captured him waving politely to a drone photographer, a tableau equal parts folk hero and parolee. [10] The clip, filmed against snow-capped hay bales, fed two national narratives at once: to supporters, he was "grounded but unbroken," to opponents ", captured yet scarcely cuffed." King himself offered no commentary; bail conditions muzzled him. But neighbours overheard him rehearsing an apology in the cold: "Sorry about the noise, Ottawa," he said to the wind, "but sometimes a horn is the only instrument a working man owns."

On Parliament Hill, MPs processed the legal cascade like meteorologists parsing storm tracks. Some Liberals mused that the trio of rulings—King's sentence, the class-action's advance, Lich & Barber's convictions—formed a barometer for public patience. One Conservative back-bencher fumed Hackland had "gift-wrapped a martyr." A New Democrat finance critic snapped that the class-action was "privatised accountability, the natural child of state timidity." In caucus corridors, aides began compiling spreadsheets titled "Convoy Vote Intention Delta," shading risk ridings in crimson and steel. The Prime Minister's Office ordered a fresh round of focus groups in Calgary Skyview and Ottawa Centre, eager to test whether the electorate read "conditional sentence" as mercy or mirage.

Meanwhile, at the Royal Canadian Mint, analysts quietly modelled lost tourism revenue against the potential bump in commemorative-coin sales should the Emergencies Act anniversary harden into popular memory. "Trauma sells trinkets," one economist sighed, tapping a calculator, "especially when the gavel's echo is still ringing."

By late March, the narrative threads—criminal, civil, political—had braided into a single rope stretching toward the election year. King scrolled through headlines about Lich's coming appeal and Barber's prospective stay in motion from the quiet of his enforced Alberta living room. Outside, a magpie landed on his porch rail and flared its wings; King, perhaps thinking of long convoys and longer winters, lifted a coffee mug in salute. Somewhere far to the east, a café owner finalised a damages affidavit; somewhere north of Toronto, a pollster compiled fresh cross-tabs; inside a drafty Parliament office, a junior aide typed the phrase "ethics implications of convoy solidarity tweets."

Thus closed the first quarter of 2025: verdicts rendered, lawsuits launched, appeals queued like trucks at an imaginary on-ramp to jurisprudence. The diesel had burned off, but its scent still hung in the national nostril, half memory, half warning. And in that lingering vapour, Canadians sensed the subsequent chapter stirring—the part where ballot boxes replace horn blasts, and silence becomes a kind of testimony.

On April 15, 2025, the House of Commons chamber felt less like a debating hall and more like an overheated greenhouse: questions, rebuttals, and points of order fogged the air until even the clerks' glasses misted. Government House Leader Karina Gould rose first, thumping a blue binder stamped *POEC— Action Matrix* and insisting that "every Canadian's security—and every Canadian's right to protest, now hang together, like strands in the same tow-strap." Her phrase echoed language the Cabinet had already planted in its official reply to Justice Rouleau's Public Order Emergency Commission report, a 70-page document promising "swift, accountable implementation" of all fifty-six recommendations. [11]

Across the aisle, Conservative critic Dane Lloyd flicked to page 214 of that morning's Hansard and said that the Liberals were "reading an after-action fairy tale" while rural ridings still nursed convoy scars. [12] When Lloyd brandished a colour-coded chart of "unanswered intel gaps," NDP MP Matthew Green shouted, "Add the Bitcoin column!" The Speaker's gavel finally cracked like a starter pistol.

By noon, the foyer's limestone walls reverberated with duelling press scrums. Reporters chased ministers down the marble ramp toward the Confederation corridor; staffers—juggling paper cups and legal pads—flashed hand signals to indicate which response line was safe to quote. Outside, a gust off the Ottawa River rattled the news cameras' rain covers. On X, provincial premiers volleyed statements: Saskatchewan's vowed to "quarantine federal overreach," Québec's demanded a revenue-sharing formula for protest policing. Ontario retweeted the commission's paragraph on "critical trade corridors," adding a maple-leaf emoji and the words "Never again."

Yet the sharpest critique brewed two blocks away in a beige boardroom where the Canadian Civil Liberties Association and Ryerson's Centre for Free Expression ran a lunchtime Zoom debrief. Projector light glinted off stainless-steel water pitchers as slide eleven warned that the draft Patriotism and Public Order Act risked creating *rolling bubble zones* around any *designated economic artery*. An activist lawyer in a corduroy blazer murmured, "That's half the country." The moderator clicked to the next slide—Charter sections 2(b) and 8—then read from a freshly posted news release urging municipal councils to resist *rights-free ribbons of asphalt*. [13] Someone in the back tapped a spoon twice on a ceramic mug, their group's shorthand for *turn that line into tomorrow's op-ed*.

Meanwhile, behind closed doors in West Block Room 207-B, Liberal caucus strategists wrestled with an uglier reality: verdicts against convoy leaders had satisfied columnists but not the polls. Aides circled a slide titled *Sentencing Bounce (Net)* = +1.8% ±3.2% and groaned. Finance Minister Chrystia Freeland warned that further tough-on-protest language might alienate Toronto's civil-liberties vote just as it soothed suburban commuters. Weighted with binders, Public Safety Minister Bill Blair argued the opposite, invoking the POEC's finding that police confusion cost the economy $3.9 billion. Someone whispered, "Does Carney have a number yet?" At the head of the table, Prime Minister-designate Mark Carney's policy director waved a *Reuters* print-out quoting the new leader's vow to *emerge stronger than ever.* [19] The line tested well in focus groups, they said, "because it sounds both Churchillian and cheap."

Out on the hustings, Conservative leader Pierre Poilievre was polishing a different refrain. On April 21, the morning's frost still silvered the asphalt outside a midtown Toronto YMCA when he promised to release his platform "Tuesday—because accountability arrives on time." *The Canadian Press* blasted the pledge within minutes, labelling it "the campaign's most punctual promise." [17] That afternoon, Poilievre doubled down, publishing a bullet-point plan to "close the Carney loophole" and force every future PM to publish seven years of tax returns. [14] Liberal war-room staffers, reading the post between Question Period votes, muttered that the move was pure theatre—yet privately logged the hashtag *#SevenYears* into their social-listening dashboard.

The theatre reached its loudest act ten days later in Greater Sudbury. Dust from half-melted snowbanks whirled across the airport tarmac as a convoy of idling minivans and pickup trucks kept heaters running against the northern chill. Inside an Air Bravo hangar festooned with red-and-blue banners, Poilievre's advance team tested the smoke machine twice, then rolled out a battered pickup to serve as a makeshift stage. When the music cut, the Conservative leader leapt onto the tailgate and opened with a line he'd honed on closed-door focus groups: "Accountability at every level—because if Ottawa can freeze truckers' bank accounts, it can freeze yours." The crowd's answer was a bright roar that seemed to flush the cold from the sheet-metal roof. [15]

Reporters counted six standing ovations in twenty-two minutes. Tyler Clarke of *Sudbury.com* later wrote that the loudest cheer came when Poilievre promised to "green-light the Ring of Fire in under six months" and a voice near the back shouted, "Defund the CBC!" [16] Poilievre's grin—half bemusement, half permission—flashed across every evening newscast. Hours later, party HQ blasted supporters with a video titled *Full Speech: Sudbury*, its jump-cuts timed to each chant of "Lost Liberal Decade." [10] [2] The clip racked up 1.3 million views by dawn. [10] [2]

Carney's Liberals scrambled to reclaim the narrative. On May 1, at a breakfast presser across from the War Museum, Environment Minister Steven Guilbeault brandished a Reuters dispatch noting that tariffs and annexation threats from U.S. President Trump had sparked an "unprecedented swell of Canadian patriotism" and given the governing party "a fighting chance." [18] Guilbeault's takeaway: patriotism sells, but only if paired with stability. He announced an extra $150 million for "green supply-chain corridors," then quoted Poilievre's Sudbury line: "If you want accountability at every level, start with carbon emissions."

Civil-society groups were unimpressed. On May 16, the CCLA convened journalists, privacy scholars, and two former Elections Canada commissioners in a brick-walled co-working loft near Dundas Square. They unveiled an open letter demanding that Elections Canada audit "all third-party campaign activity tied to convoy solidarity groups" and publicly name any MP who "fund-raised on courthouse steps." Laptops clacked while an ethics professor annotated section 486 of the Canada Elections Act on a digital whiteboard. "Transparency," she observed, "always sounds expensive until the invoice for secrecy arrives."

On Parliament Hill, caucus chairs parsed daily tracking polls with stethoscopic worry. Liberals saw a narrow two-point edge but feared "flag fatigue." New Democrats sensed space to run on civil-rights purity. Energised by northern crowds, Conservatives booked extra whistle-stop rallies in Kelowna and Brandon. Inside each party's war room, interns googled the phrase "bubble zone by-law" and tested ad copy against potential swing voters named Alex or Fatima.

Yet beneath the calculations, a quieter reckoning spread. Clerks in the Ethics Commissioner's office noticed a spike in requests for "post-convoy guidance." Crown corporations ordered fresh training on political activity policies. The Privy Council Office reopened its dormant *Peace, Order, and Good Government* briefing binder and pencilled in a new annex: *Social-Media Financial Influencers and Protest Amplification.*

By 23 May, 2025—three years after the first trucks rolled toward Ottawa—the city's lilac trees burst into bloom, and with them came a tentative sense that the convoy saga had sprouted its final chapter. But the bloom's scent mixed with diesel memory, and Canadians understood that verdicts and bills were only the middle lines of the ledger. The rest—ethics hearings, platform planks, ballot questions—waited just beyond the summer writ drop. For MPs rehearsing stump speeches, activists comparing injunctions to injunctions, and shopkeepers still tallying noise-damage claims, the frost might have lifted, but the accounting had just begun.

The numbers that dripped from *Angus Reid's* tracker felt like rainwater seeping through a cracked ceiling: Prime Minister Justin Trudeau's approval slid to twenty-one per cent, the lowest since the institute began the series in 2016, while fully sixty-four per cent of respondents told interviewers they now favoured "sweeping parliamentary ethics reforms." [21] That same morning, the institute's archive posted a brief noting a record spike—forty-two per cent—of Canadians who said federal leaders should "cede protest policing to provinces under a formal protocol," a figure up eleven points in a single quarter. [22] A *Nanos/CTV* flash poll, added salt: while half the country believed Trump-era tariffs would evaporate "before 2029," just eighteen per cent expressed confidence Ottawa could manage domestic unrest without additional safeguards. [23]

Two days later, on the third floor of a red-brick strip mall in Ottawa-Vanier, the constituency office of Liberal backbencher Isabelle Chen became an unintentional barometer of that unease. The phones rang faster than Evan, the lone intern left after staff furloughs, could click "answer." Each call he triaged onto a yellow pad: "civil-rights chill," "bank-freeze trauma," "why did no one resign?" By noon, the pad showed twenty-seven tallies; by 16:00, 16:30. As Chen hunched over an *Abacus* print-out of the April campaign's final poll—Conservatives still ahead by double digits—she rubbed the table edge until the laminate frayed, repeating, "These numbers punish hesitation, not conviction." [24]

While Chen weighed contrition against party discipline, flashbulbs crackled ninety kilometres southwest. Ontario Premier Doug Ford strode to the Queen's Park rostrum, flanked by his finance and transportation ministers. He declared the province would strike its inquiry "into every federal order or freeze letter that landed like a brick on Ontario families." Reporters shouted questions about jurisdiction; Ford replied with a shrug and a promise of "integrity first, paperwork second." [25] Behind him, aide Paige Walker distributed a press sheet citing fresh *Angus Reid* premier-approval numbers that had nudged Ford to forty-eight per cent—his highest since 2022—under a headline reading "Trump Bump or Trust Bump? Either Way, Upward." [27]

Civil-liberties advocates heard both the phones and the podium. The International Civil Liberties Monitoring Group released an open letter urging the new Carney government to "draw a bright-line firewall" between emergency finance tools and routine policing, warning that without reforms, "trust will drain faster than any convoy can honk." [26] They flagged the surge of constituent complaints logged in Chen's office and elsewhere as evidence that parliamentary committees had not yet grappled with the personal fallout of account freezes, asset seizures, and investigatory disclosures.

The debate bled westward. On the morning of May 14, in a sun-soaked seminar room of UBC's Sauder School of Business, Professor Marissa Rowan pushed aside a stack of student essays titled *Responsible Dissent: Lessons from 2022-25*, slid a *Reuters* photo of half-cleared convoy rigs onto the projector, and asked, "What happens when the state's moral authority is invoiced by tow-truck?" No one laughed. A forestry-science major quoted the Emergencies Act ruling now on appeal; a political-science minor asked whether ethics reforms without socio-economic change were "just new brakes on an old truck." Rowan scribbled notes—"procedural justice," "loss aversion," "digital restraint"—then pointed to fresh polling that found forty-three per cent of young Canadians considering abstaining from the next election unless "trustworthiness metrics" appeared on ballots. The room went silent until a commerce student muttered, "Democracy with a nutrition label."

Outside academia, the campaign machine whirred. The *Abacus* "final of the campaign" survey showed Liberal support clawed back to within three points of the Conservatives after Mark Carney's late-April minority victory. Yet, fifty-five per cent still rated the Emergencies Act response "excessive." [28] Carney's advisers pushed ethics-package drafts across cabinet tables, keen to outflank Pierre Poilievre's Sudbury vow of "accountability at every level," while watching *Ipsos* cross-tabs that showed reform enthusiasm untethered from partisan identity. Federal strategists noted that even in Alberta—a province flirting with independence referendums—support for parliamentary transparency had risen to seventy-one per cent according to a May 8 *Angus Reid* regional poll. [33]

Meanwhile, the national memory of Trudeau's decline lingered like the ghost of last winter's salt on Ottawa sidewalks. *Reuters'* video scoop—leaking talk of the outgoing PM's imminent resignation—still ricocheted through social feeds, a permanent GIF of leadership fatigue. [30] Even Carney's triumphant March 9 coronation piece, with its photo of the former central banker waving beside a banner reading "Trade Fearless," carried a parasitic caption about Liberal rescue from an approval spiral. [29] A March 6 *Reuters* analysis reminded readers that the party's turnaround owed as much to Trump's annexation threats as to ideological repentance. [31]

Grass-roots scepticism spurred parallel conversations. *LethbridgeNewsNow* op-ed pages pondered whether proportional representation might inoculate the country against another "blue-wall, red-wall" whiplash, arguing that regional sweeps had super-charged the convoy's original grievance matrix. [32] In Saskatchewan, *Angus Reid* measured prairie restlessness: half of respondents endorsed a referendum on separation "if Ottawa's emergency powers linger." However, fewer than one-third said they would vote to leave. [33]

In Chen's office, the phone finally paused, not because of the lack of callers but because the voicemail had reached capacity. Evan taped an index card to the receiver: *Switch to email—phones jammed.* At Queen's Park, reporters chased Ford down a hallway, pressing him to name the inquiry's commissioner; he ducked into an elevator, waving a thumb-up through narrowing doors. Out west, Professor Rowan published her students' essays online; within hours, the post drew comments from Chile, France, and New Zealand—reminders that Canada's winter of horns had echoed far beyond provincial borders.

That evening, a crimson sunset washed Parliament Hill, and in the rambunctious hush, MPs whispered the same word—"threshold"—as if testing its resonance. Courts had set a threshold for emergencies, polls a threshold for patience, and classrooms a threshold for faith. Canada, poised between legislative overhaul and electoral enthusiasm, now faced the quietest threshold: when memory cools into precedent. As the sky darkened, Chen left her office carrying the yellow pad of complaints and a fresh ethics-reform draft; Ford sketched talking points for his inquiry; Rowan uploaded a syllabus module titled "Post-Convoy Citizenship." And somewhere in the mosaic of north-country roads, the last convoy air horn of that era rusted into silence, leaving only the questions it had blown into the wind—questions voters, lawmakers, and students alike would bring to the ballot box, the committee room, and the following dawn's lecture hall.

ENDNOTES

[1] Baxter, D. (2025, February 19). *Pat King sentenced to 3 months house arrest in 'Freedom Convoy' case.* Global News. https://globalnews.ca/news/11024887/pat-king-sentence-freedom-convoy-case

[2] Baxter, D. (2025, February 19). *'Freedom Convoy' organizer Pat King given 3-month conditional sentence.* MooseJawToday/The Canadian Press. https://www.moosejawtoday.com/national-news/freedom-convoy-organizer-pat-king-given-3-month-conditional-sentence-10253650

[3] Baxter, D. (2025, April 3). *Tamara Lich, Chris Barber found guilty of mischief at 'Freedom Convoy' trial.* Global News. https://globalnews.ca/news/11113646/tamara-lich-chris-barber-freedom-convoy-verdicts

[4] Associated Press. (2025, April 4). *Canada trucker protest organizers found guilty of mischief.* OPB. https://www.opb.org/article/2025/04/04/canada-trucker-protest-organizers-found-guilty-of-mischief

[5] CBC/Reuters. (2025, April 4). *Canada Freedom Convoy leaders found guilty of mischief.* BBC News. https://www.bbc.com/news/aticles/cpwz5d5d8l7o

[6] Associated Press. (2025, April 4). *Canada trucker protest organizers found guilty of mischief.* WCAX-TV. https://www.wcax.com/2025/04/04/canada-trucker-protest-organizers-found-guilty-mischief

[7] The Canadian Press. (2025, April 3). *'Freedom Convoy' organizers Lich, Barber found guilty of mischief.* CTV News. https://www.ctvnews.ca/canada/freedom-convoy-organizers-lich-barber-found-guilty-of-mischief-1.6830957

[8] The Canadian Press. (2025, March 6). *Proposed class action lawsuit against 'Freedom Convoy' organizers clears hurdle.* CityNews Ottawa. https://ottawa.citynews.ca/2025/03/06/proposed-class-action-lawsuit-against-freedom-convoy-organizers-clears-hurdle

[9] Justice Centre for Constitutional Freedoms. (2025, March 10). *Court dismisses appeal of Freedom Convoy in $290 million nuisance lawsuit.* https://www.jccf.ca/court-dismisses-appeal-of-freedom-convoy-in-290-million-nuisance-lawsuit

[10] Canadian Press. (2025, February 19). *'Freedom Convoy' organizer Pat King given 3-month conditional sentence.* rdnewsNOW. https://rdnewsnow.com/2025/02/19/freedom-convoy-organizer-pat-king-given-3-month-conditional-sentence

[11] Public Safety Canada. (2024). *Government of Canada response to the Public Order Emergency Commission recommendations.* https://www.publicsafety.gc.ca/cnt/rsrcs/pblctns/2024-pblc-rdr-mrgncy-rcmmndtns/index-en.aspx

[12] House of Commons of Canada. (2024, April 15). *Debates (Hansard) No. 299.* https://www.ourcommons.ca/DocumentViewer/en/44-1/house/sitting-299/hansard

[13] Canadian Civil Liberties Association & Centre for Free Expression. (2025, May 16). *CCLA and CFE call on Toronto City Council to reject proposed "bubble zone" by-law.* https://cfe.torontomu.ca/news/ccla-and-cfe-call-toronto-city-council-reject-proposed-bubble-zone-law-unnecessary-and

[14] Conservative Party of Canada. (2025, April 12). *Poilievre's plan means accountability for a change.* https://www.conservative.ca/poilievres-plan-means-accountability-for-a-change

[15] Bertrand, D. (2025, April 27). *Poilievre warns of dark future for Canada if Liberal policies continue at Sudbury rally.* CTV News. https://www.ctvnews.ca/northern-ontario/article/poilievre-warns-of-dark-future-for-canada-if-liberal-policies-continue-at-sudbury-rally

[16] Clarke, T. (2025, April 27). *Poilievre taps into fear of Liberals during Sudbury rally.* Sudbury.com. https://www.sudbury.com/2025-federal-election-news/poilievre-taps-into-fear-of-liberals-during-sudbury-rally-10576750

[17] The Canadian Press. (2025, April 21). *Poilievre to reveal party platform Tuesday, days after release of Liberal, NDP plans.* CTV News. https://www.ctvnews.ca/federal-election-2025/article/poilievre-to-reveal-party-platform-tuesday-days-after-release-of-liberal-ndp-plans

[18] Mehler Paperny, A. (2025, March 6). *Canada's ruling Liberals move on from Trudeau with Trump boost.* Reuters. https://www.reuters.com/world/americas/canadas-ruling-liberals-move-trudeau-with-trump-boost-2025-03-06

[19] Mehler Paperny, A., Ljunggren, D., & Wa Lone, M. (2025, April 16). *Mark Carney talks tough on Trump ahead of Canada election.* Reuters. https://www.reuters.com/world/americas/carneys-tough-talk-bland-competence-boost-liberals-ahead-canadian-election-2025-04-16

[20] CTV News. (2025, April 27). *Full speech: Poilievre talks of a Conservative future in Sudbury* [Video]. https://www.ctvnews.ca/northern-ontario/video/2025/04/27/full-speech-poilievre-talks-of-a-conservative-future-in-sudbury

[21] Angus Reid Institute. (2024, December 30). *Party vote intent sinks to 16%, Trudeau approval at all-time low.* https://angusreid.org/liberals-prime-minister-trudeau-resign-election-2025-poilievre-singh

[22] Angus Reid Institute. (2025, May 13). *Archive index.* https://angusreid.org/archive

[23] Nanos Research. (2025, May 10). *Most Canadians believe U.S. tariffs on Canada will be lifted by the end of Trump's presidency (CTV News/Nanos).* https://nanos.co/2023-reports

[24] The Canadian Press. (2025, February 4). *Ottawa defends its use of Emergencies Act before Federal Court of Appeal.* CTV News. https://www.ctvnews.ca/politics/article/ottawa-defends-its-use-of-emergencies-act-before-federal-court-of-appeal

[25] Ford, D. (2025, May 13). *Premier Ford holds a press conference* [Video]. YouTube. https://www.youtube.com/watch?v=SfboyDdzm2U

[26] International Civil Liberties Monitoring Group. (2025, May 15). *Open letter: Protect civil liberties during time of turmoil.* https://iclmg.ca/liberal-government-must-prioritize-strong-unequivocal-action-to-protect-civil-liberties-during-time-of-turmoil

27 Angus Reid Institute. (2025, March 24). *Premiers' performance: The Trump bump?*
https://angusreid.org/wp-content/uploads/2025/03/2025.03.24_premiers.pdf

28 Coletto, D. (2025, April 27). *Our final poll of the campaign.* Abacus Data. https://abacusdata.ca/2025-
federal-election-final-poll-of-campaign

29 Ljunggren, D., & Paperny, A. M. (2025, March 9). *Mark Carney wins race to replace Trudeau as Canada's
prime minister.* Reuters. https://www.reuters.com/world/americas/canada-liberals-announce-
trudeaus-successor-midst-us-trade-war-2025-03-09

30 Brooks, R. (2025, April 11). *Canada's Trudeau likely to resign as early as Monday: source* [Video]. Reuters.
https://www.reuters.com/video/watch/idRW104406012025RP1

31 Ljunggren, D., & Paperny, A. M. (2025, March 6). *Canada's ruling Liberals move on from Trudeau with
Trump boost.* Reuters. https://www.reuters.com/world/americas/canadas-ruling-liberals-
move-trudeau-with-trump-boost-2025-03-06

32 Mursell, A. (2025, May 14). *No more blue wall, red wall: How electoral reform could stop regional election
sweeps.* LethbridgeNewsNow. https://lethbridgenewsnow.com/2025/05/14/no-more-blue-
wall-red-wall-how-electoral-reform-could-stop-regional-election-sweeps-2

33 Angus Reid Institute. (2025, May 8). *Referendum reality? Half in Alberta & Saskatchewan call for vote on
independence.* https://angusreid.org/wp-
content/uploads/2025/05/2025.05.08_Western_Separation.pdf

AUTHOR'S AFTERWORD:

NAVIGATING MISINFORMATION AND MEDIA FRAMING IN CANADA'S FREEDOM CONVOY

The weeks-long standoff that gripped Canada's capital was more than a clash of trucks and authorities – it was a battle of information and narratives playing out in real time. As air horns blared on the streets, a parallel cacophony of claims and counterclaims echoed online. Rumours and half-truths spread among supporters of the convoy just as fast as news of police moves. In the fog of this protest, **misinformation flourished**. Many participants sincerely believed they were answering a righteous call – some insisted **COVID-19 dangers were overblown or outright fabricated**, while others shared dire warnings of government "tyranny" and plots. These convictions did not emerge in a vacuum; a digital ecosystem where falsehood often travels faster than fact fuelled them. Indeed, researchers at MIT found that **"falsehood diffuses significantly farther, faster, deeper, and more broadly than the truth"** on social media. Emotional, viral narratives – no matter how dubious – outpaced the slower, quieter corrections from experts. The convoy's rise was a vivid illustration of this principle: sensational claims and emotive slogans ("freedom" versus "oppression") spread widely, while the nuanced context struggled to keep up. This reality underscores why media literacy is so critical for citizens and readers. Critically evaluating information has real-world consequences, a fact highlighted by impending parliamentary confrontations fuelled by misperceptions.

Misinformation during the convoy protests didn't spread by magic – it spread **because people, often unwittingly, passed it along**. In today's fragmented media landscape, the **mechanics of misinformation** capitalise on our habits and biases. In an alarming MIT study of 35 million Facebook posts, researchers revealed that users who never read the article beyond the headline posted about 75 per cent of shared links. It's a sobering statistic: In the frenzy to react or support a cause, three out of four people may share a story without verifying its contents. Researchers noted that this pattern, of users relying on headlines and social media blurbs, **"helps explain why misinformation can spread so quickly online"**. A catchy slogan or incendiary headline – "Government Declares War on Truckers!" or "Freedom Fighters Stand Against Tyranny!" – can go viral on emotion alone. When people analyse the facts, the misleading narrative has already circled the globe. During the convoy, social platforms brimmed with viral videos and memes: some showed only the most sympathetic scenes of protesters hugging and feeding people experiencing homelessness, while others depicted only the most extreme incidents or offensive symbols from the fringe of the protest. Whether true, each snippet became a weapon in an online propaganda war. False rumours (for example, claims of police actions or laws that never materialised) often leapt from one Facebook feed to thousands in minutes. **Once a narrative catches fire, it isn't easy to contain**, especially if it confirms the audience's pre-existing views. Remember that the first step in fighting misinformation is **not to hit "Share" in haste**. Pause and ask: *Who is behind this information, and do other credible sources verify it?* In an age when **false news stories are far more likely to be retweeted than true ones**, our clicks and shares have consequences. Responsible media consumption means **resisting the impulse to amplify sensational claims** before checking the facts.

Just as important as the factual truth of a story is **how that story is told**. The convoy crisis became a study in **narrative framing** – a reminder that the *frame* around facts can profoundly shape our understanding. Different narrators painted the same event in starkly different hues. To many participants and their boosters, it was the "Freedom Convoy," a **patriotic uprising** of ordinary people fed up with overreach – they invoked images of unity, peaceful protest, and grassroots patriotism. To others, especially Ottawa residents and most mainstream Canadian observers, it resembled an **occupation** or a "siege," marked by lawlessness, intimidation, and the incessant honking. The media had to choose a lens: Was this primarily a story of frustrated citizens demanding to be heard, or a tale of extremists and chaos undermining the rule of law? In truth, it was some of both, but **few outlets captured the full complexity**. Narrative framing isn't about lying; it's about selection and emphasis. A camera trained on a **peaceful, flag-waving**

family in the protest tells one story; a camera focused on a **confrontational, banner-wielding agitator** tells another. Both scenes might be real, but which one leads the nightly news will influence whether the public views the movement sympathetically. During the protests, convoy-friendly social media pages flooded followers with heartwarming vignettes and testimonies of kindness in the ranks, largely ignoring the more unsavoury incidents. Meanwhile, other outlets highlighted incidents of harassment, extremist symbols, and the palpable fear and disruption among Ottawa residents. **Each side accused the other of distortion**, and in a sense, both were framing reality to fit a narrative. For readers and viewers, the lesson is **to recognise framing and seek the bigger picture**. Ask yourself: *What am I not seeing?* If one report glorifies the protesters, find another that critiques them (and vice versa). **Truth in complex events often lives in the spaces between polarised portrayals**. By comparing multiple reputable sources, one can triangulate a more nuanced understanding. The convoy taught us that a single narrative thread is never the whole mosaic, no matter how interesting.

Beyond the content of stories and their framing, the convoy saga revealed something equally important: **where stories come from and who amplifies them**. In our interconnected age, foreign voices, and agendas **can profoundly shape Canadian discourse**. Throughout the protest, support, and enthusiasm didn't just grow organically within Canada's borders – a wave of attention, money, and influence from abroad turbocharged it, especially from the United States. One Canadian journalist observed that when American media showed up at the border blockade, it **"was like oxygen to the protesters"**, reinvigorating and legitimising their cause. Many demonstrators eagerly gave interviews to a Fox News crew, basking in the validation from a powerful foreign platform. In those conversations, some protesters echoed familiar **American culture-war rhetoric** – they railed against "tyranny," *"didn't believe there were any COVID-related deaths,"* and asked when the mainstream media would *"start telling the truth".* It was as if fragments of America's pandemic politics had blown north across the border, fanning flames in the Canadian winter. **U.S. pundits and politicians seized the narrative**, casting the convoy as a freedom fight in the grand American tradition. Fox News alone devoted countless hours of supportive coverage, and one *Associated Press* report quoted a Canadian official saying Fox had "fanned the flames" and contributed to misinformation about the protests. Meanwhile, **money poured in from far and wide**. Ordinary Americans – from wealthy suburbs in Florida and California to small towns in Texas – opened their wallets to support the Canadian truckers they saw as kindred spirits. Analyses of fundraising data later showed that **most online donors backing the convoy were based outside Canada**. One official commission found that 59 per cent of donations came from the United States for the convoy's primary crowdfunding campaign, **compared to only about 35 per cent from Canada**. This startling imbalance confirmed what many suspected: the protest had tapped into a **global grievance and ideology echo chamber**. American and other foreign donors, galvanised by social media campaigns and high-profile endorsements, helped inflate the movement's resources and confidence. Even beyond North America, copycat protests, and viral posts sprang up in Europe and elsewhere, reflecting how **contagious a narrative can become across borders** in the digital era.

This carries an urgent lesson: **we no longer have the luxury of viewing our media environment as purely local**. A Facebook post that riles up Canadians might have originated on a website in another country. Interest groups in Washington or bots in St. Petersburg could amplify a dramatic YouTube clip trending in Toronto. Being media literate today means **being aware of these hidden currents**. When we scroll through our feeds or read the day's news, we should remember that **what we see is often the product of deliberate amplification**. Sometimes it's grassroots and genuine – a neighbour sharing their story. Other times it's astroturf'd – a coordinated effort by organisations or influencers to push a certain angle. The convoy showed both at work: genuine local frustration supercharged by well-funded, well-organised messaging from ideologues at home and abroad.

So, how can we navigate this complex media reality? *First,* by cultivating healthy scepticism. This doesn't mean cynically disbelieving everything, but approaching bold claims with questions. If a piece of content screams for your outrage or your uncritical applause, pause and think: *Who wants me to see this, and why?* Check if established, independent news outlets are reporting the same claims – if they're not, there may be a good reason. *Second,* understand that **manipulative framing and emotional appeals are tools to hijack your attention**. Look out for loaded language that plays on anger or fear; recognise when an anecdote is being presented as representative of an entire issue. Ask yourself what the opposing viewpoint might say – hearing it will make you better informed, even if you disagree.

Third, consider the **source and context**. A social media meme or a partisan blog is **not** on equal footing with investigative journalism or academic research. Learn to trace information back to its origin: Is that viral quote from a reputable expert or someone with an alias and an agenda? Is that video clip edited or presented in full context? In the heat of the convoy protests, out-of-context videos or false "insider info" circulating on encrypted chat groups fooled many people. The antidote was, and remains, **to cross-verify** – a quick search or a look at fact-checking sites can save you from falling for a hoax.

Finally, we should support and rely on **trusted sources of information**. Quality journalism – whether Canadian outlets like the **CBC/Radio-Canada, the Canadian Press**, or international ones with standards – is our ally in times of information chaos. These institutions are not infallible, but they operate by **verifiable reporting and accountability**, which makes them far more reliable than rumour mills on social media. By subscribing to credible news sources, reading reports from multiple perspectives, and even reading beyond our borders, we inoculate ourselves against insular or manipulative narratives.

The convoy crisis of 2022 will ultimately stand as a dramatic chapter in Canada's pandemic politics and a cautionary tale about the power of information. It showed how quickly a narrative – true or false – can mobilise thousands, how framing can divide a public, and how foreign influences can amplify local grievances into global spectacles. But it also illuminated the path forward. **We, the readers and citizens, are not helpless** in this landscape. By thinking critically about the media we consume, we honour the complexity of truth instead of settling for easy slogans. We reclaim our autonomy from those who would manipulate our perspective by questioning sources. And by recognising how interconnected our information space is, we can better guard against outside agendas derailing our domestic discourse. The **afterword to this tumultuous episode** is ultimately a hopeful one: armed with lessons from events like the convoy, we can all become more discerning, more resilient consumers of news. In doing so, we ensure that even amid the noise of digital crowds and the **diesel fumes of discord, reason, and understanding** prevail.

www.ingramcontent.com/pod-product-compliance
Lightning Source LLC
Chambersburg PA
CBHW061135120626
46546CB00005B/1795